1973

CAN WE SURVIVE OUR FUTURE?
A Symposium

Can We Survive Our Future?

A SYMPOSIUM

edited and introduced by

G. R. URBAN

in collaboration with

MICHAEL GLENNY

ST. MARTIN'S PRESS
NEW YORK

This symposium consists of edited versions of interviews originally broadcast, in 1970–71, over Radio Free Europe, with whose kind co-operation it is here published.

The editor gratefully acknowledges permission to quote from the following publications: from Gordon Rattray Taylor's *Doomsday Book*, by courtesy of World Publishing Co.; from Jacques Monod's *From Biology to Ethics*, by courtesy of The Salk Institute, San Diego, California; from John Maynard Keynes's *Essays in Persuasion*, by courtesy of W. W. Norton Inc.; and from Bertrand Russell's *In Praise of Idleness*, by courtesy of Messrs. Allen & Unwin.

AFFILIATED PUBLISHERS: Macmillan & Company, Limited, London
also at Bombay, Calcutta, Madras and Melbourne
The Macmillan Company of Canada, Limited, Toronto.

CONTENTS

Introduction by G. R. URBAN, 9

The Impact of Science on the
Moral Options of Man

ARNOLD J. TOYNBEE
Technical advance and the morality of power, 26

PHILIP RIEFF
The loss of the past and the mystique of change, 44

NIGEL DESPICHT
Old values and the demands of new technology, 57

WERNER HEISENBERG
Rationality in science and society, 73

JACQUES ELLUL
Conformism and the rationale of technology, 89

ERICH JANTSCH
For a science of man, 103

LOUIS ARMAND
Restoring man's symbiosis with nature, 127

Growth, Controls and Responsibility

MAURICE CRANSTON
Technology and mass man, 140

EDWARD SHILS
The social control of technocracy, 153

MICHAEL SHANKS
The benefits and social costs of growth, 174

CONTENTS

ANDREW SHONFIELD
Change and social good, 187

DENNIS GABOR
Desirable and undesirable ends of technology, 196

EDWARD GOLDSMITH
Ecology, controls and short-term expedients, 207

HERMAN KAHN
On war, dissent and the control of knowledge, 225

Choosing the Future

FRANÇOIS BOURRICAUD
The preconceptions of university protest in France, 258

HELLMUTH BÜTOW
Youth and the unfulfilled expectations of German democracy, 272

MAURICE DUVERGER
The scope of technological convergence, 293

THÉO LEFÈVRE
The fallacy of technological convergence, 311

JAMES FAWCETT
The anachronisms of sovereignty in a technological world, 324

GUNNAR RANDERS
NATO and the environment, 336

BERNARD CAZES
Opportunities and pitfalls of future-oriented research, 351

OSSIP K. FLECHTHEIM
Marxism and the third road, 368

BRIAN ALDISS
Learning to live with a doom-laden future, 382

Index, 395

If this civilisation of ours is to be saved, it can only be saved by a change of heart in the whole population of the globe. Neither improvements in machines nor the jugglings of economists can do it. To have a living civilisation we must have civilised hearts.

FORD MADOX FORD: *Mightier Than the Sword*, 1938

G. R. URBAN graduated from Budapest University in 1947 and obtained his Ph.D. at London University in 1956. Between 1948 and 1960 he served with the European Services of the BBC and from 1960 to 1965 was Director of University Broadcasting, Radio Free Europe. From 1967 to 1970 he was a Senior Research Associate of the School of Politics and International Relations at the University of Southern California, where he founded the quarterly journal, *Studies in Comparative Communism*, of which he was joint editor. He is author of *The Nineteen Days* (1957) and *Kinesis and Stasis* (1963) and has edited or contributed to *Talking to Eastern Europe* (1964), *The Sino-Soviet Conflict* (1965) and *The Miracles of Chairman Mao* (1971).

MICHAEL GLENNY was educated at Radley College and Christ Church, Oxford. He has been an officer in the Regular Army; businessman; newspaperman. After three years' graduate research in international relations, he is now a Senior Associate Member of St Antony's College, Oxford, and Lecturer in Russian at the University of Birmingham. He is translator of over thirty books from German and Russian, including works by Eichendorff, Dostoievsky, Bulgakov and, most recently, a collection of *Stories and Prose Poems* by Alexander Solzhenitsyn.

INTRODUCTION
BY G. R. URBAN

Multiple authorship, like the conference-industry which begot it, is suspect. Does a convocation of professional luminaries invariably enhance the state of knowledge? Is a juxtaposition of learned articles more than the sum of its parts—or as much? Have the purveyors of the modern academic paper anything in common with the intellectual entertainers of those early drinking parties, the *symposia*, of which they have inherited the name but little of the style or spirit? Suspicion abounds and is justified. With participation running to three and even four figures, our moveable consistories seldom provide a common grid of intellectual reference. The scale of the enterprise and the demands of professional prestige encourage the formal paper, but this leaves little room for the give and take of genuine discussion. And when the paper arrives but not its author, the ensuing discussion tends to be one-sided.

Yet our taste for team-work, the conspectus and the study-group reflects an ancient and respectable trust in the superior wisdom of a collectivity of minds over those of outstanding but solitary ('unsocialised' would be the transatlantic word for it) individuals. 'Where there are many,' Aristotle argues in *The Politics*, 'each individual . . . has some portion of virtue and wisdom, and when they have come together, just as the multitude becomes a single man with many feet and many hands and many senses, so also it becomes one personality as regards the moral and intellectual faculties.' The growth of knowledge has not completely invalidated—in some respects it has reinforced—this opinion; it is still shared in its essentials by scientists in the United States and the U.S.S.R., though, in Europe, with reser-

9

vations only. Its relevance to the social sciences is less obvious, and to the humanities obscure indeed. Architecture by committee has never been a wild success, nor, *pace* UNESCO, has the amalgamated sagacity of chroniclers often attained the rank of history.

We have, in this volume, tried to avoid some of the more obvious pitfalls of the symposium-maker. First, we avoided calling a symposium; second, not having called one, we invited a number of eminent scholars and writers to share their thoughts with us on a limited number of topics from which, truth be told, we were from time to time diverted by the free flow of the conversation, but which we did, I think, manage to keep in focus for the greater part. I, for one, do not regret these detours, for some of the by-ways proved more rewarding than the open roads, and even the occasional blind alley showed an eye-opening factual impossibility here, a psychological barrier there, to press an argument beyond its stretch. Finding the points where the elasticity of subject or speaker would give no further, was one of the most revealing experiences of the exercise.

The discussions in this collection—originally commissioned by Radio Free Europe—are based on unscripted interviews. They bear the stamp of the virtues as well as the weaknesses of the spoken word. The question–answer type of conversation, even if it steers clear of the restricting dialectic of the Socratic dialogues, provides only a coarse-meshed net for intellectual discourse. It catches the gross points but allows the finer ones to slip through. Its attractiveness as sophisticated entertainment (if such it is) is outweighed by the poverty of the spoken word to render symbolic equivalents to those abstruse, and partly entirely new, problems with which this volume is attempting to deal. This, one hopes, is a temporary shortcoming of our mental equipment, but it is real nevertheless. As Nigel Despicht says in another context: 'We have taken too seriously the doctrine of Descartes that the ideas which are most close to reality are those which are clear and distinct. In fact reality is usually more akin to a massive and vague intuition.' We have, as we know from Bergson, yet to create a medium for the intuitive apprehension of reality. It is not words only that 'strain, Crack and sometimes break, under the burden', but ideas too strain and disintegrate in the inhibiting presence of words.

Yet the phenomenal growth in the volume of the written word has revived our interest in the unrehearsed discussion. The more the information-explosion threatens to engulf us, the more we are inclined to agree with Plato that, at least for a brief and pithy exposition of contested issues, the spoken word is superior to written discourses. The latter, Plato says, 'speak as though they were possessed of sense, but if you wish to ... question them ... you find them ever repeating but one and the self-same story. Moreover, every discourse ... always needs its father to help it; for, unaided, it can neither retaliate nor defend itself.'

This, and not merely a modish retreat from literacy, is behind the astonishing revival of the art of the dialogue and disputation as media excellently adapted to radio, and increasingly attractive to the quality press; clearly both reader and listener prefer a story that can 'defend itself' to one that needs a 'father to help it'. If this is part of the young generation's drive to kill hypocrisy and uncover the truth behind the judgements of those who (as they often rightly suspect with Freud) 'prop up their illusions with arguments', one has no reason to be dissatisfied, for it is a wholesome move away from the indigestibilia of the information-dispenser, and back to *Phaedrus* or *The Provincial Letters* of Pascal.

My references to the Greeks are calculated. For one thing, they shed an exceptionally clear light on the legitimacy (or otherwise) of the methods used in these discussions; for another, coming from a distance of over two thousand years, and having retained their relevance, they may help us to redress the balance between that tortuous urge for modernity of which Philip Rieff speaks, and what one would, in a less iconoclastic age, simply call the wisdom of history. But as history is at a discount, so is its wisdom too. Yet, if history is experimental politics (as I believe with Maistre that it is), a highly politicised generation would surely stand nothing to gain from an ig-

11

norance of history, unless it is assumed that our situation in the second half of the 20th Century is totally new, and that such precedents as exist are so harmful that they ought to be erased from the collective memory of mankind. But that is precisely what is more and more widely predicated.

That some idealistic dissent should feed on such assumptions is not surprising. Rebellion, like young love, is unique or it is nothing. What is more disturbing is that a decisive leap has now been made from Heraclitus's observation that no one can step into the same river twice, to a libidinous desire to stay *au courant* irrespective of where the current is taking us. The flux, one might say, is the message.

One would have no reason to quarrel with this *Weltanschauung* if it remained the property of those whose minds traffic in such matters in the seclusion of academic quadrangles. But it has not. The will to ride the crest of contemporaneity has penetrated beyond the walls of the university where the constraints of learning and tradition (such at least as the university is still able to supply) are even less in evidence than they are inside it, especially in America. Hardly a day passes without some institute or foundation enjoining us to throw away the old rule book and equip ourselves with a new set of values, one preferably drawn from the matrix of the exact sciences. This quest of an instant ethic, unsupported as it increasingly is by any contact with the habitual landmarks of a nation's history, language, art and literature, is perhaps the most chilling aspect of modernity and comes closest to Rieff's definition of barbarism.

Despicht's moral relativism ('a scale of values that is related to a limited technology is not appropriate to a situation where technology is infinitely more powerful') is not quite of this order, but it stands in stark contrast with Werner Heisenberg's denial that there is, or could be, any easy correspondence between man's tools and his morality. 'One can only make an effective revolution', Heisenberg says, 'if one changes as little as possible, and that with great circumspection . . . it is extremely dangerous, and probably also self-defeating, to try to instil in . . .

12

[man] a new consciousness by higher order, revolution or analogies drawn from science.'

What is implied here is an emphasis on the self-regulating power of continuity and a doubt whether even the most revolutionary changes in science—to which Heisenberg himself made no mean contribution—exact comparable changes in our consciousness. A whiff of qualified conservatism of this kind, coming from the author of the Uncertainty Principle, is a healthy reminder that our notions of modernity, novelty and uniqueness are too freely bandied about and need more precise definition. So is Andrew Shonfield's warning that 'in our investigations of the future we ought to identify those things which seem remarkably constant'. So is that of Edward Shils: 'complete emancipation from the past and from the limitations of human capacities is impossible. . . . It can only end in tears.'

Thus it is too readily assumed that the impact of science on society, with its repercussions on the economic, social and cultural estates of man, is unique to our epoch. Arnold Toynbee shows in these pages how far this is from being true. At the same time we know well enough that a familiarity with history has seldom prevented societies (or individuals for that matter) from repeating the mistakes of their forbears. It is perhaps this awareness of the impossibility of breaking out of the vicious circle of self-knowledge unaccompanied by self-reform—of knowing the right thing without being able to do it—that accounts for the *ennui* of our age; it is a weariness stemming from the rising expectations of a university-trained generation which sees itself cheated of its spiritual inheritance.

But *ennui* is too mild a word to express that curious blend of fear and intoxication which seeks satisfaction in a metaphysic of self-pity, spontaneity and instant experience. Have the spirits of Werther and Villon ever been evoked under more grotesque circumstances, or more unhappily married? Yet the protest is real enough. The size of our national communities, the inability of governments and bureaucracies to respond to popular feelings, the complexity of the issues of modern society which mock democracy and make the power of decision-making the privilege of an ever diminishing coterie of experts and their front-men in the political arena, all add to the frustration and increase the gap between leaders and the led. If young hands are thrown up in horror, taboos smashed and hypocrisies shown up for what they are, we should perhaps attempt to strike a more even-handed balance between condemning the naïvety and praising the idealism of the protesters, than we normally do.

To call them romantic counter-revolutionaries—'young people of the Right who happen to be on the Left' (Joachim Fest in *Encounter*, June 1971) adds to the problem; it doesn't answer the question. All dissent in the 20th Century is perforce directed against technological domination, gigantism, the de-personalisation, reification, rootlessness and alienation of the individual. There are (apart from the straightforward dictator-ships where society as a whole is in a state of latent dissent) no other worthwhile targets. If the protest movement of the 1970s shares the rejection of some of these features of our civilisation with the prophets of a distasteful past, this does not make the protest any less genuine, or the protesters unwitting accomplices of Mussolini. How does it help us to know that, for almost a century, the rejection of the modern world has been the stock in trade of conservative intellectual attitudes? It is true, but is it significant? *Of course*, in a sense, everything we can think of or say is *déjà vu*; but do the pangs of love or the fear of death ever seem less awesome because we know that others before us have gone through the same experience? Rationalism and a knowledge of precedents are tools of, as yet, limited usefulness. There is a body of experiences which each generation has to tackle with its own bare hands. It used to be war; today it is a deep moral unease at the state of society. Perhaps, as Toynbee suggests, we should not demur at the shift of emphasis.

Hellmuth Bütow and François Bourricaud show that this moral concern does not flourish in isolation: it is embedded in local politics which in turn reflects a nation's cultural and in-tellectual temper—the French dissent still nibbling on the survivals of a revolutionary mythology with the massive non-cooperation of the proletariat, and the German suffused with a high degree of impracticability and ideological perfectionism, sharing with the French an isolation from the working class that bears out Marcuse. But whether constructive or destructive (and Bütow and Bourricaud hold very dissimilar views on this point), there is little in either that would induce a reasonable man to connect them with the profundities of a Charles Reich or a Donald A. Schon. 'Consciousness III' does not make too much sense in Europe—and I doubt if it does in America outside drugland and the campuses—though it makes for amusement. By the same token, any similarity between the informal 'network roles' of Schon's peripheral revolutionaries—refugees to a man from 'stable-state' America—and the European experience is coincidental.

Here, as in other fields discussed in this volume, the American positions diverge so markedly from those held in Europe that the differences are no longer differences of quantity but rather of quality. One may welcome or deplore this—depending on one's intellectual politics—as signs of wisdom or backwardness, but the relevance (though perhaps not the persuasiveness) of the American model remains to be demonstrated. There is indeed a school of transatlantic Gaullism which believes with Herman Kahn that the time has come for the influences to be reversed—for the United States to be re-Europeanised. This may well be desirable—though I doubt whether it is possible—but it does show that, as the American and West European societies converge towards a post-industrial structure, the temper, style, inner logic and tacit assumptions of their cultures do not necessarily follow suit, notwithstanding outward resemblances. Kahn's assertion that national stereotypes still have a great deal of truth in them despite the aids of instant communication, is amply demonstrated by this volume.

To some extent the distinctions are blurred by the universal nature of the topics, the supra-national horizons of our contributors and the slightly un-typical predilections of the American contingent. But with all that, they are clear enough not only between Europeans and Americans, but equally so between the Europeans themselves (among whom I am, of course, including the British). To take one example, Maurice Duverger's emphatic refusal to see any correlation between authoritarian rule and the German temperament, is as typically liberal as it is liberal in a characteristically French context. A German liberal would have to make the opposite assertion, and that is precisely what Bütow does when he claims that the German people's instinctive respect of Authority has been responsible for Germany's recurrent disasters.

Little wonder, then, that a purely rational kind of infrastructure, on which any study of the future and any practical planning must rely for its success, is constantly bedevilled by imponderables, of which national culture is only one, and not the most elusive. The fashionable simplifications of an earlier day, such as those which ascribe human aggression to private property and war to the rapacity of plutocrats, have fallen into disrepute; not so certain undiscriminating extrapolations from the cause-effect paradigm, or even purely mechanistic models. The flat-earthers are still with us. As Bernard Cazes shows, the bulk of central planning is tied to cost-effectiveness, technical feasibility and little else.

Calls for wider perspectives, such as Erich Jantsch and Edward Goldsmith make in this collection, are of crucial importance for the survival of our race; but one wonders whether the steady march of man's irrationality hasn't leapt too far ahead of the slower and erratic progress of reason for the latter to catch up now, or perhaps ever. The world's energy resources are limited, our numbers are apparently not. One can cut the cake in different ways, but one cannot make it grow. 'The standard of affluence achieved in Western nations', Goldsmith says, 'will never be attained in the Third World.' To forestall a global class-war for scarce resources, which Jantsch and others depict as the most frightening prospect of an unplanned future, would require foresight, planning and—to make the latter even remotely effective—a cultural transformation so radical that only a genetic remodelling of man himself could do justice to the problem. But genetic manipulation would raise an even more intractable question : would we want the world to be populated

16

by a hominid more easily regimented than the present variety, or would we prefer to stick to *homo sapiens* (aren't we mocking that adjective?), with his Promethean versatility to embrace good and evil, including the evil of decimating his own species every few years by wars and other choice follies? Whether, from the ecological and demographic points of view, such pruning is really the evil it is made out to be, has been conclusively and, as we now think, illiberally answered by Malthus. The time to judge is not yet.

There is certainly a yawning gap between those for whom man's fall includes the loss of his perfectibility as a rational being, and those for whom it does not because they regard rationality, especially as it expresses itself in the rationale of technology, as a necessary but not sufficient condition of the good life. The distinction has many facets. We have Théo Lefèvre's and Louis Armand's scientific optimism, coupled with a faith that man's natural religious energies are strong enough to generate fresh moral forces to govern his activities as *homo faber*: a composite biology in the case of Armand, a Christian humanism in that of Lefèvre. We have Jacques Ellul's plea to affirm the demarcation line between the rationale of technology and the rationale of man, which he sees better protected under a Christian dispensation than under the totalitarian patronage of technology. We have Kahn's refreshingly simple view that the answer to the moral problem is 'morality, obviously, perhaps a new morality, perhaps the rejuvenation of the old'.

But nowhere is the distance between these attitudes and a straightforward science-based optimism more glaring than between Dennis Gabor and Heisenberg. Gabor's trust in the relevance and efficacy of the scientific approach both strictly within the domain of science and outside it, is classically summed up in the phrase: 'Once a dream becomes a project, the engineers can deal with it.' This is a bold claim, and Heisenberg does not directly take issue with it, but by stressing that the irrational element cannot and should not be eliminated from apprehension and human intercourse, and especially by underlining that 'reason is a very limited faculty of the human mind' with which 'we cannot grasp everything that has to be grasped in a full life', he calls in question not so much the ability of the technologist to deal with his project, as his capacity to perceive those variables in the human psyche which he can—with the rationale of science as his sole guide—neither understand nor allow for in his calculations.

This is an epistemological problem, both difficult and delicate. All recent developments in the social sciences—and less dramatically in the humanities too—have been towards cribbing the methods of the exact sciences and creating jargons comparable to theirs. Academic fashion, the computer and, as a result of these, the marked preference of the American foundations to confine their support to such projects in the 'soft' sciences as can sport some of the paraphernalia of the harder variety, put a premium on a scientism which is not very different in kind from the one that flourishes, more shamefacedly and less effectively, under Communist auspices. Lukács's *Ontology* takes up the cudgels against the latter on East European soil. In the West the counter-attack may yet be an unconscionable time in coming. That the time for it to be launched is today, not tomorrow, is persuasively argued by Shils. Great damage has already been done. When the sort of questions that cannot be quantified tend not to be asked, and academic reputations can be made (and unmade) by the simple expedient of being (or not being) on the right side of the computer-divide, it is time for the reformers of methodology to be subjected to some very searching questions, especially in the United States, because it is there that the retreat from the imprecisions of traditional methodologies to the even greater imprecisions (and distortions) of an indiscriminate quantification, had its origin.

The presumption that a rationality which is legitimate in a scientific-technological framework can be bodily transplanted into the study of man as a social and cultural animal is an irrationality of the first order. It assumes that man is more successful in endowing his artefacts with a language of *their* own than he is in creating a language for the understanding of the much more immediate and familiar operations of himself as an intelligent being. If true, this is another contemporary barbarism which must be fought.

But is it true? The history of our sensibility is the history of its development from robust sentiments and their elaboration in dramatic or epic form to subtler feelings, the shifting nuance and the fugitive melody—from the *Iliad* to Proust, from Marlowe to Rilke. The mental aura in which quantification and extrapolation from scientific paradigms flourish is hostile to this development and, with it, to the seminal stream in our culture. Quantification works from subtle data to gross data; it imposes paraphrase on statements which defy paraphrase.

The difficulties besetting quantification are clearly apparent in this volume. The inadequacy of the economists' tools, of which Shonfield speaks, to assign manageable equivalents to some of the more elusive agents of the growth and decline of economic good, is one aspect of the problem. Another, and related, aspect is the virtual impossibility to write into future-oriented research anything resembling those factors in our historic experience—the rise and fall of dictatorships, Messianic ideologies, racial and religious strife, changes in taste and cultural values, etc.—which we know are the ones that have really mattered in the past and will go on mattering in the future. The 'if . . . then' approach in future-studies is a technology, though a most useful one; it cannot act as a midwife to history. The 'soft' variables continue to be in the hands of the moral leaders and social prophets. And, as Armand eloquently points out, that is where they belong.

In the last ten years or so we have had inspired leadership in some important respects. Our concern with the environment, the preservation of the ecological balance, the ethics of scientific research, especially in biology, goes back to the work of a few far-sighted men, many of them scientists and Americans. There has been a sudden realisation that if the world's population is allowed to go unchecked, and if we go on polluting our environment at the rate we have been polluting it in recent years, we may crowd and poison ourselves out of existence.

The concern is universal, and its first benefits are slowly coming to be felt. In Europe, the British Government's decision to build London's third airport at Foulness rather than Cublington is a milestone in the reversal of cost-effectiveness and other cherished priorities. One hopes, though one dare not believe, that it will act as a precedent. The masochistic streak in the modern doomwatch should not blind us to the great good that may flow from it. Traditionally the prognosticators stand a better chance of capturing an audience if they depict the purgatorial aspects of the gods' designs with man than those which usher in Utopia. It is a good thing that we should be so conscious of the universe groaning 'in all its parts as if in the pangs of childbirth'.

Yet such hopeful signs as we see around us are insufficient to relieve a reflective man of his gloom. This is the age of the most sophisticated thinking and doing the world has ever known—of atomic power, the computer, space research and DNA. Why then, one may ask, were we taken by surprise when the Rhine refused to support the bulk of its fish population? Hadn't we been pouring lethal effluents into her waters for many years, thoroughly planned and well known to all? What was unforeseeable about the asphyxiation of our cities by the motor-car five, ten or twenty years ago, when anyone skilled enough to use an abacus could foretell with unfailing certainty that so many new car-registrations per annum, combined with a stagnation of urban road building, were bound to lead to strangulation? What is there, or has ever been, surprising about the catastrophe implicit in the 'population explosion' when, from Plato through Malthus to Sir Julian Huxley, we have been warned *ad nauseam* that the human race would not be willing to regulate its numbers by the exercise of prudence and restraint?

The sobering fact is—and this comes out repeatedly in these discussions—that there is (literally) a critical mass beyond which the clearest foresight and the wisest policy will founder on our inability to deal with large numbers. It isn't only our moral sense that has been lagging behind, or our political craft to reconcile conflicting interests (they, too, have been lagging):

we are psychologically and spiritually incapable of dealing with size beyond certain anthropomorphic limits. This may be a fault, or a virtue, in our natural equipment, but it is a fact.

Plato set the mandatory size of the city-state at 5,040 households, and this was a workable number in relation to Hellenistic culture and technology. Our own successes are peculiar to technologies which employ relatively small and homogeneous teams of men in a common enterprise. We can mount moon-shots with great precision, we can organise airlines with good margins of reliability, some of us can even run railways, postal and telephone services (in that order of imperfection) with tolerable records for efficiency. All these are homogeneous operations with a single centre, a single rationale and a predominantly one-dimensional personnel (even here, though, efficiency decreases with the number of operations and operators involved: the telephone services, in most of Europe, are poorer than the mail, the mail is poorer than the railways and the railways are poorer than the airlines).

But when it comes to coordinating the activities of large and heterogeneous societies in the common interest, we run into a barrier of incomprehension which Mao alone has so far managed to remove—at a cost, to be sure, which no Western nation could contemplate. It is not only that we know too little about how to manage large organisations, as Michael Shanks points out; we simply do not know how to deal with large numbers of people, in or outside organisations, short of putting them into uniform or concentration camps. The simplest problems elude social solutions: housing, the staggering of the working-day, of annual and school holidays, the removal of goods traffic from crowded roads to empty railways, careless and faulty driving which, as Gunnar Randers shows, claims an annual death toll the equivalent of fourteen infantry divisions in the NATO countries alone—the subject is inexhaustible.

Yet, if there is one unifying theme running through this book it is that, to avert the disasters which our myopia and apathy threaten to bring upon us, we will need not fewer but many more, and more rigorous controls.

21

Our trust in the free pursuit of knowledge as an activity that is its own justification has been too unquestioning. We believed with Plato that 'we shall be better, braver ... men if we think it right to look for what we don't know'; we believed with Bacon that 'knowledge frees the human condition'; we believed with Goethe that 'harmful truth is useful because it can be harmful only temporarily'. Today we are less sure. Enlightenment carried to excess may itself become an obscurantism. With so many of our traditional props decaying at the foundation, perhaps we should ask ourselves whether there aren't times in the history of a civilisation (and Toynbee shows that there are) when a suspension of certain types of scientific enquiry may serve us better than pushing the frontiers of knowledge beyond our moral horizons. There *are*, as we well know from common experience, harmful kinds of knowledge. Science may be no exception, nor may scientists be better equipped to be keepers of the world's conscience than politicians or bureaucrats, though it is tempting to think that the pursuit of truth guarantees the wisdom of the pursuer. But it is not so.

If, then, there is a St. Andreas fault running through the human mind dividing knowledge from responsibility, the 'can' from the 'may' in human activity, it is cogent to suggest, as Kahn does, that some sensitive problem-areas in science and technology should be left uninvestigated. Given our state of moral underdevelopment, not all truth may bear exploring. 'Harmful truth', which Goethe commends as being useful in the long run, may, in the accelerated conditions of our age, do so much damage in the short term that the human race may not live to see the long-term benefits.

We are confronted here with one of the two most formidable problems of our (and all) time: are we justified—indeed is it incumbent upon us—to use means that seems good to us if the ends it promotes are foreseeably evil? Should, for example, lives be prolonged when overpopulation is the predictable result? The opposite proposition, that worthy ends do not justify evil means, has been conclusively answered, at least for our generation. But is the use of good means self-justificatory? And if it isn't, who or what shall provide the controls?

It would be pleasant to think that there is still time so to arrange matters that, in the words of Brian Aldiss, 'the head doesn't run too far ahead of the heart', but by all the evidence assembled in this volume, there isn't. Human engineering (time was when we called it education) is a slow and taxing process, and the results do not carry the makers' warranty. If three thousand years of civilisation have not taught us to live by a modicum of reason, or to create effective buffers against the baneful components in our irrationalities, the next thirty are most unlikely to do so.

Religion, which a Machiavelli would know how to harness to the public good, is dead as a restraining social influence. So, outside China, is ideology. So is our willingness—though not our ability—to recast the consciousness of man to make him into a more rational and more malleable being. What remains is the tenacity of our race to survive, and survive at any cost.

It is not a pretty picture. It evokes the spectre of a global Los Angeles, of mass-man, of anaesthesia by remote control, of featherless bipeds huddling ever more closely together around pools of re-cycled sewage water. Perhaps it is time for us to bid farewell to the past, to turn our eyes away from the liberal polity, individualism and the dignity of man. Perhaps there *is* no difference between the lead in the head of the political prisoner and the lead in the drinking water of New York. Perhaps our sights have been set too high, appropriate to another age.

If democracy is dying of the incomprehension of the world's complexities, the day of the global manipulator cannot be far off. Our freedom may then consist of casting our vote for a benevolent despot. The real problem of the future, Maurice Cranston says, is 'not the question of putting the most intelligent men at the head of the state, but of ensuring that the kind of men likely to come out on top are suitably educated and civilised'. This is one prescription for surviving our future, and perhaps the most hopeful; but one wonders whether it, too, isn't a nostrum for the ills of simpler times.

By the year 2,000 the world's population will have reached 6,400 million of whom only twenty-three per cent will be North Americans and Europeans (including the U.S.S.R.). With every passing year this twenty-three per cent will be getting richer and the remaining seventy-seven per cent relatively poorer. North Americans and Europeans will be responsible for eighty per cent of the world's GNP (ninety per cent if Japan is included), they will be using up more than three-quarters of the world's resources and enjoying over three-quarters of the world's income, the U.S. alone accounting for more than half. It is not a question whether but how soon the impoverished and ever-growing majority will challenge the rich and ever-diminishing minority for a more equitable distribution of food, space and resources.

If Western societies were governed by a minimum of reason, or just plain self-interest, the popular issues on which political parties would run for office would be falling expectations and a ban on the ethic of the consumer society, viz. less food at higher prices, poorer housing, fewer cars, a rationing of all fossil fuels, reduced travel and holidays, restricted medical care, the outlawing of gerontology, fertility tax after the second child, a levy on all casual breeding, *and* a simultaneous and massive re-channelling of the fruits of Western technology, together with its skills, from the twenty-three per cent to the rest of mankind.

The suggestion is absurd, matched only by the absurdity of allowing ourselves to be propelled into self-destruction by the successes of technological civilisation. Yet if, with the great but legitimate benefit of hindsight, one believes with Hegel that 'peoples and governments have never yet learnt anything from history', then it is precisely that self-destruction towards which we are heading.

THE IMPACT OF
SCIENCE ON THE MORAL
OPTIONS OF MAN

ARNOLD J. TOYNBEE

Technical Advance
and the Morality of Power

Arnold J. Toynbee's reputation as one of the world's leading and most influential historians is too well established to need stressing. His many distinguished appointments include that of Member of the British Delegation to the Paris Peace Conferences of 1919 and 1946; Director, Foreign Research and Press Services, Royal Institute of International Affairs (1939–43); Director, Research Department, Foreign Office (1943–46) and Research Professor of International History at London University (retired 1955). Dr. Toynbee is an Honorary D.Litt. of the Universities of Oxford, Birmingham and Columbia (New York), Litt.D., Cambridge (England), D.C.L., Princeton and a member of the British Association (since 1937). Dr. Toynbee's best-known work is *A Study of History*, vols. I-III (1934), vols. IV–VI (1939), vols. VII–X (1954), vol. XI (1958), vol. XII (Reconsiderations, 1961). Dr. Toynbee gave the 1952 Reith Lectures *The World and the West*, and the Gifford Lectures in 1953–54, *An Historian's Approach to Religion*.

GLENNY: A new kind of terminology concerning the problems of our environment is being bandied about nowadays. Two of the words that one hears used by some of the Cassandra-figures who are warning us as to what lies ahead are the words 'biosphere' and 'technosphere'. The biosphere is defined as the entire complex of the surface and atmosphere of the planet on which we live and which provides the means whereby we and all other living organisms can maintain life. The technosphere is looked upon by some as an alien super-structure on the biosphere, created by the interaction of man upon the biosphere. Some even think that it has reached a point now where the technosphere is exhausting the biosphere to

26

such a degree (for instance, through the pollution of air and water and through the exhaustion of natural resources) that the man-made technosphere may before long become so parasitic that it will exhaust the biosphere altogether. Do you think I am drawing too alarmist a picture?

TOYNBEE: Not at all. I believe this to be the central problem not only of our time but of human history up to date, because I think today a crisis has matured which has been latent and gradually gathering force since our ancestors became human. (The biosphere used to be called nature, the technosphere used to be called tools, but these new names are convenient, and I find them very expressive.) The technosphere is coeval with human nature. If the technosphere is alien this is because man himself is in a sense alien: a self-conscious living creature is a unique and recent phenomenon on this planet, among all the vast number of different species of living creatures. The technosphere came into existence as soon as our first ancestors began to modify fragments of the biosphere to serve their purposes as tools. Other creatures like chimpanzees or beavers use unmodified pieces of nature as tools, but when you find a piece of stone chipped by some living creature to serve as a better tool, then you know you are in the presence of a human artefact. In fact, the earliest evidence of our ancestors being human is the remains of their tools, not the remains of their bones. We have unfortunately very few bones, but we have quite a lot of tools from the very earliest age.

Now here we come to two things I'd like to underline. The first is the acceleration in the development of the technosphere and the second is the relation between technology and man's ethical, spiritual and social life. This is important because man is a social creature or nothing. If he were not social he would have perished. Unfortunately he has not been social enough —anyway, not enough to hold his power in check. As for acceleration: for the first 500,000 years, by which I mean the Lower Palaeolithic Age, there was a technosphere, there were tools, but man was living under very primitive conditions and the technosphere made very little impact on the biosphere. The biosphere remained practically intact. As long as human beings are still in the food-gathering and even in the hunting and fishing stage, they are competing with other living creatures more or less on terms of equality and they are not changing the environment in which they live. But in very recent times (by very recent times I mean since the last 30,000 years, which is a short time compared to the first 500,000), i.e. since the Upper Palaeolithic Age, a much more efficient tool replaced the Lower Palaeolithic type of tool, which had been practically constant for about 500,000 years; the technosphere was gathering speed. Then came the Neolithic Age, which meant agriculture and the breeding of domesticated animals, then metallurgy, and then last of all the Industrial Revolution which started in Britain in the 18th Century and which has been gathering speed at an enormous, dizzy pace in our own time.

Now as soon as man became self-conscious he became aware, unlike other living creatures, that he was at the mercy of nature, at the mercy of the biosphere. And he naturally wanted to become the master instead of the slave of nature. This has always been his ambition, but he has never realised that he was going to achieve this to the present degree till quite recently. A few centuries ago he felt that nature was still dominant and he was still at its mercy. As fast as he has mastered nature and has replaced the biosphere, the natural environment, by the technosphere which is an artificial, man-made environment, he has acquired power. Power not only over non-human nature, but what is much more serious, over his fellow human beings —or to be more exact, some human beings have acquired great power over others. The organisation of human society means that somebody who is probably totally unknown to you is dictating how you shall live, what you shall earn, what your standard of living shall be, whether your life shall be endurable or not. This is an inevitable part of social life; but it also raises the problem of the morality of power, and I think that since the first two atomic bombs were used at the end of the Second World War everybody has realised that our power is quite out of balance with our morals. We are wondering, too, whether in so successfuly replacing the biosphere by the technosphere, we have not exchanged a moderately hard master for an *intolerably* hard one. The master we have created for ourselves may be one we really cannot endure or cannot survive. This is like the story of the artificial man who destroyed his human creator, Frankenstein.

GLENNY: Do you believe that the most urgent question of our time is whether, and if so how, we can bring the technosphere under control?

TOYNBEE: I do; but I am not encouraged by the prospects. There is a kind of senselessness about what is happening. I am thinking of the problem of traffic in and between the giant cities that are springing up all over the world now. Mechanised transport is manageable as long as it is on rails, but unmanageable now that it is almost entirely road-borne. In Britain, for instance, the motor-car industry is supposed to be vital to our economy: it employs a lot of people; it earns foreign exchange; it says it needs a home market, therefore the authorities tolerate the proliferation of millions of cars year by year on the roads of this small and congested island. The government has to build roads that can carry this traffic and this produces intolerable conditions for all the people living near these roads. Then take aeroplanes—an important industry in Britain, but a much more important industry in a super-power like the United States.

Now I am eighty-two, I can no longer travel by air because it is too exhausting even for short journeys, while journeys that cross the time zones are impossible for me. I recently had an invitation to visit Japan. I shall probably not be able to go, because I could only travel by sea, and the development of air traffic has wrecked passenger sea traffic. Liners are now only used for pleasure cruises; there are cargo boats which take passengers, but not if they are aged over seventy-five. So I cannot go to Japan. I am unable to travel because technology has become so good that it has deprived me of the possibility of travelling.

GLENNY: This is one of the ironies of progress: what it gives with one hand it takes with the other.

TOYNBEE: Yes, it is a sort of cosmic joke. Such things would indeed be funny if they were not so serious and even tragic. We must do something about it, but we haven't yet discovered what we are to do with this Frankenstein's monster. And we have left it very late. I suppose the atomic bomb, traffic congestion and the pollution of the atmosphere and of the water are the things that have woken us up, but we have come awake only at the eleventh hour and the question is: have we the resolution, the strength of mind, the imagination to be able to solve this terrible problem that we have created for ourselves? Would it not be better to be primitive man than to be us? This is a meaningless question for us because we cannot revert to being primitive man, but it is a question with a very real meaning for the less advanced countries. I fear, however, that the developmental race, particularly between what for convenience one may call the NATO powers and the Warsaw Pact powers, has reached an unstoppable pitch of intensity. Russia, and all the Eastern European countries to some degree, have been running a terrible race with the West ever since the turn of the 17th and 18th Centuries. A number of times the East Europeans (and this applies to people outside, such as the Turks or Japanese) have thought—'Well, now we've achieved it; at enormous effort we have caught up with the West.' Then, just as they thought it, the West has made another spurt forward and they have had to start all over again.

GLENNY: Since you mention Russia and Japan I should like to raise a particular question here, because I think it illustrates so well the socio-political impact of technology on traditional, undynamic societies, and that is the comparison between Russia and Japan. Russia and Japan were the two nations who decided to modernise more or less simultaneously. The emancipation of the serfs and the other great reforms under Alexander II occurred at about the same time as the Meiji restoration in Japan, both of which were then followed in both countries around the turn of the century by a period of hectic industrialisation. In the first rush of their rapid development these two expanding, modernising countries then clashed with each other in the Russo-Japanese War. Japan, whose conditions were apparently almost identical to those of Russia, was the victor of this clash. She had won the Sino–Japanese War of 1894–95, and ten years later she proceeded to beat a European, or allegedly European, nation in the form of Russia. Now whereas Russia reeled under the shock and indeed almost broke under the strain of the defeat of the Russo-Japanese War, Japan went on from strength to strength. Japan has not only far outpaced China as one of the two great Far Eastern nations to modernise, but she has advanced at an incredible pace and has now overtaken—really genuinely overtaken—many of her Western exemplars in technological development. Could we dwell for a moment on this interesting contrast between Russia and Japan?

TOYNBEE: This contrast is a very significant example for the whole world. In explaining it I would mention firstly the difference of cultural background. Russia is an Eastern Orthodox Christian country, a Byzantine country if you like. Byzantinism and Western Christianity are brothers but extremely different from each other, and there's a kind of latent hostility between them. Japan did not have this cultural handicap. In a way the Shinto and Buddhist background of Japanese culture and religion is much more easy to combine with modern science and therefore with modern technology than is Christianity— certainly than Eastern Orthodox Christianity. Although, as you mentioned, they both decided very definitely to modernise in the 1860s, there was a significant difference in the preceding chapter of their history. Russia's first decision to modernise was in the 1690s, and in the 1690s Japan took a decision to cut

31

herself off from the Western world. She sent a commission to look at the West, she did not like what it saw, and she decided to insulate herself; for about 230 years she did this very successfully.

GLENNY: This too is the reverse of the Russian experience. Under Peter the Great, Russia was the greatest industrial manufacturing power in Europe. But for some reason Russia stopped developing after Peter the Great. Indeed Catherine the Great, although she achieved enormous territorial expansion, left Russia's economy in a disastrous mess when she died. And the ruin of the economy under Catherine, plus the political stagnation which followed, right up to the death of Nicholas I, produced a kind of stasis in Russia that lasted from the death of Peter the Great in 1725 until 1855, which was a vital period when Russia lost whatever lead she had once had.

TOYNBEE: Quite so. And this illustrates another important difference between Russia and Japan; if you look at modern Russian history you see that it was an autocracy, which always depended on individuals. Russia had luck in Peter the Great; she had some luck in Alexander II, she had luck I would say in Lenin; she had on the contrary very bad luck in Nicholas I, in Alexander III and in Nicholas II. But the point is that she was dependent on these autocrats for what happened. Now in Japan there were two extremely able classes of people (a class is much more stable than an individual autocrat, and much more dependable). One class was the military class, the Samurai. The revolution which brought about the Meiji restoration was made by young Samurai. It is really very extraordinary that a feudal military class should make a revolution as they did. They were extremely patriotic and self-abnegating; they were destroying their own privilege, deliberately and with open eyes. But more important, during the period of Japan's isolation, the Tokugawa regime which preceded the Meiji regime attempted to freeze everything. Not only did it cut off Japan from the outer world, but it tried to freeze the domestic life of Japan and this was completely un-successful. During the Tokugawa regime, effective power within Japan passed from the Samurai class to a commercial class and some of the leading firms such as Mitsui and Mitsubishi were built up and created in the pre-Meiji era, so that Japan started her modernisation with experience in business organisation on a very grand scale.

This is very important in explaining Japan's successes against Russia from the 1860s and 1890s and onwards.

GLENNY: But was it not also due to the impossibility, in Russia, of trying to impose modernity on a society entirely based on the most primitive peasant agriculture in Europe? It seems to me to show that you cannot simply buy technological progress by exporting the products of a vast but inefficient agriculture.

TOYNBEE: I thoroughly agree with this. The grain trade from Odessa is an example of the absurdity of such a policy—Russian people were often hungry and yet grain was being exported. I think Peter the Great realised this fully, and attempted to modernise the *whole* of Russia, but he had just one lifetime in which to achieve it and it was not enough. I think Lenin realised it fully—but he had an even shorter life-time in power. This, surely, was the issue between the Marxist Social Democrats and the agrarian Social Revolutionaries in Russia. In opposition to the Social Revolutionaries, Lenin was quite convinced that you could not build on the peasantry, that you could not develop Russia into a modern state on a peasant basis. Considering that Russia was an overwhelmingly peasant country, this meant a very rapid and therefore drastic and brutal imposition of the technosphere in its most modern form on the almost neolithic technology of pre-revolutionary peasant Russia. We were conscious in Britain of the sufferings of the rural hand-loom workers round about the 1800s when they were ruined and forced to become factory workers instead. But this is nothing to the sufferings of the Russian peasantry.

What the Communist regime has done is to turn a nation of peasants into a nation of industrial workers. Lenin realised that the peasants not only could not form a possible basis for a really modernised Russia; he realised they were naturally attached to free enterprise ownership—all peasants are. And he was not going to stand for that. But his miscalculation was that he idealised industrial workers. He thought the industrial workers would be self-abnegating socialists who would work for society and not for themselves, and when the industrial workers, led by their trade unions, turned out to want free enterprise too, just as industrial workers have all over the world when they have had a chance, he suppressed them by military force and Russia has ever since been under a repressive regime, a continuation of the previous repressive regime—which is a great weakness for Russia. I think Russia modernised reluctantly and unevenly because she modernised at too high a speed. In a sense we have all modernised too fast, but there are degrees of speed, and in the countries like Britain or the United States or Western Europe in general, in which the industrial revolution phase of the technosphere started, at least the speed has not been so intolerable as in countries which started at the peasant stage. A more extreme example than Russia is, of course, Turkey, which in the 1920s modernised at a pace which makes Peter the Great look fairly moderate. Turkey has been suffering from psychological shock ever since, and this accounts for the troubles Turkey has had in the last fifty years and is having at the present day. She felt that her only alternatives were annihilation or modernisation—to do in six or eight years what the Western world had done in four hundred years, but she had to do it.

GLENNY: The Tokugawa regime in Japan of the late 17th Century, which sent a commission to examine Western civilisation, then made the decision that, in the words of one of our other contributors to this symposium, Professor Dennis Gabor: 'History must stop.' Some people are so alarmed at the way things are going today that they take refuge in this rather simplistic but radical statement that definite action must be taken to arrest historical advance, and for this they use this catch-phrase 'history must stop'. What is your reaction to a statement of that nature?

TOYNBEE: My reaction as a historian is to look at the past to try and see what experiences of this sort there have been. Experience shows that you can stop history by a tremendously repressive government for a time and to a certain extent, but the noticeable thing about the Tokugawa period of Japanese history is that in reality it was not possible to stop history. Fortunately for Japan, the history that did move on, in spite of the regime's determination to repress changes of all kinds, was economic history of a kind which prepared Japan, contrary to the regime's intentions, for entry into the modern world. This was an unforeseeable stroke of good fortune. But there have been other regimes which have been put into power and tolerated because they stood for stopping history.

GLENNY: What examples do you call to mind?

TOYNBEE: Besides the Tokugawa regime in Japan I am thinking of the Roman Empire and the Chinese Empire. The purpose of those empires, the reason why they were tolerated, why they lasted as long as they did (and the Chinese Empire lasted a very long time), was that on the whole their peoples felt that they must tolerate them because history had to be stopped. For two centuries before Caesar and Augustus, the Graeco-Roman world had been destroying itself by utterly ruinous wars and by political and social revolutions. The choice was world autocracy or the dissolution of society, so they chose world autocracy. There is an interesting story about a Roman Emperor who was told by his secretary that somebody had invented unbreakable glass, so he said, 'Oh, put him to death.' When the secretary did not understand, the Emperor said, 'Don't you see that if unbreakable glass is made it will put the glass-makers of Alexandria out of employment, there will be riots and revolution and the world will relapse into anarchy again? What do we stand for? To stop anarchy. So put him to death.' And this was done.

I think that when the Chinese Empire deliberately restricted the ideology of China to the single Confucian form, restricted the running of the administration to Confucian-educated scholars who all had to pass one examination which qualified them for the civil service, that again was a case of stopping history. This was paralleled in the Chinese attitude to technology. China invented a number of key techniques which have been taken up and eagerly used by other people, like gunpowder and the compass and printing, but Imperial China saw them as a menace and, in the light of the experience of anarchy and destruction and suffering that had been caused by using them recklessly and in the wrong way in earlier periods of Chinese history, they were repressed in China. Greek and Roman technology also stopped developing. That is why the barbarians succeeded and why the Mediaeval Western world forged ahead of the Byzantine world, because the Byzantine world retained the Roman Empire's attitude towards technology. The Western barbarians had no prejudice against technology and produced numerous vital inventions, such as stirrups and a more rational way of harnessing horses.

GLENNY: You imply that there were great difficulties in stopping history.

TOYNBEE: In a sense there were, even in the relatively simple technologies of the past. On the other hand, we have one tremendously stark fact that in our day, in the technologically advanced part of the world, tomorrow in the world as a whole, organised human power is quite out of balance with our social and moral and spiritual performance—not with our standards but with our performance. This is menacing the human race with self-liquidation, and we have to do something—we have to make a pause in the development of our power, and also to redirect our attention and energy from the mastery of the biosphere and the imposition of the technosphere on it, to the mastery of ourselves and of our relations with each other. This is what all the historical religions and philosophies have been telling us with one voice for a very long time. This has now surely become obvious to everybody. Why have science and technology developed so tremendously in the Western world? Because so many people have put their hearts and minds into that and not into other things. Now we must take out a lot of that heart and mind from developing technology, and put it back into making our social life and our behaviour in general come up to the standard which is necessary for creatures who have this enormous power in their hands. We realise we are simply not fit to exercise the power that we have, and this is the most menacing thing in our present situation.

GLENNY: You mention the conscious effort to arrest technological development that occurred in the Chinese Empire. In the Chinese Empire strict ordinances were issued, for instance, by which potential warlike materials, such as bronze and gunpowder, could not be made in ways which might have had military uses. As a result, Chinese civilisation, technologically speaking, remained static for thousands of years. Then suddenly China was faced with the 20th Century when she was technologically still in the first millennium B.C.

TOYNBEE: Yes, in the stage of the Greeks and Romans.

GLENNY: Now, in the short term this appeared to put China at a tremendous disadvantage, because she twice suffered defeat by Japan, first of all in the Sino-Japanese War in the 1890s, and then again in the 1930s. She also suffered psychologically by being apparently so backward compared with the other nations of the world, although implanted in the Chinese psyche was the conviction that the Chinese were infinitely more civilised and, in a certain sense, the most advanced people in the world. Ever since the Opium Wars this blatant dichotomy between Chinese political thinking and technological backwardness has caused

37

constant tension and disturbance in China. However, when we look back in a few decades' time, I wonder if in fact China has not been most fortunate in having missed out on a great deal of technological development, because she is still in a largely agricultural state and her technosphere, as it were, has not yet had time to start to ruin her biosphere. Do you think that this may give China an enormous advantage in the future?

TOYNBEE: I do think just that. I think China has the chance —whether she will take the chance or not we do not know, but the Chinese are a wise and intelligent people—she has the chance of profiting by the unhappy experience of the Western world and particularly of her next door neighbour, Japan, who is Westernised. China has her biosphere more or less intact. Though agriculture has transformed the biosphere, this agricultural stage of the technosphere has not obliterated the biosphere or wrecked it. It has inserted technology into the biosphere in a way that is not destructive. Now this is just what the human race as a whole has to do now, and perhaps China may have a chance of experimenting in this in ways which will be very valuable to the rest of us, of somehow reconciling the most advanced technology with keeping the biosphere intact.

The Chinese were very immoderate and violent during those five centuries, the so-called Period of the Contending States, before the foundation of the Chinese Empire in the 3rd Century B.C. In that age China was as violent as the modern Western world and the Graeco-Roman world in its stages before the foundation of the Roman Empire, and the Chinese never forgot this. You have illustrated the ways in which they sacrificed technological development in the cause of keeping moderation in social and political relations. After all, Confucius was convinced that social relations were the fundamental aspect of human life because man is a social creature. Of course, the Chinese system of life and of government had its drawbacks. I think the administration by the Mandarins was economically top-heavy and there was rather oppressive landlordism, but on the whole during those two thousand years of the Chinese

Empire the Chinese were far more successful than any other part of the human race in keeping hundreds of millions of human beings together politically in peace. No other people has achieved that. The Roman Empire was very short-lived and very small in population compared to the Chinese Empire.

GLENNY: Perhaps the typical example, the epitome in fact, of our destructive effect on our environment is the phenomenon of the city. Not the manageable, organic *polis* of Greece in the 5th Century B.C., but the modern megalopolis, which, although it has very marked cultural and social advantages, now appears to be creating disadvantages and, to use a fashionable word, diseconomies which are now so tremendous as to call into question the whole concept of the city, and to prompt the thought that we may be forced, maybe in some catastrophic way, to find an alternative to the city.

TOYNBEE: I agree that the city is the supreme present illustration of the technosphere getting out of control. As you say, there have been cities from a very early stage; there were even one or two Neolithic cities, Jericho for instance, and there have been cities all through history. But there have been very few big cities. Of course, there have been the capitals of empires or big national states, but these were exceptional, and they were not centres of large-scale industry, so they did not have the problems of the modern industrial city. But the typical city, till the end of the 18th Century, was a city from which you could walk out of the city walls within ten minutes from the centre of the city. And the city had an organic relation with the countryside. I could cite a novel by Thomas Hardy, *The Mayor of Casterbridge*, which has some eloquent passages about the relation of a small market town in the south-west of England with the countryside, and how town and country were beautifully interdependent. There was no question of one wrecking the other or menacing the other; each was necessary to the other. I think of the German poet Goethe, in his loving account of his childhood in the city of Frankfurt, which for the 18th Century in the Western world was a rather big city, and how he then spent the rest of his life in the tiny capital city of Weimar in Eastern Germany. He too was living in an urban environment which was not a threat to the biosphere but was a stimulus to the biosphere. People who lived in cities of that kind were proud of their cities, they loved to live in them, they hated to be away from them. The English poet Robert Browning has written a poem about Italy called *Up in the Villa, Down in the City*, in which an impoverished Italian nobleman has to live in his country house instead of in the city. The poem describes how he hates it and how he longs to be back in the city again— one of these tiny cities of course, not a modern industrial city.

Now the ominous feature about industrial cities is that everybody who can escape from them does. People will make their money in the cities, but if they can afford it they will live in a suburb and retire far way to the Riviera or Southern California or Florida, and during their working life they will commute— every industrial city in the United States is surrounded by a ring of separately incorporated suburbs which are barricaded, so to speak, against invasion by the industrial workers, by factories and by pollution. This shows you how hateful the new industrial city, the city of the last two hundred years, is to mankind.

GLENNY: Earlier you referred to the way in which the Roman Empire coped with the problem of social and political control, also the impact of technology, in this particular instance of agricultural and military technology, on the society of the day. Now to most ordinary people looking back, the Roman Empire is a very long time ago. Looked at from the time scale of the common man, we have had two or three thousand years in which to work out systems of social and political control to keep our house in order. Yet it would appear that we have failed to do so, because, if you regard our present age, together with what is normally referred to as antiquity, this is merely a speck on the great biological or geological time scale of the history of the planet as a whole. Assuming then that we have not had enough time to become truly civilised, how do you rate the chances of three possible outcomes of our situation? Firstly, that we shall blow ourselves up with an enormous nuclear explosion. Secondly, that we will smother ourselves in our own waste products, and thirdly, that perhaps there may be some other solution that is equally unpleasant. What would you suggest that this solution might be at worst?

TOYNBEE: First I must again stress the time scale, because it is almost impossible for any of us to imagine the truth that all but a minute fragment of human history has been passed in the Lower Palaeolithic Age, in which control of technology was no problem, but in which control of *nature* was a problem. Only in the last thirty thousand years has this become a life and death question.

The possibility of our obliterating ourselves by an atomic world war: we all know that this exists, we all know that nobody wants to do it, and we know that the two people and their governments, the United States and the Soviet Union, which at present are the only ones who could do it, are determined not to do it, but we also know that circumstances might overcome them. There have been many wars in which both sides have drifted into war while realising that such wars would be completely disastrous. The confrontation, or possible confrontation, in the Middle East is an instance of the possibility that America and Russia might be drawn into a war with each other despite their extreme efforts to avoid it. So we cannot rule out the possibility of the so-called big bang and the self-liquidation of the human race, though the crime and the folly of it is almost beyond imagining.

The possibility of suffocating ourselves by pollution is much more menacing. It would be caused by the immediate prospect of economic gain, and this applies not only to free-enterprise societies but to Socialist societies, because Socialist societies are in competition with each other *and* with the free-enterprise societies, and are therefore tempted to take short-term views of economic and technological development rather than long-term

41

views. This is a very serious menace. Fortunately we are beginning to become conscious of this. The question is how—are we to provide safeguards against these two alternatives—the rather more likely alternative of suffocation by pollution and the rather less likely alternative of self-liquidation by a nuclear war? I am always impressed by the fact that everything has its price—you have to pay, in the metaphorical as well as the literal sense, for anything that you want to achieve. And I fear that the price of guarding ourselves against both these dangers will be an extremely repressive government of the Roman or Chinese kind, and this is what we have to face. Such a government could not be permanent and it could not control every side of life, as these historic examples show. But it may be, shall we say, the lesser evil to which we shall have to submit. In fact, according to my expectation, this is our third alternative choice, and I guess that we are more likely to choose this than to choose either of the other two.

GLENNY: All the time that we have been discussing the dire future which may await the inhabitants of the developed Western world, behind us and treading on our tail is what is referred to as 'the Third World'. What should those who think about these things in the developed world say to the leaders and the citizens of the Third World, in the hope that they will avoid the mistakes that we have made? Because they are hell-bent on following the same course and making the same, if not worse, mistakes, that we have made in our treatment of our environment.

TOYNBEE: They are indeed hell-bent on this because they reasonably feel that, unless they get even with us in technology, which means in material power, they will be at our mercy and we shall continue to abuse our power and to exploit them—treat them as 'natives' as we have done in the past. And these people who are still in the agricultural stage of society, the neolithic stage you may call it really, are the vast majority of the human race still, in spite of the immense industrialisation and urbanisation of the more advanced countries. This new-found anxiety over technology has so far been a dialogue between representatives of the more advanced countries. Unfortunately, I fear we are the blind leaders of the blind. We have not found our own way and yet we have to advise a great majority of the human race, who have not reached our stage yet, on which way they should follow. We can advise them, we can point to our mistakes and advise them not to do that, but what positive advice can we give? The positive advice I would give in very general terms is that the human race is far more able at technology, that is in dealing with *non-human* nature, than it is in dealing with itself. In other words, far more able in technology than in religion, politics and social relations. We must somehow master ourselves—master ourselves in the sense in which the historic religions and philosophies all beseech us to master ourselves, and, until we can do that and unless we can do that, we shall be under threat from the technosphere which is our own man-made creation.

PHILIP RIEFF

The Loss of the Past
and the Mystique of Change

Philip Rieff is the Benjamin Franklin Professor of Sociology at the University of Pennsylvania, Philadelphia. His many distinguished appointments include those of Fellow at the Center of Advanced Study in the Behavioural Sciences, Palo Alto, California (1957–58); Fulbright Professor at the University of Munich (1959–60); Visiting Fellow, Center for the Study of Democratic Institutions, Santa Barbara, California (1963–64) and Fellow of All Souls College, Oxford (1970). He has published *Freud: The Mind of the Moralist* (1959), *The Triumph of the Therapeutic: Uses of Faith after Freud* (1960), and edited *The Collected Papers of Sigmund Freud* (1961).

GLENNY: Most of the contributors to this symposium may be classified, in their attitudes towards the future of society under the impact of technology, as those who foresee either the apocalypse or paradise, pessimists and optimists. The pessimists tend to foretell almost total doom, whereas the optimists, although never so extreme as the pessimists, express a guarded belief that man contains within him powers which will enable him to control the monster that he has unleashed in the form of modern technology. Where do you stand on this great divide between opinions?

RIEFF: Certainly it is easier to be a pessimist than an optimist and perhaps intellectually less interesting. Intellectual pride demands that one be an optimist, but honesty seems to me to demand a certain pessimism. I expect the apocalypse long before I expect paradise.

44

GLENNY: You imply that the situation is going to get a good deal worse, with regard to the possible social and environmental effect of technology, before it gets better.

RIEFF: I have no special knowledge of the physical effects of technology; I am, rather, an analyst of the social structure of technology, and it is to that kind of question that I can best address my intellectual energies. It seems to me that the first step towards an adequate sociological analysis of the crisis of Western culture with special reference to technology, is to look at what has happened to the technological cause itself. As early as the 18th Century we have very powerful figures, not least among them Benjamin Franklin, with what might be called, if the paradox is permitted, a transcendental faith in the power and future of technology to transform both the outer and inner life of man. We are seeing very clearly that faith is now challenged if not abandoned. Where does one now find a technocratic movement, the kind of hopes that Veblen had in his time? The technocrats, so far as both the outer and inner life of man is concerned, are on the defensive.

Firstly, the outer life of man, the 'culture' of the technologists, is in ruins. Here others have spoken with considerable precision on the question of the risks involved in the continuous transformation of our physical environment. Those risks are literally in the air now, and I leave it to the ecologists to extrapolate from those risks.

But the technologists of the 18th, 19th and first half of our own century also expected to transform the inner life, to transform consciousness. This, it seems to me, has not happened in any way that they themselves expected. Certainly Benjamin Franklin expected such a transformation, and in fact the University of Pennsylvania, for one institutional example, was the first American University founded specifically as a secular university by Franklin and his associates. It was to be a university that was not to emphasise systematic training in the religious and philosophical traditions of Western culture, but rather in the more practical arts; in short a more technologically oriented institution was envisioned.

GLENNY: But did Franklin and his fellow-rationalists of the Enlightenment have any inkling of the possible dangers inherent in unlimited technological advance?

RIEFF: Indeed they did not. Franklin was of course a powerful optimist, as were his colleagues of the American Revolution. But technology as they understood it was not a technology of total transformation. They expected the inherited religious and social capital of Western culture to continue to be indefinitely amortisable. So on the basis of the notion that mankind lived on a great and stable moral and cultural capital, technology could then extend itself indefinitely and beneficently. What has happened is not a challenge to the capacity of technology to extend itself indefinitely, but rather beneficently. That is bound up with the badly shaken belief in the stability and the largesse of the moral capital of our culture. The fact that men can capitalise on his technological opportunities may be the most dangerous capacity he has. It is precisely this suspicion about his capacity to capitalise as a technologist on opportunities that occur in the continuum of technological effort that worries the technologists themselves, and not merely the latter-day Luddites who are so afraid of the advance of technology that they want to stop it.

The doubt that there is a great and stable moral capital upon which we can depend was certainly present long before the rise of the technological barbarians of Nazi Germany and of our European culture generally. This unease was also understood in the 19th Century by conservative philosophers of history, figures like Burckhardt, who would not have thought of themselves as philosophers of history but nevertheless saw a new barbarism rising. And this barbarism must be very closely understood as the barbarism of what I would call 'radical contemporaneity'.

GLENNY: How would you define this concept of 'radical contemporaneity'?

RIEFF: Well, in America it is a kind of ingenuous will to transform, without regard to what is being destroyed and what is being constructed. America has been the place to which people have gone to escape the past; in this sense American culture is the cemetery of many pasts. This was certainly true in colonial America, and it has been true ever since. The characteristic feature of the technological ethos (and it is the cultural context of technology that is my concern) which is so typical of American culture, is what I would call the trap of radical contemporaneity. It means a systematic rejection of the past and of the constraints of the past, the constant opening up of new opportunities that are implicit in the dynamics of technology itself, and a feeling that the constraints applied by the traditional culture are hostile to the demands of technology and therefore are somehow reactionary and regressive.

This outlook is certainly an essential element of the bourgeois ethos. Marx was right to understand the middle class as an endlessly revolutionary class to whom nothing is sacred. And this fusion of the bourgeois ethos and the technological ethos can be seen in a figure like Comte, who saw in the social technologist a savant who would stand by the side of the technologist of the mechanical world (and for Comte the world was to be understood in mechanistic terms) and would advise him on the social implementation of industrial, or if you like, technological processes. And there is a tremendous sense of confidence in Comte in the 1820s, the confidence of a young man seeing an entirely new role for a social technologist, and seeing a transformation of consciousness that occurs because the old constraints of the Catholic consciousness of European civilisation were somehow destroyed. The systematic entity that might have been called European culture fell with the French Revolution, and these new intellectuals of the post-revolutionary period saw themselves not as shoring up some elements of that constraint, or capitalising on some elements of it, but really building a scientific culture.

GLENNY: But is not the expression 'scientific culture' a contradiction in terms?

RIEFF: In a sense, it is. In the particular cultural history of Western society, science seems to me constantly to operate against the established constraints and towards the kind of radical contemporaneity that I, with perhaps others even more pessimistic, would call barbarism. What precisely do I mean by barbarism? Barbarians are not, as some of my naïve students sometimes consider, people with primitive technologies. Barbarians are people without a constraining sense of the past, the mistakes of the past, the follies of the past, who are thus able with fewer inhibitions to attack the potentialities of the present. Therefore what characterises barbarism is an absence of historical memory. And this is precisely what characterises the mechanistic mind of the technologist—in so far as he is a pure technologist. Of course he may be many other things. There are highly segregated psychological and moral systems within each of us as individuals, and the technologist is only a technologist perhaps in his outward life; he may be quite traditional in his attitudes to his inward nature. But the early thrust of technology was towards a transformation, not only of the outward life but —and that is clear in the 19th Century already—of the inward life, too. And this thrust has not taken adequate account of the great discoveries of the nature of the irrational by Freud, for example, and other features that have changed our notion of what the moral and psychological capital of Western man is like, and have made us question how his ego might be able to withstand the dynamics of change. In fact a mystique of change has been created which may itself be psychologically unmanageable for a great many people in Western culture.

GLENNY: You have talked of the barbarism of 'radical contemporaneity'. This seems to me a very telling critique of one particular strand of Western culture, or more precisely of Anglo-Saxon culture as it exists at the moment, which is a kind of thrusting, no-nonsense pragmatism. And it has produced its own brand of barbarism. However, there is another culture, which claims to be deeply imbued with historicism, which is not only historicist in content but also claims to be specifically scientific in its methods, namely the Marxist analysis of society and of man's place in society. Being also a materialist-based philosophy, it gives particular emphasis to the interaction of man with his environment through technology. Now there are many ways in which one might claim that the forms of economic management derived from the Marxist rather than the pragmatist tradition are rather better than is the more diffuse but older Anglo-Saxon tradition. I refer in particular to the amazing speed for instance with which a country like Soviet Russia, which was an underdeveloped country in 1917, has thrust itself forward into the ranks of super-powers. And it has been thought by many leaders of developing countries that Soviet-style development is the one best able to bring them rapidly forward industrially and the devil take the social consequences. How do you react to this?

RIEFF: There are two points to be made here. Firstly, as to the material achievements of the Soviet Union under the Marxist doctrine in one shape or another (Stalinism seems to be a long way from Marxism): that material achievement was well under way in the capitalist phase of Russian history, and there is good evidence to support the generalisation that the pre-Stalinist and the Stalinist phases actually set back what was already a quite healthy development of Russian industry. So what would have happened had the non-Bolshevik Russian meliorists held power, and just how Russian Capitalism might have developed, is a question that can't be pushed further. One can't argue back to the Marxist theoretical alternative from the development of Soviet state power.

The second point interests me more. Just what has been the attitude of Marxism to technological development? Certainly to encourage it, certainly not to view it with the kind of suspicion with which it was viewed by Marx's conservative European contemporaries. There's no doubt about that. But in fact there is no doubt either about the eschatological elements in Marxist theory. The one condition to which Marx referred sparingly, but which he nevertheless regarded as necessary, was a new man. All other developments are consequent upon the development of a new man, of a new consciousness. That new consciousness does not seem to me to have emerged in Marxist culture. In fact what I find so striking about Marxist culture is that while it is so powerful in terms of transforming the external environment, it seems to have done little to transform the internal life of man. Looking at Soviet culture, for example, I think one sees a remarkably conservative element in Soviet society. When one goes to the Soviet ballet one can never see such beautiful aristocratic gesturing as that performed by Soviet dancers. The democratic capitalist bourgeois West has lost that capacity to make aristocratic gestures, the wave of the hand, the inclination of the body—it is from another world. And Soviet culture is resolutely conservative; whereas Anglo-American culture is resolutely radical. And there is no doubt that official Marxism is culturally conservative.

GLENNY: If Soviet Marxism has not produced a 'new man', what *has* it produced?

RIEFF: My impression is that the creature which has emerged from Soviet culture looks strangely like Babbit, the epitome of petty-bourgeois America, immortalised in the novel by Sinclair Lewis. And the American Babbit may be said to be most comfortable with the Soviet man. The Attorney General of the United States, speaking perhaps with the consciousness of his wife, indicated that he much preferred Soviet bureaucrats, that is Soviet Russian Communists, to the home-grown irrationalist American radicals by whom he finds himself terribly confused nowadays. So there is perhaps an elective affinity between the bureaucrats of the Soviet camp and the American technological mentality.

Aside from that question of elective affinities between certain decision-making groups within each culture, what has Marxism, in its later developments, offered? It has offered the Party, the successor institution to both Church and State in many ways. One of the most pathetic and telling lines written by the Italian Marxist Gramsci, is the passage in his splendid short work *The New Prince*, in which he says in effect that the new prince is the Party, and this new prince, able to do everything in its infinite tactical wisdom, is itself a great problem within Marxist theory. The place of the Party in society, and the monopoly of the Party of all wisdom in the culture generally, seems to me to render this Leninist invention exceedingly suspect.

Nevertheless, the Soviet technologists are able to go their own way within a culture dominated by the Party—and this is the telling point—apparently with no less intellectual efficiency (at least viewed from the outside) than the American technologists. So technology appears to be able to thrive under conditions of Party monopoly of the arts and of social wisdom, and in a situation very unlike that of the Anglo-American situation. This further indicates that technologists themselves, who once flew a banner that had inscribed on it something that led people to believe that a totally new culture and a new man would emerge, are a total cultural failure. There is nothing on that banner; rather they always march under other banners.

GLENNY: You are implying that such great innovators as Edison, Bell, Ford, Marconi and all the other pioneers of 20th-Century technology were incapable of putting any cultural content into the apparatus that they created, and our imposing edifice of modern technology is essentially hollow; although sounds are going out over the air waves, and images are being brought to everybody's home, there has been no cultural equivalent of the technological revolution in the 20th Century which would satisfy the enormously greater number of people who, through technology, now have access to the forms, images and sounds of our culture. Would you agree with this?

RIEFF: Yes, I think so. I'd go further, I suspect. I should say that what the technological revolution has helped to do is to fill up and render more superficial the interior life of man. If you can walk along with a transistor radio held to your ear, then you resolve the problem of interior thought, of contemplation as you walk. There is simply no room for it. Your life, the interior life, has been displaced, externalised and trivialised, and this seems to me a model of what technology can do. In that sense it is a very revolutionary instrument. It does not leave man alone in his depths. The constant stimulation available to the ego through technology will negate the interior life so that man will truly lead a more exterior existence. This hollow kind of man certainly can exist; the society of hollow men is quite conceivable and could be rather well ordered.

GLENNY: This was one of the nightmares of the anti-Utopians, of writers like H. G. Wells, Zamyatin in Russia, Aldous Huxley and George Orwell, whose fear was that, provided man's attention could be permanently seized by broadcasting means, this would lead not only to cultural domination by one single source, but also that this would bring with it political domination.

I should have thought that the greatest danger lies not so much in pollution of the atmosphere and our environment as in the recurrence of despotism, with all the instruments of technological control at its command. Surely this seems to me in human terms a greater danger than the destruction of the environment.

RIEFF: I think the problem of the destruction of the natural environment is inseparable from the question of the interior life. The inseparability may be expressed most briefly in this way: all classical cultures as we have known them in the Western tradition, the cultures that ultimately derive from

Athens and Jerusalem, and also the cultures we know of in other societies through the work of the great 19th-Century ethnographers and anthropologists of the 20th Century, all appear to have established certain limits, to have developed certain mythologies of limits, and to have organised their activities around those limits and within those limits. What is characteristic of the cultural revolution of modernity, to which technology has contributed in a unique way (perhaps the unique factor *is* the technological contribution) is the abandonment of limits, to which we are only now returning.

The technologists themselves were, until very recently, not concerned with this question, and yet it is at the very centre of all cultural invention; and so the one science we do not have is the science of limits. In this sense the argument between the apocalyptic and the optimistic polemicist of the present is itself misleading. There is a certain contradiction among the apocalyptic thinkers because they themselves do not propose any limit, but see the inherent destructiveness of a limitless power of technology: in short, they are making an implicit cultural criticism in that there is nothing with which to resist the internal dynamics of the technological order. The optimists on the other hand are still trading implicitly on the exhausted capital of a culture no longer able to constrain the technological dynamic, and perhaps hoping that man in his infinite plasticity can be rendered more superficial, more controllable, and that we can therefore construct a society with fewer problems by simply weeding certain defects out of so-called human nature.

GLENNY: When you discant on the word 'limits', you are echoing what some of our more pessimistic contributors have said in these discussions. In the words of one of them, Professor Dennis Gabor, 'History must stop.' By this he means that the way technology is driving us at the moment is too appalling to contemplate, and therefore controls must be exercised on the unrestrained application and development of technology. However, when they are asked to be more specific and to say how such controls might be applied, it becomes a more subtle and difficult matter to discuss. And in particular it is the political and the social implications of the controls on a global scale that some people are now proposing, which raise doubts. In other words we move into the realm of global politics. Now is this growth of what must eventually be a totalitarian kind of control something that you fear in society's future under the impact of technology?

RIEFF: There are easy answers, swiftly given, that mask difficult answers. The question is so immense that let me give one of the easy answers first and then immediately go beyond it. I think there is, to take a handy example, no solution for the automobile that does not involve other parts of the economy. In America, and I would say in England too, until the automobile is rendered a vehicle for occasional use, for pleasure, an assistance of public transport, totally reorganised in a way that is both logistically and economically feasible, it will continue to be a destroyer of cities and will not be controllable as a factor in our social life. But the really important question you asked was: Who is to forbid? And this breaks down into the problem of the structure of prohibition, and the question of the execution of prohibition. Of course, this is an immense question. It is both particular to our time and general to the human condition, as all figures in the history of the discipline to which I am related from Plato to the present have witnessed. There are great mysteries about this question. If one reads Solzhenitsyn's *The First Circle*, one finds Abakumov confronting Stalin in what is to me a novel of truly Tolstoyan stature. How was it possible that not only Abakumov, but so many millions of Russians, Rumanians, Bulgarians, but also Frenchmen and Americans, people all over the world, should have danced such grotesque dances at Stalin's bidding? How was it possible? What is the mystery of such a tyranny? There is something horrifyingly attractive about a transgressive figure, about a great criminal. Hitler had that quality in one way, Stalin in another. A figure like Stalin, once in power by a process we cannot discuss here, is the very locus of the disorganisation of a culture—of the destruction of its particular constraints on what can be done. So anything can be done. And Stalin did everything. This was also true of the Nazis.

GLENNY: But totalitarian rule depends on much more than mere cultural disorganisation.

RIEFF: Yes. Therefore the abandonment of received constraints in the art of governing is the key to understanding totalitarianism, which leads to a new kind of control, the control by terror. But then what is terror? It is not simply the devices; after all other cultures have had terroristic devices. But what is most characteristic of modern totalitarian control is the absence of competing constraints. So long as the controls are used externally—manipulated, say, by a Communist party or some consistory of technologists sitting at the Massachusetts Institute of Technology deciding on just what level of pollution is acceptable to society—we have endless trouble, because this is in fact the parody, at best, of the Platonic vision of the philosopher-king and, at worst, an expression of totalitarian reality, of a Stalinist or a Hitlerian dictatorship, or others to come. Between the best and the worst there is the muddle that all cultures in the past have managed to achieve and that rests on the notion of internalisation. Unless controls are deeply internalised in a culture, unless there are in fact what I would call 'pastoral guides' who are able to establish internal controls, the problem of control seems to me to be unmanageable.

And so the great problem of technology is that it is irrelevant to this problem of, if I may use such barbaric words, the internalisation of control. The problem of controls, so deeply installed that to abrogate them is psychologically a very costly business, is precisely the one that is avoided when we think of technological problems.

GLENNY: Why is this so?

RIEFF: Because there is no interior control within technology; it is itself (as I tried to say earlier) in its very principle the abrogation of interior controls; what can be done will be done. It is in this sense, I think, that Professor Gabor said, 'History must stop.' But history does not stop at the command of the scientist. It stops at prophecy, irrational prophecy. It stops at a certain kind of emotional reconstruction, psychological reconstruction, for which technology has no room within its intellectual ambience. And there is our problem.

In a modern technological society the great movements nowadays are themselves forms of dismantling what controls exist. Take, for example, the sexual revolution or the legalisation of pornography. At every point these movements are against the established but failing constraints, very much as a neurosis operates in exactly the same way. It arises because the established restraints are failing and then compounds the neurosis. Technology has no interior constraint that can serve to order the interior life. It has no relevance to the interior life, except to abolish it. The nature of the control of the dynamics of technology, if resolved in a model that is intellectually the equivalent of the technological model itself, must also be a form of tyranny of one sort or another. The true historical and cultural alternative is another deeply installed interior ethic which spins out its own controls. But it is precisely to that sort of ethic that the direction of contemporary history is most clearly opposed. And no professor of physics and no professor of sociology can, by saying, 'History must stop,' stop this history.

NIGEL DESPICHT

Old Values and the
Demands of New Technology

Nigel Despicht is Director of Transport at the Economic Commission for Europe and a former Senior Research Fellow at the University of Sussex where he worked on the project 'Regional Policy in the European Communities and the United Kingdom' (1968–70). His earlier appointments include that of Principal for Town and Country Planning and Roads Programme (1955–65), Deputy Rhine Commissioner (1962–65) and Head of Urban Planning Division (1965–68), Ministry of Transport. Mr Despicht has published widely on urban problems, transport policy and European integration.

GLENNY: Can society survive technology? Do you believe this is a proper question or have we drawn a false distinction between society and its technology?

DESPICHT: I would call it more provocative than proper and real. It can be misleading if people answering it make too clear-cut a distinction between society on the one hand and technology on the other. You cannot really think of any human society except in terms of its technology. How can a human society be considered, if not in terms of its ability and skill to manage itself and its environment? If you look at the matter this way, then I think you will not make a false distinction between technology or skill on the one hand and values on the other. The values which a society holds are dependent upon what it thinks it can do and what it cannot do. No society is going to demand as a matter of moral or social values that its members should do things which amount to sudden death or suicide. In other words, values can only exist above a certain

57

level of what you may call the level of necessity or absolute prudence.

GLENNY: Perhaps the question should be put in terms of the argument of some of the other contributors to this symposium, in particular that of Edward Goldsmith: he is what one might call a cosmic pessimist, who believes that although our use of technology may hitherto have been dictated by some form of necessity, it is quite unaffected, in his view, by prudence. He sees the general direction in which technology is moving at present to be almost wholly imprudent in regard to the resources of the planet and the effect that the technological transformation of these resources is going to have on society.

DESPICHT: I think this view really puts what you have at the back of your mind in asking the question 'Can society survive technology?'

What any society regards as prudent is determined by what it regards as its ultimate capability for changing or transforming its environment. If you go back several centuries, the ability of even the most advanced human societies to alter their environment was extremely limited. As a result, it was not only possible but quite appropriate that their scale of values and their notion of prudence should be conditioned by a realisation that they had a very limited capacity to alter the environment. Today it is not true to say that human technology has only a limited power to alter, and even destroy, the world in which human beings live. A scale of values that is related to a limited technology is not appropriate to a situation where technology is infinitely more powerful. I would therefore like to rephrase your question as follows: is society likely to survive if it tries to use its new technological skills in accordance with values and notions of prudence appropriate to the very much less powerful technologies of the past?

GLENNY: Thank you for rephrasing my question: it is improved by being made more precise. By your rephrasing of it, however, you have put another question—namely, the question of whether the cultural equipment which we inherit from the past enables us to deal with our present state of technological power, or whether the latter is so new, so revolutionary that it is *sui generis* and we are therefore dangerously unable to control the monster of technology that we have unleashed.

DESPICHT: This is a very fundamental point and is really what used to be called metaphysics. Modern European society seems to be unfitted to deal with metaphysical problems. In fact, metaphysics has become a rude word and one is accused of it in order to be discredited. I would like to look at certain basic attitudes which we have inherited unconsciously from the past. I might say here that a very good exposition of this sort of theory is given in a book by Jean Fourastié called *La Moral prospective*.

Let us take three areas of technology. The first is that of the technology used to satisfy human material needs for food and heat, etc. If you look at the attitude displayed by virtually all Western Europeans, even 150 years ago, it is obvious that they assumed that the world was a world of shortage. The great danger was literally that you would not have enough to eat tomorrow or that in the winter you would die of cold. In this sort of society, the amount of mining you do, the amount of artificial fertilising you do and the amount of waste you create are something which nature can safely absorb without harmful effect. Modern technology in this field can, apart from questions of financial and political control, supply the food and all the heat that people need (certainly which Western Europeans need), but the application of this advanced technology is something entirely different from old-fashioned agriculture and old-fashioned mining. If you seriously set about giving people everything they demand in the way of food and heat, etc., you will risk physically poisoning the earth by the pollution resulting from mining waste, industrial waste and petrochemical waste.

Now let us consider a second area—the control of natural

forces which, 150 to 200 years ago, were considered to be un-controllable by man. Take two examples: nuclear energy and bacteria. With nuclear engineering and modern medical science the extent to which man can create energy and control bacteria is very great. This can have a transforming effect on the capa-bilities of industry and on the spread of disease. But, as we know very well, these two technologies can be used to replace rather cruder ones in other fields of application. You do not even need a nuclear bomb to destroy the world. You only need to unleash chemical warfare, and that will have the same or even worse effects. As a result, the capability of human beings to destroy each other was nothing like as serious two hundred years ago as it is now.

Now let us take a third area—what one can call very gener-ally the control of life itself. In my grandparents' day, they reckoned that five out of ten children died either at birth or before they reached the age of two. You have only to read the memoirs of Casanova to know that his contraceptive technology was what we would call today rather risky. In that sort of society, people's personal and sexual morality was geared to two basic assumptions. The first was that you could not really avoid unwanted babies, so it was better not to do anything which could risk producing them. The second was that, even if you got married and had babies, you could only count on half or less surviving. Modern hygiene, medical technology and con-traceptive technology now make it fairly certain that you can avoid conceiving children if you do not want to have them and that those children who are born are most likely to survive. The effect of this change in the basis of the most fundamental of all human moralities—sexual morality—is obvious. It is useless to tell your daughters now to be chaste on the grounds that it is dangerous not to be. They know it is not so dangerous. You have to tell them to be chaste because chastity is a good thing in itself, regardless of whether you conceive children out of wed-lock or not.

These are rather random examples, and I will try to draw a general principle from them. Two hundred years ago when

human societies were considering the social and moral values
involved in the uses of their skills and technologies, they could
rely upon nature being far more powerful than man. Nature, in
fact, was so powerful that man's own personal morality had to be
subordinated to it. Quite frankly, this is not the case today.
Technology is so much more powerful that one is beginning to
have the illusion that mankind is in actual fact the Lord of
nature. The basis of human morality has changed. In order to
have values appropriate to modern technology, we shall have to
change our conception of human society from one where human
beings are subject to the inscrutable and uncontrollable forces
of nature, into one where mankind can control nature at will.
In fact, to survive, or let us put it in moral terms, to do good,
mankind must adopt a positive morality. It is no longer a question of avoiding the bad. It is a question of deliberately choosing
the good. The excuse that we cannot do good even if we want
to is no longer there; we can do it, and therefore we are under a
moral obligation to choose what we do. Hence we have a situation where society must become what the French have called
'*La Société volontaire*'.

GLENNY: There have been moments in the past when man's
development has appeared to pose him with what you are suggesting, namely, a totally new set of moral imperatives. Would
you say, for instance, that the appearance of this new category
of moral imperatives can be paralleled in the past? Might there
perhaps be an analogy with the upheaval which occurred at the
end of the 18th Century, when the ideas of the Enlightenment
culminated, in political terms, in the French Revolution; when
the Ancien Régime which had hatched out the cuckoo's egg of
the Enlightenment was in turn thrown out of its nest by the
cuckoo? Are we at such a climacteric moment in history now
and would you characterise the 'technological revolution' in
such terms?

DESPICHT: Your historical analogy is a good one. There is,
I believe, a certain parallel between the situation today and that

at the end of the Enlightenment. The message of the 18th-Century rationalist was that man had at last mastered the universe. He knew it was a wonderful mathematical machine which had been started by some prime cause and had been going according to Newton's laws or Leibnitz's laws or someone else's laws ever since. I recall what Alexander Pope said:

> Nature and nature's laws lay hid in night.
> God said—Let Newton be, and there was light!

There is an analogy between this sort of attitude and the attitude of some of our technologists of the present day who imagine that they now have nature in their grasp. But at a certain point the analogy falls down, or rather there is a very important difference. The concept of the Enlightenment that it controlled nature was in a way an illusion. What it meant was that it had satisfied itself that it understood nature rationally. The 18th Century did not control nature. The situation today is that we are quite happy to admit that we do not understand nature but we are not happy to admit that we do not control it. We may not know what the atom is but we can split it. Thus the 18th-Century revolutionaries were a menace in the sense that they could upset society, but the French Revolution did not in fact produce a very great difference in the ability of the French to feed themselves and to avoid starving to death in the winter. Nowadays, our revolutionaries of modern technology are capable, as far as we can see, of blowing the earth to smithereens at any moment. This is a very different matter.

There are other analogies between the late 18th Century and the present day. One of the apparent effects of understanding the universe as a rational machine was to make everybody very bored and emotionally frustrated. One of the cuckoo's eggs hatched out of the Enlightenment was the Romantic movement. This was preceded, if one recalls one's literature, by a period when the enlightened persons were very vulnerable to fits of hysteria, bursting into tears and what we would now call the most mawkish sentimentality. The unhappy story of Manon Lescaut is not the invention of an irrational romantic but of a good rationalist priest of the 18th Century. Now if you think of what the moral pundits complain about today, it is precisely the boredom and excessive emotionalism of the youth.

I would suggest another possible analogy. The 18th Century Enlightenment introduced in practice, and as it were by accident, a social revolution which was anything but mechanically rational. It was almost as if latent in the very illusion of the rational understanding of nature there were all sorts of principles which were contradictory to it. One might even say that the French Revolution and the Romantic movement were not so much the product of Enlightenment as the emergence of its fundamental contradictions and illusions. Now if you look at the basic attitudes to modern technology today, one is struck by the almost hysterical way in which people who are obviously convinced of the power of modern technology wish to denigrate it (at least in the developed Western countries). One hears as much today about the destructive power, the danger and the pollution of modern technology as about its possible beneficial effects.

If I may, I will leap into what may appear to be a *non sequitur*. This curious dichotomy between an almost slavish admiration of technology and a hysterical resistance to its so-called destructive power appears to me to spring from a basic contradiction or muddle in people's outlook. What they seem to be doing is to conceive of man as something autonomous and separate from his environment. The whole problem of technology is conceived in terms of man controlling or destroying his environment. By implication, the social and moral values of man are themselves something which man invents autonomously from his environment.

It could be that this way of conceiving man as something autonomous within an environment is just a metaphysical muddle. Perhaps reality is not like that at all. If one goes to the leading metaphysical philosopher of the 20th Century, Alfred North Whitehead, one finds a doctrine put out in good mathematical, scientific and epistemological terms which casts considerable doubt upon this autonomy of man from his environ-

CAN WE SURVIVE OUR FUTURE?

ment. If one wants another version of this, one can try Alan Watts, an American who has written a most amusing and vivid book called *The Taboo Against Knowing Who You Really Are*. He repeats in a more popular way many of the tenets of A. N. Whitehead, who was after all hardly everyone's idea of a popular writer, having been thrice a Professor in different subjects and taught Lord Keynes on the way. But essentially for ordinary people like you and me, Whitehead was telling us that there is in fact a taboo against knowing who we really are.

I will try and put this in a different way. What these philosophers in their very different ways are saying is that mankind has become far too intellectualised. We have taken too seriously the doctrine of Descartes that the ideas which are most close to reality are those which are clear and distinct. (In fact reality is usually more akin to a massive and vague intuition.) As a result, our outlook on technology and our outlook on moral and social values is over-intellectualised. We tend to reject that which is not immediately clear and distinct. As a further result, we have grown, during a period of perhaps two centuries, to disregard the derivation of our moral values from the environment of which we form part. We fail to see the very close connection between our prescriptive values concerning what we should and should not do, and our sense of what we can and cannot do. Hence we feel a sort of opposition between moral values and technological capabilities, whereas there is no genuine opposition. What we are feeling in fact is the strain placed upon values appropriate to one level of technologies by our capability in technologies at a new and quite different level. What is wrong is not the destructive power of technology, but the sluggish attitude of human beings who will not adjust their moral values to changing realities.

GLENNY: Perhaps a good example of the unthinking application of an outdated attitude which no longer corresponds to reality is the almost universal preoccupation among governments and bureaucracies throughout the world with economic growth as an end in itself. There are critics now writing in the

West who maintain, sometimes in rather idiosyncratic terms, that economic growth is no longer a rational aim and that indeed it is not so much inhuman as anti-human. Such thinkers have proposed various criteria by which economic growth should be modified or even in extreme cases halted altogether. Do you regard the preoccupation with economic growth as one instance in which we are applying useless old-fashioned tools to cope with a situation which requires entirely new ones?

DESPICHT: Not entirely. This obsession with economic growth is nothing very new. To me, economic growth is usually a new, rather fancy, term for getting rich and powerful. It is nothing peculiar to this century that just getting rich and powerful, for no other reason than that you want to be rich and powerful, involves you in quite inhuman relationships with your fellow men. If by getting powerful you mean increasing your economic output and technological power (which you usually do), then an obsession with economic and technological growth is the same thing as just getting rich and powerful for no other reason than that you want to be a bigger fish than the other fish in the sea.

If you want to make economic growth a decent human activity, it must be related to the purposes for which you want to grow economically. Now the question is : is this process happening in Western Europe today? By this I mean : are the authorities responsible for economic growth relating that economic growth to worthy human purposes? I am not pessimistic about this. It seems to me that there are distinct signs that politicians and governments in Western Europe are doing that. If one compares post-war Europe with pre-war Europe, there is a very distinct improvement. In pre-war Europe Nazi Germany and Fascist Italy were both concerned with economic growth. But this sort of growth was unrelated to any purposes which we would call humane or civilised. Since the war, Western Europe has been characterised by planning. Now the process of planning, if it means anything at all (which I sometimes doubt) is in fact a conscious relation of capabilities and resources to purposes. It is in effect an attempt to impose some sort of rational choice of values and ends on what would otherwise be chaotic and spontaneous processes.

The preoccupation with economic growth started after the war and had originally very good and human purposes. In the early 1950s economic growth meant for the populations of Europe better housing, more food, better jobs, the reconstruction of war damage. This was a good thing. Once the momentum was started, however, it got into the hands of the technicians and the economists, whose whole training and work in life is devoted to the technicalities of economic growth. They succeeded in many ways in convincing governments that economic growth was somehow a good thing in itself. They did this usually by pointing out that the absence of economic growth created difficult problems like inflation or lack of money, conjuring up, of course, the bogies of the 20s and 30s. So politicians, being sensible people, immediately took the path which they thought would help them to avoid all the difficult problems such as inflation and unemployment which they had never really been able to solve before. But in the 1960s there has been in Western Europe a very distinct change in attitude towards economic growth. Right up until about 1965, you find that governments are talking about medium-term economic planning, as if economic planning by itself was the great instrument for directing society. But from 1965 onwards, all sorts of social considerations creep in. These considerations have tended to acquire a label—'regional'—for reasons that in many ways are obscure. This label seems to come from the experience of what purely economic planning does not do. And the first thing it does not do is to ensure that everybody gets a fair share of the cake. Secondly, economic planning to be effective tends towards a centralisation of decisions affecting the development of society. This of course is the opposite to liberating initiative and giving people a say in deciding their own future. This is a 'regional' question in the sense of the devolution of power from the centre to the people actually being affected by decisions.

It seems to me that this new, more socially conscious attitude

made a breakthrough in about 1967–68. At that time the statesmen of Western Europe realised that the previous five years,
which had been referred to as a recession, had actually been a
period of growth, only at a slower rate. It suddenly seemed to
sink into people's minds that a steady rate of growth of anything up to four per cent per annum was an accepted fact of life,
replacing the old concept of society as subject to great slumps
and booms and with the prospect of a complete collapse always
around the corner. As soon as you make steady growth the
basic concept of society, you are at once faced with the problem of how you are going to deal with twenty years' accumulated growth in a generation's time. As a result, long-term
planning ceased to be a day-dream about what might happen
at the millennium and became an urgent problem.

The reasoning is this: if your economy is growing steadily
and your population is growing steadily in numbers and affluence, and modern technology permits you to achieve extraordinary things in the way of material development, then now
is the time to start planning what you want if you want the
world to be a decent place in twenty years' time. If you wait
another five years, it will be too late. It takes in fact not months
but decades to implement the enormous material and social
engineering required for a highly affluent urban and industrialised society. Medium-term economic planning is not enough.
You must have strategic objectives. In fact you must go in for
technological forecasting, or as some people call it futurology.
The Americans initiated this at government level with the
famous report entitled *The Year 2000*. In the European context,
we also find curious adventures being embarked on by hitherto
quite respectable governments. In 1970, in Bonn, there was a
Conference of European Ministers of Regional Planning. Super-
ficially this looks to be a fairly technical subject. When you look
at the definition given of regional planning by the organisation
which launched the whole exercise, the Council of Europe,
you find that it is not at all technical. They start their report by
quoting a French Minister who said simply: regional planning
is in reality the planning of our society. This so-called regional

planning, which ten years ago was just one aspect of economic planning, has graduated to a position where it is becoming almost a framework within which economic planning itself is fitted. In other words, the latest trend in European thinking, both at the European level in the Council of Europe and the European Communities, and also at national levels, is to move towards a comprehensive strategy designed to direct not only the economic development but the physical, social and cultural development of the European population towards the creation of a great new society, which is conceived in the glowing terms of the millennium.

We find, for example, that the old preoccupations with economic growth, inflation and employment are now joined with intense concern for the elimination of pollution, the conservation of nature, the creation of a habitat for mankind which will enable it to flourish and develop its cultural possibilities. You will even find that economists and governments, when assessing practical problems like the advantages of different places for the location of modern industry, are now regarding the environment, educational facilities, amenities and cultural criteria as more important than the older economic factors of transport facilities, raw materials and so on. See the British Government's decision to put London's third airport at Foulness rather than Cublington.

GLENNY: Here I would like to throw a basinful of cold water over the splendid prospect which you have been describing. I suggest that what you are proposing is almost irrelevant to the much bigger problems which face the world. For example, the population explosion. At the end of the 18th Century, there were about eight hundred million people in the world—a figure which took a million years to reach. A hundred years later, that figure had doubled. Seventy years after that, it had doubled again. And nowadays it only needs eight years for the population to rise by eight hundred million. There are other horrifying predictions of an absolutely cosmic scale, such as that in approximately thirty years' time—one generation from hence

—in our lifetime perhaps and certainly in the lifetime of our children, there will be no more gold, silver, platinum, copper, zinc and perhaps no manganese, tungsten, molybdenum left in the world at all, and that in seventy years there will be no more fossil fuels: no more coal, no more oil, no more natural gas. Faced with cataclysmic predictions of this kind, do you not believe that the nice-sounding proposals for social engineering, which you describe under the title or regionalism, are in fact mere tinkering with the future—or worse still, are a wilful refusal to face the real dangers, an attitude which has been called 'the ostrich syndrome'?

DESPICHT: Yes, there is this danger. You are right in the sense that many people who are now asserting the priority of social values above economic and technological ones are in fact really being ostriches. But this is not the attitude which I take. You will remember that right at the beginning of our discussion, I asserted a general principle which was that moral values are closely related to, or depend upon, technological capabilities. What backward-looking social engineering does is to apply to modern problems moral values and concepts of amenity appropriate to an old form of technology. That clearly will not work. What we must do is to develop together a technology and a moral attitude which can cope with these horrific problems which you have just mentioned.

I think there is one legacy from the past which is called in English common-sense, or scepticism, which makes one suspect predictions of a horrific nature. I do not myself believe that the population explosion and the exhaustion of minerals will come to pass exactly in the way you have just quoted. On the other hand, to assume that these predictions can be disregarded would be folly. It will not happen just like that. But something of that scale is facing us. What then is the moral message? I think it is simply that, rather than curse modern technology or try to curb it, you direct it to solving these problems. In fact, the horrific problems which people allege are being created by modern technology and modern society can only be solved by a great advance *in technology*. For example, take fossil fuels. We would not need fossil fuels if we could harness even a tiny fraction of solar energy. The fact that it might take us fifty years of extremely costly and intensive research to learn how to do that seems to me to be the kind of moral decision which we ought to take. Here there is a link with space research. It would be nice to think that one of the side-benefits of space research was a technique for harnessing solar energy. In practice we are more likely to achieve unlimited energy resources from imploding the atom than from solar energy. But the first part of the moral message is the same—we must go on developing modern technology as intensively as we can.

But there is also another moral message implied. If we really develop modern technology to the pitch where we could, for example, harness solar energy, it is very unlikely that the average citizens of the world would stand the remotest chance of being able to control intelligently what was done with this technology. The degree of skill required to run such technology would be so great that only a few people could ever acquire it. We are, therefore, up against the age-old problem of who controls the controllers: how do we guarantee that the men who control this extraordinary technology, on which our very existence depends, will do the sort of things that we as the citizens want them to do with it? This is one of the oldest problems of political science.

Let us look into the past and see what went wrong with the people who controlled the older technology. It is true to say that the average citizen has never had much say in the great decisions which govern the conditions of his life. If you go back far enough, the only people who were allowed to have a real say were those who controlled large numbers of men armed with axes and swords. Later in history you had to have great wealth in order to have a say in the control of affairs. But if there's *one* thing which modern sociology has indicated to us, it is this—that the people who were nominally in charge of the world's resources did not actually make the decisions. The decisions tended to be made by rather mean little people known as bailiffs, lawyers and bureaucrats. These people knew how to make the decisions to deploy the resources. In fact they were the social technologists. But unfortunately, this is where their knowledge ended. They were the people who ran the social machine and became devoted to its mechanics.

Take, for example, the basic one—the bailiff. A large agricultural estate is there for the simple purpose of feeding and giving a happy life to the people who live on it. I ask you, is this the attitude of the average bailiff in charge of an estate? You know as well as I do that the attitude of the average bailiff is usually the very opposite of devotion to the welfare, affluence and ease of his tenants. This same narrow sort of attitude is also characteristic of lawyers. Try and talk to the average hack lawyer about the nature of justice. He just doesn't know what you mean. He will tell you what the law is. Finally, in modern times, the bureaucrat fulfills this essential social role. With modern technology governing the sort of life we can expect to lead on this planet, this essential role of society's bailiff will be played by the technocrat. There is real cause to indulge in cosmic pessimism if one assumes that the technocrats of tomorrow will have an attitude to their work similar to that of the average estate bailiff in, say, Western Sicily.

The problem of social engineering boils down to a quite simple one: how do you ensure that the technocrats of tomorrow will have the quality of vision and the quality of personality which will enable them to use their skills to make the great technological machines do what the citizens want? This surely is a matter of education. I will not go into the question —education is a moral universe and a technology all of its own.

I will end with a subversive thought. Being an old-fashioned person, I do not have too much faith in the moral attitudes of the average citizen either. So I think we shall have to create a new category of citizens with high moral values to educate the technocrats. Take, for example, the average citizen's attitude to one very important technology, that of diet. One of the scourges of the modern world is obesity. What does the modern citizen do about it? He is very worried about it. He wants to slim. So he goes to the technocrats of nutrition and asks them what to do. He is happy if he gets from them highly complicated and sophisticated diets. But what happens if a great technocrat of nutrition says to him: 'My dear chap, just eat one meal a day; your problem is simple—you eat too much.' The technocrat would be dismissed, because the real fault is human gluttony —not the technology of nutrition.

WERNER HEISENBERG

Rationality in
Science and Society *

Werner Heisenberg is one of the most influential physicists of the 20th Century. He was awarded the 1932 Nobel Prize for Physics 'for the creation of quantum mechanics' and is best known as the formulator of the Uncertainty Principle. Professor Heisenberg's work on quantum theory profoundly influenced the development of atomic and nuclear physics. He has held a variety of important posts at German and other European universities. Since 1958 he has been Director of the Max Planck Institute for Physics and Astrophysics and Professor at the University of Munich. His publications include: *Wandlungen in den Grundlagen der Naturwissenschaft* (1935), *Vorträge über kosmische Strahlung* (1943), *Die Physik de Atomkerne* (1943), *Das Naturbild der heutigen Physik* (1955) and *Der Teil und das Ganze* (1969) (English title: *Physics and beyond*, 1970).

URBAN: One of the most striking features of the interaction between science and society is the difficulty ordinary people experience in trying to understand the language and concepts which scientists and technologists use. We are given to understand that most problems that merit a scientist's and technologist's attention are too involved for the layman to grasp. We are handed down answers by the specialists which we are expected to take on trust, and, *faute de mieux*, do take on trust. Nor do our troubles end there: even the different technologies and the different 'hard' (but now also the 'soft') sciences are less and less able to communicate with each other because the symbolisms they use are private to their specific scholarships. Worse, within each discipline there has been further fission into even smaller units, each with its special grid of reference

* *Original contribution, unrevised.*

73

---

and a vocabulary which means little to the uninitiated and nothing at all to the men and women whose future depends on the uses to which the work of the scientists and technologists are put. Now it seems to me that this erosion of a common language and a common conceptual framework began, in its grosser forms, with the advent of modern physics, for it was there that the common-sense uses of notions such as causality, simultaneity and our sense of time and space were first seriously challenged.

There are two questions here that interest me. First, how far have the common-sense uses of causality, time and space been, in fact, invalidated by the physical sciences? Second, can we hope to pull down some of the semantic barriers that have built up around specialised knowledge? Incomprehension between the scientific and lay communities gives cause for special concern for it has made a great many people feel intellectually disinherited, not only because their cultural antennae are ill-attuned to the message of a scientific culture, but for the more pressing and alarming reason that they no longer understand what is going on around them.

HEISENBERG: I do not quite agree with the word 'invalidated'. The layman should go on using words such as space, time, causality just as he has always used them; modern physics should only make him aware of the fact that in some circumstances the validity of such words is limited. The word 'simultaneous', for instance, becomes problematic when one refers to events that are happening at a great distance from one another, say on different stars. But modern physics does not change anything in the everyday usage of these words. The difficulty which you mention—that the layman cannot understand technical terminology—has existed for centuries and did not lead to the kind of problems you describe. The common man never understood his doctor when he talked about the specifics of an illness in medical terms. Nor can the common man understand when the engineer talks about parts of an aeroplane, and yet he trusts the doctor and the plane he boards.

So this basic confidence which the man in the street has for the specialist has always existed, and I do not see why it should disappear in the future.

URBAN: I wonder whether the analogy with doctors and technicians really applies. People like doctors and pilots are, in the last analysis, technologists. Doctors take the Hippocratic oath when they qualify. This is a warranty that the physician knows what he is doing but also a pledge that he will follow an ethical code in dealing with his patients. Pilots and aero-engineers also take highly specialised examinations which guarantee their fitness to do the work they do, and their integrity to do it safely for the people who rely on them. Can we say that the men and women who run our lives for us in government and administration—the sociologists, psychologists and bureaucrats of various descriptions—are comparably qualified, and that we can put our trust in them for the same kind of reasons that make us trust a doctor or even a bus-driver? We are touching here on the kind of problem Plato discusses in *Protagoras*—whether political 'virtue' is a thing capable of being acquired.

HEISENBERG: The distrust of those who actually hold the levers in their hands, for the men who rule a country, will always exist, and it is easily stirred up because people have different opinions about their political interests. But I can't see why one should not meet the challenge of mistrust, particularly in a democracy, by letting individuals have a say in the replacement of people they do not find suitable. The qualifications for steering the affairs of a nation are not as easily tested as those of a doctor or pilot. The criterion of success in public life may not be an ideal criterion, but it is an acceptable method for testing a man's ability to exercise responsible leadership. Democracy, with all its shortcomings, is still the best way of giving minimum cause for distrust, but it will probably be impossible to eliminate it altogether.

URBAN: It is interesting that in some of the older democracies the technologist is mistrusted precisely because it is felt that he is too highly specialised. In some countries it's traditional that a general should be minister of war, that an engineer should be minister of technology and so on. Now in England, for instance, this has never been the case. There has always been an assumption here that if you want to be an effective minister of, say, technology, you must be a good classicist first or a good musician, that you've got to have the ability to think away from your special field, because it is the broader outlook that guarantees your humane, and therefore ultimately effective, approach to human problems. How do you see this as a physicist and a practising musician?

HEISENBERG: I think it is a good principle to choose people for leading positions who can see the whole and not isolated parts only. Particularly when political decisions for a whole country or even large parts of it have to be made, it is not enough to be a good expert on social or technological matters, but one must be able to balance the interests of the whole, and over and above that, to perceive life in all its variety, to probe into its deeper meaning and to make decisions from there. But one has to remember that this broader outlook can be the result of either a scientific or a humanistic kind of education, or, of course, both: it needn't be tied exclusively to either. But the difficulty still remains that the man in the street cannot always understand the reasons that lead to certain public decisions. This is probably inevitable.

URBAN: You don't think, then, that there is any hope that we may find a common language that people might at least basically understand?

HEISENBERG: Again, I do not want to appear too pessimistic, but finding a common language is certainly very difficult, and I would say that it has always been very difficult. This predicament goes back to two thousand years ago, and it continues to be with us today. The man in the street cannot follow up things the way the élite have to. His way of thinking is simpler, he has less interest in familiarising himself with complicated matters, and he probably has no accurate sources of information. What is worse, the gap between élite sophistication and the relative unsophistication of the general public is growing, and I can see no way of reducing it to manageable proportions.

URBAN: My second question concerns the relationship between a scientist's image of the structure of the physical world and a layman's image of the structure of the physical world, including, of course, his own place in it. I am struck by a theme which is recurrent in your books (and is perhaps a feature shared by some of the most distinguished mathematicians and physicists of our time)—the theme that the most complicated relationships in the organisation of matter can be reduced to very simple, and, as you often stress, satisfying mathematical statements. You even imply in one of your books that the sensation of beauty which derives from these formulae is not merely an aesthetic satisfaction that delights the physicist, but that it also supplies a kind of warrant for believing that the world is, after all, capable of being understood in very basic terms such as $E = mc^2$ and the like.

Now put into a layman's language this kind of simplicity would seem to satisfy another need, the need to be reassured that the measures and dimensions which apply when men deal with each other in their daily lives also apply to the understanding of man's place in society and of his future on earth.

You say, in one instance, that there is in nature an impressive proclivity for certain elements to assume identical or near-identical shapes—such as drops of water. How would you describe the broader implications of this proclivity? Are we faced here with some code written into the structure of nature which is universal?

HEISENBERG: The simplicity of the basic laws of nature is certainly a central point in natural science. That nature tends to reproduce the same symmetrical forms is the first indication of this underlying simplicity. An analysis of atomic phenomena has led us to the conclusion that this simplicity is connected with certain operations, for instance in time and space, the possibility of which is embodied in the laws of nature. By operations of this kind I mean operations like shifting, turning and so forth, which we consider as self-evident possibilities. A symmetrical form may then be defined by its invariance (or more general behaviour) subsumed under such operations. These symmetrical forms are reproduced time and time again in different contexts.

Such experiences make us aware of the existence of a central order, and I would believe that is also the central order to which all religious parables refer us, although their language and symbolism are quite different. So, on the one hand our actions are subject to the laws of nature, but on the other, when we exercise our free will, our actions must still be guided, in one way or another, by some reference to a central order of things. And this is probably how standards of values and all religions came into being.

URBAN: There is a lot of speculation among scientists, especially among biologists, that science demands a new code of values, that our values are simply old-fashioned, that they no longer apply in the light of scientific discovery, particularly in biology. It is suggested, for instance, that the structure of the family, the way we co-exist in society, are outdated because they are not in harmony with certain laws in the micro-structure of living matter.

HEISENBERG: I am highly sceptical every time I hear that we ought to change the values we use in our daily lives on the grounds that the world has changed around us. Since you mentioned biologists as pioneers in this search for a general revaluation of values, let me stick to your example and leave out for the moment the religious aspects of the matter.

I think there is a good case for saying that the conduct considered as right, just and acceptable among human beings at any particular period has asserted itself in a selective process. In other words, man has learnt by long and bitter experience that he must behave in such and such a manner to have a tolerably good chance of survival. Our values and our individual and social ethics are functions of this selective process. Of course, it is possible that man's situation in the world, especially in the contemporary world, has changed so radically—through mechanised travel, electronic communication, affluence, urbanisation, the conquest of disease, etc.—that these external changes must be reflected in some way in his ethics, i.e. in his conduct *vis-à-vis* his fellow men. However, my own opinion is that such changes, in so far as they require legal sanction, should be made with extreme caution or else accepted only if the pressure of events leaves no other alternative. The confused talk about revolution leaves me unconvinced. One can only make an effective revolution if one changes as little as possible, and that with great circumspection. There are, of course, situations where—for social, national or bureaucratic reasons—the need for change runs into obstinate and mindless opposition. One is then, as it were, forced by the situation to force a change and, with it, cause some new values and conventions to arise. Yet, it would seem to me that such action must be the exception rather than the rule. On the whole, man's behaviour has developed by slow stages, responding to the changing conditions of his survival, and it is extremely dangerous, and probably also self-defeating, to try to instil in him a new consciousness by higher order, revolution or analogies drawn from science.

URBAN: Do you think that the revolutionary changes which have taken place in our century (and those that may occur in the remaining decades) have been, or can be, effective unless they present themselves equipped with the paraphernalia of religion? Marxism–Leninism, and especially Maoism, can be looked upon as religious constructs in the broad sense. Would radical change in the future have to resort to this, what one might call, opium technique, or could it be carried out in the framework of a purely scientific-technological rationale?

HEISENBERG: All radical change, no matter how scientific or technological, sets out to win the loyalty of people, and that can only be acquired by appealing to the irrational, as well as the rational, component in the human mind. This can, as you hinted, lead to absurd situations, but such are not new in history.

Now if you use the word religion in the broad sense, if you apply it to the sort of common language people use when they talk about the meaning of life and death and of human existence, then I should, in fact, consider it quite possible that in the coming hundred years or so such a new common language will evolve, this time probably for all civilisations; then you can, if you like, talk of the emergence of a new religion. Personally, I would have nothing against calling it a religion. We have not reached that stage yet, however. We still have a plethora of religions in the world, inherited from our ancestors and over-laid with traditions; my own belief is (as I have said already) that they all point to one basic theme, but use different parables and different spiritual languages. But I suspect a common language in this sphere of our thinking—common both to different civilisations and to the lay and scientific communities—will re-emerge in the quasi-religious form we have discussed, and I could well imagine that this might happen within the next hundred years.

URBAN: It is paradoxical that the changes our modern revolutionaries demand are rational in substance, yet the psychological context of their 'revolution' is wholly irrational and their methods and slogans are irrational too.

HEISENBERG: This irrational behaviour may be a natural reaction to the mystique of rationalism of our time: one runs into the postulate at every turn that only rational activity, only rational modes of thinking, only rational associations are acceptable or even permissible. The irrational, it is said, is dangerous and should be eliminated or, at the very least, ignored. I think, first, that it cannot be eliminated, and second, that it should not be eliminated. Reason is a very limited faculty of the human mind. It is a highly useful faculty but we cannot grasp everything with it that has to be grasped in a full life. So we must be constantly aware of the limitations of this human instrument.

URBAN: How does this apply to your work as a creative physicist?

HEISENBERG: Well, I prefer not to talk about my personal *modus operandi* but rather of the methods of a science which is considered to be a model of rationality, namely pure mathematics. I know from several mathematicians that their discoveries have not been made by rational processes alone. They start off with a vague idea that certain correspondences, certain symmetries, certain equations *must* be true, and it is only much later that they manage to render proof of their conceptions. The discoveries of the young Indian mathematician, Srinivasa Ramanujan, are a famous example of this. He worked under Hardy in Cambridge (England). He put forward several startlingly brilliant theses without offering rational proof, and it was left to Hardy to render the evidence very much after the event. Ramanujan simply sensed that things must be the way in which he imagined them to be. You can call this intuition or inspired invention or what you will, but it is certainly true that scientific activity is far from being a purely rational activity. 'There is,' Hardy wrote, 'no place in the world for ugly mathematics.'

URBAN: In your book, *Das Naturbild der heutigen Physik*, you show very convincingly that the Cartesian dualism between the outside 'objective' world and man's inner world, between *res extensa* and *res cogitans*, can no longer do justice to the world as it appears to a physicist today. The methodology of the physical sciences, you argue, stresses the relationship between man the observer and the thing observed, removing therefore the natural sciences from their traditional realm, 'nature', and shifting their emphasis to what one may call, for want of a better word, the 'inter-face' between nature and man.

What has caused this shift of emphasis and what are its broad implications for the future of scientific enquiry and technology?

HEISENBERG: The shift of emphasis from studying 'nature', to studying man in the process of observing 'nature', is due to man's encounter with the atomic world. The experiences gained in atomic physics just cannot be objectified in the same way in which one can objectify those of classical physics or, indeed, the experiences of everyday life (and by 'objectify' I mean the attempt to make something into an object and deal with it without reference to the way in which it is observed). The main characteristic of atomic physics is this interplay between 'nature' and ourselves. It is a complicated matter and I won't attempt to discuss it here. As to the implications of this shift for philosophy, technology and society, I would not dare to make a forecast. I will, however, say one thing: what impressed me most in studying the atomic world is that the verb 'to understand' itself has assumed a shifting meaning. The content of 'understand' changes with the development of science and has changed enormously in the last two hundred years. No doubt it will change further.

URBAN: In the book I have just quoted you claim (with what I think is great literary elegance) that, 'for the first time in history, man on this earth is facing nothing but himself'. In the physical sciences as elsewhere, you argue, 'the object of research is no longer nature, but nature exposed to the process of human questioning'. These seem to be fundamental assertions from which consequences of very great moment may flow for man as an individual, as a member of a family, a nation, a race or, indeed, of humanity. What are the scientific bases for these assertions and how are they likely to change our image of ourselves in the world that surrounds us?

HEISENBERG: The sentence you quote has, in the first instance a very obvious meaning: life on earth has changed completely under the influence of man. The great dangers to our lives come no longer from natural disasters or wild animals. They come from human enemies or from the results of technical progress. Then we have, as I said earlier, the lessons of nuclear physics which tell us that we cannot observe atoms as they are in themselves, objectively as it were, for there are no such things. We can only seize them in the act of observation, and we can say meaningful things about this relationship only. We are deeply embedded in this interplay. As Carl Friedrich von Weizsäcker once put it: 'Man may be subsequent to nature, but then natural science is subsequent to man.'

However, it is one thing to be aware of these correlations and quite another to make forecasts about their likely consequences for human thinking. It is riskier still to philosophise about them. Nevertheless I would go so far as to say that in my estimate the rift between the humanities and science and technology will decrease. It is already widely realised that the kind of questions philosophers and artists ask, the mental processes they follow, are important for the scientist; and that the scientific mode of arguing and scientific discoveries are directly relevant to men who write history or aesthetics. There is a convergence between the two, and here again one may look forward to the slow emergence of a common language.

URBAN: Could this possibly mean that we are going back to a mediaeval type of a unified world-view? If there is convergence between the sciences and the humanities, might we expect a new Thomism to arise on the ashes of the scientific age —a synthesis, like that of St. Thomas, between faith and reason?

HEISENBERG: I think it would be rash to place any convergence between the humanities and science on the one hand, and that between faith and reason on the other, under one intellectual umbrella. Both the humanities and the sciences try to use rational methods. Faith, however, has not primarily to do with what we believe, but with the nature and degree of our commitment, with the fundamental assumptions of our lives. It is true that we can base our lives only on something we trust and take for granted, but it is certainly neither necessary nor possible to render rational proof of this underlying essence. When the historical religions were born, they were in harmony with the empirical and scientific knowledge of their time. Later this harmony was disturbed by the vast increase of knowledge. Many people nowadays trust science more than religion, yet at the same time they feel that science and technology do not satisfy some of their essential needs. The convergence between science and the humanities may be the first step to a new understanding of these needs. When that step has been taken, we may be on our way to a new harmony between faith and rational knowledge; but for the time being this is no more than a hope. However that may be, it is certainly true that in the coming decades man will be more intensely involved with his fellow human being at every turn and will depend on him much more than he did in the past.

URBAN: Will this greater involvement entail a kindlier involvement—a new humanism?

HEISENBERG: I hope that it will but one cannot be sure.

URBAN: You say in one of your lectures that the extension of man's material and intellectual powers should not be lightly equated with 'progress', and you depict man's predicament in the following metaphor: 'With its seemingly unlimited growth of material power mankind finds itself in the situation of a skipper who had his boat built of such heavy concentrations of iron and steel that the boat's compass points constantly at herself and not North. With a boat of that kind no destination can be reached; she will go round in a circle, exposed to the hazards of the winds and the waves.'

I find this a most telling image. In what sense does modern science put dampers on Bacon's optimistic assumption that knowledge frees the human condition? What are those concentrations of iron and steel around the ship of which you speak that prevent us from acquiring a proper understanding of our predicament? It is a sobering thought—one now widely held by scientists, especially in America—that 'for the first time in three hundred years a large part of educated mankind, perhaps even a majority, may be actively hostile to further advance in science and technology' (Harvey Wheeler).

HEISENBERG: It is, in fact, true that people in the 19th Century, and some in our own, believed far too readily that progress was automatically beneficial and that it would be continuous. Today we know better, or so one likes to think. We will certainly have to make colossal efforts to cope with future progress—morally and politically—for our inventions, our technology, have run away with us.

You mention my metaphor of the boat that is built of so much steel that its compass has ceased to work. It has many meanings. The one I should like to stress here is that calculations of utility and practicability are obviously inadequate and dangerous guides for our actions. Every time we are able to make a new gadget, we should ask ourselves before embarking on its manufacture: what purpose and whose purposes is it going to serve? It is not true that everything that can be invented should be invented, or that everything that is technologically feasible should be manufactured and marketed.

As long as we were powerless in the face of nature we could say that, to the extent that we would interfere with nature and control its processes, we would do so for the good of mankind. But now we have achieved a very complete control over nature and we are aiming at total control which seems to be within our grasp. This changes our entire situation, and I must stress it again that the notion of utility will no longer do. The harmful consequences of an unrestricted technological progress stare us in the face: polluted lakes and rivers, poisoned air, atomic weapons and the rest. Clearly our actions need new guides. It is terribly difficult to say what those guides should be, and I dare not go into this question in a short discussion, but there must surely be another code of values, other goals than mere practicability.

URBAN: Would this new code of values have a religious, spiritual framework, or would it be something completely away from our past religious experiences? Would a simple trust in man's good-will and reason offer sufficient scaffolding for a building like this to be erected?

HEISENBERG: The reason why it is so difficult to answer your question is that almost all the words in our vocabulary in this field have been misused and exhausted, so whatever we now say can at once be misunderstood or misrepresented.

What I personally believe in this matter I have already broadly stated; the substance of what the great religions say points to a common centre. This point of confluence, if you like to call it that, will continue to play an important part in our future. It is bound to guide the actions of men. I have no idea how this will happen in detail, nor do I know whether the idea of a personal god will somehow re-emerge or whether we shall incline towards some oriental conception of the divine. But both reason and instinct tell us that the mere practicability and utility of human action must no longer be allowed to rule our lives.

URBAN: In the traditional religion of China there is no supernatural world and the concept of god itself is hazy and unimportant. Nevertheless Confucianism has vigorously cultivated the same type of values, the same social and personal do-s and don't-s as Christianity. So the argument that the ethical actions of man are exclusively tied to Christianity is not convincing.

HEISENBERG: I agree. I also believe that one should not make prognoses of what the new 'language' will be. But I am convinced that a new framework is about to be born in which the traditional and new problems of man will receive a fresh meaning. And one hopes a reassuring meaning.

URBAN: And you, as a physicist, Professor Heisenberg, would you not find a quasi-religious framework of this kind slightly anachronistic, even objectionable?

HEISENBERG: No, on the contrary, I would say that what we have learnt from modern science fits in well with the basic conceptions of the traditional religions. In fact, some of the deeper implications of modern science invite extrapolations into a spiritual dimension.

URBAN: The important discoveries you have made in quantum theory, unsettling as they have been for many a received notion in physics and the philosophical interpretation of 'nature', seem to have left you personally not only entirely unaffected by anything as fashionable as an identity-crisis or a loss of confidence in the worth of rational discourse; on the contrary, you emerge from your book as a man singularly balanced, cautiously optimistic and possessing what I suspect is something akin to faith, though perhaps of an unconventional kind.

I am impressed by the amount of loving attention you devote to describing your walks in the Bavarian Alps, the birth of formative ideas in your exchanges with Bohr and Weizsäcker in your skiing hut near Bayrischzell, the aesthetic satisfaction you derive from a flawless and simple formula, and from your enjoyment of music as a practising musician. There is a great sense of peace and quiet joy about your attitude to your work, your friends, the woods and lakes that form the background to your thinking. Are all these things parts of a whole? How, in fact, to quote the German title of your most recent book, do *Der Teil und das Ganze* balance out in a man who has reached the frontiers of knowledge but has retained the humility of unknowing?

HEISENBERG: The *aperçu* you have given of what I am trying to say in my book is so accurate that I could do no better. One of the points I make is that modern science and technology aren't in any sense upsetting or unnerving. They do not lead to extremism in the cultural-political field or to pathological cults of any kind. Nor should they be allowed to serve as a shield for those who want to cultivate extremism for ulterior purposes. Listening to young people nowadays a cry of woe and despair

87

is very much in the air. One has, of course, to take this mood into account, but I can see no substantial justification for it. Their world is no worse than ours was in our youth. There *are* difficulties and they are partly at least due to scientific and technological progress. But, at the same time, they are a challenge which requires our response. My feeling is that it is the very act of responding, the act of getting a purchase on the reality that surrounds us, and the joy which comes from a creative response, that may regain for us that 'harmony of life' of which the ancient philosophers have spoken.

JACQUES ELLUL

Conformism and the
Rationale of Technology

Jacques Ellul was born in 1912 in Bordeaux. He studied at the University of Bordeaux and at the University of Paris, and holds degrees in Sociology, Law and the History of Law. Since 1938 he has been associated with the University of Bordeaux as Professor of History and the Sociology of Institutions.

During the Second World War Professor Ellul was a member of the French resistance movement, and since then he has been active in politics in his native city. He is prominent in the world Ecumenical movement. He published *The Technological Society* (original title *La technique ou l'enjeu du siècle*) in 1954 and *Propaganda (Propagandes)* in 1962.

URBAN: The word 'convergence' in these discussions has been used as a shorthand expression for the idea that the size and sophistication of technological societies—whether they are supported by a capitalist or socialist economy—make them grow more and more similar. Your use of 'convergence' in *The Technological Society* takes one into an entirely different field.

ELLUL: I would agree with Duverger and other convergence-watchers that the similarities between industrialised societies are more important than their differences. However—as you will probably discover in the course of this discussion—my reasons for subscribing to the theory are different from theirs.

I use the word to show that in a technological civilisation the different techniques with which man has to deal in his day-to-day activities are entirely unrelated to each other and often even pull in different and seemingly incompatible directions; yet, in the end, they all come down to man, they converge on him and threaten to reduce him to an object of techniques. In other words, it isn't man so much dealing with technologies as the technologies dealing with man. This does not mean to say that there is some conspiracy here between technologies or technologists. There is no conductor to the technological orchestra—the convergence is spontaneous. In fact, most technologists are not conscious of what they are doing, and those who are usually believe that their particular technique serves the good of man or, at the very least, leaves the integrity of the human being intact. Nevertheless the conjoint result of man's exposure to technologies of various kinds is an operational totalitarianism which may lead to, or may facilitate the rule of, political totalitarianisms, though not necessarily of the overtly dictatorial type. We know what technologies have already been used by totalitarian governments, but we'd do well to expect more of such to be used both in those societies which are dictatorships and those which are nominally free.

URBAN: You seem to be saying that it is not so much the particular content of any technology that affects man as the fact that he is ceaselessly assaulted by a variety of technologies. I'm reminded of MacLuhan's *The Medium is the Message*, for you too ascribe in your book an almost mystical significance to technique—to the signal rather than what the signal is about.

ELLUL: I have some reservations about MacLuhan's method but I'm in full agreement with his basic ideas. As to his phrase 'the medium is the message', I had put forward the same idea, almost the same phrase, in my book on propaganda. I tried to show there that what matters in propaganda is not the content of any particular item, but the fact that the deployment of a propaganda technique brings in its train certain effects. What are they?

Propaganda in a technological society is called upon to integrate the individual in a technological world, and from this point of view it hardly matters whether the state is a democracy or some kind of a despotism of left or right. Propaganda is a means to persuade the individual to submit to the exigencies of an increasingly mechanised, artificial world with good grace and even with enthusiasm. How does it do this? Under the effect of a certain amount of propaganda the individual closes up. He becomes insensitive to TV, radio, posters, newspaper articles, etc.: he is rendered immune to the poison by tolerating gradually increased doses of it. The question is: has he been rendered immune to the *themes* of propaganda or to propaganda itself? Experience shows that though after a certain time the individual becomes indifferent to the content of the signal, he is by no means indifferent to the signal itself. He obeys the catchwords of propaganda though he no longer listens to it. He no longer needs to see and read a TV advertisement—a simple splash of colour will do to awaken the desired reflexes in him. In short: though the toxin–anti-toxin process has immunised him to ideological content, he has been sensitised to propaganda itself. And once his attitude and behaviour have been broken and new responses determined, the smallest doses suffice to keep him in the desired condition.

URBAN: I would tend to question whether the signal alone is as effective as you say. One could see in Czechoslovakia in 1968 that the content of radio and television was all important, while the stimulus as such played a minimal role. Up to about 1967 official propaganda in that country was all-pervasive—and ineffective. But when the reformers were given the freedom of the press, radio and television, the public lost no time in picking up the message and putting its weight behind the reform movement. The media used under Dubcek were exactly the same as under Novotny, but the message was different. If MacLuhan is right, there should never have been a 'revolution' in Czechoslovakia.

ELLUL: In the short run the message is obviously important; by giving publicity to certain ideas one can induce action. But there is another, a deeper influence which persists when the

91

message has worn away, and that is the psychological impact of the medium itself.

URBAN: What exactly is this psychological impact?

ELLUL: It acts on many levels. At its most general I would say it foists on the individual a whole range of patterns of thought and action which make him conform to a technical rationality. Now one can safely say, without going into the complex problem of what is the true nature of man, that this type of rationality is alien to man if it arrogates to itself the right to be a life-philosophy, which it does. And basically the irrational movements we see in our society seem to me to be spontaneous and rather ineffective reactions against this imposed rationality. They are a form of orthopraxy—a reluctant assertion of corrective practice.

URBAN: You say somewhere in your book that the disproportion between the leisurely ways of the bourgeoisie and the explosive tempo of technology has produced a state of 'war' which is with us all the time. Is this another side of the battle between the demands of technical rationality and man's instinctive refusal to subordinate his whole self to it?

ELLUL: Yes, the rationale of technology drives us into rational behaviour, but we are not happy with it. Countries that have reached great perfection in their technology—and I'm thinking here of Sweden as a typical example—sometimes feel that perfection to be intolerable. It bars the outlets to some of the deepest impulses of human nature. When that happens, a revolutionary, and usually irrational, reaction to the too perfect universe is almost inevitable. I have called these reactions 'ecstatic phenomena': when the constraints of a technological civilisation reduce the number of ways in which religious sentiments can be released, these sentiments concentrate on opposing the technological mode of thinking itself and acquire enormous intensity.

92

URBAN: The ecstatic rebellions you mention are variously attributed to the hypocrisy of democratic institutions, to the surfeit of our civilisation, to the manipulative power of hidden persuaders. You seem to ascribe them to technology alone. Is this in fact the underlying cause of dissent?

ELLUL: I think it is. A technological society obliges the individual to make vast sacrifices—sacrifices of what, in pre-technological societies, were considered the prizes in life: pleasant contact with nature, personal relations easily maintained over short distances, the compactness and solidarity of the extended family, work satisfaction, personal independence and so on. I am not saying that the possession of these made man happier, but they were there and could be taken for granted.

Technological society, with its rigorous ethic and high degree of organisation, has stripped us of all this. A deprivation of that magnitude cannot be accepted without protest, and it is naturally the young who react most vigorously against this kind of sacrifice because they have the most to lose. They don't easily vote for an existence which requires them to spend forty years of their lives making technology function. What value is there in such slavery? What possible interest? Hence they rebel, and the cause of rebellion is their rejection of the ethos of the technological mode of living. But there are two paradoxes here. First, the young cannot see the advantages of going into a technological society because they are, without realising it, already the beneficiaries of that society: a young Chilean would not be against it. Second, technological society has shown itself to be perfectly capable of absorbing and disarming contradictory currents of opinion, even those directly questioning its own *raison d'être*. The 'underground', for instance, is now part of technological society which does not seem to be cracking under the strain. Technological society has a complex enough system of rationality to make room for the irrational without in any way providing constructive outlets for man's non-rational aspirations.

URBAN: Your reading of the intellectual and political permissiveness of technological civilisation is similar to Marcuse's indictment of the American type of consumer civilisation, with its tendency to absorb its enemies, adjust the misfits, take the acid away from whatever is uncongenial to its social ethos and present it in acceptable form. '... the supreme luxury of the society of technical necessity,' you say, 'will be to grant the bonus of useless revolt and of an acquiescent smile.' However, in your presentation this incorporation-by-anaesthesia is done exclusively for reasons of technology whereas Marcuse's accusation is directed against several factors that make up the civilisation he describes, only one of which (though perhaps the most important) is technology.

ELLUL: The American model is simply an extreme case of the tyranny of the rationale of technology. American society is, in its non-political aspects, the most conformist we have seen in modern times, and I ascribe this conformism to the circumstance that in the United States technology has reached a pitch of perfection which it has not reached elsewhere, and that perfection demands a faster and more effective assimilation of even the most discordant elements than is the case in the technologically less developed countries.

URBAN: Your use of the word 'technology' would appear to refer to something much wider than simple nuts and bolts mechanics. In fact, in your books you do not talk of technology at all but of 'technique', and this would seem to have something to do with the technical way of doing things, the technical cast of mind.

ELLUL: Yes, in my vocabulary 'technique' has a much wider range of meanings than technology. Up to about the end of the 18th Century one could legitimately talk of technology, for it applied to solving practical problems by mechanical means—gadgetry would be the word today. But at the turn of the 18th Century people began to look for efficient ways of doing things in the whole domain of life, and basically the technical mind is one which looks for this kind of efficiency as an end in itself. As society is more and more geared to this efficiency, the objectives tend to get lost sight of and, after a time, cease to matter. Whether it is a question of business or a question of politics, the search for the most efficient way of doing things becomes *the* paramount consideration; and this search is what I call 'technique'.

Now this does not at all mean that there isn't a profound relationship between technique and technology. Today technique is the general *modus operandi* and is applied outside industrial life—the growth of its influence has little to do with the growing use of the machine. Yet the machine is profoundly symptomatic: it is the ideal to which technique aspires. The machine is pure technique. Technique sets out to build the kind of world the machine needs. It does in the field of the abstract what technology did in the field of labour.

URBAN: Aren't you condemning rather more than the tyranny of the machine? Aren't you questioning the rational mode of intellectual enquiry?

ELLUL: I am not condemning technique or technology—I'm not trying to pass judgement. I'm trying to describe the rise and nature of technique in order to gain a better understanding of the structure of our society; I am trying to see how the individual, who is the main victim of technique, could be spared some of his suffering. But technique is here to stay. It is the result of an evolutionary process which has also given us much we ought to be grateful for. But, I repeat, it is only by understanding exactly how the technical system works that we can determine how man can live with the technical system.

URBAN: Having read your book I'm not so sure that you really hold it desirable that we should learn to live with the technical system. I have certainly been left with the impression that you regard it as a wicked system and that you could think of a better one.

ELLUL: Of course I could *think* of a better one, who couldn't? The problem is: to make a moral judgement, to say that the technical system is inhuman, I would have to have an exact idea of what *is* human, I would have to have a reliable reading of what is man. Now I have no definition of man that I'm sure about. All I can say is that up to now man has succeeded in making his own history. With the rationale of the technical system pervading his entire life—a rationale he is not even beginning to grasp—I'm not so sure that man can go on making his own history. It is not through a new morality that man will manage to save himself, but by making use of his conscience and intelligence. When man manages to dominate the technical system by understanding it, he will also gradually determine what is essential to his humanity. But one has to stress the importance of understanding technique before one can go any further. Think of it in this way: every time there was an epidemic in the Middle Ages, religion and morality were brought in to explain and expiate for the disaster. When, in later centuries, science was brought to bear on such afflictions, their causes were understood and remedies were found.

URBAN: This is a telling parallel but doesn't it rather confirm my impression that you'd be happiest if we could do away with technical civilisation? If technique is an epidemic, our first duty must be to find its causes and then to stop it.

ELLUL: No, technique is not an epidemic and it would be entirely wrong for you to think that I'm yearning for a pretechnical civilisation. Technique is a phenomenon that can be dangerous to man, and the danger is by no means alleviated— it is in fact made the graver—if we think that mystical and moral kinds of reactions can shove it out of the way. We have to understand it, and understand it rationally in the same way as medical science investigates the causes of disease. That is all my comparison was meant to convey.

URBAN: I sense a dichotomy in your attitude to rationality. On the one hand you seem to deplore any attempt to criticise or reject technique for moral and emotional, i.e. non-rational, reasons alone, but on the other hand you recognise and, by implication support, the irrational elements in human behaviour. You say in *The Technological Society*: 'Man cannot live without a sense of the secret ... the invasion of technique desacralises the world ... mystery is desired by man' and so on. This means that a society based on the rationality of technique cannot do justice to human nature, and that in turn would imply some knowledge on your part of what human nature is. However, you deny that you possess such knowledge and I tend to question your denial. Let me press you on this point for it seems to me important.

It seems to me that you give us a fair indication of what human nature is by telling us what it is not. You say, for instance, that 'No technique is possible when men are free ... Technique requires predictability and, no less, exactness of prediction. It is necessary, then, that technique prevail over the human being ... Technique must reduce man to a technical animal ... Human caprice crumbles before this necessity. The individual must be fashioned by techniques, either negatively (by the techniques of understanding man) or positively (by the adaptation of man to the technical framework), in order to wipe out the blots his personal determination introduces into the perfect design of the organisation ... The individual who is a servant of technique must be completely unconscious of himself ... True technique will know how to maintain the illusion of liberty, choice, and individuality ... The solitary is a useless mouth and will have no ration card—up to the day he is transported to a penal colony' and so forth. So, by a process of elimination, we have here *a* picture of man as you see him. Does this picture stem from a Christian, or Hellenistic or Confucian conception of man?

ELLUL: Well, there is of course a conception of man behind my reflections. I am a Christian but I cannot say that I have a Christian conception of man. I don't think man's nature is permanent; it can be changed and perhaps it has changed. Nevertheless, there is a kind of minimum programme which man has always set himself in history and which is now threatened by technique. This programme doesn't tell us much about human nature, but it does tell us something about the human condition. Well, it seems to me that every human ambition to understand the world in some new frame of reference, to change man's surroundings, to plan for the future, is an expression of man's freedom. I am not saying that man is free, but his ideal has always been *to be* free, and this aspiration to the state of freedom has been his supreme goal in history. It is going against this historic experience to shut him up in a system, the rationale of which makes no allowance for the rationale of man. A system modelled on the pattern of a purely technological rationality is too perfect, hence too limiting and oppressive, to allow man to function along the lines we have always known him to follow. Now it can be argued that man ought to adapt himself to the rules of an entirely new situation, that there is, in what we know of human nature, room for a great deal of improvement. This is a hypothesis which implies a multitude of value judgements and is no fit tool for analysis. All we can say with certainty is that any attempt to curtail man's freedom —real or imagined— is bound to collide with his ambition to extend the area of freedom he has already attained.

URBAN: You say repeatedly in your books that man needs outlets for his religious sentiments, and you also say that technique has robbed him of most natural (or shall we say 'habitual') outlets. Are these sentiments then permanently suppressed or are they diverted into other channels?

ELLUL: The popular assumption that modern man is unholy and entirely secularised is false. On the contrary, man is in the process of creating new forms of religious expression, but instead of relating his religious needs to his natural surroundings —of which he experiences less and less—he relates them to his new habitat. Western man is no longer in daily contact with nature—he is in contact with technical objects. He lives in the town and he uses technical methods of work. It is to these that his need for the sacred is gradually transferred. The artificial satellites, the *Apollo* programme, even jet travel lend themselves to mystical interpretation. Man invests these with a powerful aura of belief. For the technician par excellence, the power of technology, which covers the earth with its network of telstars, waves and wires, is the locus of the sacred and a source of pride and satisfaction.

URBAN: Isn't this mythologisation of whatever seems most admirable and most coveted to man an age-old phenomenon: the rain-god in primitive cultures, womanhood in the mediaeval court lyric, the Great Mother in early French Socialist literature, now the moonshot and genetics?

ELLUL: It is of course a general phenomenon, but given the fact that today it is technique that is the object of worship, it is a most insidious phenomenon, because a religious attitude to technique prevents us from seeing it for what it is: we blow it up and trust in it instead of simply trying to understand it as a rational process. If a technical object is nothing more than a technical object, it is not a force we have to worry about, but if it is an object in which we believe, which we mythologise, and to which we hand over control of our destiny, then the object becomes powerful and dangerous.

URBAN: I think we are touching here on a related problem: the transformation of means into ends. We have come a long way from Socrates's reassurance of Phaedrus: 'But surely, my friend, if the ends be glorious, all that befalls us in seeking them is glorious also.'

It is by now a platitude to say that Christ, if he could walk down the corridors of the Vatican, would be greatly astonished to find a hierarchy of churchmen and libraries of dogma raised on the revolutionary poetry of the New Testament. By a similar token Marx, who said 'I'm not a Marxist', and who was squarely against any idea of setting up a party of the proletariat, would gasp at seeing his portrait worshipped in Red Square and would probably join the opposition. *Mutatis mutandis*, the rise of technology seems to have followed a similar path, and the lesson I would draw from all this is not about technology, or Christianity, or historical materialism but about human psychology: if we want something badly enough, or fear something badly enough, we turn it into an end and surround it with sacred symbols, however menial the origins of the object of worship may be.

ELLUL: It is indeed man's great weakness to surrender himself to some force beyond him. But technique is an ususually powerful seducer for, unlike Marx and some of the old religions, it has already given proof of its ability to solve a vast number of practical problems. It has credibility. The trouble is that from its usefulness as a minister to our needs we tend to infer that it could do even better if we allowed it to rule us. At this point man renounces his independence, hoping that this mysterious new force will do all the thinking for him. But this is not so. Technique will think for *itself*, but it will not do man's thinking: the order it has created was meant to be a buffer between man and nature, but it has evolved autonomously and has created its own laws which aren't the laws of either man or nature. We are still ignorant of these laws but it is quite clear that a new necessity has taken over from the old. The morality it imposes on us demands unquestioning loyalty to technique and the technician, and the road to that loyalty is paved with an educational system which induces us to comply with the technical environment. In practical terms this loyalty demands a behaviour which is dedicated to and dictated by work and a high degree of social conformity. All other values a technical civilisation creates revolve around these two central factors.

URBAN: I now have a clear picture of the values and qualities you contrast with the essential, or at any rate the desirable, nature of man. But a positive formulation of your position still escapes me. Let me approach the matter from another angle.

In the last chapter of your book *The Technological Society* you say: 'When our savants characterise their golden age in any but scientific terms, they emit a quantity of down-at-the-heel platitudes that would gladden the heart of the pettiest politician . . . "To render human nature nobler, more beautiful, and more harmonious." What on earth can this mean? What criteria, what content, do they propose? . . . "To eliminate cultural lag." What culture? . . . "To conquer outer space." For what purpose? The conquest of space seems to be an end in itself, which dispenses with any need for reflection.'

May I put the same questions to you and ask you: if and when technique has been conquered, what is the culture you would put in its place? What purposes would it serve? I'm sure you would not wish it to be thought that the conquest of technique is an end in itself any more than technique is.

ELLUL: I sympathise with your effort to lay bare behind my criticisms some ideological axe you suspect I am grinding. But there is none. I have already said that personally I'm a Christian, and I believe that the truth is revealed in Jesus Christ, but that statement can have a variety of interpretations, and I would hesitate to relate them either to the understanding of a technical civilisation, or to the way in which the rationale of a technical civilisation may be overcome. However, if there were to be one value which I regard as the most important, it is freedom, because, although freedom (one might say) is the precondition of error, it is also the precondition of the correction of error, which is more important. Now I would not claim that historic Christianity has lived up to the revolutionary message of the New Testament, or even that it has been an agent of non-conformism—no human institution that has lasted two thousand years can be that—but Christianity has always kept man a certain distance apart from his social environment. The Christian was encouraged to participate in the concerns of society but also to keep his critical faculties intact. Of course, from time to time, he has been subject to great social pressures to conform, but the fine balance between the positive and negative features in his attitude to society has never been destroyed. In other words, Christianity has guaranteed *a* form of freedom which, it seems to me, is worth preserving.

As to your question: what spiritual goals is a post-technical civilisation likely to set itself?—I cannot give an answer because I would first have to ask myself whether, in our new, technicised, situation it is at all possible to think of investing life with a new meaning. My suspicion is that this meaning will emerge only in the process of shedding what is unacceptable in the rationale of technique. This may give us a fresh reading of the nature of man, but one cannot be sure that it will, and one can be even less sure what it might be. We are on the defensive, and all we can do at this stage is to see to it that the tyranny of technique does not destroy our options.

My personal aim has been to help one generation of men and women to preserve their sense of criticism *vis-à-vis* technical civilisation, but the step from that rearguard action to a fresh departure is a long one. New civilisations do not evolve overnight, nor are they the work of a small number of men. Ours too, if there is to be one, will be the result of a slow and laborious process, with many false starts and setbacks. In the meantime we have to make sure that we are not engulfed by a world-wide totalitarian dictatorship which would give technique its full scope and take care of all our problems.

ERICH JANTSCH

For a Science of Man

Dr. Erich Jantsch is the author of *Technological Forecasting in Perspective* (OECD publications, 1967) and editor and co-author of *Perspective of Planning* (1969). Dr. Jantsch was educated in Vienna where he obtained his Ph.D. in Astronomy. He worked with industry as a physicist and engineer, and was for several years a full-time consultant to the Directorate of Scientific Affairs in OECD. He held visiting appointments at MIT in 1969, at the Technical University of Hanover in 1970, and is currently with the Department of City and Regional Planning, Institute of International Studies, at the University of California, Berkeley.

URBAN: Communist parties in the Soviet Union and Eastern Europe have been planning their economies and societies from the day they came to power. In Western Europe and especially in the United States we are now being warned that unless we too heed the voices of the long-range planners, we might find ourselves in deep trouble as creators and consumers of the social product, as consumers of the world's energy resources, as men with a stake in the cultural heritage and educational resources of our civilisation. Have we just discovered what the Communist parties have known all along?

JANTSCH: I don't think so. The philosophy underlying the development of all future-oriented thinking in the West is entirely different both from the Communist type of planning and from its first cousin: industrial product planning which has been employed by Western enterprises for a long time. This old type of planning—whereby you determine the likely consumption of soap-powder in New Jersey if the average man continues to buy five shirts a year, or the number of university places France will need when the results of the post-war baby-boom reach the university admission offices—this type of planning is a purely mechanistic affair. Communist planning (I always have to add: 'as practised in Eastern Europe') operates on almost identical lines. It is mechanistic because it assumes that the framework in which the planning has to be done is already given. Marxist planners presume that there is an objective law running through the lives of societies, that there is an objective framework of values and norms, and the question they have to ask themselves is simply: how do we attain our ends most efficiently within that framework? It is, therefore, a religious framework in all essentials, for the sort of questioning it permits does not extend beyond the mere operation of the system. The system itself—the hypothesis that there is in our time only one correct ideology for man to live by, and one natural state towards which society has to develop —is not called in question. So while the general framework of Communist planning is basically a religious affair, its execution shares a method with the linear product-planning ways of our more old-fashioned industries. In fact, it combines the worst of both worlds.

URBAN: So both Marxist planning and the product-planning process in Western industries have a teleological principle running through them. They know their ends and the future will be bent to those ends.

JANTSCH: They do. I should make it clear, though, that at a low level of planning, at what we call the operational level of planning, this rather elementary approach is valid. If you take industrial product planning, there is a time when you have to freeze in some of your options so that you can devote your resources to products which have a higher priority in your planning. It is then that a mechanistic model comes in handy.

URBAN: You said a moment ago that the ideas governing future-oriented thinking in the West are entirely different from the kind of planning we have in the Soviet type of societies. What are the differences?

JANTSCH: My answer to that, at its simplest, is that we try to develop a 'human-action' model, which is our way of saying that it is man himself who takes the responsibility for designing his future and of finding ways of making that future just and liveable.

URBAN: He is not governed by historic necessity or any goal which would pre-determine his actions?

JANTSCH: No, he is not. Mankind is now pushing against limitations which are global in character. We are encountering the fact that the planet Earth has limited resources to feed us and house us and keep us warm. We are running up against boundaries when we talk about the world's population or the balance between nature and the man-made world. We are discovering that it is not only the normally peaceable chimpanzees that start fighting and then dying off of disease if they are forced to live in an overcrowded cage, but that over-population can, and already does, have the same effect on human beings. These are vast and pressing problems and we cannot hope to do justice to them with the old methods, Communist or Western. Man and his surroundings have to be conceived as one single whole, a system, in fact, in which changes in one part have an impact on all other parts, directly or indirectly. The picture we should have of our state on this globe is one of interdependence as between nations and regions, and also between man and the natural world which sustains him. We are all our brother's keepers.

URBAN: How would you spell out the moral, cultural and aesthetic consequences which follow from perceiving man's situation in this way?

JANTSCH: Before we can talk about the ethics of our situation we must have a clear picture of what is wrong with the direction we have taken so far. For it is clear that in many important respects the technological engine has landed us in a blind alley. Take our attitude to growth. We never question the proposition that economic growth, the growth of the material standard of living and the resulting competition between individuals, companies and nations are good things and ought to be encouraged. This is surely a prescription for disaster. We are already straining against the limits of growth: economies cannot go on growing much further, consumption and the exploitation of the earth's resources cannot increase indefinitely. So what we have to do is to sit down and think again. It is then that the need for fresh values and a new orientation impresses itself on us with very great urgency. We'll have to ask ourselves whether, for instance, the ethos of competition and growth should not be replaced by an ethos of responsibility, whether the scramble for squeezing the last inches of usable land out of the earth's surface and the last drops of unpoisoned water should not give way to some view which pays due attention to the overall ecological balance between man, society, technology and nature.

URBAN: But aren't we then talking about a complete and almost revolutionary transformation of our values, our business mentality, the collective goals of society, the norms that guide us in our dealings with foreign races and so on?

JANTSCH: Indeed, I'm talking about the need for a complete cultural, I might almost say anthropological, transformation. And this goes for the Eastern countries no less than for the West because the Communist growth-ethic is a replica of our own, pursued even more fiercely but perhaps less efficiently. And the tragedy is that the more highly developed the technology, the more intricate the interactions and the more difficult to undo the damage. So you can launch an ecologically misconceived production method in Japan and the results will be felt five years later in Europe and they may well be irreversible.

URBAN: All this would militate for a fully international type of cooperation between governments, planners, data-collectors and digesters. How can this be done without world government or, at the very least, a voluntary but binding kind of international cooperation?

JANTSCH: I have no ready-made solutions to these problems but I can indicate some ways that seem to me feasible. One need not go the whole hog and demand world government. It would not be realistic at the present time. There are enough problems that can be dealt with internationally on a delegated basis for us to make a start without wanting to write off nation-states at this stage. Some of these problems will demand the creation of new institutions, others can be farmed out to existing ones. I'm not saying that we'll have an orgy of nation-states voluntarily relinquishing their sovereign rights. National governments don't normally behave like philanthropic institutions, but they can be made to yield if public opinion is sufficiently roused and the consequences of the collision course on which we are now set are made clear to the passengers. It is not enough to tell the driver.

URBAN: The Communist governments have been pioneers in trying to map out the future for their societies. Are they responsive to this highly dynamic, non-class approach to man's life on the planet Earth?

JANTSCH: I have visited some of the Communist countries and spent time in Moscow on an official invitation. Certainly the Soviet Government is much concerned with the future. They argue from the fact that they have made considerable progress in giving their population a higher standard of living and made spectacular progress in some fields of technology. They don't want to see those achievements endangered. They are much more conscious than most West European governments that national interests may be defeated if global interests are not taken care of.

URBAN: If the Soviet Government, and perhaps some of the other Communist governments, are aware of these problems, the peoples of Eastern Europe are certainly not. In Poland or Hungary one knows from personal experience that the man in the street wants more pollution rather than less, more technology rather than less provided that he can get the car he is dreaming of buying, or the refrigerator, or the weekend cottage. His standard of comparison is the Austrian worker who has many of these things, and he will dismiss all talk about unclean rivers and impure air as typical concerns of the rich. He would be most unresponsive to any suggestion that the Gross National Product ought to be tested against the Gross National Pollution, or the Affluent Society against the Effluent Society.

JANTSCH: This may well be so, but I should hasten to add that what the little man feels in Russia, Poland or Hungary is shared by what little men feel about this problem in most developing countries. I have heard the argument in countless places in Asia and Africa, and it is very much in evidence at the United Nations.

Even in Japan one hears the kind of view you have just quoted. I remember a phrase used by the Director of the Japanese Economic Research Institute at a recent conference: 'Harmony and progress: harmony for the developed countries, progress for the developing world.' In other words, the developing countries want economic development irrespective of what systemic interactions it may cause; once the development has reached a certain level, they will, they say, take care of the harmony.

I, for one, don't believe this is a viable philosophy. The rapid progress of technology in the advanced countries has already brought us to the crossroads. It is, in terms of a global ecology, impossible to bring the living standards of the developing world anywhere near the standards enjoyed by the Western nations. Reflect for a moment on American statistics. The population of the United States is six per cent of the world's population. Yet it consumes forty per cent of the world's resources. If everybody in the world consumed on the scale of the United States, the world's consumption of resources would increase sevenfold and that would mean instant disaster.

Where do we go from here? The conclusion I draw, and I think it is the only possible conclusion, is that we shall have to get the Western countries not only to prevent their economies from growing, but that the West will have to take several steps backward, lowering the material standard of living of the population, cutting back on consumption and taking a share in a more equitable distribution of the world's resources. This is going to be very hard on the Western governments and even harder on the people.

URBAN: It runs counter to the rising expectations of the Western countries all of which, with the possible exception of the United States, have themselves just escaped from centuries of grinding poverty.

What worries me more in what you are saying are the long-range prospects of growing populations fighting each other for practically static or diminishing resources of food, minerals, water, etc. Does this not spell the spectre of class-war on a global scale—have-not Asians ravaging the cities of well-fed Europeans and Americans? It is a horrifying thought, but if it is true that the world cannot satisfy *both* the Swiss *and* the Bolivians, then the larger part of the world's population would seem to be doomed to eternal and probably growing relative poverty, and we know that sooner or later such inequalities lead to violent eruptions. You are, in a sense, confirming what Maoists like Lin Piao tell us: the world's hungry countryside encircling and destroying the world's cities—the developed and bourgeois West.

JANTSCH: I fear you may be right. The gap between rich and poor is growing throughout the world and I can readily believe that in ten years' time we will not be able to visit the developing countries for they will have accumulated an explosive hatred for us. It isn't that we can keep them in ignorance of our welfare. We have given them radio and television, and they can see for themselves that even though they may be slightly better off than they were five years ago, they are, compared to the American Express traveller, much worse off than they were five years ago. All our aid to these countries —Western or Eastern—hasn't had any real impact. It hasn't been given fast enough and the methods used were ineffective. In the UN Development Decade the advanced countries increased their *per capita* income by more than three hundred dollars per annum, whereas per capita incomes in the developing countries were stagnant. I can see no hope that a second UN Development Decade would do any better, unless it started with a completely fresh philosophy and a vastly increased programme of financial and technical aid. At the moment we are offering less than one per cent of our GNP.

URBAN: So we are talking about the need for a fundamental reappraisal of our moral and cultural attitudes both as individuals and as nations. The individual would have to lower his sights, consume less and find a new balance between himself and his surroundings. The rich nations would have to make similar sacrifices on a collective scale. These are daunting prospects which neither individuals nor nations would readily adopt unless their very lives were endangered.

JANTSCH: They *are* daunting prospects, but what are our options? We could muddle along as we have done so far, postponing the day of reckoning. However, it isn't that we have to start from scratch. We can draw on the economic experiences of the wealthy countries both in their own development and the experiences they have gained in the developing world, and we can go on using them for a few more years.

But I would regard it as more important to inculcate a different spirit, not only in the donor nations but also in those that are at the receiving end. I'm thinking, for instance, of the lessons we may draw from examples such as the Asian cultures

110

offer. They are very different from the life-ethos we have deduced from Christianity. Christians talk of a beginning and an end of the world and the span between the two has to be filled in with productive achievement. The Christian ethic, especially the Protestant ethic, concentrates on concrete activity on this side of eternity, and the usual concomitant of that work is to create something out of nothing and, as the next step, to make things grow: it may be the growth of a man's wealth, the status of his family, his clan, his city or his nation. The strictly Catholic equivalent of this ethic is perhaps less clearly programmatic, but even there the rewards of thrift, good husbandry and wise planning—i.e. growth and achievement—are well recognised.

Now all this is different in some of the Asian cultures. There man is believed to be destined to have more than one sojourn on earth and therefore he is in no particular hurry to fill his life with feverish activity. He disdains competition, he cannot see much point in a multiplication of his tools or possessions. Rather, he values the unspectacular virtues of learning and contemplation which would seem to me to be much more in tune with the ecological requirements of the coming centuries than our growth-mania.

URBAN: I would agree with you and go a step further. After all, man's exploitation of his natural environment is sanctioned by the Bible. In the first chapter of *Genesis* God says to man, 'Be fruitful, multiply, and replenish the earth and subdue it: and have dominion over the fish of the sea, over the fowl of the air, and over every living thing that moveth upon the earth.' Here we have a faultless Judeo-Christian prescription for the population explosion, for the pollution of the water and the air and for ecological disaster. True, one hears theologians argue that this picture is greatly modified by Christ's attitude to nature in the New Testament, and also by the dire warnings we are given of the impending environmental nemesis in the *Revelations* of St. John the Divine ('Hurt not the earth, neither the sea, nor the trees . . . And the third part of the waters became

111

wormwood; and many men died of the waters, because they were made bitter ... and the day shone not for a third part of it, and the night likewise ... and the sun and the air were darkened by reason of the smoke of the pit' and so forth). Yet, in the most highly developed, industrialised countries it was the Protestant view of the world that set the public ethic, and that meant relying on *Genesis* more than on any other Biblical source. So, until quite recently, nature was looked upon as something to be overcome and suppressed. Taming the wilderness, cutting down trees, harnessing rivers were thought to be not only lucrative activities for man, but also attuned to God's purpose with man.

JANTSCH: I agree with you, and when one remembers how Max Weber deduced the growth of capitalism from the Protestant ethic one has yet another reason for thinking that we may do well to look for cultural stimulants to India and China if we want to find a life-philosophy that would help us to do justice to our ecological problem. I'm reminded of Professor Chomsky's recent experiences in North Vietnam. As you know, Noam Chomsky is one of the most brilliant dissenters in the United States, an eloquent and influential opponent of American policies in Vietnam. Recently he was invited to North Vietnam, and in the course of his visit he asked the North Vietnamese Communist authorities what sort of technical help, what sort of engineering help they would need after the war has ended. To his surprise he was told that they didn't want engineers but rather the type of person who is well up in modern thinking in more general ways—scientists, philosophers, even artists. My guess would be that the North Vietnamese, with their tradition of sturdy independence, may not want to repeat the pattern of large-scale industrialisation which the Soviet Union and the East European countries have taken over from the West. They may want to try another alternative. That would mean not entering the race for increasing your GNP; it would mean the first conscious effort on the part of a developing nation not to join the suicide club.

And this takes me back to the spirit of cybernetic planning which we have already briefly discussed. The spirit of this modern planning does not set man apart from nature. There is no question of man subduing the earth or slaughtering the fish of the seas. On the contrary, it is realised that the man who subdues nature also subdues the human species. This is perhaps the easiest part of cybernetics to understand. But cybernetic planning applies the same philosophy to man-made systems and to the interplay between the man-made world and the natural environment. Its fundamental tenet is that systems— social systems, cities, industrial conglomerations and so on— are in permanent interaction with each other, with the earth, the air, the world's energy resources, and have to be continu-ously re-designed to protect the ecological balance and, through it, man's freedom. Quite obviously, this freedom presupposes the loss of *some* of our freedoms. An unbridled, competitive economic activity is clearly incompatible with that freedom for the simple reason that, within a very short time indeed, it would lead to quite crippling restrictions and worse. I can't do better than quote to you the opening paragraph of Gordon Rattray Taylor's new *Doomsday Book*:

Put bacteria in a test-tube, with food and oxygen, and they will grow explosively, doubling in number every twenty minutes or so, until they form a solid, visible mass. But finally multiplica-tion will cease as they become poisoned by their own waste pro-ducts. In the centre of the mass will be a core of dead and dying bacteria, cut off from the food and oxygen of their environment by the solid barrier of their neighbours. The number of living bacteria will fall almost to zero, unless the waste products are washed away.

Mankind today is in a similar position.

Here we have it all summed up in a few sentences.

URBAN: You are saying that if men want to be free in the long run, or at any rate free within the possibilities of what our planet can afford to give us in terms of food, air, water, shelter and other resources, we must relinquish some of our freedoms in the short term, such as the freedom of untrammelled competition in the economic sphere, the pursuit of selfish national and individual interests and the like.

This, it would seem to me, is the sort of problem that exercises the rebellious young a great deal, but I perceive in their attitude a profound paradox. On the one hand the young are against anything that smacks of organisation. On the other hand, however, they are for the sort of freedom from environmental troubles which, according to what you have told us, only a proper understanding of the interactions between man, his technology and nature can secure, and that, you are arguing, imposes strict limits on our freedom. So even if the young managed to free the world of every trace of government and authority, they would still have to put up with, indeed they would have to create, agencies to curtail the freedoms they want.

JANTSCH: Yes, I would say the romanticism and anarchism of the young is best understood as one manifestation of the spirit of competition and growth of which a free-enterprise economy is another. Now the paradox you mention is perhaps real but it gives me no cause for worry. One principle which is gradually emerging from the philosophy of future-oriented studies simply underlines the impossibility of solving certain problems with any finality and the necessity of learning to live with them. Our intellectual heritage is a great bind for us here, for, using the physical sciences and technology as our models, we have got used to the idea that conflicts are open to resolution even if they occur in complex systems. But this is not so. The paradoxes are numerous: the system I attempted to describe is weighted in some of its aspects against individual liberty, yet its whole purpose is to safeguard liberty. As Sir Geoffrey Vickers recently put it in *Freedom in a Rocking Boat*: 'all human liberties are social artefacts, created, preserved and guaranteed by special social and political orders'. In other words, liberty is created, not given; and it is as well to remember that freedom should not be confused with a situation free from all strains and pressures. There is also the dichotomy between instinct and rationality. Here again one has to realise that we can't hope to create the kind of consciousness that our ecological situation demands unless, like every good artist, we combine the two. By living these paradoxes rather than resolving them we may be approaching a kind of *modus vivendi*. This is no prescription for an easy life. It assumes that men, ordinary men, can be taught to live in a state of creative tension and perhaps taught to like it. This is the spirit of the ancient Greek tragedy, revived through ecological necessity, but of course enacted on a very different stage. It is the story of man rebelling against the system yet realising all the time that there are systemic boundaries to his actions. We understand that we are a part of nature yet we possess free will to contest the frontiers of our liberty. This may be a creative and constructive act or it may be mechanical and end in tragedy.

Now this may strike you as being slightly far-fetched but I believe that our dilemma is, basically at least, similar to those of the Greek tragedians.

URBAN: I think this is a most stimulating analogy. It reminds me of one of Max Weber's books *Wissenschaft als Beruf*, and a rejoinder written to it by Erich von Kahler, *Beruf der Wissenschaft*. Kahler was passionately arguing that science—he was thinking of both the hard and the soft sciences—is not, cannot be and shouldn't be, a morally neutral activity. Scientific work, he was saying, is value-laden. It should adapt its method to man and his emotional needs. Objective truths are irrelevant to its purpose. It should work in 'homologies', not analogies. If my understanding of what you have said about man interacting with his social and natural environment is correct, then you should be agreeing with Kahler's point of view.

JANTSCH: Yes, this type of thinking is entirely in line with what the new, future-oriented philosophy would seem to demand. The traditional view, as expounded by numberless scientists, has been that science is value-free, that technology is

CAN WE SURVIVE OUR FUTURE?

neutral and that only the use to which technology and science are put is loaded with moral issues. This is a false distinction. Science is a creation of man. It is not given in raw nature. In one way or another, every scientific activity creates anthropomorphic paradigms. Knowledge may be understood as a way of doing things, a mode of questioning, an approach to nature which implies, precisely because it asks certain questions, also the rejection of others. In other words it is a selective activity and therefore deeply influenced by the tastes, predilections and interests of the men who do the selecting.

I am not praising or condemning the subjective element in science, but it is as well for us to know that it is there because from it we may develop a quite unashamedly anthropomorphic kind of science which may become a culturally creative factor in the civilisation of the future. It will counteract the, to my mind, damaging influence of behaviourism and empiricism in the social sciences. It will have only the most tenuous links with practicability and will reaffirm our identity as men and not, as Professor Skinner would have it, as rats who happen to be bipeds endowed with an outsize cranium.

URBAN: This is a very elevated view of scientific activity and I hope you will not think that I am disrespectful when I say that I am not sure that it is practicable.

JANTSCH: Well, I happen to believe that defining and understanding the boundary conditions of science is a highly necessary practical activity. The system we want to design embraces every form of life and every type of society, and its purpose is to make it possible for man to continue living on this planet without destroying it, and with it, himself. So we have to shape an anthropomorphic system. But here is the snag: what is anthropomorphic? We have an elementary knowledge of what man is about: he needs to breathe air, if possible clean air. He needs food and he needs clean food. But over and above these simple facts our knowledge of human nature is very imperfect. Man can shape the environment. Is this a natural or

116

an unnatural activity? And when the artificial environment he has created reacts back on him—is that so removed from the nature of man who has created it that we can say that it is alien to him and damaging to his nature? Let me quote another example. In the last hundred years we have adapted to vastly changing environments, and of course before that we have adapted to environmental change for thousands of years at a much slower pace. But we haven't the ability to adapt indefinitely. Some geneticists believe that eighty-five per cent of our genetic heritage is constantly in reserve to make it possible for us to adapt to new environments. Only fifteen per cent of it is actively engaged at one time. The mutations are extremely slow and man is in all essentials the same as he was in the stone-age, three hundred generations ago. But we don't know how far we can go in adapting to artificial environments; we only know that there is a limit.

Futuristic speculations don't pay enough attention to such factors. We are told that in fifty years' time we shall all be living in vast, push-button glass and concrete environments, but we have no notion how that will affect us. There is, as René Dubos insists, a new science to be founded to study this kind of problem—the science of humanity. It will be a study of man as he encounters himself in an increasingly man-made world.

URBAN: What kind of values would underlie the new civilisation you envisage?

JANTSCH: Well, bringing new values into play is a difficult question and it is at the very core of this new planning philosophy. By going into a highly technological world we have given up the possibility of acting on instinct alone. Instinct gives you certain unerring certainties. Bees know precisely what they have to do to survive comfortably. We have lost that. We are now searching for something to give us a tolerably reliable yardstick, and that yardstick, that method is rationality. The great modern bet is that rational understanding can tell us what the world is about and, what is more important, that men will heed rational advice.

URBAN: One would like to believe that man is a rational animal but there is little in history to confirm that he is. When the chips are down, when action has to be taken on essential issues, whether it be on the national or family level, the irrational element usually takes precedence over rational considerations. Khrushchev, as we know from his memoirs, ran the awful risk of a nuclear war with the United States for highly irrational reasons—he was out to humiliate the Americans and to teach them a lesson. American presidents have repeatedly stated that they won't be the first to lose America a war. That supposedly most rational of planning exercises, planning in the Communist countries, shows a pattern of irrationality and arbitrary tergiversations, compared to which the market economies of the Western countries are models of economic rationality. One could go on. My suspicion is that the colossal transformation we need is not likely to come about before we are reminded that it *must* come about by some huge ecological disaster or a nuclear war.

JANTSCH: I'm afraid I have to agree with you. What disturbs me most is our lack of foresight. When man fell from Paradise he appears to have been endowed with a surprising light-heartedness about the consequences of his actions. He was taught to live in the present. This protective wrapping has now become a liability. Today we can foretell the consequences of our actions in many cases with unfailing certainty. We *know* that so many more cars will simply poison the inhabitants of London by the year 2050; we *know* that at the present rate of consumption the world's easily recoverable oil resources will dry up in so many years. Yet we are so poor in rationality, or, if you like, we are so heavily protected from seeing the results of our follies, that we refuse to see what really stares us in the face. We still hope, quite irrationally, that we'll muddle through.

URBAN: But hasn't this protective mechanism served us extremely well? If a child were capable of being made *fully* conscious that he was heading for death from the moment he was born, could he bear to live a normal life in the first place? If every soldier who was killed in the First and Second World Wars had taken to heart the statistical forecasts, wouldn't the world's armies have disintegrated, or turned into psychiatric wards the day the war broke out? In 1939 everyone knew perfectly well that if the war were to last three or four years, a very large proportion of the young men drafted into the forces would not survive. And they didn't. But every soldier had this protective wrapping around him believing that *he* would be spared. This is surely something we ought to be thankful for.

JANTSCH: I don't doubt for a moment that throughout the ages this protective shield has served us admirably, but our situation is essentially different from all earlier situations.

URBAN: Hasn't this uniqueness been the cry of every age? Every new civilisation, like every young man in his teens, believes that he is unique. But on closer examination the neophyliacs turn out to be old hats.

JANTSCH: The uniqueness of our situation is quite easy to explain: the time-scale on which we work has undergone a sea-change. In earlier times we had time to react to slow changes in our environment. It took thousands of years for man the hunter to become an agricultural worker, and for the latter to become an engineer in electronics. Today we have such a dangerously short time-factor at play that we have to act in anticipation. To spread the word around about this is going to make some of us highly unpopular. I have already said that the full satisfaction of short-range demands will almost automatically involve us in long range disaster. So, to protect ourselves against long-range trouble, we ought to take restrictive steps right away, which people will not like. They will appeal to their protective shield ('hope' if you like) and shove the really

119

important problems under the carpet. Alas, these problems will not go away.

URBAN: This brings us back to an idea we have already touched on and which I would now formulate in slightly different language, namely that collective myopia is the original sin of mankind. The changes your new civilisation would demand in our consciousness seem so large that it is difficult to believe that they can be accomplished not in one but perhaps even a hundred generations. Why should we have any hope on this score when we cannot solve the simplest of techno-social problems, such as shifting freight transportation from our over-crowded roads to the railways which are running empty and at a great financial loss to the tax-payer? What could be more reasonable, economically sound, technologically feasible and more likely to save lives? We *all* want it (private road hauliers excepted), and yet no country has managed to do anything about it.

A book recently published in Hungary makes great play with the phrase 'cosmic alienation'. The author, Imre Magyar, is an eminent physician, and his message is that while we can now go to the moon, we can't get our telephone system working, or our trains to run on time, or taps installed that don't flood our bathrooms, or organise the smooth distribution of even the simplest commodities. So, he says, man is cosmically alienated : he possesses 'big science', which is of absolutely no use to him, but sitting in his prefabricated apartment he isn't really better off than was his grandfather on the farm. In fact he is worse off, because television tells him he lives in the space age, but his five senses tell him he is just beginning to drag himself into the 20th Century. Now I realise that this 'alienation' is a European, especially an East European (and Third World), phenomenon, and that it applies much less to the United States, and I'm quoting these examples simply to stress the point that closing the gap in our consciousness between *knowing* about some long-distance contingency and getting this knowledge into our *bones*, is immense. Perhaps you are more hopeful.

JANTSCH: The alienation you mention is part of the mismanagement of the global system. The little man feels that moonshots are a spectacular waste and dangerous distractions from our real problems, and I can't blame him for his cosmic alienation. But remember that there is also a perennial trait in man's ambition, his perfectionism, which urges him from time to time to do a superlative thing that has no real bearing on his daily life. Landing a human being on the moon was a faultless, one-shot operation. It required superb technology and organisation, well within the control of a small number of scientists. The result was a stunning demonstration of what men can achieve under optimal conditions.

The trouble is that this sense of the perfect operates only within very small dimensions. Your example of the road–rail controversy is a good one : the number of interests to be consulted, the number of ingrained habits to overcome is too large for effective action, and the end-result promises to have nothing perfect, nothing uplifting about it. So the malaise is allowed to continue. We would, thus, have to add to the dichotomy we have already discussed—that between rationality and instinct—another and perhaps equally important, namely the duality between man's urge for the inspiring, finite, perfect whole, and his need to go on tinkering, mending and improvising in his daily work. But this again simply gives added urgency to my view that an entirely new outlook is needed to establish the balance we need before a point of no return is reached in our mismanagement of ourselves and of our resources.

URBAN: Are there any signs that this change in our consciousness is on its way?

JANTSCH: Well, there are some signs. The whole young generation in Europe and America lives in a state of intense unease. They feel that our values have to change although they are less certain what our future values should be. Now some of this feeling can and should be funnelled into constructive channels.

121

One such channel, an essential one to my mind, is to combine a decentralisation of initiative with a concern for the impact of that initiative on society as a whole. It implies a two-way traffic. My model would be a large industrial corporation in which every employee is, or ought to be, aware of what his contribution (or the lack of it) may mean for the overall objectives of the enterprise, while on the other hand the objectives of the corporation are conceived with the employee's social needs, his health requirements and his cultural ambitions in mind. It would require an efficient feed-back mechanism and a fine sense of balance between initiative and responsibility.

URBAN: Wasn't there a similar idea behind Soviet Man whose existence has been heavily called in question by Klaus Mehnert? Soviet Man was also supposed to be a serious and upright kind of gentleman who would curtail his material interests to serve the state which is his, in theory. He would not strike, for the factory is his, so why damage your own property, and so on.

JANTSCH: Ah, but I can't allow you to put an equation mark between the two. Soviet Man has never been given a chance to show any real initiative. In fact, he has been the victim of a tight, mechanistic kind of planning which made a mockery not only of his initiative but of his humanity too. I believe it is possible to create a spirit of responsibility in man if you put the right challenge to him. Once his basic creature comforts have been satisfied, he will not be content with the challenge to 'get rich', or 'get yourself a perfect technology'. We can see from the rebellion of the well-to-do young in America, France and Germany that affluence, like Dante's Paradiso, is a dull condition. But it is possible to go beyond it by being aware of the problems that surround us and doing something about them. Of course, one cannot redesign a system, or the individual's consciousness, by a stroke of the ecologist's wand. We cannot hope to motivate people for noble and responsible action by preaching at them.

122

But it is my profound belief that men will listen to reason provided that the challenge is put to them in a way which they understand. Take the matter of pollution. It was a non-problem and a non-subject ten, even five years ago. Not that the problem didn't exist before, but people simply hadn't been educated to recognise it. Within the last three years the world has brought forth ecologists and environmental scientists of all kinds, and ministries to employ them. There is intense concern with what the motor-car and the oil refinery are doing to the air we breathe, with the pollution of the rivers which supply our drinking water and so forth. There has been legislation in many countries, and the public, at least the opinion-making sections of the public, have been mobilised. This is a vast and very encouraging change for the better, the more important because it has succeeded in the teeth of opposition from very powerful interests such as some of the world's greatest industrial polluters. True, this is just scratching the surface of one of many problems, but if we have woken up to this one, I can't see why we should not tackle others.

Surely we can make a similar impact when it comes to explaining the consequences of the growth of the world's population. To feed the growing number of mouths each year, we are pushing agriculture to invest more in certain high-yield crops. Crops have been developed which yield three and four times the amount of the earlier species. But what we are developing here harbours very great dangers for the world's ecological balance. Chemical fertilisers and pesticides have poisonous ingredients. At the moment only the United States and Europe use them on an extensive scale. But supposing the rest of the world—and that is where the real food shortage is—started using similar techniques: the ecological equilibrium of the world would be very seriously affected. In other words, the land can bear only a limited amount of disequilibrium before it starts reacting against its exploiters. All this sets a definite limit to the amount of food we can ever hope to extract from agriculture, and this amount will be roughly enough to feed us up to about 1990, possibly the year 2000, if the population goes on growing at the rate we envisage.

After that time we will have to go short, which means in plain language that some of us will go on living as we do now, while others will starve in very much greater numbers than they are already doing. And this is where future-oriented research comes in. We know that there are ways of checking the growth of the world's population but we are already too late with our measures if we want to have any practical impact by the year 2000. We also know that there are alternative sources of food-production which are non-agricultural. But if we want to make use of them in thirty years' time, we must make a start now. What we do not know at the moment is how to restrict the growth of the population and at the same time do away with the most effective pressure which restricts population growth, namely food shortage. A little later the same problem may present itself in a different form: how to prevent the population from growing to the level of food production. The question is: how do you bring this view home to the politicians and the public and how do you get them to fight off the vested interests —commercial, military and plain psychological—which constitute the fatal myopia you have mentioned. But, as I say, we have done it with pollution and I'm fairly confident we may do it with other issues.

URBAN: In bringing the message home to the governments and the public, do you expect to encounter different sorts of difficulties in the Western and Communist societies?

JANTSCH: When I talk about large-scale planning for the future, I become unpopular both with the Communist planners and the leaders of commerce and industry in the West. People on the ideological Left tell me that I'm ignoring the most important point, the class struggle. From the ideological Right I'm accused of pushing Socialism. Well, if socialism means a concern for the future of society, by all means let's call it Socialism. However, the Western attitude to the systemic change I advocate is very different from what one gets in Eastern Europe, and induces more optimism. In the West we can engage the individual. We can do something about de-centralisation. Also, we have the people, a great many people, who are burning to make a contribution. We have the ability to shift our attention and our methods from the corporations to the whole body of society—from product-design to social planning. Also, we are, at our universities, preparing the ground for a systematic study of macro-planning. These are considerable assets, so I would say we are in a more favourable position than the East European countries where, for decades, democratic centralism and the centralisation of planning have killed all initiative. It is only in the last two to three years that Hungary and Czechoslovakia have tried to escape from the straitjacket. Alas, their escape aims at imitating some of the features of the Western economy, so they'll probably have to go through our troubles before they can hope to pull their weight in extricating mankind from the quagmire in which we have landed ourselves through our rapacity, lack of foresight and sheer inertia.

URBAN: Are you implying that the East European economies, even when they try to reform themselves, are consistently a step behind contemporary thinking?

JANTSCH: You are being too kind: some of them are a generation behind. A certain amount of industrialisation and technological proficiency is, of course, essential in poorly de-veloped countries (of which Russia was one), for technology is the only means given to man with which he can get a grip on nature. The Asian and African peoples are, by and large, still in a state where they cannot begin to live like human beings unless they have more technology. The danger comes with the next phase of development—the industrial take-off—and it is here that the East European reforms are not convincing.

Man's proper concern is with the quality of life. The United States has twice the GNP of Western Europe but, judging by what my American friends tell me and what I can see for myself, it does not at all follow that the quality of life in America is twice as good as it is in Europe. It is probably the other way around. There is a level of development where quantitative goals do not lead to better quality, where more money does not mean more wealth. None of us can eat more than three square meals a day or wear more than one pair of shoes at a time.

To sum up: the West has to settle for falling expectations; in the developing world we may do well to go on supporting growing expectations up to the point where the development threatens to become counter-productive. And when the balance is reached, we may, with some luck, congratulate ourselves on having averted disaster. But until then we have a hard row to hoe.

LOUIS ARMAND

Restoring Man's
Symbiosis with Nature

The late Louis Armand was a Member of the French Academy and
one of the most distinguished and influential administrators of post-
war Europe. M. Armand began his career as a mining engineer and
worked in the French resistance during the occupation. In 1949 he
was appointed Director General of French Railways. In 1958 and
1959 he was both President of EURATOM and Chairman of the
International Union of Railways. His election to the French Academy
in 1963 was in recognition of his career as an administrator and his
activities as a writer. M. Armand's publications include *Plaidoyer
pour l'avenir* (1961), *Simples Propos* (1968) and *Le Défi européen*
(with Michel Drancourt, 1968).

URBAN: The wheel has come full circle: technological progress has become a loaded expression, and it is revealing that
those who object most strongly to the further spread of technology are the people who have it and enjoy it. Thus the 'knock
technology' school has an uncommonly heavy ring of hypocrisy
about it, and one wonders whether the calls for technological
disarmament don't really rank on a par with those pious declarations of universal disarmament which we have learnt to skip
in our daily papers for the best part of half a century. After all,
the technologies men use have no will of their own (or so one
would like to think): tanks, like motor-cars, are in themselves
morally neutral forms of hardware, and what makes them potentially dangerous are the intentions of the men who drive
them. At the same time, however, it is true that the fact that a
weapon or some instrument of locomotion has been manufactured raises the stakes enormously in favour of its being used.
So one is confronted with the familiar dilemma of how to make

moral pigmies learn to deal with the problems of technological giants.

ARMAND: Technological progress has been the result of the haphazard progress of science and this is linked with the ease with which objects produced by this progress can be sold. But we have a very imperfect knowledge of how to use these objects. Humanity has been caught unprepared, in a state of immaturity. We have not been alerted to the dangers of technology, and even now the realisation that we may need new moral values is only beginning to dawn on us. It is an unfortunate fact that humanity, when faced with the fruits of technology, is like a child. At the risk of appearing to be patronising, I would also say that a child needs a tutor or else he will not make proper use of the objects he finds about him. He will amuse himself hiding glasses instead of drinking from them.

We know how to make cars, we know how to make them better and cheaper all the time. We also know, and knew from the beginning of motorisation, that there is nothing people would more wish to possess than motor-cars and there is nothing the manufacturers and their shareholders would more wish to sell than motor-cars, or governments to export to boost their foreign earnings. Yet no one had the foresight or courage to warn us that the congestion of our roads would choke us. And those who did were not listened to because the dangers seemed long-term while the benefits were thought to be immediate.

This is a political and moral question and has to be dealt with at the highest level. Some years ago I suggested that in modern society there ought to be a council of wise and independent people who would give their governments some idea where technological development was taking us. I proposed that this council should be set up for the whole of Europe and that its members should be given the freedom of Europe's radio and television stations, an hour each day, so that their reading of our situation would get the widest publicity. If men act like children, they need tutorials, and these broadcasts were meant to be one way of giving it to them. There is nothing in democracy to make us shun the views of men of the calibre of Arnold Toynbee or Jean Rostand. The chances are that they could tell us something useful about our civic responsibilities and offer moral advice.

URBAN: You are depicting an élitist type of society, and one wonders how far that is in tune with the egalitarian demands of Western democracy. In England Lord Reith held somewhat similar views when he was Director General of the BBC, and he put them into effect to the great benefit (or so it seems to me) of British society. Today the BBC's estimate of how much the public would tolerate of Reithean tutoring is very different from what it used to be, and I'm not sure that the other European countries would react differently. Our threshold of tolerance of responsible thinking is being gradually pushed back, and this is happening at a time when, as you say, more, not less, of it is needed.

ARMAND: Democracy cannot be allowed to mean the debasement of values or the deflation of responsibility. The need for guidance in matters that affect the whole of life is a natural need of man and democracy has certainly not done away with it. For many centuries it was the church that satisfied that need, and the broadcasters of those days were the ministers of the church who spoke to the people from the pulpit and fulfilled the kind of function I have been talking about. Their voices were heeded by king and bondsman alike. Our need to be warned about the genie we have allowed to escape from the bottle is greater than were the needs of our forefathers, and our methods must have an accordingly greater urgency about them.

URBAN: If you were to write a modern sermon on some theme such as 'Technology and the Reorientation of the Moral Purpose of Man', what would be the main points you would be making?

ARMAND: I would stress two ideas—what we call in French 'la socialisation' and 'la planétisation'.

I   129

Now 'socialisation' has nothing to do with Socialism. It describes the fact that work has become mass-activity. Fewer and fewer people work in the fields or in small workshops. They work in factories and offices. They eat their meals in works canteens, they go to the same beaches, they look at the same television programmes; in fact most of their waking life—whether at work or at leisure—is spent in some kind of social activity. They have to take notice of their neighbours, yet we have not taught them how to behave in relation to their neighbours. People do not realise that this socialisation is going on and they have to make do with reflexes which stem from a morality that does not fit their real situation. There is a gap between moral values and civic spirit. Of course, civic responsibility is an elusive quality, and our classics don't tell us how to go about developing it to help us with our present problems. I can think of one unusual initiative, though, that of an Italian priest who was so upset about careless driving and road casualties that he let it be known from the pulpit that any driver crossing the continuous white line in the middle of the road was committing a mortal sin and should confess. And I think the spirit in which he acted was the right one.

The second point I would stress is 'planetisation'—the fact that the world has become a global village, that millions of people could simultaneously watch Kennedy's funeral or the World Cup in Mexico where radio and television chalked up seven hundred million listeners and spectators. Now there is a vast change here from earlier times. In the Colosseum in ancient Rome there were never more than sixty thousand people to watch some spectacle, but now we move from that sort of figure to hundreds of millions of people simultaneously attuned to the same image and the same sound. This implies a profound psychological difference, the impact of which we have not even begun to understand. What happens to men when they share the same electronic signal thousands of miles away from each other —do they share the same emotion; does the signal subliminally feed the growth of some planetary solidarity?

One thing we do know is that the idea of global solidarity has not entered at all into people's consciousness. The simultaneity of the electronic signals of television is, needless to say, not the only thing that should call for a global consciousness. There is the runaway growth of the world's population, our mindless husbandry of the world's resources, the despoliation of nature. All these call for new responsibilities, but before we can feel these in our bones, somebody has to spell them out vigorously and, I would add, spell them out vigorously especially for the benefit of the white man. It is amazing that white men are totally absorbed in busying themselves with white men's problems, forgetting that each year there are fifty, sixty and seventy million extra mouths to feed and only ten per cent of these are the mouths of white children.

I am a great believer in the power of the word and in appealing to man's rational self. We need men with the conviction and eloquence of a Saint Bernard to tell us the truth about the state we are in. The United Nations cannot do it—no organisation can do it. So we are back, in this respect, where we left off not so many hundreds of years ago, searching for prophets and preachers.

URBAN: Changing the values of a society is a very slow process. God's enjoinder in *Genesis* for man to multiply, replenish the earth and subdue its creatures has imprinted a lasting ethic on us. For thousands of years it has been supported by the authority of religion and more recently by the needs of industrial society. Can a few wise and eloquent men change all this in a matter of years or even decades, especially when the choices they would have to depict for us would call for a very sophisticated and painful judgement of the various options open to us? They could not, if they were to be honest, present us with either/or kinds of alternatives; they would have to bring it home to us that for every gain in the environment some price would have to be paid in comforts foregone, growth restrained and so on. And I wonder whether the average man is capable of dealing with sophisticated choices of that sort. Wouldn't your modern preachers have to be great simplifiers, and wouldn't that bring us close again to the great *political* simplifiers of unhappy memory?

ARMAND: I am totally unpessimistic: man has shown that the most important of his qualities is his ability to adapt. Only ten or fifteen years ago one talked of pollution and the protection of nature at the risk of being made to look silly and ridiculous. In less than five years all that has changed. Today anyone who does not utter the word 'ecology' ten times a day isn't up to date. What accounts for this abrupt reversal? There has been a reappraisal of man's situation, a real act of conscience—there is no other word for it. And it has been a universal act of conscience—not American, French, German or British, but one shared by all nations. For the first time in our history people are being forced to talk of man's *common* responsibilities towards nature, towards other men and towards future generations. Now one thing we can be fairly certain of is that if there is a pressing need in the affairs of men, they will respond to it. Here is our opportunity to design a new morality. There is a pressing need to refashion our attitude to nature: respect for nature will, or can, lead to respect for other men. It need not end in demagogy. We have the means to guard against it.

The Biblical story cannot be allowed to justify man's collective suicide. That is not what Creation is about. The bonds between man and nature have shown themselves to be strong. No nation has plundered its natural resources more ruthlessly or ruined its landscape with greater relish than the United States. Yet the American reaction has been very powerful. The American people and their government are now fully aware of the consequences of what they have been doing and they are beginning to rehabilitate their lakes and forests, clean the air and restore the landscape (in so far as that is possible) at enormous expense and effort. Even in France, where green grass used to be thought of as something Englishmen admired, the rage is for lawns to be laid out in the public gardens where formerly Frenchmen were content with gravel.

URBAN: You don't think this a passing fashion?

ARMAND: No, I don't. For thousands of years man lived in
a state of symbiosis with nature from which technology is now
separating him. A horse's smell is a natural one, a car's isn't.
Man was made to travel at four m.p.h., he goes at six hundred.
Beyond the walls of the mediaeval city was open country. Today man lives in a world of stone. A window giving on a maze of
concrete blocks, pylons and cooling towers is not a natural landscape. It clouds man's horizons. It deprives him of his roots.
The freedom not only of his movements but of his gaze is
shrinking.

Fortunately there is a balancing mechanism in man's activities: when the pendulum has swung too far in one direction
there comes a reaction in the other. The swing towards more
and more technology is now being followed by a period of rest
and retrenchment. Technology has run too far ahead of our
moral faculties and reflexes. It is ruining the ground which sustains us. Here is where we can turn man's innate respect for
nature into a force that can and must put a brake on technological growth. And it is up to us to take advantage of this respect. The facts are very simple: man's greatest joy is to live
with nature. He expects to bathe in clean and cool water, he
expects to breathe fresh air, he expects to find deserted sea
coasts and lonely mountains. And if we expect man to remain a
human being as we have known him, he has every right to expect these things.

No doubt, the vested interests will fight back and a great
deal of nonsense will be spoken about the price we'll have to
pay—for *saving* ourselves, for nothing less is at stake. I notice,
for instance, that some people have had the temerity to argue
that the protection of nature in Europe would raise retail prices
by twenty-five per cent! Scare-mongering and obscurantism of
this kind—and worse—has to be expected. But it has to be overcome and it can be overcome if we manage to alert man to his
new, collective responsibilities. In the last analysis, technology,

like most issues, is about ethics, and that is where we'll have to attack the problem.

URBAN: There is no shortage of voices calling for a re-orientation of our values, but when it comes to saying where these values are to come from, we are usually stuck for convincing answers. Of those who discount religion and all metaphysical thinking as possible sources of moral rejuvenation, the biologists are perhaps the most vocal or, at any rate, the most listened to. Some of them now urge us to draw our ethics from the life sciences, and their argument is usually coupled with scathing attacks on religion and traditional cultures of every kind. A. Sargent, for instance, says: 'The life-sciences bring together certain means of knowledge and action. All doctrines which draw their inspiration from abstract conceptions have already betrayed their fundamental incapacity to organise the human world. Biocracy, that is, organisation in accordance with the basic laws of life, represents our only chance of salvation at a moment of our development in which the various metaphysics and systems left over from archaic cultures still corrupt human life.' Would you agree that biology is in a position to be our salvation?

ARMAND: Yes, I would, although I have serious reservations about Sargent's way of formulating his point.

To start with the educational value of biology, I would say Biology, not Mathematics, Greek, Latin, History or French grammar, should be the basic discipline in our schools, because biology teaches us to respect life. This would require a revolution in teaching but one that would benefit all mankind. With biology as our basic science we could draw up a programme which even the Chinese wouldn't turn down. Flowers grow in the same way in China as they do in France, and the mystery of life is something to which all men react with fascination and respect. Biology is also a middle way. It makes for balanced judgements, it discourages fanaticism.

We must instil in man a new respect for humanity and for

man's natural surroundings. Do we achieve that with constitutions, declarations, with words like freedom, equality, fraternity? Clearly, no. It is through respect for life in the most general sense that we'll find new forms of respect for man, and biology unquestionably has within it a concept which implies respect for life as well as a concept of man's progress. Biology is a humanism in the profound sense of the word, for it is not setting man apart from nature as something to be chained or exploited; on the contrary, it militates for the restoration of man's symbiosis with nature.

URBAN: I rather suspect the Chinese might not agree with you that flowers grow in the same way in China as they do in France. This would strike them as bourgeois thinking. One of the heresies of the 'hundred flowers' movement, later cut down by the Cultural Revolution, was precisely the view that there is such a thing as human nature or a non-class approach to science.

But coming back to Sargent, I feel there is a discrepancy between your conception of biology and his. His attack on 'archaic cultures', which he claims corrupt human life, would seem to be at variance with your insistence that it is technology that corrupts it. Earlier you were saying that we have not been alerted to the dangers of technology, and you were implying that technology is, and should be, a means, not an end. Yet, Sargent's conception of what biology is about is distinctly technological, for all he is saying is that instead of learning from the Sermon on the Mount, we should emulate 'certain means and knowledge of action' (it could hardly be less clearly defined) which the 'life sciences bring together'. What does this mean? It means that the techniques used in the experimental science of biology have some innate claim to be regarded as man's moral guides, but it does not imply any denial of the fact that we are dealing with a technology—a means—but one that is trying to foist on us its particular ethic through the back door.

ARMAND: My reservations about Sargent's argument concern precisely that point. If the biologist regards himself as a narrow technician, obviously he is not our man, for he would contribute to a further fragmentation of man whereas our aim must be to rebuild his essential unity. But I am not sure whether Sargent's 'basic laws of life' refer to bio-techniques or to something more profound.

URBAN: Another distinguished biologist, Jacques Monod, the French Nobel Laureate, holds views which are perhaps even more disturbing. I am rather labouring this point because you have been saying that biology has in it the capacity to develop certain humanitarian values—respect for man and respect for the correlation between man and nature. In a lecture he gave at the Collège de France, later reprinted by the Salk Institute in California (*From Biology to Ethics*), Monod seems to say that biology is a morally neutral and self-sufficient activity. 'In the ethic of knowledge', he says, 'the single goal, the supreme value, the "sovereign good" is not, let us admit it, the happiness of mankind, still less mankind's temporal power or comfort . . . it is objective knowledge itself . . . this is a severe and constraining ethic which, though respecting man as the sustainer of knowledge, defines a value superior to man.'

ARMAND: With all respect, this is again a bio-technician's point of view and no less dangerous than the application of the standards of any technology to the whole of life. It is an example of the popular fallacy of 'the part for the whole', but when the part is that of biology the fallacy is especially insidious because it is so terribly misleading. If the technician of the internal combustion engine were to claim that some combination of his particular skills should furnish society with its ethical standards, we would not take him very seriously. But when a claim of that sort comes from biology, we tend to listen. And there lies the danger. There is much to be said for the idea that the scientist should take an ethical vow on the lines of the Hippocratic oath for doctors. Like the doctor, the scientist would have to agree to use his own conscience to judge the ethics of the consequences of his work.

136

When I talk about biology I have something much broader in mind than either Sargent or Monod. I'm thinking of the universal science of the future—a mixture of zoology, palaeontology, anthropology and sociology. But speaking in 1970, even if one were to speak from the profoundest knowledge of the life sciences, the essential thing to remember is that we know too little to be able to support a philosophical theory. We must learn to respect ignorance, and we must learn to be humble about what we do know. The intellectual arrogance of the 19th Century is well summed up in the biologist's dictum: 'If God existed, I would have found him at the end of my scalpel.' Today we are very much less confident. All we can say is that we cannot demonstrate that God doesn't exist.

URBAN: You are saying biology is too new a science to support a philosophy, yet you are hopeful that a new code of values, more in harmony with man's needs in the present situation, is implicit in the life sciences.

ARMAND: One of man's fundamental aspirations is to religious experience. Biology, precisely because it touches on so many unsolved problems which affect us at every turn of our lives, possesses a quality to which man's desire for the spiritual can be and probably will be harnessed. It will replace respect for the Creator by respect for the Creation. And if this is a case of transferring our loyalties from a conjectural to a nearer and more familiar object, as psychoanalysts would tell us, so be it; it makes the end-result no less desirable.

GROWTH, CONTROLS
AND RESPONSIBILITY

MAURICE CRANSTON

Technology and Mass man

Maurice Cranston is Professor of Political Science at the London School of Economics and Political Science, where he occupies the chair once held by Michael Oakeshott and Harold Laski. Professor Cranston's published works include *Freedom* (1953), *Human Rights Today* (1954), *John Locke: a biography* (1957), *Jean-Paul Sartre* (1962), *Rousseau's Social Contract* (1967) and *Political Dialogues* (1968). He is editor of *Western Political Philosophers* (1964), *A Glossary of Political Terms* (1966) and *The New Left* (1970).

GLENNY: I would like to begin by quoting at you a remark made by Alexander Herzen when he was thinking about the future. He said. 'What I'm really afraid of is Genghis Khan with a telegraph'—by which he meant the absolute autocrat with all the apparatus of technology at his command, and thus able to exert total dominion over his subjects; is this one of your fears?

CRANSTON: Yes, it is my fear; but it is worth remembering that it was precisely this policy that was recommended at the beginning of what we call the age of reason by Francis Bacon, in the early 17th Century. Bacon was, I think, the first great prophet of the idea that science can save us. Bacon thought that the way to benefit mankind, to 'improve the life of man on earth' was to harness the discoveries of science to the service of human welfare, and Bacon also thought that this required not only a vast number of scientific institutes, colleges, laboratories and so forth, but a government with enough power to enforce the rule of science. Bacon was very much against maintaining what he regarded as the old-fashioned, parliamentary-type government because he thought this form of government interfered with progress, and that the kind of progress he wanted could only be achieved by an enlightened despot.

GLENNY: Of course, in the early 17th Century Bacon was speaking of a pre-technological world, a world in which the 'take-off' had not yet occurred. Therefore he was advocating the means whereby the growth of science and technology could be encouraged. The situation today, however, is rather the reverse: technology has been encouraged and has flourished to such an extent that it is becoming a political and social threat. Today the problem, surely, is how to control the technological Frankenstein that the scientists have created.

CRANSTON: Perhaps I might mention another name, that of Rousseau, who was as important a prophet as Bacon and said exactly the opposite. Rousseau believed that the growth of technology and science was dehumanising mankind. He said this long before we had all the manifest evidence of the 20th Century that science and technology is in fact dehumanising mankind. Both Bacon and Rousseau were gifted with prophetic vision, because what Bacon recommended has in fact been put into practice in many of the advanced societies of the present century. Communists also believe that science can serve mankind. They call themselves humanists, but they achieve this end by the Baconian method of political despotism, and the question that we must ask ourselves is whether the true interests of humanity are really served by the sovereignty of science. I myself do not believe it. I am more impressed by Rousseau's arguments.

GLENNY: Would you say a little more about Rousseau's views on how the political structure could curb the excesses of applied science and technology? In a certain sense Rousseau is one of the spiritual ancestors of Soviet Communism. What were his prescriptions, if any, for preventing technology from getting out of control?

CRANSTON: A spiritual ancester of Communism? Well, perhaps it is true that Rousseau's notion of the total state was incorporated first into Hegelian and then into Marxist thought; but on this particular question of science and liberty that we are discussing, Rousseau's position is as distinct from that of modern Communism as it is distinct from that of Bacon. Bacon believed that if you have science you cannot have liberty, and he wanted us to choose the rule of science. In a way Rousseau agrees with this; he says you cannot have both the rule of science and liberty, but says: let us have liberty and not the rule of science. For this reason Rousseau is what many people would probably call a reactionary; he believed that mankind could best fulfil its destiny in small integrated communities that were close to nature and without the corruption and sophistication of city life. In other words he wanted man to live without the so-called advantages of science. Both Rousseau and Bacon offer the choice: are you going to have scientific progress or are you going to have freedom? You cannot have both.

GLENNY: However, you would no doubt agree that in the modern world the technological clock cannot be turned back. We cannot return to the idyllic, natural life which Rousseau would recommend.

CRANSTON: We perhaps cannot turn the clock back, but why should we not try to put a stop to the unchecked advance of many of the more inhuman features of modern life? Surely it is possible to have an architecture, for example, that is related to human needs and human dimensions, rather than the kind of architecture which now prevails, an architecture governed purely by economic and technological factors? I regard it as inhuman, for example, to make people live in tiny rooms in very high buildings, so that they seem to live in plastic boxes like ants. I think it is inhuman to build vast multiversities and comprehensive schools where the children are forced into a pattern of education geared to allegedly 'economic' considerations and so forth. In 'progressive' circles today the traditions of the past are regarded with suspicion as being reactionary and anti-egalitarian. It is argued, for example, by modern progressives that equality requires uniformity, as indeed in certain circumstances it must, but the result of the ideological pursuit of equality is bound to be a synthetic, uniform culture which hardly deserves the name of a culture at all. It will not even be a folk culture. Rousseau had a great belief in folk culture because he thought it sprang from tradition, from the contacts of people with their neighbours, from traditional means of recreation, traditional music, art and design; whereas what we have now is mass-produced entertainment devised by shrewd, soulless impresarios, an experience in which people play a totally passive role, the style and pace being dictated to them by the mass-communications industry. As a result people as cultural objects become 'mass men'. I think it is technology which has produced mass man. This is a feature of modern life which was foreseen by Rousseau, and all his warnings seem to be very relevant to our present predicament.

GLENNY: Indeed, we have created mass man and I believe that mass man is here to stay; we are stuck with this new culture, this successor-culture to the humanist culture of the past five centuries. Is it not so powerful and all-pervasive that it is too late to attempt to modify it according to the criteria of the old culture?

CRANSTON: I do not think we have yet completely created mass man. I think we still have in Western Europe the co-existence, so to speak, of mass man and the individual. Indeed one of our tasks in Western Europe is to maintain the individual and all those institutions and forms of life which encourage individualism side by side with the mass man, who, as you say, has already come into existence, especially in the big industrial and commercial centres. However, there are other parts of the world, the less 'developed' parts, where it is perhaps still possible for men to learn the lessons of the industrial West, and to resist the various temptations of industrialisation and to maintain their more agricultural way of life. If this is possible, it is very desirable.

GLENNY: Although there are parts of the world where technology and its social and political concomitants have not advanced as far as they have in the developed industrial countries, and where there is still hope that the phenomenon of mass man may be avoided, is it not much more likely that a leader of a developing country will, in the face of his electorate, choose the material benefits to be obtained from Western-style industrialisation?

CRANSTON: Yes, this is true because the social situation in the developing countries is very similar to that which Bacon envisaged—namely one in which you have a very small but predominant political class, a group of men who can in fact rule the country without much interference from representative bodies. They will tend to seek popularity both with their own people and with the exporting countries of the advanced industrialised West by promoting the policy of rapid industrialisation. But technology, as we are all beginning to realise, cannot perform miracles, and I think that development in these countries is going to be slow; therefore it may be possible, especially when economic recessions loom up, for them to conserve a good deal of their simpler ways of life. This perhaps applies more to Africa than to Asia, where the problem of population is more pressing than it is in Africa. But I am not without hope that in any part of the world where people live close to nature they can retain their humanity and resist being turned into mass men.

GLENNY: Let us turn to another disturbing aspect of the advance of technology, and that is the prediction made by some thoughtful people that before very long automation and control mechanisms in industry will have reached such a stage of perfection that the bulk of our present work force, which now does the repetitive and largely mechanical labour in manufacturing, will have no work to do because its work will be done by machines instead. There will, it is claimed, be a small élite, in which intelligence becomes virtually the sole criterion, who will design the machines, maintain them and keep them going, while the rest of the proletariat will in fact have nothing to do. We will have moved towards a kind of beehive state, in which there is a small group of workers, and a great number of socially useless drones. Some say that there will then be a situation where work has to be devised for them as a form of occupational therapy, simply to prevent them from going mad with boredom. Do you not think that this implies a very great political threat, in that the degree of control over these people's lives will have become even greater than it is in, say, a Communist state today?

CRANSTON: It is difficult to visualise all the implications of this, but I think it is true that this development was perhaps predictable when factory methods were introduced, and brought about the situation which Aristotle once referred to as machines doing the work previously done by human labourers. Aristotle spoke of machines as an alternative to slavery, and people have gone on regarding them as a means of eliminating drudgery. Of course, at a certain stage machinery does have a liberating effect, but now mechanisation has got to the point where it has not only released men from dreary, repetitive work and labour, it is also beginning to deprive them of what one might call satisfying labour; since it is man's nature to do something constructive with his time, he is bound to be unsatisfied if he does not spend at least a large part of his waking hours in creative activity. I suppose in a Utopia of the kind that you are hinting at, a benevolent despot would in fact provide working gardens or allotments or various forms of hobbies which could serve as a form of therapy for the people who would be thrown out of productive work as a result of the advance of industry. This is part of what I spoke of just now as the dehumanising effect of industrialisation, of industrial progress.

GLENNY: What do you think of Professor Gabor's suggestion that the future society will be a hierarchy based on differences of intelligence, with the tiny minority with IQ's of 130 + ruling, the middle range acting as machine minders and the rest, with IQ's under 80, filling up their time with the kind of therapeutic labour you speak of?

CRANSTON: I have no faith whatever in intelligence measuring. Intelligence, whatever that may be, is one of the factors in the formation of what might be called natural hierarchies, but only one. In France, since the Revolution, efforts have been made to produce an 'élite of brains' to take the place of the 'élite of birth' which existed in the ancien régime; but even there, the distinction is not a distinction of measurable IQ's. In France there is a whole system for the formation and encouragement of talent, a system of republican élitism, which is quite different from the English hierarchy, which has tried to merge the free competitive struggle for privilege with an ideal of the gentleman derived from the aristocratic ethos, and which believes that 'character is more important than intelligence'. And this again is different from the U.S.A., where the egalitarian individualist spirit rejects both French *étatisme* and the vestigial aristocratic notions of England in favour of an élite which simply emerges from free competitive struggle. Of these three societies, America is the most 'modern', yet is also the one which gives the least thought to the formation of its élite. This seems to me to suggest that future élites, far from being chosen by an IQ test, will emerge from some increasingly Darwinian struggle for supremacy. There are various types of personality—ambitious, public-spirited, bossy and so forth—who *want* to be leaders; such people have been political leaders in the past, and I have no doubt that such people will be the leaders in the future. The real problem for the future is going to be the familiar problem: not a question of putting the most intelligent men at the head of the state, but of ensuring that the kind of men likely to come out on top are suitably educated and civilised.

GLENNY: Might it not be better to ensure that everybody is suitably educated and civilised?

146

CRANSTON: My argument is that if everyone is to be suitably educated, they cannot all be educated in the same way. I am not an egalitarian. I am an unashamed élitist. I think if you have a uniform system of education, as you have in many parts of America, the result will be that the ruling class is inadequately civilised. I do not think there is any natural tendency at all for the most intelligent to rise to the top in the political sphere. A certain mixture of political talent and ambition and luck produces the political leadership everywhere when the hereditary principle is abandoned. It seems to me essential to have an educational system which can both cultivate and tame these exceptional personalities. The French system does this with its heavy emphasis on the culture of the mind, and the English system does it, at its best, with its emphasis on moral qualities. But both the French and British educational systems are now under heavy pressure to 'modernise'—in other words, to Americanise themselves: to abandon 'selectiveness' and so forth, and gear themselves to the supposed aspirations of the mass man.

GLENNY: We keep on talking about 'the mass man'. Is he a reality: or is he some kind of abstraction, like 'economic man'?

CRANSTON: I think it was Michael Oakeshott, my predecessor at the London School of Economics, who described the 'mass man' as the 'anti-individual'. His point was that the individual is a creature of modernity. The individual did not exist in the ancient world or the mediaeval world. In those ages man was really a social animal. But in the modern world, the individual emerges. He emerges in Protestantism, when every man is a priest unto himself; he emerges in the political philosophy of Thomas Hobbes, for whom civil society is conceivable only on the basis of a pact between competing individuals; and he emerges in Lockean liberalism, where every man is a little empire of rights. Now the individual is a solitary person, and it might have been a good thing if he had never come into being. But in this context there is no turning the clock back. The choice for the individual, once he has emerged, is to live as an individual, or to try to escape from his individuality by becoming a mass man, or what Oakeshott calls an 'anti-individual'. The burden of being an individual is undoubtedly too great for many people: and the search for a collective identity in the crowd, or in the totalitarian political society, is perfectly understandable. If people are not helped by their education to be individuals, if their education positively hinders them being individuals, or worse still, if their education turns them into anti-individuals, then mass man is likely not only to dominate the future, but gradually to eliminate the individual altogether.

GLENNY: Would it be fair to say that you are not a believer in progress?

CRANSTON: The word 'progress' is a difficult word to use in this context, because by definition progress means beneficial or desirable development; but we are talking of development which may or may not be desirable—which in certain senses is desirable and in certain senses is undesirable. Therefore we are using words which sometimes trap us into saying what we do not always mean. It is a very difficult subject to discuss, because if you take the view, as I do, that what is called progress has now become for the most part undesirable, then one seems to be adopting a paradoxical attitude in denying the merit of something which by definition is good. This is our difficulty.

GLENNY: In that case perhaps we could discuss a more easily identifiable problem. I refer to the very increasing mobility of the work force in modern industry. For instance, for technical reasons a large factory may close down and may move to another location. The workers must either move or find alternative jobs, and this is a process of which countless instances can be produced. At the executive level it is quite normal for a man making a career in a large firm to expect to move his whole house and family maybe five, six or seven times during that career; and movement from one firm to another is now much more common than it was forty years ago. In other words we are all becoming much more footloose. The effects of this in Western developed countries is that there has been an almost complete break-up of the extended family, and now the pressures of mobility are being felt on the nuclear family. Are we breaking down even that unit in our society, to arrive at the atomised individual?

CRANSTON: What you have just said is very interesting because it reminds me of what I myself have observed in Italy in the past twenty-five years—the movement from the country to the city: for example, from the countryside of Tuscany, where my wife's family comes from, to the big cities like Turin and Milan. There are now vast areas of the beautiful Tuscan countryside which are being depopulated. It's impossible, for instance, for the farmers to find people to pick the olives for olive oil; the agricultural workers who used to be there have moved to hideous blocks of flats on the periphery of Milan and Turin, and there they become either contented or discontented workers in industry. They become members of the trade unions, of the Communist party perhaps, and at the same time they become, as you say, isolated and uprooted. True, they also become members of a mass body, in which they try to recover their sense of communal social existence in a political party or trade union, but they have lost the sense of membership of a larger family, of the village and the commune, which they had when they lived in the countryside. They have not become *citizens* in the sense of being fully integrated town-dwellers, which is perhaps the ideal. They have lost much more than they have gained. Of course, if you speak to them they will tell you they moved because they wanted more money, either to save for a better future or to buy things which they now esteem, such as televisions, radios, refrigerators, air conditioning plants and above all cars. The car is now the symbol, not only of social status, but of this very mobility you speak of. It enables man to live as a mobile animal, which is the part cast for us by the dramatists of our times.

However, in reality this process makes people much too

subservient to the values of the machine. I think the machine is more the master than the slave now, because in a way people no longer quite know what they want. Perhaps they never did, but at least they did not have to ask themselves this question because they were free from the kind of anxieties that they now have, anxieties largely caused by mass man's growing subservience to the reign of technology. Therefore I think that although they may tell you they are happy, it is only because they have made their bed and realise they must lie on it.

GLENNY: So you are, I take it, rather pessimistic about the significance of technology for the future of our society.

CRANSTON: A question I often ask myself is 'at what point does technological development begin to turn sour?' In aviation, for example, I think no one can deny that jet aeroplanes like the Caravelle and the VC10 are better than the DC6's and other propeller aircraft which were made before them: but equally, the jumbo jet is manifestly worse than the VC10. It is beastly in almost every respect. With the jumbo jet civil aviation begins to become a curse rather than a blessing. Similarly, broadcasting, in the days of sound radio, was a cultural medium of the highest value—it took music and a knowledge of current affairs into the homes of millions. But then television comes along. And what does that take into the homes of millions? Bad movies. Bad imitations of movies. And the people who run television stations are so slavish towards the mass man, so eager to attract big audiences easily, that they themselves become brutalised. Compare the men who used to work for the BBC in the golden age of sound radio with the kind who flourish in the television world today.

GLENNY: Does technology have its own momentum?

CRANSTON: It does seem to have. Up to a certain point, technological change seems to improve man's life on earth: then it passes through some mysterious kind of sound barrier and becomes a hindrance to good living. I have a feeling that nature does not want to be mastered beyond a certain point. Nature is hitting back nowadays because we have abused it. Nature can be cultivated: but not exploited indefinitely. I am not a Luddite. I believe in the consumer society. Unlike Marcuse and other such intellectuals on the Left, I think it is a good thing for the working classes to be affluent. When technology helps to feed people better, I am all for it. But a great deal of technology means that people live less well. Think of things we are forced to eat nowadays. Battery chickens, for example; or the veal produced in factory-farms; and even the beer and wine that is made by the latest mass-production methods—all these things diminish life. The actual quality of food people eat or drink in Italy and England—even in France—is going down every year: and in America it has become nauseating.

I think this kind of situation develops because technology has produced the reign of technocrats—people who think only in terms of the measurable, of quantity, and have no idea whatever about quality. And one of the worst aspects of it is that such people are impervious to argument. If you complain to a modern architect, for example, about the ugliness of his buildings, he will not know what you are talking about.

GLENNY: One of the implications of what you have said is that in the past our political thinking has lagged behind our technological development, and has been little more than palliative in effect. In other words, we have not been capable of devising anything better than *ad hoc* political remedies to cope with the problems which our scientific and technological progress have produced. What political institutions or political machinery might check some of the more horrifying aspects of the advance of technology?

CRANSTON: We have in England, and in some other Western countries, succeeded in having both industrial progress and the maintenance of parliamentary government and civil liberties. We have performed this very difficult act of doing what

Bacon thought impossible, namely of having a very fair measure of scientific progress without introducing despotism. This is one ground for hoping that we in England can maintain this in the future, and that it may be maintained in certain parts of the world as well.

So long as the state confines itself to the role of policing and upholding some form of minimum welfare, then it will be possible to reconcile a fair degree of industrial progress with political liberty. However, this may only be possible in countries where there is a strong tradition of liberty to maintain. It may be difficult in the new countries, such as those in Africa, to introduce industrialisation and political freedom simultaneously —in fact I very much suspect that it is impossible. I have great hopes for what may be done in Africa, but the realisation of these hopes depends on there being only a moderate degree of industrialisation there. As you say, we in the West inherit industrialisation as part of our way of life, and since we in England also inherit a feeling for freedom, I think we can avoid the situation predicted by George Orwell in *1984*. We can avoid it if we realise the importance of maintaining our political institutions and traditions of freedom and our cultural values against the vulgarity of the mass man. We must defend the individual as much as possible, and prevent excessive state control from taking over in the West. If this is done, we may perhaps preserve this delicate balance in the future. Therefore I am not without hope, although I do believe we shall have to fight a constant battle against the advances of so-called 'popular' culture, against the advance of excessive industrialisation and of the scientific ethos into modern life. I think that we have to fight in a defensive attitude more than in an aggressive one, but it is, nevertheless, the most important task that faces us.

EDWARD SHILS

The Social Control
of Technocracy

Edward Shils is Professor of Sociology and Social Thought at the University of Chicago; he is also a Fellow of Peterhouse College, Cambridge, in England. One of his principal occupations is as editor of the journal *Minerva*, which is published in London and deals with questions of science policy and education. Shils is the author of *The Torment of Secrecy* (1955), which is a work on the social and political background of American security policies, and *The Intellectual Between Tradition and Modernity* (*The Indian Situation*, 1960).

GLENNY: I wonder what your reaction would be to the remark that Alexander Herzen is said to have made when contemplating the effect of technology in the word of the late 1860s. He said, 'What I'm really afraid of is Genghis Kahn with a telegraph,' and many people have seen his prophecy fulfilled a few decades later in his own country. Do you feel that the absolute autocrat, wielding all the apparatus of technology today, is the principal bogey which we have to fear?

SHILS: Much as I esteem Herzen, I do not share his apprehension. Modern technology has increased the power of tyrants but it has not created tyranny. Of course, for a tyrant to be effectively cruel and oppressive, he needs helpers to carry out his wishes. Successful tyrants have never lacked such helpers. In societies like those in which Stalin, Hitler, Mussolini and such 20th-Century tyrants have ruled, the more advanced techniques of 'electronic surveillance' have been less significant than old-fashioned techniques like denunciation, blackmail, torture, exile and brutality. Mrs. Mandelstam's memoirs do not show the brutes who drove her husband to his death as using any technology more elaborate than the telephone and the telegraph. Couriers on horses would not have made Hitler's or Stalin's regimes any less monstrous. Technologists and scientists did not contribute much or anything special to those terrible tyrannies.

It is true that technological developments which have come about since the end of the Second World War permit a closer surveillance through direct observation, e.g. long distance photography, 'radio-active tailing', miniaturised sounding, recording and transmission—and through the more comprehensive recording and processing of information about individuals by computer systems. These surely could be very helpful to tyrants. It must also be said that some technologists and social scientists are rather enthusiastic about these things, in both instances because their own professional purposes of technological advance and of improved data for social research are thereby served. It is possible that such technology might be used by tyrants in the future; it is also very likely that, should a tyrant so desire and have the financial resources to carry out his desires, there will be some technologists willing to perform his bidding in the course of pursuing their narrow professional ends. The danger to the human race from science and technology, if there is such a danger, comes not from the aspirations of scientists and technologists to rule the human race through their fiendish devices, but rather from their narrow definition of their professional obligations, from their desire 'to do their own thing', to put it in a recent slang phrase.

The fact is that many scientists and technologists are great enthusiasts for the things they do in their professional capacities. It is admirable that men and women should be enthusiasts for their work; that indeed is a precondition for their doing it successfully. There is a tendency among scientists and technologists to regard the tasks on which they work as of overriding importance as well as extremely interesting and gratifying to themselves. They often fail to appreciate, however, that their enthusiasms are not equally shared by others and that their pet schemes are not necessarily of the same benefit and advantage to the rest of the human race as they are to themselves. These men are somewhat naïve or disingenuous, and they are very ready to take advantage of their fellow citizens, not so much for the purpose of manipulating them, as for getting their hands into the public treasury for forwarding their own ends of discovery and invention. It is my impression that scientists and technologists—like most human beings—are self-centred, and they are therefore also self-serving. But whereas businessmen and trades unionists look out for their own advantage and make little claim that they are serving universal human interests or the national interest or some other higher, transcendent interest, scientists and technologists do both, claiming that their work is to the advantage of others, while obscuring its advantage to themselves. I do not mean the latter in any base sense; they do not seek financial gain or power for themselves. They do, however, think that, however costly their research, it is an obligation of society, i.e. of government, to provide the necessary funds. They simply regard this as self-evident. For a quarter of a century, they have been cossetted by society, and they accept it as their right to be supported on a grand scale. They have come to believe what politicians, social scientists, publicists and some of the 'elder statesmen' of science have been saying about the centrality of science in modern society. But, despite their belief in their right to constantly increasing financial support, they are not concerned to dominate society. In fact, there are very few, and those by no means very important, figures who have fantasies of dominating society by means of the technology developed from their research. What they want is an increasing share of the treasury of society at their disposal, so that they can do the research which is interesting and pleasing to them. Some of their research is of fundamental intellectual value in that it reveals something vital about the nature of the universe or of the earth or of man; some of it, even much of it, is beneficial to mankind. Some of it, however, is neither of these and some of it also contains potentialities for harm.

Scientists are motivated by the delight of discovery, the pleasure of the search, and some of them believe profoundly in the metaphysical value of penetration into the nature of existence. Only a few of them would ever say this, however. They have become used to saying that their scientific work will produce practical benefits for mankind, while they actually regard their scientific work as a challenge in a great and expensive game which they wish to play and which they think society should support.

This is certainly true for many scientists in the rich countries; it is also true for some of the scientists in the poor countries where there is much talk of the contribution of science to economic development. The links between science and economic development are complex and obscure; some research done in these countries does contribute to economic development but much also hides under that justification. In India, for example, a large system of national laboratories was established on the grounds that the research they could do would contribute to the economic development of India. A little bit has in fact done so; much of it hasn't, but none the less large claims on the public treasury continue to be made. This is probably true also of the intellectually rather superior research done at the Tala Institute in Bombay. Some of it might well contribute to India's economic development and it is difficult to know in advance what will and what will not do so. It does, however, seem to be the case that large sums of money are requested and granted for scientists to do what interests them and themselves alone. I do not disapprove of the generous support of pure research. On the contrary! But I do think that scientists often exploit their prestige and the somewhat mythological dependence of technology on scientific research to obtain funds to do what they themselves want to do.

To return to the original question: I do not think that it is the absolute autocrat using scientific technology to fortify his position that we have most to fear. We have of course to guard against the tyrannies of dictators, with or without scientific technology, but as regards science and technology what we have to fear is the excessive prestige of scientists and technologists and the attendant belief that they can or will solve our problems. Science and technology cannot substitute for a strong moral sense throughout all of society and above all in the élites of the different spheres of society—political, economic, cultural, religious, etc. Scientists and technologists are not going to displace these, however poor an opinion the scientists and technologists have of them.

I don't see in the future of any Western or Oriental societies, any displacement of politicians. The nature of human society is such that there will always be politicians; some will be struggling for power, and others who are more skilful and more lucky will be in power. Those who are more able, either by influencing voters, or by manipulating arrangements within the party bureaucracy or within the Politburo, are going to be on top. They are almost bound to be laymen *vis-à-vis* practising scientists and technologists, and although some might have studied engineering, some might have studied science at university, they are no longer scientists and technologists, and it is they who are going to hold the sovereign power in society. In order to exercise their power effectively they must have self-confidence. Now one of the great consequences of the scientism and the technologism of the present age and the fantasies about technocracy is that many persons have become too deferential to scientists and to technologists. If politicians come to believe that the scientists have the solution to the secrets of the world at their disposal, that they have the key to El Dorado and to eternal life and that therefore they must have everything they ask for, scientists and technologists might well gain the ascendancy over them. Aware of their prestige, scientists and technologists sometimes bully the politicians. This is part of the story of NASA in the United States. The politicians can be too easily mesmerised by the excessive prestige that surrounds scientists and technologists. They might lose their self-confidence, just as in democratic countries the politicians have been losing their self-confidence before public opinion polls.

Even though we may hope that scientists and technologists will show more of a sense of responsibility in attempting to estimate the prospective benefits and potential dangers contained in their discoveries and inventions, it would be wrong to expect them to do this entirely on their own, or to give them the exclusive power to do so. That is a major task for politicians and industrialists; it is a task to which lawyers, social scientists, especially economists, and publicists must contribute, as well as scientists and technologists working in fields other than those in which the discoveries and inventions in question have been made.

GLENNY: But don't you think that the politician now has a dangerously widening gap in his personal armoury of knowledge of the world, which puts him at a disadvantage when it comes to assessing what the technocrat asserts to be a desirable course of action?

SHILS: Yes, what you say is correct as far as the ordinary politician is concerned, although it is not a recent phenomenon. It is much older; it really originated in the epoch when organised bureaucracy came into existence. The members of an organised bureaucracy have specialised knowledge of particular subjects, whereas politicians come and go. They don't remain at the top for a long time, and they don't have a very long period of being the head of one ministry or another. This means that they are at a disadvantage where specialised knowledge is concerned. None the less, sometimes politicians are very intelligent people with strong personalities, and they succeed in establishing ascendancy over the experts. This has happened repeatedly in the late 19th and 20th Centuries. Furthermore a politician who develops an interest in a particular subject, let's say, hydroelectric power or agriculture or medical services, can learn a very great deal about the subject even without formal qualifications, and thus if he is shrewd can gain the ascendancy over his experts.

I know that some matters are extremely difficult, but I be-

158

lieve a layman can understand what is essential in them provided he is prepared to make the effort. The real danger, I
think, is the aura of insuperability, indomitability and super-
confidence of the expert technologist and scientist—the myth
that he has knowledge which is not available to a layman. There
isn't such a sharp distinction between the knowledge available
to a scientists and the knowledge available to a layman in so far
as that knowledge available to the scientist bears on some practical matter. Unfortunately politicians often do not have the
self-confidence needed for dealing with their subordinates in
the civil service or with their scientific consultants. It is partly
a matter of intelligence, of capacity to reason and to absorb
knowledge, and partly, above all, of self-respect and self-
confidence. The fantasy of the present age is that a university
degree is better than no university degree, and hence being a
layman without having a university degree is thought to be a
disqualification. It is a new kind of social stratification, just like
the old distinction between those who owned landed property
and those who didn't own landed property: those who owned
it being more estimable, more worthy, obviously more favoured
by God than those who didn't own it. We now have exactly the
same situation: a new basis of social stratification which is just
as unfair, just as immoral, just as baseless.

It is important that scientists and technologists learn not to
take advantage of their prestige—otherwise they might become
the victims of a hostility something like that which overcame
the landowning aristocracy. It is important that they should
learn to understand something about society, about the other
sections of society with which they must share responsibility,
both in the making of science policy in fields other than basic
research, and in the effort to foresee and to forestall the injurious
consequences of their discoveries and inventions. They must
learn to be more circumspect in the interpretation of these consequences and they must above all not appear to gloat over
them, as some computer experts do when they imagine a universally comprehensive amalgamation of information about
every member of society, or as some biologists do when they

speak about extra-uterine conception or genetic engineering.

GLENNY: In view of the present proliferation of technocrats and pseudo-experts who claim to know best, what is your prescription for restraining them?

SHILS: You've asked an extremely difficult question. I don't really have a ready and satisfactory answer, except to say that it is necessary to increase the scientists' and technologists' self-critical faculties, and to educate them to see the limitations of their knowledge and their powers. Almost up to the present the whole world has been moving in a contrary direction. We have been flattering those with a scientific education, making it seem as if they were the saviours of mankind. And naturally mediocrities, as well as gifted men and even geniuses, if they are not restrained by some sense of moral responsibility, will take advantage of their fellow men. Not necessarily to get power over them, but to get a larger part of the resources than they ought to have, to divert these resources from other purposes, which are often known to be desirable, so that they can indulge themselves and act without regard for any consequences except their own advantage. I do not mean to say that they act cruelly or malevolently, only that they act to realise things which will be most gratifying to themselves and which might not be—often are not—equally good for others. In the case of scientists and technologists the temptations are many, the pitfalls deep because, since the 17th Century, the acquisition of knowledge has increasingly been accorded the dignity which saintliness and the mastery of sacred texts possessed for much of the history of civilisation; technologists, particularly in the present century, have been looked upon as benefactors. The widely accepted doctrine of progress gave a central position to technology. It is therefore not so easy for scientists and technologists to look upon whatever they wish to do as not necessarily identical with man's highest calling and with what is conducive to the progress of society. Nor is it made easier to attain this discrimination and

160

detachment when there is in fact a fair amount of truth in the inherited idea. Yet, it is necessary that it be done. Scientists and technologists must become more discriminating about the values of what they are doing.

Thus some of the controls must be internal—within the minds of scientists and technologists and within their professions. There is really no recipe which can be given aside from the old one of moral self-restraint, and the more modern one, a Benthamite one : the principle that 'the eye of the public is the virtue of the statesman' restated as 'the eye of the colleague is the virtue of the scientist and technologist', and 'the eye of the public is the virtue of the scientist and technologist'. What Bentham meant was that politicians who are kept under the scrutiny of those whose disapproval they fear, are also kept up to scratch by that mechanism. To bring this maxim to bear on our problem we could say that the eye or the opinion of the morally and socially circumspect scientists and technologists will set standards and help to keep their colleagues on the strait and narrow path. Just as the opinion of their peers is the force which helps to guarantee the scientific integrity of the scientist, so it must be with regard to science policy and what is now called technological assessment.

But in those scientific matters which concern not only the scientific community—these must be left to the scientific community—but which concern the wider society, there is no substitute for an alert and informed public. The main—not the sole—custodians of the public interest in any decent society are the politicians and public-spirited citizens of all professions and occupations. The politicians and the representative institutions which they man are in the most crucial position. If they are reasonably well educated, if they are willing to study the subjects, and if they do not cringe before scientists and technologists, they can do much to maintain a balanced view. To maintain a balanced view means to keep a balance between the interests and enthusiasms of scientists and technologists, and the interests of economic well-being, health, general culture, aesthetic value, national security, good order in society and social justice. To do this, they must be sustained and aided by an alert public, by journalists, lawyers *and* scientists and technologists as well as by military men and businessmen.

In all that I have been saying, I postulate the value of a pluralistic society. Pluralism is at a discount today for no good reason—the only reason is the hidden fantasy in the value of a dictatorial wisdom, which is not a good reason at all. Pluralism in the field of science and technology entails a plurality of more or less autonomous institutions which can act fairly independently of each other. That is where universities have a great part to play.

GLENNY: Let us hope that our society can continue to maintain sufficient checks and balances to counteract the *hubris* of scientists. However, some people maintain today that Western Capitalism and Soviet Communism may be said to share a common rationale, namely that maximum economic growth plus the maximum utilisation of technology equals good, and that that is as far as any government, of either East or West, can see at the moment. What is your feeling about that?

SHILS: I think there is some truth in that, but it is very far from the whole truth. There are marked differences, of course, between the Soviet Union and the United States and their cultures. For one thing, the United States is a very free society; the Soviet Union is not. That is the greatest difference. There are numerous others. For example, looking at it from the outside, there is still a considerable amount of Victorianism in the culture of the Soviet middle classes. There is still the appreciation of labour, of modesty, of diligence. Such old-fashioned virtues are rather less respected in the Western Capitalistic countries, at least among intellectuals.

Most important is the fact that in the Western Capitalistic countries, and especially in the United States, there is far more freedom for a widespread exercise of initiative. The pluralistic system in the United States permits far more inventiveness, resourcefulness and adaptability than exists in the Soviet Union. It also permits far more open criticism. But, none the less, the two cultures do have something in common: namely this profound hedonism, and the belief that the goodness of man's life can primarily be measured by his state of material well-being. The remnants of the kind of Victorianism to which I refer in Soviet culture and which the Soviet élite does not like to acknowledge, but which is there none the less, in a way makes them appear a bit more respectable. Also the remnants of Christian culture in the United States also prevents the foolishness of unrestrained hedonism and self-indulgence from operating to the full extent of its capacity for destruction.

Does this hedonism make the two cultures identical? I don't think so. Technology and the belief in the fruitfulness of technological research is only one factor in determining the form of human life. Moral and religious traditions are certainly more important elements, and they are certainly not exhausted, although in Western countries at present they seem to have their backs to the wall. And the political system—political values and political ideals—also make a very great difference. But, none the less, the very strong utilitarian trend which in 19th-Century Russia was represented by Turgenev's hero Bazarov, was also found in the United States in the numerous virtuous inventors like Edison and Henry Ford, and all the rest of them who were going to transform human life—and who did. It mustn't be denied that scientific discoveries and technology have brought about many very great improvements. Human beings are less subject to pain now, they live longer and live far more comfortably. They eat much better, more become educated. They have a wider range of choice in occupations, in style of life, in personal associations. That is all to be welcomed, and our great task is to find some way in which these benefits can be preserved and can develop further, while not losing our humanity and our capacity for moral judgement.

GLENNY: Do you think that the acceleration of technology, and above all its effects in the size and location of productive units, is introducing a far greater social mobility than we have witnessed in advanced Western countries in the past? And if so, do you believe this is having a fatal effect on social cohesion? But what is social cohesion? Do we want to stay as in an old walled mediaeval city, or might our personalities expand in a more fluid, mobile society?

SHILS: I think it is true that technological change, the development of new natural resources and new modes of production, do change the distribution of population. But there is also a mania for urban residence, which isn't necessarily required by technology. All over the world the prestige of urban culture and the poverty of life in the countryside attracts people to cities. There is the fact that agriculture is either (as in the United States) very productive, or (as in other countries) so unproductive and has so much hidden unemployment that there is a surplus rural population which finds its way to the cities. Life in the big cities might be a poor thing from the point of view of a sophisticated, well-fed and fastidious urban intellectual. For those who are not so sophisticated, city life has a tremendous attraction. It is the centre of light. The mediaeval German proverb '*Stadtluft macht frei*' had much truth in it and it still does. Cities might appear to be cruel, terrible places. They have a very poor press right now, but those who denounce them usually can't stay away from them; in any case, they have to be in the city in order to be able to spread and diffuse their denunciation of city life. The poor of the cities, the *clochards*, the Algerian labourers in their *bidonvilles*, the Negroes and Puerto Ricans in the United States, the miserable creatures who sleep on the sidewalks of Calcutta—at least those who are refugees —they all find something in urban life. According to the critics of bourgeois society, those who speak of the *lumpenproletariat* of the great cities as if they represented all society, that *lumpenproletariat* is more degraded and impoverished than human beings have ever been. This view is nonsensical, but there is a *Lumpenproletariat* in the great cities, and the fact is that most of them have come there because they thought that in some way or other city life would be better for them than life in the countryside. It is.

There are employment opportunities in big cities which the countryside cannot provide. Life in the city is more interesting. There is more of a surplus which can provide alms, welfare services, educational opportunities for self-advancement which the countryside could not provide. (There is also more to steal and probably a better chance to get away with it.) The most important of these are the occupational opportunities. The cities began from the division of labour, and they still are its locus. Industrial, commercial, administrative differentiation and specialisation all have their primary seat in the city. They are partly a result of technological development, i.e. new tools, new machines, but they are also products of ingenuity and imagination about institutional arrangement, and of new tastes.

There has been a great expansion of what Colin Clark has called the tertiary occupations, i.e. those occupations which are concerned not with extraction or cultivation of raw materials or with their processing, but rather with their distribution, with the organisation of the primary activities and with the performance of services very remote from extraction, cultivation and processing. Some of these tertiary occupations have arisen from or been made possible by new technology, e.g. typewriters, telephones, telegraph, wireless. Others not so or at least not so to the same extent and mode, e.g. administration, accountancy, and book keeping, social services, education, publicity and promotion. Some of these latter occupations utilise complex mechanical technology of the more recent sort but that is not central to their practice.

Many of these occupations are a luxurious form of hidden unemployment. They are not very valuable; the demand for them is a product of new fashions and they are made possible by the productivity of the economy, which in turn is partly a function of technology. This is very obviously true in the poor societies in which the governmental administrative and auxiliary corps is much larger than it need be for the effective administration of the country. Since the educational institutions produce persons who have to be employed—such are the status and connections of the educated and such are the dangers of frustrating them—the governments swell the ranks of their employees. In the richer countries it is not political prudence which produces this multiplication of posts in the tertiary sector. The belief that advanced education is a nearly universal necessity creates aspirants for employment simultaneously with the growing readiness to provide employment in categories thought fit to be occupied by educated persons. For example, the prestige of research helps to create many spurious research posts, the incumbents of which do not do research of either intellectual, scientific or practical value. It is difficult to estimate the exact numbers of such posts in the rich countries but the growth of statistical and research departments in governments and business enterprises is striking.

All this means that urban life provides far more opportunities for mobility into middle-class occupations—for upward mobility—than is possible in predominantly agricultural life. These are not technological posts, but they are made possible by technological progress. This aspiration towards a higher position in society is part of a more general process of what I have called elsewhere 'the closing of the gap between centre and periphery'. The desire to enter into or to come closer to the centre of society is an aspiration to come closer to the charismatic centre of existence. The growth of our technological power aids this process, it has not created it.

You mentioned, in the last part of your question, the expansion of personality which is very closely connected with this phenomenon. The expansion, i.e. 'the realisation' or fulfilment of the self has been an ideal, for several hundred years, and it has been an increasing, more widespread reality since some time in the 19th Century. This is partly a function of the increased productivity of the economy, which in turn is very much a function of improved technology and better organisation of the economic system. The improvements in the standard of living increase the level of desire.

The 17th-Century English political philosopher Thomas

Hobbes saw that man's wants are inexhaustible. At any one point in time they can be satisfied, but no sooner are they satisfied than they expand further. There is no such thing as the 'natural' cessation of human wants. That might be preached by Buddhism as an ideal, but it is not very effective once an economic system becomes more productive and the standard of consumption begins to rise. As human wants expand and as they get increasing gratification at the more elementary levels, there also develops a cult of personality, not in the Soviet sense —there it was concentrated on one person—but in the sense of a widely pursued ideal. The cult of the personality of a leader is an old thing, but the cult of personality in the whole population is a new thing, a 20th-Century phenomenon. It is an effort to expand and enrich the personality, to widen the range of sensibility by widening the range of experience. Of course, it derives ultimately from European romanticism of the 18th and early 19th Centuries, which in turn comes from Christianity: the belief that every single human organism has a spark of divinity in him. In the course of time this spark of divinity grew into a flame, but in becoming a flame it lost its divinity, and became an end in itself.

The expansion of the self through the enrichment of wider experience with greater sensibility as its results is attended by a demand for the autonomy of the self from the external powers which hem it in. The process of the expansion of the self is also an expansion of the sphere of independence from the pressure of tradition, expectation, convention, law and coercion—from all those processes by which institutions bring individuals into conformity with their rules.

This enrichment of the personality, this raising of man above the level of being a clod, an animal, a creature to be ordered about, is a very great improvement. It permits the justification for our existence by the realisation of our best capacities. But we have to recognise that it has limits, that human beings cannot be completely self-sustaining. It is erroneous, it is self-deceiving as well as arrogant to believe that any human being can be completely self-governing, and no less so to believe that any society in any particular generation can be completely self-governing. Man could not be formed into what is human in him without the aid of institutions, and this means that he cannot wholly annul his past—which is what he would have to do individually or collectively if he were to be wholly self-governing. It is simply beyond human powers. No technique of psychotherapy, no religious self-discipline, however severe, no religious conversion can create a wholly new man, wholly different from what he was before. Some human beings who have great moral self-discipline, great creative powers and great wisdom can come as close as it is humanly possible to make their lives into 'works of art'—but works of art exist in a tradition too. Most human beings lack the strength of character, the wisdom and the imagination to become wholly self-governing, and no techniques of pedagogy will change that much. They might improve them in this direction or they might make them rebellious, but they cannot free them from what the past presents through contemporary institutions, through memory and the inclinations of human beings to cling to the past.

It is damaging to human life, to the attainment of such individuality as is attainable, and to the social conditions which permit that attainment, to believe that there is nothing beyond human powers. This belief is very widespread at the present time—the very time when the New Left which promulgates this belief in an extreme form also tells us that man has never been as enslaved as he is at present. The belief that institutions can be dissolved and abolished and that life will then really begin is a romantic, anarchist ideal which is also contained in Marxism and Leninism. It is not peculiar to them alone. It is part of the view of life of which scientism is a major element. Scientists and technologists, regardless of their political positions, sometimes espouse this belief in the possibility of the complete emancipation of man from the trammels which have hitherto encumbered his existence. Certain publicists of science and technology, the greatest of whom was Lord Bacon, have preached this doctrine; distinguished social and natural scientists like Thorstein Veblen and J. D. Bernal, and popular pedants like Herbert Marcuse have preached it in the present century. But it is not true. Such complete emancipation from the past and from the limitations of human capacities is impossible, and it will lead to disappointment and disillusionment. It can only end in tears.

GLENNY: You say that human beings need institutions, need frameworks in which to exist happily. In a country such as Italy, where there has been a massive shift of population, largely for combined economic and technological reasons, from the South to the North, the first casualty of this migration is a social unit of organisation very characteristic of Mediterranean countries, namely the extended family. As the workers move in their droves from Calabria and Sicily into the Northern cities such as Turin and Milan in a very short space of time, the nuclear family too begins to come under pressures, social pressures which didn't exist in the South, and which these families are ill-equipped to cope with. This creates an entire stratum of proletarian Italians who are disorientated, and whose supporting social units have fallen apart around them. Can you not see this as a danger elsewhere?

SHILS: I think it is a danger. Italy is now going through the experience which England went through in the 1830's and 1840's, the kind of thing which Engels wrote about in *The Condition of the Working Class in England in 1845*. And this existed in France and Germany and in the United States at the turn of the century. Great demoralisation occurred among these uprooted peasants, particularly when they were separated from their families, their wives were left behind and their children neglected. However, I don't think that this is necessarily a condition arising exclusively from the recent developments of scientific technology. It already occurred as a result of the first great technological revolution of the 19th Century which was fairly independent of scientific research. As to whether such displacements of population are necessarily a result of technological innovation is another matter. The location of natural

169

resources is an important factor in the determination of industrial location. And this has been an important cause of migration. Reduced transportation costs and changes in the kinds of raw materials used in industry might reduce the necessity for frequent and large-scale displacement of population. Much of the displacement in recent years has been a result of political, religious fanaticism and of the increased productivity of agriculture which has rendered large sections of the rural population unemployable in agriculture. Industries can nowadays be located closer to the source of labour supply than was economical in the 19th Century, when labour was in one place and the natural resources, which were bulky and couldn't be economically transported, were in another place. In any case, a very great deal of internal migration as a result of the development of science and technology does not seem to me to be an unavoidable necessity over the coming decades.

To turn, however, to the other part of your question, I do think that the breaking of institutional ties does damage to human beings. Not that the inherited institutions didn't depress and oppress people. They did; they were often restrictive, they prevented good potentialities from developing, they often made people miserable and cramped them. But none the less the opposite, namely the person completely without any ties or bonds to control him or to help him to control himself, isn't good either.

The disruption of institutions is affected by internal and international migration. It has many other causes as well. One of these causes is the strong surge towards the denial of the legitimacy of authority in the state and in social institutions. (This is also an important consequence of the disruption of institutions of the sort touched upon in the question.)

The 'dislegitimation' of authority is a process of long standing in Western society. The rejection of the theory of the divine right of kings was an early stage—and a very good one too. The process has gone steadily forward—it has been a moral step forward for humanity—but, at the same time, the capacities of the state have been increasing. In the present century, the populations of Western society have been demanding more of the state, and at the same time they have been increasingly critical of its performance.

The deference granted to institutional authority has diminished in the present century while the deference granted to the educated and particularly to the highly educated has increased. Politicians have become increasingly deferential to the learned, to those with university education and particularly to those who are masters of scientific and technological knowledge. I might cite in passing the statement made by former president Lyndon Johnson when, in explaining why he decided not to contend for the presidency of the United States in the elections of 1968, he said that he felt that he could not unify the country because he had come from an inferior college. He was implying that had he been the equal in education of the Harvard professors, he would have been more capable of exercising authority with effectiveness.

The new pattern of social stratification in Western countries which gives more weight to education than to any other factor makes politicians grovel before the learned. Politicians still defer to those who own knowledge, real or false. And nothing unsettles society as much as being ruled by an authority which lacks legitimacy. To be effective, authority must have self-confidence, must appear to know what it is doing, and be able to do it with a semblance of self-confident effectiveness. Nobody can act perfectly and without error, but at least authority should avoid the appearance of continually fumbling, making mistakes and of having lost its grip on the situation. I would refer to two great politicians of the present century, Franklin Roosevelt and Churchill. They were not angels, and they were certainly not men with perfect knowledge; they made many mistakes in the conduct of the war, and Roosevelt made many in peacetime in the 1930's in the United States. Both of them, however, were men of great self-confidence, self-esteem and indomitability of spirit, so that however often they were in adverse conditions —as was Churchill in 1942 when the Germans were sinking so many ships—they never appeared depressed (although they often *were* depressed). They were always ready to fight hard, and the appearance of being on top of the situation was an extremely important element in maintaining the solidarity and morale of their fellow-men. That is why Britain had such a high morale in the Second World War; that is why Franklin Roosevelt was able to rescue the American people from the profound demoralisation into which they had fallen as the result of the great depression. Roosevelt always gave an impression of moral strength, and by the fact that he always appeared either to know what he was doing, or if he failed, to be ready to try something else in which he also appeared to know what he was doing. He never appeared depressed or beaten.

Now what do scientists and technologists have to do with all this? Most of them are persons of modest aspirations or none at all as far as political power is concerned. They want to get on with their scientific and technological work and to have the resources to do so. But some of them, including those who are taken to be their spokesmen, act and speak as if there is no proper role in society for politicians or for political authority. These 'spokesmen' spoke that way when science and technology were the petted and heavily subsidised darlings of their societies, and they still speak that way in the face of the surge of 'anti-science' of the past few years. The more clamant ones —not necessarily the most distinguished ones although the clamant do include some who are very distinguished—insist that it is the politicians—with the military and businessmen —who have corrupted science and landed the world in its present mess. They proclaim their own innocence and their own superior wisdom. Their claims are full of fallacies and arrogance but this does not stop them, in the United States above all, from disordering the public mind about the tasks to be faced and the means necessary and available to deal with those tasks.

Man cannot live without membership in a larger society. It is very true that the family is of profound importance; personal relationships are important, and neighbourhoods are important, and workshop groups are important. None the less, a sense of membership in a larger society is very important too. Man, as Aristotle said, is a 'political animal'. His nature requires it. And one of the greatest dangers, because of the increase in population, is that this sense of membership on a larger order will shrivel; otherwise modern societies might come closer to falling apart. That is why the effectiveness of politicians and of legitimate authority is so important. By authority I must emphasise that I do not mean repressive or harsh authority, because we know that brutal authority, despite appearances, does not necessarily legitimate itself enduringly.

Authority is not going to be abolished, least of all in the state from which so many services are demanded. An authority which is thought to be illegitimate will not be able to do what it has to do, which is in any case very difficult. When authority in the state and society becomes illegitimate, conflict becomes more severe and authority becomes even more ineffective and inefficient.

Many scientists and technologists have been indifferent to this problem, because they have thought only of 'their own thing', and regarded themselves as the proper and ultimate arbiters of the future of their societies. It is because of this that I bring my scatter of observations to a halt by wishing that they should become as circumspect and civil-minded as they are gifted and indispensable.

MICHAEL SHANKS

The Benefits and
Social Costs of Growth

Michael Shanks was educated at Blundells and Balliol College,
Oxford, with a period of commissioned service in the Royal Artillery.
He lectured in economics at Williams College, Mass., before becom-
ing a journalist, first on *The Economist* and subsequently on the
Financial Times, where he worked as industrial editor until 1964.
During this time he published *The Stagnant Society* (1961), *The
Lessons of Public Enterprise* (1963) and, with John Lambert,
Britain and the New Europe (1962). He also published a number of
pamphlets and became well known as a lecturer on current affairs.
In July 1964 he joined the *Sunday Times* as economic correspon-
dent. In 1965 he was seconded to the Department of Economic Affairs
as Industrial Adviser, and in May 1966 he became Co-ordinator of
Industrial Policy. He left the Government in 1967, and shortly after-
wards published *The Innovators* (a Pelican book). He is currently
director of marketing services and economic planning at British Ley-
land, and also writes regularly for *The Times* on business and
economic subjects.

GLENNY: Does the advance of technology, which is worrying
many people now, represent a wholly new experience in human
history? Are we faced with an utterly new set of problems
which our institutions are rapidly becoming incapable of
dealing with, or are we merely seeing new variations of problems with which we have dealt, with varying degrees of
success, in the past?

SHANKS: The problems are really the same ones which have
occurred throughout human history, but I believe there is a
considerable difference in degree, though not of kind, in that
the pace of change is accelerating so rapidly. Moreover we are

174

having to live with the consequences of past technology which are revolutionising our world. I'm thinking of the changes in population caused by medical technology, and the enormous influence of the development of communications, both in the material and also in what one might call the spiritual sense.

Now this is also revolutionising the environment of industry, the market is changing at a pace we've never before experienced, and we have the great problems of accommodating the inventions and discoveries which are pouring out at a rate never before known, and at a rate which is constantly accelerating year after year. Now it seems to me that our basic problem is this, that in order to cope with these changes in our environment caused by technology, mankind is creating institutions— political institutions, trade unions, financial institutions, educational institutions, industrial institutions. And when one creates institutions, one is creating organisations that have a built-in tendency to maintain the *status quo*. The great problem of modern government is that it has to try and deal with a rapidly changing society, it has to try to organise change to make sure that the change is beneficial, and it has to do so through institutions which themselves are proving much too slow at adapting to the changes in the environment. And so we see throughout the world a situation where man-made institutions are not changing rapidly enough to cope with the changes which are being forced on them. We've seen this in the educational establishments throughout the world; we see it in the inflexible political system of Eastern Europe; we see it in the great cities of the United States, in Great Britain we see it in our industrial relations; we see it in the attempts to adapt the international financial system to a totally new situation. Wherever one looks, one sees this problem of institutional rigidity in the face of the dynamism of technologically-induced change.

GLENNY: One of the characteristics of institutions over the world nowadays is a growing tendency towards ever greater centralisation where important decision-making is concerned. As these ever-larger units grow, decision-making moves further and further away from the people who are affected by the decisions. There is also a feeling that some of the essential values of democracy are being undermined by the growing gigantism of corporations and other decision-making bodies. Do you see an inherent conflict between democracy and non-representative decision-making bodies which may override democratic institutions?

SHANKS: This is a very complex question, involving a number of different factors. One factor is of course the importance of the increasingly technical nature of the decisions which have to be taken, and this does mean a danger that power will concentrate on the people who have the techniques. There is the danger, for example, that people who know how to operate computers will, because of this specialised knowledge, acquire an excessive degree of power within corporations and in the political field as well. I think this is a danger, though I don't frankly know what the answer is.

Then there is a different question, which you implied in what you have just said, and that is what I would call the economies of large scale: the tendency for institutions, particularly business institutions, to become larger and larger because of economic factors. Now, there is no doubt whatsoever in my mind that there are economies of large scale, and that the tendency towards gigantism in business is an irreversible one. But I don't think that this necessarily means that these large organisations are bound to be inhuman and uncreative. They have tended to be up to now, but this is largely because we don't know very much yet about how to manage very large organisations. The same is true of educational establishments or local government, where there is obviously a danger of remoteness with increasing size. I don't think this is necessarily so; I know of some very large organisations which are far more creative and offer far more genuine participation than a lot of smaller ones. But this is not something which will happen automatically: we need to acquire a lot more knowledge of how to run large organisations, and I don't know how one acquires this knowledge except by practice—by creating large organisations and going through the difficult process of making them efficient and creative bodies.

The other question to which this applies very much at the political level is that, although society is changing very rapidly and the problems are changing, we are saddled with history; we are saddled with a situation where, if you take Britain for example, certain types of operations have always been considered the prerogative of central government. Others have been considered the prerogative of local government. Education, for example, police, housing, we have always tended to treat as a function of local government in Britain. Other operations we have tended to deal with on a centralised basis. Now because this has historically been the way we've organised things, it doesn't follow at all that this is the right way to organise them now. In other countries other subjects are treated centrally, and a different set of subjects are localised. The Swedes, for example, decentralise to agencies a number of things which in Britain are dealt with by government departments. We need to look at the totality of the problems facing government at any one time and then try to sort out how those problems can best be tackled. In some cases this would lead to decentralisation, in others to centralisation. But what we have at the moment is a whole series of decision-making operations and systems which are a function of history rather than of an intelligent response to present-day problems.

GLENNY: One of the things which worries people nowadays is that both Soviet-style Communism and Western Capitalism to some extent share a common philosophy. Both want maximum economic growth and both want the maximum utilisation of technology. Between them the two are supposed to produce the good life. Now there are critics of economic growth as the one and only rationale of our behaviour, one of the best known in this country being E. J. Mishan at the London School of Economics, who claims that the answer to the problem of controlling the socially adverse effects of unbridled technological

M 177

advance is, among other things, to calculate into the cost of any product or process its social disadvantage. In your opinion, is it possible to calculate into the price of a motor-car a factor which represents its social diseconomy? And how, in anything other than a totally controlled command economy, could such a thing ever be achieved?

SHANKS: Well I don't think Mishan really is against economic growth. What Mishan is saying, although I don't think he realises it, is that he wants economic growth to be channelled into certain directions and away from certain other directions, and I have a great deal of sympathy with a lot of priorities which he would like to give. I think they are in many ways better than the strictly materialist priorities which have sometimes tended to be adopted in the past. Now I believe that economic growth does equal good, because economic growth means people becoming richer, and the richer people are the greater the degree of choice they have, and this it seems to me is the whole essence of economics; it widens the range of choice available to people, provided—and this is where perhaps I do have most sympathy with Mishan's approach—that in the process of creating this extra wealth you have not in other ways damaged people's well-being by forcing their life into certain patterns which may not be the ideal ones, by exploiting them in one way or another, or by so damaging the environment that in creating one form of wealth they have lost another form in the way of social well-being. It seems to me that this is the object of every government: to provide some kind of a balance.

Now you raised the question of motor-cars. Ought one not to put into the price of a motor-car, or into the cost of a motor-car, the social cost which motoring imposes on the community? Well, to a large extent governments do this already by taxing petrol, by licensing motor-cars, by imposing taxes of one kind or another on owners of motor-cars. I believe this is going to go much further. I think governments throughout the world are going to impose much stricter controls on the safety of cars and on the pollution caused by cars. I think that the

178

motor-car is going to come increasingly under pressure from government to conform to social requirements, and I believe this is highly desirable. It means that people will have to pay more for their motor-cars. This is going to make the cars more expensive, but it is going to make them socially less undesirable. This seems to be a perfectly reasonable cost to ask people to pay and to ask the motor manufacturers to pay.

In this whole debate over economic growth we are talking about priorities; we are talking about the directions into which the wealth-creating ability of a population ought to be channelled. Now this poses a number of problems, because of course what is one man's good may be another man's harm. It raises questions of the distribution of wealth, and of the diseconomies, if you like to use the word, caused by people having to give up their traditional pattern of life, accept disciplines of working to a particular pattern and so on. It is a question of choice, but all these choices become easier if there is a greater degree of wealth in the community. I think one of the dilemmas which we face is that we *seem* to have a choice in front of us: either to aim for a high rate of economic expansion or to maintain social stability. But we don't really have this choice, because the changes forced on us by technology will occur whether we like it or not, whether we consciously try to expand our economy or not; we will have to face the consequences of technological change. It will be more difficult in my view to face these consequences if we have a stagnant economy than if we have an expanding economy.

GLENNY: Can you give me an example of what you mean?

SHANKS: Yes, I can. One of the traditional industries in Britain, as in other Western European countries, is coal-mining, and coal is becoming technologically obsolete. What happens therefore to all the people employed in the coal-mines? One possible solution would be to say we will shut ourselves off from alternative fuels; no matter how expensive it is, we will continue to give a very high degree of priority to coal, and this means that we will keep people working in the jobs in which they're accustomed in the coal-mines, although we all know this is a highly unpleasant and dangerous job. However, you can't go on doing this if you live in a competitive world economy, because it simply means that this increases the cost of manufactured products and prices them out of world markets, so this option isn't really open to you. The other option is to phase workers out of coal-mining into other occupations. Now it is much easier to do this if the economy is expanding than if it is stagnant and there are, therefore, no other jobs to which they can go. So the pains of change are more likely to be acute if the economy is stagnant, than they are if the economy is expanding. And this is one of the costs which have to be taken into account.

So my answer to your question really is this: economic growth in itself is not an inhuman rationale; it is the object of economics to achieve a faster rate of economic growth. The question is, how do you measure economic growth? If you confine your estimates to those aspects of economic growth which can be measured, that is the numbers of tons of coal produced, and the number of motor-cars produced, and you ignore the ones which can't be measured, such as the growth of education, the growth of culture, the improvement in the quality of life, then you are distorting the pattern of growth and you are harming your welfare and your real wealth in order to create the illusion of wealth in the sense of the material objects which you may even not really need. This, it seems to me, is where some of the East European governments have tended to go wrong.

GLENNY: What do you suggest are the right priorities that should be given to economic growth?

SHANKS: A wise policy of economic growth would identify what are the main priorities in improving human welfare and improving the overall quality of life in the community and then try to maximise these. But this will also involve changes; you cannot maximise the welfare of the community by standing still, by refusing to accept change, by sticking to traditional methods, traditional social arrangements. This is not a recipe for maximising the welfare of the community and in the long run, if you live in a competitive world, it will be self-defeating anyway.

GLENNY: There is one economy in the world which can be said to have achieved, in relative terms, one of the highest growth rates, and in absolute terms the highest degree of national wealth, and that is the United States of America. And yet, despite its economic dynamism, the U.S.A. is at this moment socially and politically in an extremely unhappy state. To take the Negro problem alone, the Americans have here a sub-proletariat left over from a previous stage of the economy which they don't know what to do with. Now this seems to me a typical example of one of the socio-political relics of advancing technologies which have not been dealt with in the correct terms. The Negro problem of the United States may well be repeated on an even vaster and in some ways more frightening scale when technology advances even further, and large areas of the present working population also find themselves both economically and socially redundant. Looking at the United States, how do you think that such a situation might be forestalled, both in the United States itself and in other countries where an analogous situation is liable to arise?

SHANKS: Well, whatever has caused this American situation, it has not been too fast a rate of economic growth in the United States. The problems of the Negro minority and of the other members of the sub-proletariat in the United States become more acute whenever America stops growing, for the simple reason that this means that there are fewer jobs available for these people to do. What has caused this situation in the United States is partly the racial mixture, for which the reasons go right back to the slave trade, which does create a peculiarly explosive situation; the other reason is the distortion of the pattern of growth in the United States due to the excessive concentration of expenditure on the private sector, and the ignoring to a very large extent of the public sector. The American pattern is complicated by the division between Federal expenditure on the one hand, and State and local expenditure on the other, which I think accounts for between sixty per cent and sixty-five per cent of the total public-sector budget in the United States.

Now this is something which we in Western Europe must avoid at all costs. We must not allow a situation to develop in our countries where a substantial section of the working class become unemployable through being inadequately educated and inadequately trained and, as has happened in the U.S.A., produce children who themselves never have the opportunities of proper education, thus creating a hereditary class of virtually unemployable people. As automation develops, and therefore as the amount of capital per worker increases, the threshold below which it will not pay to employ a worker (because you cannot employ a moron to look after extremely expensive machinery) is certainly going to rise. Therefore our educational programmes and our training programmes must develop at least in the same ratio as the degree of new capital investment in industry. I see no reason why we in Western Europe, with our ethnically much more homogeneous populations and our much stronger traditions of public education, should not meet this problem. But we do need to plan ahead for it, and we do need to be prepared to allocate very large sums of money (which I must say in this country I think we are doing; one of the things which is most encouraging about Britain in recent years has been the development of training in industry); and unless we concentrate on this and keep at it, then I think we shall run into the same dangers as the United States.

GLENNY: How do you account for the fact that some societies are more dynamic than others?

SHANKS: It seems to me that in every society you have in a sense a balance of forces between those sectors of the

182

community who benefit from a faster rate of growth and who
are therefore dynamic in pressing for change, and other sectors
in the community who do not benefit from economic growth,
or who feel that they do not benefit, the ones who will be
hurt by change or who are psychologically resistant to change
and who therefore are, if you like, the static element. Different
societies weigh the balance in their institutions between the
dynamic and the static in differing ways. In Britain, it seems to
me we have traditionally given greater weight than in the
United States or most other countries to the *static* forces, to
the rights of those who stand to lose by change. In many ways
this gives British society its attractive quality, because it is
undoubtedly a very tolerant community in which to live. It
also makes it a slow-growing, a rather undynamic society, and
I think we are now paying the price for this. Just to give an
example : in this country it is much more difficult than it is in
the United States or in most European countries to get government permission to build a new road, to build a new aerodrome
or to build a new power station because the ability of local
residents who might be adversely affected to delay such
decisions is much greater within our constitution than it is in
most of the countries with which we compete. Now as I say,
in many ways this makes Britain a stable and rather attractive
society, in which the rights of the individual, even when they
conflict with the rights of the community, are given a very
great weight indeed. But this has been a significant factor
contributing to Britain's slow rate of economic growth compared to most of our competitor-countries. And I think that
every community must decide where it wants to strike a balance
between the rights of the individual to resist change and the
rights of the community, or of the dynamic section of the community, to impose change. I personally think that in our case
we have weighted the balance too far against change; other
societies like the United States, for example, have probably
weighted it too much in favour of change. What is absolutely
certain in my view is that you can't have it both ways :
you can't have stability of the kind that we have in Britain

and at the same time have a very fast-growing, dynamic society.

GLENNY: Granted that there must be a true balance between the static and dynamic elements in society, we must nevertheless not lose sight of what happens to people, both as individuals and as members of small communities (because all people are primarily members of small communities rather than of large units) when dynamism 'gets the bit between its teeth', and wrenches people out of their familiar, traditional communities as a result of technological change. Does this not strike you as being a danger which is going to increase? If so, can you suggest a means of mitigating the social and individual disturbance caused to the workers who are forced to move as the industrial pattern changes?

SHANKS: I don't think it's quite fair to say that they are forced to move; on the whole they move because they see greater opportunities in other parts of the country or in other parts of the world. The movement is in general a function of greater opportunity rather than of greater pressure at home. I believe that this kind of mobility is going to increase; and this brings me back to what I was saying earlier: namely that institutions must change more rapidly. The problems that you find in Italy and the problems that you find in Great Britain with coloured immigrants are really due to the inability of our institutions to adapt themselves quickly enough to these changes, and particularly to the inability of institutions for example to create new loyalties to replace the old loyalties of the communities from which these people come. Above all this is due to the inability of government to create enough decent housing conditions, decent schools etc., to enable these people to live in the new environment to which they've come, without appearing to shoulder out the people who are already there and therefore causing friction.

What worries me much more is this: certain economies in Western Europe (I'm thinking particularly of Switzerland and

Western Germany) have now created a situation where the hardship caused by the ebb and flow of business activity falls completely on the migrant worker. Western Germany, I believe, has now created a situation where they have full employment and will continue to have full employment of their own people; when demand expands they merely suck in more workers from Italy, from Greece, from Turkey, from Spain, from Yugoslavia. When demand contracts and they have a recession, the people who are dismissed and who get sent back to their own countries are these migrant workers. If there were to be a recession in Western Europe now, this would not be felt by the workers of Germany or France or Northern Italy, it would be felt by the migrant workers who would lose their jobs and would be sent back to their homes. And the degree of friction and hardship that this would cause would be quite appalling. In this sense the most advanced countries of Western Europe are 'riding a tiger'. We must continue to run our economies in advanced industrial countries in such a way that we can provide full employment and decent living conditions for all the workers we have attracted into our industries from other countries, or in the case of Italy from remote peasant communities in the South.

GLENNY: What are the other disruptive social effects of technological and industrial advance?

SHANKS: One effect is that as technology develops you find that whole layers of age-groups are becoming technologically outmoded because they haven't had the opportunity of absorbing the latest knowledge. This is going to pose increasingly serious problems, particularly in business management. Ten years ago the leading posts in British industry were held in the main by people in their fifties; now the leading posts in British industry increasingly are held by people in their forties, and we already have a problem of the redundancy of highly qualified executives in their fifties who simply are not quite good enough to keep abreast of rapidly developing technologies. And there is a significant growth of new heads of industries being appointed

185

in their thirties, which ten years ago would have been absolutely unheard-of. This is not only happening in Britain, it is also happening in other countries, and I think one of the problems we're going to have to face is re-educating people at ages where in the past they had stopped learning, people in their forties or even older. This is going to be an educational challenge which will be extremely hard to organise, but which must be done.

Of course, in the broader sense, all technological advance is disruptive in its impact on society, in that if it is to be effective it must modify existing patterns in society, and this modification process, which has existed throughout history, is now being greatly accelerated; and what is in question is the speed of adaptation and response of which human beings individually and collectively, through their institutions, are capable. That is why I believe biology is the most useful of the sciences for us today—far more so than physics or chemistry, which have dominated the scientific field for so long. I am, as you may have gathered, an optimist. I believe society *will* learn to harness technology, and that a civilisation enriched by science can and will survive. But it will only do so if we devote far more effort than in the past to the study of people and society, rather than the study of things. Otherwise, in mastering the universe, man may destroy himself—if not physically, then culturally and morally.

ANDREW SHONFIELD

Change and Social Good

Andrew Shonfield is a distinguished economist, now Chairman of
the British Social Science Research Council, and a former Director
of Studies of the Royal Institute of International Affairs, Chatham
House (1961–68). Mr. Shonfield was Foreign and later Economic
Editor of the *Financial Times* (1947–57) and Economic Editor of
the *Observer* (1958–61); he served on the Royal Commission on
Trade Unions (1965–68) and the Foreign and Commonwealth Office
Review Committee on Overseas Representation (1968–69). Mr.
Shonfield published *British Economic Policy since the War* (1958),
Attack on World Poverty (1960) and *Modern Capitalism* (1965).

GLENNY: A number of thoughtful people in the West have
been writing in a prophetic strain on the probable fate of our
society, mainly as it is affected by the accelerating impact of
technology. Some of these predict changes which are quite
apocalyptic. Others are more measured in what they foresee.
Would it be true to say that you yourself are disturbed by the
changes which are ahead of us, and which are coming so fast
that perhaps our institutions are incapable of dealing with
them?

SHONFIELD: Indeed it is true that the rate of change has
accelerated greatly, that there are technical possibilities whose
future social and psychological consequences are extremely
difficult to foresee, and they might be disastrous. On the other
hand, I think I'm impressed, when I look back over the enormous rate of change that we've had in the last quarter of a
century, by how much has *not* changed fundamentally. The
young are supposed, for example, to have developed a new kind

of sexual morality, they are accused of being promiscuous. I then ask myself realistically whether they are more promiscuous than my colleagues were, not to speak of myself, when we were very young. I think not. I observe on the contrary that attachments form very early. It is certainly true that sexual activity is more actively pursued by the eighteen-year-olds today than in the past, but I find that it is pursued in a remarkably comradely and indeed monogamous fashion. I have been immensely impressed by the evidence of continuing concern with sexual fidelity. I use this merely as an example. It isn't that, merely because people are easier in their sexual behaviour, the basic desire for a certain kind of intense attachment between a man and woman, or between homosexuals, has suddenly ceased. It doesn't seem to be so. It is simply taking place in another context. Therefore I think that in our investigations of the future we ought to identify those things which seem remarkably constant.

Now on the other side of the medal it is true that such a development as the ready availability of drugs, which profoundly alter people's moods and behaviour, and may permanently alter their character, does represent for me a possible change in the whole quality of existence. So on the one hand I think that with an accelerating rate of change human beings, if left to themselves, will show a large number of constants. To put it in a word, they will continue to appreciate Homer and Shakespeare a hundred years from now: that what they will be talking about will not be utterly different from what we are concerned with. At the same time the technology of chemicals might do something profound and destructive, just as the technology of nuclear weapons might mean that we will have no significant future a hundred years from now.

GLENNY: Since your concern is very much with social questions, I wonder if you have some thoughts on the effect of what technology in its broadest sense is having on the social units that up till now have represented the basic structure of our society. I am thinking in particular of the effect that changes in technology bring about when, for instance, large-scale migrations of population occur and great numbers of people move from traditional to a new environment: for instance in Italy, where there has been since World War II a constant and massive shift of population from the dying agricultural regions of the South, such as Calabria, to the great cities of Lombardy. The traditional cultures of Southern Italy have been entirely broken up and the main social grouping, the extended family, has been destroyed when the migrants move North. This, it would seem, is a typical example of technology-induced social breakup. Do you see this as a continuing trend, and what would you have to say, for instance, to developing countries who may be moving into exactly this situation?

SHONFIELD: I will take the Italian case first, and then move on to the more general question of how the more rapid rate of technological change in our kind of society is likely to affect the family structure.

About the Italian case, what strikes me is how normal, how ordinary, how usual such phenomena are. They have been going on for years and years: in fact I would have thought that the present was not a period of particularly great migrations. I am excluding the immediate wartime and post-war migrations, let us say up to 1950, such as the great migration from East Germany to West Germany. But if we take it from about the middle 1950s onwards, the migrations induced by the magnetic attraction of the highly prosperous areas of Northwestern Europe, or of comparable areas in the United States which have brought the Negroes up from the South to dominate and become the majority in a number of American northern cities, these movements were not on a scale greater than the movements associated with the early Industrial Revolution. I would have thought the destruction of the English village as a productive unit, which took place during the first two-thirds of the 19th Century, was on a far more drastic scale than what has been taking place in the South of Italy. It is true that in the South of Italy the men go away and you get this curious impression of going into towns and villages which are entirely women-dominated. One does not object to it as a visitor, but it must be not at all pleasant to live in. On the other hand, I did observe, when I went to Düsseldorf round about Christmas time, that the announcements on the loud-speaker in the station were primarily in Italian, Turkish, Serbo-Croat and Spanish. These people are going home. They are affluent enough to travel all the way to the South for one or two, or even three holidays in the year. And this we know from the migrant workers in Switzerland, who by now make up as much as one-third of the working population of Switzerland, that they are typically people who do go back home. This is not the inhuman movement of population with which we were familiar in the earlier Industrial Revolution, of the poor moving into great cities where they continued very poor and very miserable, with no means of maintaining any contact with the place that they came from.

One is therefore faced with this curious paradox, that one of the consequences of the affluence of these rapidly growing societies in Northwestern Europe is that other societies in the border-lands of Europe are able to change at a slower pace than they otherwise might have done. Because the menfolk who go and work in Northwest Europe send back money, are able to educate their children in new ways and are able to maintain their houses, the rate of change is typically rather slower. Now in case that sounds as if I were taking an idyllic view of the situation, I want to say that if one goes to a place like Milan and one sees families which have been moved in exactly the fashion that you described, plainly it is worrying, unpleasant and difficult for these people. I am just saying that if we are looking at the world and how it is changing, and above all how Western Europe and North America are changing, I would have thought that the scale of change has had fewer deleterious social consequences than previous changes of comparable magnitude.

Now may I continue with the more general question of what

our type of society does to the family unit. It has been observed by sociologists that in the typically affluent society the consequence of the new great toys of civilisation, the motor-car and the television set, is not to break up the family but to induce what they call much greater 'privatisation'; that the family, for instance, tends to move together as a unit in a motor-car, it tends to group itself around the television set. And the most recent study that I know from my own country, the study of the affluent worker in Britain, which is based on a close survey of the habits of the population of Luton, published by Goldthorpe, Lockwood and other sociologists, is remarkable in the evidence that it gives of the reinforcement of family life as a result of affluence. These people are taking notice of one another, are aware of each other's moods and are trying to do things together for pleasure in a way that they did not in the past. Very often in the past they had to be together for work, more than they are today, but for pleasure and for choice they now behave in a quite different way. And if they appear, for instance, to be more ready to challenge the authority of the old, this is partly because they are so close together—out of choice—in their spare time. I would see our civilisation in this phase, whatever may lie ahead of it, as tending on balance to reinforce the privacy of these social units, of which the most typical is the family. I would have thought that the *kibbutz*—to use that as a symbol of another way of living in which there is a larger community and which operates a different set of social relations —was not at all characteristic of our time.

GLENNY: As we have been discussing the question of the affluent worker in Western societies, I think it is probably fair to say that this affluence is a concomitant of economic growth. Now, there are some people who are worried at the prospect of ever accelerating economic growth without checks and balances being placed on it by society. I am thinking in particular of some of the very interesting suggestions thrown up by Mishan in his book *The Cost of Economic Growth*, in which he suggests that we must find ways of adding the cost of its social diseconomies into the price of a particular product. How do you react to this critique of economic growth?

SHONFIELD: Part of the difficulty with the argument over economic growth is that there are two different aspects of the question which are commonly confused. One is the aspect of measurement. How does one measure accurately the growth of economic goods? Surely the way that we do it at the moment is crude and unsatisfactory. We measure things, for example. We measure the number of units of things and we put them into the calculations of the real change in the gross national product. When we take a service like education, we do not put it in as a product which improves in quality because, for instance, the number of children in a class goes down. We just put it in at cost price. In fact, if you just use our crude measures one would say that as a class of children drops from a typical thirty-five to twenty-five, the productivity of teachers goes down. This is because we can only think of a unit of teaching as being an hour of instruction. Now we have obviously got to devise better methods of measuring collective welfare, which is what the national product purports to do. That it is not doing it well means that economists must think how to do it better, and I believe certain improvements of the last ten years point clearly in that direction. It seems to me that a lot of what Mishan says is about that, and on this matter there is no disagreement at all.

There is another and more subjective aspect of the matter, namely that one does not like many of those things which happen to go into the measurement of the national product: the motor-car, the television sets, the worldly goods in the form of furniture or high fashion products where the advertiser induces people to change more frequently than we believe they really would change if they had complete free-will. Now this brings us right into the middle of big moral questions; and I find that economists who happen to hold strong moral positions disguise these by talking about the *first* problem as if it were the *second* problem. Now what we must do, for instance, in order to get these diseconomies that Mishan is talking about properly costed, is to make sure that when manufacturers create a public nuisance, this is 'internalised' into their own accounting system; that if they emit tons of smoke, somebody is there with arrangements to measure this and to say: 'This costs you so much to put right.' Or to say: 'We forbid it altogether because the hazard to health is too great.' But equally, when there are external *economies* which are produced by industry that too should be counted, in their favour. And in this connection I want to tell briefly a story related to the recent examination of the site of the third London airport which is now being considered by the Roskill Committee. The Committee has been working on the factors which should influence a choice of airport, such as trying to measure the social costs of noise, trying to measure the diseconomy created by vibration over ancient and beautiful churches which will probably be damaged by aeroplanes passing in large numbers overhead. The Committee has approached this job very much in the spirit of Mishan and has tried to do a number of useful operations in calculating these costs. At a certain stage, however, in the course of the investigation a youngish man came along and gave evidence in the following spirit. He said something like this: 'This is a very poor area to live in, and many of us would like an airport here. You see the beautiful countryside, and you say what a shame it would be if it were urbanised. You fail to notice that much of this countryside has fences round it and belongs to private land-owners and we don't penetrate into it. You look at the roads and you say how pleasant these winding country lanes are, with so little traffic on them. What you don't observe is that in this countryside the last bus to the nearest town is at 6.30 p.m. We can't go to the cinema. We can't even go to our friends, unless we happen to have a car. Now we would like to have cinemas. We would like to have better public services. We would like to have a whole lot of things, such as better services, which go with towns. And we would regard this as being a social good which you ought to cost as a plus. You of the middle classes, you who are already affluent and who monopolise the services and goods which already exist, are calculating the losses which *you* will suffer as a result of bringing in a lot of vulgar people connected with the new airport, but you don't calculate the benefits that go to us vulgar people.' And I think that there is a tendency to do precisely that. We economists, members of the professional middle classes, have many tastes which we reflect when we calculate costs. But if we are to do it fairly we must take both sides into account.

My story is only intended to illustrate a general bias. Now if we are going to suffer from the pursuit of high economic growth, if high economic growth means growth of economic welfare, of the goods and the services that people want, then I think we have little reason to feel alarmed about growth. What should cause us concern, however, are the techniques of bargaining among the different groups with different tastes who live in crowded societies. This is a political problem. The economic problem is to find the proper methods of measurement, to make sure that you properly calculate both social costs and social benefits—and that's a very big job which economists, I think, are going to be busy with for the next twenty years—and to give a proper costing in the national income account to the item of services. And many services are collective services, which have to be bought by people in groups. They can't be produced for individuals to consume. If you want a school you must have at least five hundred children to go to it, and if one family opts out it can't say 'I'm not paying for that'. That family must be compelled to pay for the collective service, whether it uses it or not, and this introduces a new element into economic relations, because the service sector of our affluent societies is going to grow very fast. It's already growing very fast and it's going to grow, I think, continuously over the next period. And we're going to find that many of the things we want are typically collective, and this creates a new set of problems. The measurement of services is, as you can imagine, a more difficult thing than to measure goods, because goods come in units which you can actually see, weigh, feel and count. But if *services* improve in quality it's very difficult to say 'We've got more' or 'We've got less'. If my laundry is delivered on Saturday because I happen to be at home on Saturdays, rather than on Monday, Tuesday or Wednesday (when the man happens to want to deliver it), the improvement in the service is very great and worth a lot to me, but it's very difficult to measure as a national income factor. This is at the simplest level. If my children are being educated at better schools than they are now, what can I say about it except that there is a better teacher. It is difficult to measure these things but we could, I think, devise better means of doing so than we have at present.

While I'm on education, which is my last point, it seems to me that those who despair of our societies becoming more and more materialist, and who complain that people are merely accumulating more goods, should examine the main trends of demand among the newly affluent. Their demands are going into the services sectors as well as into the consumption-goods sector. And the biggest boom of all is in a very desirable service —in education, above all in higher education. Perhaps the most serious problem that Britain faces in the next ten to fifteen years is to find university places for those who will be clamouring to enter university between now and 1985, and who, on all our calculations, will be fully qualified to do so. What we are facing is the prospect of a doubling of the number of people in universities, better qualified than today to be there, within ten years. This is our problem. And this is a typical collective service for which we have to find room by a collective decision of our society. It is to the solution of this sort of problem that we must address ourselves in the future. Although rooted in technological change, these problems are social in effect and their solution is ultimately a matter of politics—a state of affairs which has been with us since civilisation began.

DENNIS GABOR

Desirable and Undesirable
Ends of Technology

Dennis Gabor, who was born in Hungary and is now a British subject, is a Fellow of the Royal Society and Professor of Electron
Physics at the Imperial College of Science and Technology in London. He is most famous in the scientific world as the inventor of a
method of three-dimensional photography using lasers, known as
holography. Professor Gabor also has a wide following among non-
scientific readers, thanks to such stimulating books as *Inventing the
Future* (1963) and *Innovations* (1970) in which he speculates on
the likely social and economic effects of scientific advance.

GLENNY: It is the aim of these discussions to consider what
many people see as a threat to humanity, which I would like to
express by using two terms which are gaining currency today—
the biosphere and the technosphere. The biosphere means the
Earth's crust, its surface and its atmosphere, in other words the
environment for the maintenance of life on this planet, and the
technosphere refers to the super-structure that man has created
by his ingenuity, and which through the advance of technology
has become something resembling a parasitic growth on the
biosphere; in other words, the technosphere is consuming its
parent body, the biosphere.

Now in your book *Inventing the Future* at one point you use
the phrase: 'History must stop,' by which I think you mean that
some brake must be put on technological development if we are
to survive and the biosphere is to remain intact for the foreseeable future. Is this a misinterpretation of your views or am
I approximately right?

196

GABOR: Well, you have put this question very provocatively; there is no harm in that, but I must say it is greatly exaggerated: the technosphere is not a super-structure. It is itself the basic structure—the substructure. Marx is not so entirely wrong when he thinks that the whole of society is built on the economic substructure and that the ideologies constructed on top of it are a super-structure.

However, you are right in so far as the enormous development of technology is on an entirely new scale. History as we have known it was the history of relative scarcity: our forbears could get richer only by taking something away from somebody else. Now we have reached a point where to go on playing the old power game is sheer madness which cannot be allowed to continue. The problem lies not in technology but in the fact that man is not prepared for it. Technology gives us the means for everybody to get rich and happy; the trouble is that man is not cut out to be happy.

GLENNY: I am glad that you begin by reverting from technology to come back to its starting point—man. Man has always been aware that he must in some degree control his own activities. This is the starting point of all politics; indeed, some would say that it is the starting point of art and culture—an urge to impose order on a disorderly or apparently disorderly universe. There are now people who think that if the technological explosion is not to smother us, a much more severe set of controls must be placed on man's activities, above all on man as *homo faber*—man the tool-maker, man the technician. This might be summed up under two headings: firstly, control of science and technology, and secondly, much more far-reaching controls on man himself, not only as a social creature but also as an individual. There would then inevitably be further controls and further restrictions of our individual liberties, because one control tends to engender another. All such predictions, it is felt, pose a very great threat to democratic values. In other words, the far-reaching nature of the controls that may hold back science and technology and stop man himself from destroying his environment would be such as to produce a totalitarian political structure. Does this alarm you?

GABOR: There is no doubt about it, the development of technology and of science could lead to a new tyranny if it got into the hands of the wrong people.

What science can do is to solve the extremely difficult problem of creating the right conditions for the development of culture; this should enable us to keep the maximum possible individual freedom. Though a very difficult proposition, I see this as something technology can do. I said the *maximum* possible freedom, but how are we to determine the maximum possible freedom? By its very definition, freedom means proceeding by trial and error. Up to now it has not been possible to experiment with the social system because it was too precarious to be used as a laboratory. But now science has given us the computer and methods of computer simulation which enable us to play out the game of the future in millions of variations. With these aids we may be able to determine what is dangerous to man and his freedom and what is not.

GLENNY: Let us start by looking at the present where it seems that those in power right across the globe can see little further than the immediate short-term goal of economic growth, with its concomitant of increased material well-being. They appear, however, to have very little notion of the pollution, diseconomies and disadvantages which this is going to entail. Certain developing countries are doing their best to move as fast as they can along the same road that the advanced countries of the West have taken, without regard for the errors and dangers which this course brings with it.

Do you see any feasible political alternative to a policy of all-out economic growth?

GABOR: Here I must use two rather delicate words—'rational' and 'irrational'. I hope you understand why I regard them as delicate—no one likes to be called irrational. Well, to desire economic growth in an African country or in India is perfectly rational because there is no real alternative: people must be lifted above starvation level, and they must be given some creature comforts. But in our Western civilisation economic growth has become a fetish—a sort of fixation which is dangerous. To quote one example, every American will tell you that the economy of the United States is now based on nine million motor-cars being produced annually in Detroit and about five or six million being scrapped; this is a 'whirling dervish' economy. If it goes on, long before the end of the century the United States and Japan, and perhaps even this country, will reach the point where there are two big cars to every family, so that all our roads will be jammed. But road-blocks of a more dangerous kind are in wait for the technological society. At the present rate of production America can provide work for about ninety-five per cent of its population—and this is with a fairly big war in progress, and a system of rapid, built-in obsolescence which makes even the most complex product useless after a year or two, so that the consumer is forced to replace it. Any good engineer can make a plan that would maintain the present rate of production based on a twenty-five-hour working week, and later on a sixteen-hour-week and so on. What will people do then? They cannot be kept busy just by increasing consumption. Sooner or later, whether we like it or not, quantitative growth will have to stop. It is already slowing down for several reasons, one of which is that near saturation point people are less willing to work. Many people, and not only the young, are coming to realise that economic growth pursued as an end in itself has become senseless. Unfortunately the youthful rebels in America and other Western countries have no constructive alternative to offer; their protest is negative and emotional, and this is where one must use the term irrational. Many of them, who really ought to know better, think it is enough to smash up the existing system to make everything come right. Well, it isn't! Anarchy has never produced anything but chaos.

GLENNY: If I understand you rightly, it is your belief that at some point (and the point is rushing towards us at great speed, indeed we may even have passed it already) the people who control the world's economy must consciously make a decision to decelerate its growth, perhaps even to put a halt altogether to certain areas of economic activity. Now it is difficult enough for governments nowadays to take such an unpopular measure as an alteration in the methods of paying social security benefits; how much more politically undesirable will it therefore be for a government to place, for instance, a crippling tax on motor-cars, in order to slow down the process of swamping us in chromium-plated four-wheeled monsters.

GABOR: It will be very difficult indeed, for technological development is advancing under its own momentum and is going entirely the wrong way. It is really heart-breaking to see that, for instance, the railways do not pay any longer. In America the Pennsylvania Railroad has gone bankrupt. This is forty per cent of the U.S. rail network and far and away the biggest transport company in the world, with nominal assets of two hundred million dollars. New development ought obviously to be in the direction of fewer motor-cars and much more electrically-driven public transport, yet it just does not pay. The first job of government, however much it may hurt the public and industry, will be to make public transport pay and to make the chromium-plated monsters *not* pay. This will be very difficult and require such a high degree of governmental foresight that I really wonder if it will be forthcoming. I'm afraid, as always in history when there is a big turning point, change will come about only after a major breakdown.

GLENNY: Therefore you foresee that we must experience some appalling crisis, or shall we say the United States, as the pacemaker of the world's economy, must first experience some really disastrous crisis in order to bring people to their senses. Would it be too much to hope that somewhere in the upper reaches of the governing élite of the United States, and indeed of the Soviet Union—because the U.S.S.R. is also moving in the same direction—there are men with enough foresight to bring about a sane, rational deceleration of economic growth without a crisis?

GABOR: The problem is not so much one of putting a brake on growth as of diverting the gross national product to other purposes. It must be diverted to the quality of life; unfortunately nobody knows exactly what this means—or rather no one can agree on what it should mean. To me it means one thing for certain—education. Education is already nearly the biggest industry and it must become by far the biggest industry of an advanced country. Rich societies can and must afford to spend very much more money on education than most of them do now. There is, however, a financial difficulty because schools and universities do not pay for themselves. They must be financed out of taxpayers' money, and taxation in the U.K. at any rate is already so heavy that any increase will encounter very strong resistance.

In the Soviet Union one might say there is no such difficulty, because the state controls everything. Unfortunately there is no guarantee that any state will spend its funds on improving the quality of life of its citizens. The U.S. now spends sixty-five billion dollars on armaments. The Soviet expenditure has been estimated at sixty billion dollars, which is about twice as much related to the whole economy. Though the Soviet Government announce in every plan an increase in consumer goods, in 1970 the share of capital goods in total industrial output was still seventy-four per cent, while the share of consumer goods was only twenty-six per cent. The Russians carefully maintain an overgrown armaments industry. One of the results is three billion dollars' worth of arms exported to the Middle East, a policy that could have the direst consequences for us all.

GLENNY: You said, 'Technology is advancing under its own momentum.' Is not technology, in fact, a mere shell, a vehicle, whereas what moves it forward is the power of the human will? This brings us back to the question of how to channel man's

201

inventive powers and his boundless ingenuity away from the false or dangerous path in which they're now moving.

GABOR: Technology advances by its own inertia, for two reasons. One is that the old industries must be maintained, for instance an overgrown heavy industry, or an aircraft industry. The other is the principle of technological civilisation itself: 'what can be made, will be made'. 'Progress' tends to apply new techniques and to establish industries regardless of whether they are truly desirable or not. The clearest example of this is the space race. With the development of rockets and computers, space shots have come within the reach of technology, although they have no economic importance whatever apart from giving work to the aircraft industry at a time when their main product, manned aircraft, is declining. It so happens that space shots have great prestige value and therefore a very considerable amount of money is devoted to them, mostly in the United States and in Russia: perhaps fifty thousand million dollars. I must admit though that perhaps the only event in which the whole world joined as enthusiastic spectators on both sides of the Iron Curtain was man's first landing on the moon, and even more the perilous adventure of *Apollo 13*. But this exploit is more or less played out. It is very likely that after the so-called conquest of the moon there will not be much more left to do in space. The material benefits for mankind were marginal, and the same resources spent on solving the really difficult problems of man could have brought much greater profit to the world as a whole, instead of merely giving a boost to a certain sector of the electronics and aircraft industries. The world's really pressing needs are a long way away from space, such as finding a cheap method of re-cycling industrial waste.

Now a ray of hope. The moon flight has shown that people can achieve an unbelievable degree of coordination. For the *Apollo* Moon programme about six hundred thousand people worked together as one team and made the project run with split-second accuracy. No wonder these people are very proud of their achievement and say: 'Let us now apply our methods to social problems.' I am quite convinced that by taking an equally gifted set of people—even taking the same people, the same engineers with, of course, a sprinkling of economists and social scientists and the like—and giving them social problems to solve, such as for instance the race problem in the United States, the social integration of the American cities, the building of new cities with adequate urban transport etc., that all these problems could be solved, because these engineers and scientists have evolved effective methods of integrated planning and they have an absolutely wonderful system of cooperation. Once a dream becomes a project, the engineers can deal with it!

GLENNY: In your book, *Inventing the Future*, there is behind all your thinking a streak of fundamental optimism about man's future. However, perhaps we might test your optimism by seeing how you react to a rather more pessimistic view of the future. To revert once again to the sort of civil war that some people claim exists between the biosphere and the technosphere—this is the question of whether man's biological and cultural adaptive mechanisms, which have been relatively successful up till now, are not in fact now in danger of atrophy and malfunction. I would like to give two examples of such a thing. One is our over-dependence on technology, of which perhaps the most striking recent example was the power breakdown which took place along the whole of the Eastern seaboard of the United States a couple or so years ago. Another more recent example was in Johannesburg, when the municipal slaughterhouse broke down and for days Johannesburg was rendered almost uninhabitable by hundreds of thousands of dying cattle which were piling up in over-heated freight cars all round the city, and which posed the kind of monstrous catastrophe which at the moment only science fiction writers have dealt with. How would you comment on that kind of problem?

GABOR: It is true that such terrible things can happen, because we have reached a point where technological methods are so universally applied that particular breakdowns are common. To take another example, we are now faced all over the world with the pollution of the air and water. Here the problem is how to make anti-pollution measures pay. The only thing that can help is appropriate legislation. You cannot expect the good citizen to pay more for lead-free octane fuel or to pay more for a car with improved combustion and computer-controlled emission so long as others are allowed to pollute the air with cheaper cars and cheaper fuels. I would not consider such legislation as an infringement of personal freedom. One could make a good case for saying that one of the human freedoms is, for instance, the freedom to breathe fresh air.

You said you wanted to test my optimism. It is nowadays very easy to decry any sort of optimism because it hangs on a very slender thread. But I can still see some reason for optimism, and one of my reasons is that I think I can see a change of mind among my fellow-scientists and engineers. Only twenty to thirty years ago, engineers—not just in this country but all over the world—were a culturally underprivileged minority; they even felt very smug about their station and had a clear conscience. Now the first change is coming. Engineers are beginning to have a bad conscience. Some of the older generation manage to resist it, but the young ones have started to develop a feeling of moral unease which I welcome. After the atomic bomb had been made and used, scientists got such a guilty conscience that they are now almost all universally pacifist; they are trying to behave with a sense of social responsibility and advise their political leaders accordingly. That a great amount of scientific intelligence in the world may be directed towards social and environmental problems certainly gives cause for hope. Unfortunately, governments are so overwhelmed by the *visible* instability of our system and the need for short-term measures that they are now less capable of taking a detached look at the prospects ten or twenty years ahead than they were ten years ago. For instance, all the attractive plans for 'The Great Society' in America have been nearly swamped by the present danger of inflation. And yet, perhaps this small setback is enough to make people aware that society just cannot go on as it is.

GLENNY: The unspoken reproach that has lain behind much of your criticism of the lack of control over technological advance in recent years has been aimed at what some people might call the profit motive, the free enterprise economy, or the price mechanism. Admittedly even in so-called Capitalist countries this has been greatly modified lately. Nevertheless, it still dominates our economic system. Are you hinting that this form of liberal, free-enterprise economy should be so strongly curbed as to be reduced altogether and changed into something else—into perhaps a command economy on the East European pattern?

GABOR: That would certainly be going too far. It is true that socially irresponsible economic activity must be curbed, but it would be folly to abandon the free-enterprise economy altogether. It is, after all, basically the most efficient system we know. Look at the East European states; their system works very badly indeed. It works, of course, in some ways: there is no trade union pressure on wages, there are no strikes; but at what a price! Everybody is concerned with looking after 'number one' and little else. There is even less social responsibility, less social cohesion than on our side. I know from personal experience how many East Europeans are exclusively preoccupied with their personal interests and work as little as possible, doing the minimum consistent with keeping their jobs. What we must do—and it is very difficult (compromise is always difficult)—is to curb the obviously destabilising factors in our economy such as the Stock Exchange, where a small amount of selling can bring about a catastrophic breakdown, and a small amount of buying can cause a totally irrational temporary upswing; or the 'free for all' of the trade unions, with one after the other presenting their claims and driving up wages and prices in a vicious spiral. But we must not curb the enormous benefits which our civilisation has gained from individual enterprise, from individual effort spurred on by the hope of advancement. The rules of the economic game must in future be modified by social criteria, but let us not throw out the baby with the bathwater!

EDWARD GOLDSMITH

Ecology, Controls
and Short-term Expedients

Edward Goldsmith was educated in a variety of schools in England,
France, Switzerland, the West Indies and Canada, before going up
to Oxford University to read Politics, Philosophy and Economics.
For the past six years he has devoted his entire time to his main
interest in life: the development of a unified science—and he has
written a book and a number of articles on the subject, as well as
lecturing widely on more general ecological matters. In 1970 he
founded *The Ecologist* magazine, of which he is the editor.

GLENNY: Could you give us a very brief definition of the
word Ecology, and then an explanation of the philosophy that
lies behind your journal that you have entitled *The Ecologist*?

GOLDSMITH: Ecology is normally regarded as the study of
the inter-relationships of organisms between each other and
the various resources on which they live. We propose to use
the term in a somewhat different way, in accordance with a
newer use of the term already current in certain universities. We
want to regard it as the study of the whole effect of human
processes and actions of different sorts on the total environment.

Used in this sense, ecology is more of an approach than a
conventional discipline. And this approach could be used to
study absolutely everything in the world in which we live; for
instance, an ecological approach to medicine would be to study
not the specific effects of acts undertaken by doctors, but the
total effects on the body as a whole and possibly even the social
effects of doctors behaving in a particular way. Unfortunately,
people have been looking at things in quite the opposite way,

207

especially in recent times. The result has been to see things from the very short-term point of view and in terms of specific targets, rather than from a long-term standpoint and in global terms. We want to influence them to look at the whole rather than the parts and to see the long-term future of man, which unfortunately has been very seriously compromised in every field by the short-term approach. This narrow attitude is typical of politicians who are merely interested in obtaining votes, or businessmen who only want to make quick profits, and of trade unions who are interested in getting the maximum benefits for their members regardless of the cost to society. Scientists are also too interested in short-term results; they look at their own little subject and are not particularly concerned about the effect of what they're doing on the world as a whole. I think the scientists must be held very much responsible for many of the things that are going wrong at the moment.

GLENNY: Your initiative is obviously an extremely important one. Who do you believe is going to read your journal? What will be its effect?

GOLDSMITH: Our magazine is aimed at the general educated public, the sort of people who in this country would read the serious weekly journals. It is also aimed at academics. I don't think one can expect politicians to pass the necessary legislation to solve our various environmental problems unless there's a very strong and highly organised public opinion—a very strong lobby, in fact. We would like public opinion to be seriously awakened to the extreme urgency of man's position on the planet Earth at the moment, and I think it is conceivable that the correct measures will be taken by industrialists and by politicians when public opinion is so awakened. Whether we shall be able to achieve this or not is another question. I am fairly optimistic. I think that youth is going to be very responsive to our message and that it will arouse great interest in schools. This is perhaps the most we can achieve, because changes are bound to occur slowly; but it is on youth, who will be running this country in the next ten or twenty years, that we can count the most.

GLENNY: You are, I suppose, one of the front runners in a trend of public opinion which is beginning to make itself widely felt. However, there are centres of power both in the East and in the West which are as yet unaffected by your message. I am thinking in particular of many of the Communist countries and the countries of the Third World who would simply dismiss your message as irrelevant to their problems.

GOLDSMITH: I don't think the people in the Communist countries would dismiss the message as irrelevant. They are responsible for a considerable amount of environmental disruption, certainly in the Soviet Union. It appears that the Communist countries are having problems very similar to those of the Capitalist countries. Undoubtedly in Capitalist countries the profit motive does lead to very irresponsible behaviour, but in Communist countries where there is not the same profit motive, you will also find that there is irresponsible economic development whose object presumably is to give people more jobs or to increase their standard of living in accordance with present cultural values.

However, I agree much more with what you say about the Third World. That's a quite different problem, because there they are only beginning to be industrialised and have not yet been disillusioned as to the benefits of so-called progress—by which I mean economic expansion. This is going to be a major problem. In fact, *The Ecologist* refers in one issue to what it calls *The Biggest Confidence Trick of All Time*: our efforts to destroy the cultural patterns of 'primitive' tribes in 'underdeveloped' or developing countries. Such cultural patterns have enabled these peoples to lead ecologically sound existences for a very long time—until they are interfered with by industrialised nations, who destroy these cultural patterns and inculcate in their place a set of values which is inextricably linked with the notion of economic growth.

o   209

We are going to create an enormous demand for things that we simply will not be able to give them, because the standard of affluence achieved in Western nations will never be attained in the Third World. It is absolutely impossible, for many reasons. First of all, the pollution generated by the amount of economic activity this would involve would be intolerable. Take, for instance, the case of radio-active pollution. A Russian scientist, Professor Polikarpov, has recently written a book called *The Radio-Ecology of Aquatic Organisms,* in which he shows that the effect of radio-active waste on such organisms is much worse than anyone has hitherto suspected. While scientists are very concerned with observable effects, too little attention is paid to non-lethal long-term effects; yet these can be very very serious, especially on the larvae. According to Professor Polikarpov, it is inadmissible to put any more radio-active waste into the seas without compromising this, the most important bio-mass in the world, which is responsible for ten per cent of the world's protein intake—and for some countries like Japan and the Phillipines, over fifty per cent.

Britain, with about 1½ per cent of the world's population, is producing at the moment *half* of the world's nuclear power. Imagine what would happen if everybody was producing nuclear power at the same rate as Great Britain and dumping the radio-active waste in the sea. This would probably lead to the disappearance of all life in the seas; think, too, of the effect on the people subjected to radio isotopes in the air. Then take another aspect of it: the heat generated—thermal pollution. In thirty years' time it is considered that in that vast urban conglomeration which has spread between Boston and Washington (to be called BosWash, I believe) fifty per cent of the atmospheric heat will be man-made. It appears that only a small change in the temperature of the atmosphere, about two per cent, is sufficient to cause the polar ice-caps to melt, flooding most of the world's major cities.

The question arises as to how much man-made heat can be absorbed before such a climatic change takes place, and at our present rate of economic growth, how long will it take for this to occur? Various calculations have been made. Some suggest that it will take another seventy years, others more. What is important is that a point must eventually be reached when no more man-made heat can be absorbed and this point is not that far off. Therefore if you propose that all the countries in the world must achieve the American standard of living, the answer is that such a state of affairs is simply beyond the physical capacity of our planet.

Consider it from another point of view—natural resources. There are not enough natural resources available in the world to enable the people in the Third World to achieve the standard of living that we think they should have. The world's oil reserves, for instance, can only last another seventy years, and about ten out of the twenty minerals in greatest use in industry today will no longer be available in thirty years' time. We will have to depend on recycled scrap metals, and perhaps on tapping uneconomic sources, which means that mineral prices will be much higher. It is true that with advanced technology we are capable of utilising sources of copper, for instance, that were deemed totally uneconomic twenty years ago, but nevertheless, a point comes when returns diminish beyond zero and eventually become negative.

You cannot go on applying more and more technology to less and less natural resources. Already we in Britain, for instance, are feeling the effect of negative returns on technology applied to agriculture—our so-called intensive agriculture, which we are trying to persuade the Third World to adopt. We are trying to force the latter to relinquish their very sound methods of agriculture in order to intensify their farming—which means more machines, more artificial fertilizers and more pesticides. In the long run, though, this is no substitute for sound husbandry, and by applying more of our methods they will eventually obtain smaller and smaller returns.

GLENNY: The agricultural policies that we are offering the Third World will also presumably lead to more rural unemployment in these countries, with a consequent increase in urbanisation.

GOLDSMITH: I should think this is possibly one of the most important problems we have to face today—the problem of rapid urbanisation in certain parts of the Third World. The population of some cities is increasing by more than ten per cent per annum, and it is becoming impossible to find jobs, houses, provide sewage facilities, education and medical services for so many people. Apart from this, when they get into cities, their cultural patterns break down; the rate of delinquency goes up, crime, drug addiction, alcoholism and all the various manifestations of social disorder increase radically. We must realise, which I believe some people are realising already, that it is better to pay a little more for our food than to have social chaos in the cities of the Third World.

GLENNY: Obviously there are dangers involved in disrupting the traditional agriculture and cultural patterns in regions such as Africa. Yet there is another side to the coin as well, namely that many of the rural economies of Africa have for centuries suffered from acute in-built defects, such as chronic protein shortage in some areas of East Africa or endemic deficiency diseases such as beri-beri, yaws and kwashiokor. The efforts of modern medicine and changes in agricultural patterns are beginning to eliminate these curses, which are surely just as debilitating to human ecology as are some of the dangers which are threatened by technological progress.

GOLDSMITH: What I shall say now is not going to be very popular. I believe there is no evidence to prove that modern medicine as we are practising it in Africa is going to improve the long-term health of the people there. For instance, it is easy enough to wipe out certain diseases like malaria or yaws. But in many areas where malaria was endemic, people did not die of it, they were just debilitated. By introducing massive antimalaria operations, we have done two things: firstly, we have destroyed the people's natural immunity against malaria, which means that when an epidemic comes in from the outside, the population is going to get the disease really badly and die from it. I was talking only yesterday to a friend of mine, a radio-doctor in Lagos, who was telling me that people coming in from rural schools to the capital were subjected to anti-malarial treatment, and when they went back to their homes they caught malaria and died from it. Why? Because they had lost their natural immunity.

Secondly, the widespread use of chemical insecticides such as DDT is having a very serious effect on the ecological balance, by destroying certain extremely important species of animals and birds, predators that are essential for controlling insect pests. This means that in some cases we are actually creating pests, in that insects that were once perfectly well controlled by their natural predators are now appearing in plague proportions.

GLENNY: Some people would interpret what you say as being somewhat callous. You maintain that the measures taken to control disease and to raise agricultural productivity in the short term are actually harmful; but surely what is happening is that a great deal more people are being fed and are able to lead at least halfway reasonable lives who otherwise would simply be dead.

GOLDSMITH: This is true. But it must be understood that these short-term methods, these expedients that are in use today simply succeed in putting off the day of reckoning, and the more you put it off, the worse it will be. On the other hand, I do agree that there is a very good case for using such methods on humanitarian grounds. Obviously we cannot allow people to starve; but only on condition that we take the necessary long-term measures as well, so as to prevent this final day of reckoning. If we take the short-term measures without the long-term ones we are heading for catastrophe.

GLENNY: I take this point, but nevertheless, I would still not like you to get away without conceding that there is a more positive aspect of present policies, such as those which are aimed at restoring ecological systems which have been destroyed not by wicked technological man but over the centuries by ignorant non-technological man. I refer for instance to the denudation that is occurring over large areas of East Africa by the uncontrolled herding of cattle by such people as the Masai who, when their herds have destroyed all the pasture in one area and have induced erosion, then move off *en masse* to another area to repeat the process. Before very long there will not be any pasture left for them. Is there not a case for guiding them into better and more rational practices in a way which need not necessarily upset their cultural patterns?

GOLDSMITH: There is, but I still maintain that any interference with the way of life of the Masai or other pastoralists is likely to have very serious consequences on their social structure and on their way of life. If you break down the society of the Masai they will just pour into the cities, live in shanty towns and simply become members of the impoverished and depressed proletariat—which is what you want to avoid. Every effort should be made to maintain the essentially healthy social structures of these people. Now before we can modify the customs of the Masai, the problem is to understand the function of their customs. One must furthermore understand that all behavioural traits are functional, that a culture itself is an adaptive response to a long-term environmental situation; this is something which very many anthropologists in this country would refuse to accept. They refuse to look at these things in a functional manner, though, in fact, the founders of British anthropology such as Malinowski would have certainly agreed with the functional approach.

You cannot simply pass a law and tell the Masai not to have any cattle; what you can do—and it would have to be done with extreme care—is to find a functional substitute for the possession of cattle, which of course can only be done when you understand the exact cultural role of owning cattle. I give you an example of the lines on which this might be done. In one of the islands off New Guinea there were head-hunters. The Dutch thought this very immoral and tried, with considerable subtlety, to get rid of this custom. The reason why these people indulged in head-hunting was that they considered their ancestors to require company in their graves, and a head was apparently suitable company for them. Once they were told that they could not cut people's heads off, they were in a terrible quandary, because they were caught between the fear of their infuriated dead ancestors who would take revenge on them, and the fear of living Dutchmen who would send them to gaol. Their cultural pattern might quite easily have collapsed but the Dutch, as I have said, were quite subtle; they introduced a functional substitute for a human head in the form of a little dried bird, and they succeeded in persuading these people that a dried bird was just as satisfactory company for their dead ancestors. So the whole cultural pattern remained intact, with just a slight change. In the same way, the ancient Egyptians, like the Sumerians, used to bury all the courtiers with their dead king, until eventually someone hit upon the good idea of burying small ceramic effigies of the courtiers, which were regarded as acceptable substitutes. A similar thing would have to be done with the Masai: you would have to persuade them that prestige and economic benefit could be achieved by other means than keeping cattle—for instance by accumulating other things that are less harmful to the land. Ideally it might be eland, for instance, or other game. We know that the African bush can support a vastly greater amount of game than it can domestic cattle. To solve this problem in the right way means introducing cultural controls, which are infinitely more effective than coercive measures.

GLENNY: The question of controls is undoubtedly the crucial aspect of what we are discussing. In your leading article in the first issue of *The Ecologist* you write a sentence which seems to me to contain the nub of the problem:

'Thus to control population, we may have to interfere with "personal liberty", while to reduce economic expansion, we are forced to curb the march of "progress". But surely all this is but a small price to pay if we consider the long-term alternative to such a policy.'

Looked at from one angle, the price may indeed be a small one; nevertheless, it will be an extremely difficult one to pay, certainly in political terms. You are proposing controls at two levels; firstly, a control of science and technology at the administrative level, or shall we say at the economic level if one uses fiscal rather than administrative measures to control it; the second form of control is quite simply the control of *people*. This is a very sensitive area, particularly in a world which has seen the rapid rise in this century of totalitarian systems. You say that we may have to interfere with personal liberty. I think that if what you are suggesting were put into effect, the encroachment upon democratic values and their safeguards might be most unwelcome in certain societies. For instance, you might have to control people's child-bearing habits in a way which now is simply not contemplated. You would certainly have to control people's economic lives, hence their social behaviour, and gradually the logical result could be the control of people's behaviour in its widest sense. Any government will arouse insuperable opposition if it tries to put such controls into effect.

GOLDSMITH: Let me deal with this on a theoretical level. A stable society is subjected to as many controls as an unstable one. Let us take a 'simple' society—an African or an Australian aboriginal tribe. Such a society displays order and is capable of adapting to environmental changes of a predictable sort, that is to say within given parameters. When I say it displays order, the different parts or individuals are subject to constraints which limit their range of choices, which I think is a normal definition of order. What is important is that each of these constraints is in turn subjected to the constraints of the system—in this case, the society as a whole. These constraints are basically what

216

keeps such a society behaving in an adaptive way, and they are embodied in its traditions—traditions such as fear of the ancestors and of other forces invoked to make people act properly in accordance with tribal behaviour-patterns. All these forces or constraints which make them behave in this way are part of the society's self-regulating mechanisms—in which public opinion plays a big part. This is tremendously important, because in such conditions there is no need whatsoever for any of what are known as 'asystemic' controls. A simple society of this sort will not have a dictator or tyrant. In fact one of the themes of Aristotle's *Politics* is that there is no need for dictators until society breaks down. Simple, ordered societies do not normally even have kings, and when a larger or more centralised society does have a king, he only has limited power. The king of a traditional African society can be dethroned if he breaks any tribal tradition, simply by a show of hands, which is exactly what happened to a king of a Homeric city, who in traditional Hellenic society ruled with only a minimal degree of sovereignty which was always subordinated to the opinion of the people. The king had to abide by that opinion or he was thrown out. Now what is important is that you cannot have real democracy unless the society displays all the characteristics of a stable society: including a powerful public opinion, patriotism and a strong sense of duty towards the society. Our citizens today do not feel they have any duty towards society. They feel only that society has a duty towards them, that they must be given everything they want whether they deserve it or not. Demosthenes was complaining of just these things when he was speaking to the citizens of Athens and attacking them on their degeneracy and their refusal to face their challenges.

When the structure of society breaks down, when it ceases to display the essential features that enable it to behave as a stable self-regulating adaptive system, then you need external or 'asystemic' constraints, and if these are lacking you have chaos. Look at the world today. Look at the South American or Middle Eastern nations. They do not have a choice between dictatorship and democracy. The choice is purely illusory. Their choice is between dictatorship and chaos. When one authoritarian regime is overthrown by a revolution, its place is taken by another equally authoritarian one. And if there is an interregnum between such regimes, it is one of pure anarchy. The institutions of democracy, of which they are proud, are a façade and nothing more. They may have tried to adopt the institutions of countries like Britain which have been reasonably stable for a very long time, and they think that simply by virtue of having these institutions they can develop a stable society. It is not the case. What is lacking is an appropriate cultural pattern. The institutions are secondary. Now, we know what disorder is like, for instance in industrial slums where society has broken down completely. There you see the opposite of a stable society: the institution of marriage has almost broken down, most of the children are illegitimate and there is a very high crime rate. This sort of society has been described for us by a number of writers —best known is possibly Oscar Lewis, the author of very revealing studies of life in Mexican shanty-towns.

Localised disorder of this kind, however disagreeable it may be, is relatively tolerable; but not so on a global scale—especially among vast societies that possess all sorts of technological skills which would enable them to destroy the world we live in. Now it is already sufficiently terrifying to know that a few scientists sitting in laboratories in different parts of the world are capable of producing something like poly-water, which was recently produced in Russia. We don't quite know the implications of poly-water, but at one time people thought that if you put a little poly-water into the sea, the sea would be wiped out and all life with it. This may not be true, but nevertheless it is quite conceivable that people could invent similar things which could destroy life in one fell swoop. The idea that it is possible to do these things is truly terrifying, because on purely theoretical grounds, when a definite possibility exists for something to occur, it is simply a question of time before it in fact does so.

Now when the technological skills involved are in the hands of societies that are totally disorderly, where no sorts of constraints either of a systemic or asystemic nature are applied to the behaviour of the scientists and technologists with these skills —then the situation is even more alarming. What is to be done? I agree with you that dictatorship is unpleasant and should be avoided at all costs. I believe that the whole object of political endeavour is to create self-regulating societies—societies which display the features required for them to be stable and adaptive without any external or asystemic constraints being applied at all. When this is not possible, what do you do? It is useless to introduce an unsound short-term expedient to deal with a long-term situation. It must be unsuccessful in the long run, unless at the same time you introduce the necessary long-term measures to bring about a stable, sound and self-regulating situation.

Let us consider the population question as an example. In certain countries like Britain, population need not be so much of a problem. All that is necessary in this country to get a stable population is for average family size to be reduced to 2·1 instead of 2·5 children. Organised birth control or family planning, however, has not been a great success. Its failure has been world-wide. The reason, of course, is that it has provided people with a short-term means for keeping down population; but it cannot succeed in the long run if the motivation is not there. In countries like the Phillipines where women want more than six children, why give them contraceptives? Even in America, women want three or four children. It is useless to give them pills; it has absolutely no effect at all. Instead, we must introduce the correct cultural controls to prevent them from wanting so many children. It is a sort of cultural engineering, and I believe it could be done. Abortion, of course, which is now legal in Britain, will have a very important effect. It has already succeeded in the U.S.S.R. In the Soviet Union, when there was completely free abortion, they had to change the law because they were worried about the population going down. In Japan the same thing has happened. Abortion will certainly have an important effect, but this is not likely to be so in the countries which really have a vast population problem —I mean in countries like India, where there is something like a 2·6 per cent increase per annum, and in South America, where population increases by over three per cent per annum. Obviously some method of control is essential, and we may have to make use of something like a licensing system, whereby people would need a licence to have a child. This has already been proposed by, among other people, the American anthropologist Margaret Mead. After all, you need a licence to drive a motor car; it is a far greater responsibility to bring children into this world, yet there are no constraints on procreation by anyone, however irresponsible or unstable they may be.

GLENNY: You suggest in your leading article that control of science and technology will be necessary. Some such controls, of course, are already in existence, although you will no doubt be the first to say that they are generally inadequate or misapplied. Surely the crucial question is whether the degree of control which you regard as necessary is enforceable, particularly if you do not interfere very drastically with the nature of the economy. Could an adequate system of control be applied in the present type of modified free-enterprise economy that exists in the West?

GOLDSMITH: It is important to realise, on the subject of control, that all sorts of *natural* controls are going to become operative in a short time unless we act ourselves. The population will be controlled by famine, massacres and epidemics in the not too distant future. Technology will be controlled, and industrial growth will be controlled very shortly by the total exhaustion of our natural resources, by the radically increasing cost of combating pollution and by the difficulty of running businesses in an increasingly unfavourable social climate.

Now the sort of controls that I am proposing are simply aimed at making these natural controls, if you like, less necessary. The controls that would be necessary today are probably not too harsh and need not upset too many people's susceptibilities. In twenty-five years' time, the sort of controls needed will be far more radical. In thirty or forty years' time—God knows what sort of controls we shall need. Eventually it will be too late for human controls to be effective at all. We have seen for instance how ridiculously short-sighted, greedy and irresponsible man is with regard to activities like whaling. Whalers have been told by countless international commissions that they must reduce their catches, but with no success. We know very well that in a short time there will be no whales left. Such unbelievable short-sightedness, such hideous greed and total irresponsibility should simply not be allowed. And it is not only businessmen who are the culprits, because governments are behaving in just the same way. Recently, Denmark has refused to abide by certain fishing quotas, and the Soviet Union, Japan and Norway are particularly irresponsible in their behaviour towards the seas.

It is extremely important that people be made to realise that technology does not provide a solution to the environmental crisis. There are no purely technological means of solving man's problems—of this I am absolutely and totally certain. I do not say that technology has not a very important role to play; it has an essential part to play. In the next few decades, for instance, we must learn to recycle all our waste products. Let us take a typical example. Sulphur dioxide is emitted in vast quantities into the air today in England—something like six million tons a year. This is a very dangerous substance. It is not only harming agriculture very severely—in certain cases it can reduce plant growth by as much as fifty per cent—but it may produce lung cancer and mutations in living organisms. It is clearly a matter of urgency to control sulphur dioxide, and if possible to do so by technological means. The Monsanto Chemical Company has developed a device called the Cat-Ox which can be used for recycling sulphur. Unfortunately, re-cycled sulphur would sell at roughly twice the current market price—and therefore would be uneconomic. What is the answer to this problem? Should we allow our air to be poisoned by sulphur dioxide or should we be willing to pay more for our sulphur? Surely, only people concerned with short-term economic problems can really believe that we can allow ourselves to be poisoned, simply in order to save a bit of money on sulphur. It is perfectly evident that the government must increase the price of sulphur so that it can be properly recycled. This is only one example out of many.

However, if we think that because of these technological developments we can simply go on expanding and increasing economic growth, then these technological devices are actually harmful, because they are merely enabling us to adapt to a pathological situation by making this situation tolerable —which can only serve to perpetuate it.

GLENNY: Do you then believe technology is inherently harmful?

GOLDSMITH: I do not say that technology is harmful in itself; but there are certain theoretical reasons why technology is not a panacea and cannot solve our problems by itself. One of the reasons is that technological processes are very clumsy by nature's standards. The waste generated by a technological device is infinitely greater than that produced by a self-regulating device that is a natural component of the biosphere. In a way you can regard technological devices such as factories, aircraft, cars etc., as vast machines eating up the planet's stock of negative entropy and replacing it with random parts or waste. Eventually, if we go on ravaging the earth long enough we shall be left with something looking like the moon. Interestingly enough, the moon is an ideal place for industry and technology because, since there is no lunar biosphere, everything there must be provided by technology.

Next, there is the problem of natural resources. For instance, where is the energy to come from for all the vast technological programmes of the future? Where are we to get the minerals, the water, the land? All of these will soon be in short supply.

There is one other factor which tends to be ignored by everyone except ecologists : that is the concept of simplification. One of the basic laws of ecology is that stability is mainly achieved by increasing variety or complexity. This means increasing the range of environmental changes through which adaptive responses can be mediated. Now when you replace complex natural controls by simple artificial ones, you are simplifying your eco-system and thereby making it less adaptive and more vulnerable. For instance, there are two thousand million micro-organisms in a teaspoonful of soil, all interrelated in countless different ways. If you replace this unbelievably complicated eco-system by a little artificial fertiliser, you are simplifying it, and by simplifying it you make it that much more vulnerable.

The same thing happens when we replace the natural controls that keep down insect populations by our crude pesticides; those that maintain a balance between ourselves and our bacterial populations by unsubtle antibiotics; also those that maintain social order in simple stable societies by asystemic controls like bureaucrats and policemen. In each case the system involved must become correspondingly less stable, and hence more vulnerable to unexpected changes of any sort.

Another reason why technology cannot solve our problem is that natural controls are self-regulating, while technological ones have to be regulated asystemically from the outside, in other words by ourselves; combined with our notorious human fallibility, this makes our society even more vulnerable.

Thus, once we start using artificial fertilisers, we have to go on doing so. Once we start eradicating malaria with DDT we have to go on spraying, year after year. (Ceylon stopped doing so in 1969, with catastrophic results: a million out of a population of ten million people suddenly got malaria. An SOS had to be sent for ten million pounds of DDT to recover control.)

Once we depend on sewage works to ensure the cleanliness of our rivers, and purification plants to provide us with drinking water, we simply have to keep them functioning year after year, or we end up with no fish-life and no water to drink. Now these devices can only be kept functioning if certain very specific conditions are maintained:

Raw materials and, in particular, sources of energy, must

be available. There must be enough food for our increasing industrial population. The environment must be capable of absorbing ever larger quantities of industrial wastes, and people must be willing to and capable of fulfilling their respective functions in the economy.

None of these conditions are likely to be maintained for very much longer; and as a result that vast and elaborate technological super-structure that we have built to replace the biosphere we are so methodically destroying, will slowly collapse.

In conclusion, I would stress that the sort of society that technology has enabled us to build is a highly unstable one, and can at best be but a localised and temporary phenomenon.

HERMAN KAHN

On War, Dissent and
the Control of Knowledge

Herman Kahn is Director of the Hudson Institute and one of the
founders of games theory and future-oriented research. His publications *The Year 2000*, *On Thermonuclear War*, *Thinking about the
Unthinkable* and *On Escalation: Metaphors and Scenarios*, have
shaped American national defence planning and public policy making for more than ten years, not only through their specific recommendations, but also through the methodology that Herman Kahn
and others, in centres like the RAND Corporation, created after the
Second World War.

URBAN: Gaston Bouthoul, a leading French sociologist of
war, says in one of his books that war breaks out in a social
group when there is a 'plethora of young men surpassing the
indispensable tasks of the economy'. That is to say, war breaks
out when these men are not employed: it is the multiplication
of men excluded from labour processes which makes them
ready for war. I'm quoting this view for a special reason. Professor Dennis Gabor shows in his book *Inventing the Future*
that before the end of this century there will not only be a
continuous decrease in human participation in the technical
operations, but also that a very large percentage of able-bodied
but low IQ'd men and women will have no useful work to perform in society. So we may be heading for a congenital kind
of permanent unemployment disguised—it remains to be seen
how effectively—by a therapeutic employment of the unem-
ployables.

KAHN: We know of many societies which have chronic problems of unemployment and yet do not go to war. Every

agrarian society has a problem of non-employment or under-employment, especially between November and March when the farmers and peasants are mostly idle. Yet, generally, these societies have been the victims of war rather than the aggressors or instigators of war. You may, of course, argue that non-employment during the winter months in a traditional and stationary society isn't unemployment at all but part of the rhythmic pattern of life, in which feverish activity in one part of the year alternates with relative inactivity in another, and that peasant societies have learnt how to deal with these cycles. I would agree, and I would also agree that unemployment in an industrial, densely populated setting is more likely to release the springs of aggressiveness, as we have seen in the early 1930s in Germany. Also, it is a fact that the European nations (and the United States) harbour great piles of aggressive energy, and it is undeniable that if you don't have tasks for large numbers of achievement-oriented people, they will look for tasks, and one of the tasks might be war. With all that, the process is not automatic even in the industrial societies. In Britain, France and the United States the depression of the 1930s did not produce a German-type of situation for the simple reason that in Germany unemployment was coupled with a sense of national grievance stemming from Versailles, which Hitler could and did exploit.

But whatever unemployment may do to the collective psyche of society, modern war may be safely discounted as an anachronism. For one thing, you can no longer conquer a nation in the traditional way and use it for plunder and slave-labour. It just doesn't pay. It did once pay, but it doesn't any more. Those who could make it pay don't have the ability, and the ones that have the ability haven't the social system.

I would say that today most of the traditional causes of war among the major nations have pretty well disappeared. In Europe the territorial boundaries are firmly set and, with some exceptions, they have been accepted by public opinion. Nations no longer go to war because they have been insulted, and most of the prestige arguments had to fall by the wayside. The basic remaining causes of formal war would stem from considerations of defence: one nation feeling threatened by some crisis which it could only resolve by force or because it feels threatened by the pre-emptive strike-potential of its rival. But it is highly unlikely that any military request for nuclear weapons to be used to achieve positive gains would be condoned either by the United States or the U.S.S.R. For all these reasons it is very difficult to write credible scenarios for formal nuclear war in the 1970s or 1980s. Now, this has not been true throughout history. Aggressive war has often paid.

URBAN: When you say it is difficult to think of a credible scenario for nuclear war in the 1970s, are you making some allowance for the imponderables which, in history, have accounted for many more wars than an aetiologically minded historian would care to admit? Scenarios I have seen of the Bosnian crisis were far from providing conclusive evidence that the First World War was inevitable. Yet, in retrospect, many of us tend to think that it was, though for reasons very hard to quantify.

KAHN: It would be entirely unreasonable to argue that, because we find it difficult to write a plausible scenario for nuclear war in the coming decades, such a war *cannot* take place. It can be argued that the specific historical concatenation of events which led to the outbreak of the First World War was implausible and that a scenario embodying those events would not meet the standards of my Institute. By the same token, it is possible to think of a specific sequence of events which *might* lead to nuclear war in the 1970s. But this sequence would be fraught with so many irrationalities, and a war, if it did result from it, would so blindly ignore the penalties, that for practical purposes it would be impossible to incorporate a sequence of that kind in a plausible scenario. One can, naturally, use the 'if ... then' type of prediction and design acceptable alternatives, and this is a useful approach, but it can only provide a number of surprise-free variations.

Having said that, my personal feeling is that nuclear war has been ruled out less by the effectiveness of nuclear technology than by the basic context in which nuclear technology would have to be employed. There are, to sum-up, three factors involved here: first, those who make the decisions are no longer under pressure to increase national territory; second, there is great pressure on them to avoid any risk of nuclear war; third, there is a high degree of doubt among military planners whether it is, in the nuclear context, possible to make realistic military calculations. If any of these three factors changed, nuclear war would still be possible, but I do not expect them to change. Also, one cannot rule out nuclear war by accident or miscalculation. Bluffing and intimidation may backfire, especially if this makes accident or miscalculation more likely.

URBAN: I am trying to go back to the social causes of unrest and aggression and I wonder whether you would subscribe to the 'twenty-five-year itch' school of thinking. This holds that every twenty-five to thirty years memories fade, the scars and the horrors of war die with the generation that was involved in it and young men are again ready to defy the institutions which their fathers bequeathed them. It was Arnold Toynbee who said a few years ago that we shouldn't really be too unhappy about the restlessness of the younger generation because theirs is a relatively harmless way of letting off steam at a time when these young men might well be spoiling for a more dangerous sort of confrontation.

KAHN: It is an attractive theory but I don't think it is accurate. I suspect the analogy is drawn from one single instance—the time that elapsed between 1914 and 1939, and I for one would hesitate to generalise from one observation. If one goes further back in history: in the Napoleonic wars young men in France had been blooded over and over again but were still willing to go to war. They liked war in some real sense. In America, on the other hand, twenty-five or thirty

228

years after the Civil War there was no sign of any generational unrest, any thirst for a fresh conflict coming to the surface.

In any case, there is, in your proposition, an implicit belief that the human race dislikes war. This is not quite true. Certain classes and certain societies do like it. There is an element of truth in your assertion that young men tend to forget the experiences of their fathers if they are not taught history, and in the modern American education system they are certainly not taught it. So a whole modern generation has grown up free from the kind of restraints which constitute, if you will, the wisdom of history. However, this generation has been taught that war does not pay and this may furnish a corrective.

URBAN: This vanishing sense of history is perhaps the most alarming aspect of the mismanagement of education especially, as you say, in America where the sense of history has never been very strong. The sophisticated attitude is to ask 'problem-solving' questions and hope for problem-solving answers in political science and sociology. History is for the antiquarian—a collector's item for people retired from the serious business of living. One wonders, then, whether it isn't a misnomer to talk of our information-dispensing system as 'education': if our young people are not expected to know about the past, if they are led to believe that their situation is unprecedented, their predicament unique—what, apart from pot, is the mind-expanding stuff they are getting at our schools and universities?

KAHN: It is very clear that the situations are not unique. The ideology these young people have is a rejection of all 'irrational' restraints, all 'non-functional' structures and, to a remarkable degree, of all reality-testing; part of that renunciation is the rejection of history. What 'irrational' and 'non-functional' are meant to convey in their vocabulary is not readily apparent unless one sets these words against a non-existing or highly superficial knowledge of history and an astonishing unconcern with any serious literature.

These young people think of man as infinitely malleable

229

and infinitely good. Now, if you start from this premise of man's innocence, you have little use for history which tells a very different story. Man's history is not a story of his innocence. This almost instinctive rejection of the past is then reinforced by certain educational trends both in America and in North-west Europe: the emphasis on the social sciences as practical aids in social planning, the prestige of scientific methodology, the technicisation of knowledge all militate against the study of history.

URBAN: Isn't there, at least in Europe, a subtle rebellion in all this against two attitudes of mind which may well need rebelling against? First, there is the professional historians' high-handed dismissal of contemporary history as mere journalism. At the University of Strasbourg, for instance, contemporary history starts (or has started until recently) with 1792, which makes a mockery of contemporary history. Second, there is a feeling, especially among the keen young 'Europeans', that too much history—and history has usually meant national history—distracts from European unification. That the independent histories which have been commissioned by UNESCO and other international bodies have not been too successful, does not invalidate the suspicion with which the old type of histories were and are still being treated by the younger generation. They have a lot to be suspicious about.

KAHN: This may well be true for Western Europe but in America the rejection of history is much more spontaneous and much more naïve. We have to allow for man's wilful ignorance, the durability of his fantasies and his indolence. The intelligent attitude for the young generation would be to say that all history is contemporary history and to build up their case from there. But for that they would first have to read a great deal of history, which is hard work, and even then, the finest sieve of intellectual prejudices could not prevent some of the lessons of history from percolating through, and that is a risk they would surely not want to take. Rebellion must often start from a certain ignorance, wilful or real. Dealing with facts is a high-risk form of activity. It often debilitates.

URBAN: Do you see in this ignorance some constructive preparation for religious experience? Are we faced here with the mystics' 'dark night of the soul'—some mortification of the practical mind as a first step to a higher vision?

KAHN: There is a conscious attempt to maintain the qualities of childhood in adulthood: the directness, spontaneity and creativity of the child are now valued and encouraged, at least by the *avant-garde*. Like most Americans, I like children, and I like these child-like qualities unless, of course, Frankie is pushing forty and his spontaneity is a form of self-indulgence, a shedding of inhibitions set by responsibility.

Now it seems to me there are some forms of religious disposition which are constructive: reverence, idealism, altruism, perspective, openness are healthy forms of religious sentiment and you will find some of these in the Hippy movement. On the negative side you have naïve mysticism, passivity, unworldliness, fadism, superstition, and these are mixed up with the more constructive attitudes. Do they add up to a 'religion'? I don't think so. At best they are an unstructured aspiration for religious experience, a 'religion' without a tenet, without a book, without authority. The religious impulse is there but it is overlaid with fantasy and self-indulgence. However, the search is taken seriously and some of these young men and women will probably find a religion to which they can hold on for life. It is hard to say what forms it might take. At the moment we are faced with a variety of vaguely experimenting cults. That is all. But then Christianity too was a cult at one time—and, if you are a Roman, it is hard to tell whether Christianity is going to make it. In fact, it seemed very unlikely that it would.

URBAN: I should be slightly reluctant to bring early Christianity and the Hippy movement under one umbrella. For one

231

thing, the majority of our young rebels suffer from a very negative sort of metaphysical discomfort: they don't like the world as it is and they want to opt out of it. If this were accompanied by the saintly life, the abnegation of human desires, the mortification of the soul and body, they might command our sympathy. But they are hitting the bottle (or marijuana as the case may be) *and* they are sanctimonious about it. It is an unconvincing combination and has, on the face of it, little to do with religion. On the more positive side of the metaphysical complaint there is this quest for—well, I would not call it religion but the paraphernalia of religion and the emotional satisfactions of spiritual commitment. But it is hardly more than that, except in the case of a very small and intellectually ambitious minority who are looking for that very unoriginal combination: the irrational aura of religion filled in with a practice consistent with rational theory. I am saying 'unoriginal' because it has been tried before, by the eclecticism, for instance, of Chinese religious reformers in the 19th Century who tried to fuse the most elevating aspects of aesthetic experience into a religion without giving any thought to the supernatural.

KAHN: Well, whether a religion is religion without a concept of God and the supernatural would lead us far from our subject. The fact is that the retreat from the supernatural has been characteristic of the religious experience of both Protestants and Catholics in Northwestern Europe and Latin America for most of the 20th Century and particularly in the last fifteen years: the young generation are continuing in that tradition. Everywhere in the world, except in Eastern Europe, the churches have suffered a sharp erosion of the articles of faith. People, including the younger sections of the clergy, are more interested in religious humanism than in dogmatism. That our would-be-religious are muddle-headed is beyond doubt, and that they think they are breaking fresh ground is due to their ignorance of history. But that ignorance is sincerely held— which offers one little consolation, or *a* little consolation, depending on one's sympathies.

232

URBAN: Why has the appeal of religion not suffered a similar decline in Eastern Europe? 'Faith thrives under oppression' is a popular belief, but is it true?

KAHN: I think it is. Almost all the erosion is due to affluence and safety and a certain lack of reality-testing in excessively secure environments. I don't think it is a natural development, for man's excessive security is not a natural state for us to live in. I'm reminded of some of the South Pacific cultures which suffered from an exceptionally high degree of social feather-bedding. They lacked external constraints and had to compensate for them with totems and taboos, that is, with *internal* constraints of a religious kind.

URBAN: So religion is invoked when security is eroded, which is Marx's position: if you are suffering, you need hope and consolation and that is what religion offers. Those who *can* walk need no crutches.

KAHN: There is something in that but I would put it in almost exactly the opposite way: in the post-industrial civilisation of America, for instance, people live in a highly artificial climate; the first effect of living in an artificial environment is sensory deprivation and the second effect is value deprivation. I am assuming, as you will see, that the quest for a religious type of commitment is one of the *données* of human nature in much the same way as the wish for natural sensory experience is. Now one aspect of the value deprivation produced by an over-protected and unnatural environment is the disappearance of religious values. I will readily concede that in Eastern Europe the continued strength of the churches may well be due to a combination of poverty and a wish to challenge the established institutions of the state which happen to be materialistic and anti-religious. But I suspect that the affluent sons and daughters of the new class in Russia are irreligious in the same way as the affluent in the United States.

233

URBAN: I take it you would agree then that faith thrives under poverty and oppression but perhaps for the more general reason that poverty and oppression make demands on you while over-protection and a state of satiety do not.

KAHN: I think that is a fair way of putting it, but I would add that the demands have to be real demands that challenge you at the existential joints of your mind or body. A baseball game, even a moon landing, are vicarious forms of challenge for the vast majority of people.

URBAN: Aren't we then inexorably set for a hopeless confusion of values, for the things most dearly wished for by West Europeans are precisely the same comforts, the same armchair pleasures, the same artificial environments which you deplore because of the effect they have had in America?

KAHN: It is not for me to make a moral judgement. All I can say is that *if* Western Europe follows the American example, the erosion of values, with the whole syndrome of attendant problems, will also follow. But perhaps one is allowed to be slightly cynical: England has shown, though I would say much against her will, that social planning, socialised medicine, subsidised housing, old age pensions, etc. can go together with a real sense of poverty, squalid housing, low morale and frustrations that should suffice to keep everyone on edge for a long time to come. The challenges, if you will, are there, but whether the British people will want to rise to them is another matter.

URBAN: The third view on which I should like to hear your comment is the 'spoilt child' type of philosophy. It has many spokesmen but Keynes is perhaps the best known and most convincing. Writing in 1930, at the worst time of the depression, Keynes addressed himself to a problem which is already with us today and will be very much more with us by the end of the century: when poverty and insecurity have been eliminated from our lives, will we not get up to worse forms of mischief, because we have too much time on our hands, than we did when the daily grind consumed most of our energies? Keynes put it like this: '... the economic problem, the struggle for subsistence, always has been hitherto the primary, the most pressing problem of the human race. If the economic problem is solved, mankind will be deprived of its traditional purpose. Will this be a benefit? ... I think with some dread of the re-adjustment of the habits and instincts of the ordinary man, bred into him for countless generations, which he may be asked to discard within a few decades ... for the first time since his creation man will be faced with his real, his permanent prob-lem—how to use his freedom from pressing economic cares, how to occupy his leisure ...'

KAHN: The problem is grossly overstated. Boredom, or rather the thought of it, is an upper-class affliction. As I have said, peasants around the world have a great deal of leisure; farming occupies no more than about six hundred hours of their work-ing time each year—the rest of their time is free, and they fill it rather well. It is true that most of the time is filled with rituals, with religion, with games which are 'out' in the modern Ameri-can sense. But I think they may be coming back. As far as young people are concerned, we notice that when they are given a year's sabbatical, they have the time of their lives: they visit relatives, they repair their houses, they go fishing, they play games. Time does not hang heavily on their hands.

Also, I would deny completely the remark of Dennis Gabor that, in a post-industrial culture, the relatively untrained in-dividual with a low IQ has difficulty in getting a job. Everything would seem to point the other way. A rather high-powered U.S. commission made a study of this problem. They were going through the evidence with a very fine comb indeed and could find no sign of the low-priced occupations disappearing. On the contrary, the jobs are there but there aren't enough people to fill them. The hardest kinds of work to eliminate are personal services—I'm talking about the elevator operator, the baby sitter, the maid, the cook. Those are, it is true, disappearing in America and Northwestern Europe, but it isn't because the demand isn't high. It's because there is no supply. People can make better money elsewhere. In Scandinavia, if you get off at a small airport, there is nobody to carry your bags for you. If you are sick, the pilot will do it, but you can't tip him for he is making more money than you are.

Now Gabor is absolutely right in saying that the technology of the coming decades will provide work for only a smallish, and shrinking, part of the working population. In the post-industrial civilisation industry becomes a small part of the social effort, but as far as we can tell there will continue to be an inexhaustible demand for people in the services, in maintenance types of work and the like. The problem is a rather different one : because there is a scarcity of people willing to go into these service industries, the cost rises sky high.

URBAN: There would still remain a problem though. Modern technology is making it possible to diminish the amount of time spent to secure the necessaries of life. In less than a hundred years the working week has been halved and by the end of the century it may be halved again, leaving the average office worker with twenty out of every twenty-four hours on his hands. Now people like Paul Lafargue and Bertrand Russell could see nothing but benefit accruing to mankind if men could only be persuaded to be idle, but the idleness *they* had in mind wasn't the kind that would worry a Keynes, for they were convinced that man would put his leisure time to constructive use and be happy in the process. But would he? Russell, for instance, says *In Praise of Idleness* that in a world where no one is compelled to work for more than four hours a day 'there will be happiness and a joy of life, instead of frayed nerves, weariness and dyspepsia.... Since men will not be tired in their spare time, they will not demand only such amusements as are passive and vapid.... Ordinary men and women, having the opportunity of a happy life, will become more kindly and less persecuting and less inclined to view others with suspicion. The taste for war will die out, partly for this reason, and partly

because it will involve long and severe work for all. Good nature
... is the result of ease and security, not of a life of arduous
struggle.'

Well, one could take these statements point by point and
show how more leisure has come to mean more television, a
phenomenal growth in cardiac diseases and mental illness. In
the U.K. today, almost one in every two (forty-five per cent)
hospital beds is occupied by a mental patient. One could show
how greater wealth and more security have done nothing to
depress the crime rate—rather the opposite seems to have
happened—and one could also show that man's aggressiveness
has not noticeably decreased because he works less. The interesting point is that Russell wrote these optimistic sentences in
1932, only two years after Keynes had expressed his fears.

KAHN: Well, the comparison is stimulating. My first comment would be that we are faced here with men with very
different intellectual temperaments. Keynes took a more pessimistic view of human nature than Russell and, on balance, if we
take 1930 as our starting point, his fears have been borne out
by facts, whereas Russell's hopes have remained largely unfulfilled. Of course, it is as well to remember that these are not
forecasts in the modern sense. In Russell's case it is also true to
say there was an element of propaganda in his prediction: by
asserting that, unburdened by excessive labour, man is a
basically good and happy animal, he was hoping that his
prophecy would be self-fulfilling.

It is pretty clear from what we have experienced between
1930 and 1971 that—by the rather elevated standards of a
Bertrand Russell—the great mass of mankind will not make intelligent or creative use of its spare time. The vapidities and
trivia will be with us in the future, and man's good nature will
not necessarily increase with the growth of his wealth and
security. It may decrease. At the same time one ought to bear
in mind that the people who indulge in these vulgarities and
spawn the trivia will find them both interesting and satisfying.
So they may be happy according to their own lights, and per-

haps we ought not to quarrel with them for having those lights rather than others of which we may more readily approve.

However, all this is very different from saying that the chances of large-scale war are on the increase—and that was the starting point of this discussion. For the reasons I have already mentioned, nuclear war, though not ruled out by the nature of nuclear technology, seems a less plausible and less practical proposition than it is generally thought to be.

URBAN: But it is—is it not— the balance of terror that makes it an ultimately impractical proposition.

KAHN: It is not the balance of terror by itself that makes war and war-like crises unlikely. After all, Hitler used the balance of terror between Germany and the Western powers to violate the integrity of his smaller neighbours. The balance of terror has offensive and defensive uses. In our situation the point to remember is that the nations which possess nuclear weapons appear to be tolerably satisfied with the *status quo* and are unwilling to rock the boat by trying to exploit the balance of terror for offensive purposes.

URBAN: I appreciate your insistence that the balance of terror makes it difficult for the smaller evils to assert themselves. Yet, going by the examples of Korea, Vietnam and the repeated upheavals in Eastern Europe, it is a question worth asking: what are the kind of conflicts that may produce war-like action in our time? If, as you imply, there is nothing congenitally war-like in modern society, nothing, at least, that we can pinpoint and measure with our present tools of analysis, what are the sources of future conflict—small or large—most likely to be?

KAHN: In Africa and Asia we have to expect nationalism to be the main source of conflict. Nation-states are made of blood. People who have not yet made their nation-states will fight. The four divided states are clear-cut cases of the possibility of war. Their conflicts are not going to be easily resolved peacefully.

URBAN: Including Germany?

KAHN: Yes. We tend to think of these countries as each con-
stituting two separate states, but the citizens of these countries
don't think of them in that way. In Eastern Europe, too, the
problem of nationalism could cause wars without any trouble
at all. Then there is the sensitive question of investing in the
Third World. The underdeveloped countries need Western
investment but they resent it when they get it. Even the
Canadians, who are far from being underdeveloped and have
now been made rich through American investment, resent
American capital. That kind of resentment gets a great deal
worse when investments are made in a North–South context
where racial and cultural factors exacerbate the psychological
climate in which the two parties operate.

As far as the large and highly developed countries are concerned, war may occur out of miscalculation. In American
society for instance there is a lack of reality-testing which can
get us into trouble. Our people just aren't careful enough in
foreign policy. They can allow situations to occur which should
never have arisen. How does this come about? Well, there is a
refusal to face problems in time. There is a lack of seriousness.
But there is no law in any of this, there is no mechanism that I
know of. Perhaps it is in the nature of democracy that foresight
is at a discount, especially when the things foreseen demand unpleasant and unpopular measures in the short term.

In America you also get the problem of emotionalism at high
levels of decision-making. There is a piquancy in this if you
compare it with the way decisions are arrived at in the Soviet
Union. In Russia, as far as we know, decision-making by committee still obtains. Committees have a built-in rationality, and
it should be easy enough for a responsible leader to stand up in
committee and say that such and such a course of action might
hurt the achievements of Communism, that Communism is too
important to throw away in a fit of anger and so forth. In
America, national policies tend to be conducted on a more im-
pulsive basis; this may be an over-reaction to the ordinary

American's lack of emotion in his private life, or a refusal to believe that anything America does in her foreign affairs can physically hurt her except all-out nuclear war. Or else it may be a sign of political immaturity. Possibly all of these.

However this may be, there is, on all sides, a very great reluctance to fight a modern war. No large country is going to be rushed into one. People would have to be forced into it screaming, and for extremely good reasons. This means there should always be time and elbow room to back down.

URBAN: Khrushchev's emotional approach to the Cuban problem would not seem to confirm what you say about Soviet caution. He put his missiles in Cuba, very nearly provoking war with the U.S., primarily to spite the Americans. There does not seem to have been any committee decision.

KAHN: This is true, but it is also true that he backed down and was later dismissed, and one of the main factors which appear to have hastened his dismissal was his irresponsible action over Cuba. I am not saying that the Russians are always rational but they have more to lose than the Americans or any other country. Putting Russia at risk is risking all the works of Communism throughout the world. The U.S., if she lost in a large-scale war, would be losing as a nation, not as the seat of a papacy. And in Soviet official eyes the survival of Muscovy *is* identical with the survival of Communism. In America and the Western world we have reason to have slightly more faith in the durability of our system, imperfect as it is.

URBAN: War is a great catalyst both within nations and between nations and races. You make a very important point in your book by showing how Russia's defeat by Japan in the 1905 war, and more recently China's possession of the atomic bomb, profoundly changed the non-white races' estimate of their strength and self respect. The 1905 war demonstrated that a formerly backward Asian country could master the West's technology and use it to defeat the West. At the time, this came as a great shock to the Western world and especially to Russia. But 1905 showed only the tip of the iceberg. With Japan's spectacular advance to great power status perhaps we are about to have even greater shocks. Writing as late as 1936 Trotsky was still able to say that the 'brutal exploitation' of the peasants in Japan (he also mentioned China and India) 'never produced an industrial tempo remotely approaching that of the Soviet Union'. Well, today there would be beaming faces in the Kremlin if the rate of Soviet industrial development were anywhere near that of Japan. How do you see Japan's position in the industrial and power league, and what are the lessons, if any, that the Soviet Union might learn from the Japanese example?

KAHN: My estimate is that some time in the '80s the Japanese will pass the Russians and become the second largest economic power in the world. This will be a very great shock to the Russian Communists, intellectuals and the managerial class. It was interesting to see that when Japan passed West Germany about three or four years ago, and Britain even before that, nobody got upset. I think they will get very upset in the Soviet Union.

URBAN: Why do you think they will get so upset?

KAHN: For one thing, the Russians are great chauvinists and the memories of 1905 still rankle. For another, there is an important ideological issue here. The Russians didn't make their revolution and suffer for fifty years to become number three.

URBAN: What you are saying is that Stalin, the camps, the terror, forced industrialisation, the extermination of the kulaks were all unnecessary because the Japanese have achieved all the Russians have, and much more, without any of the Russians' terrible sacrifices.

KAHN: I wouldn't put it quite that way for some of the features in the traditions of the two nations are not comparable. Stalin, the terror, the camps, the starvation in the Ukraine, the poverty were unnecessary in the sense that between 1890 and 1913 economic growth in the Czarist empire was extremely rapid, and I suspect that if the Russians had never had their revolution but had tolerably competent management, they would be materially as well off today as they are. There would have been every reason for Russian governments to encourage growth. There would have been a slow evolution on democratic lines and probably a bourgeois liberal revolution, which might have been a failure for various reasons. Of course it is possible that, in an authoritarian type of reaction to that revolution, economic growth might have stopped for a while and Russia would have marked time rather like Spain and Portugal. But it is most unlikely. By the time the First World War broke out Russia had been launched as an industrial power. But whether, if the revolution had never taken place, Russia would have achieved the egalitarianism which Soviet citizens enjoy, nominally at least, it is hard to say. My personal guess is that the inequalities would have been greater, certainly on paper, but that the average Russian would have suffered less than he has suffered under the nominal egalitarianism of the Soviet system.

Now if my thesis is correct, I should imagine the Ukraine would have done especially well because Russian governments would have had reason to encourage Ukrainian growth in sensible ways. There would have been a large European participation in Russian development which would not have hurt Russia. The growth-rate would have doubled with very much less sacrifice. And the misinvestments, due to faulty concepts of centralisation and dogmatism, would have been avoided. There is a lot of misinvestment in the U.S. too, but the economic ruin which misinvestment has wrought in the Soviet Union is beyond compare.

The parallel with Japan is incomplete in another sense too. The Japanese have shown that by taking their own culture and adapting Western, industrial civilisation to it, they can outperform the West. It doesn't mean that the Russians could have done it—this is a peculiarly Japanese development. But it does show that there are certain Capitalist devices and institutions which are tremendously efficient in producing economic growth and that the Japanese can use these without giving up the characteristics of being Japanese. I would say that Chinese culture as a whole—and that includes Japanese—is very well adapted to modern, industrial systems. We must not go by what we see in mainland China where the government itself sabotages a Western type of economic growth. But everywhere else in the world the Chinese are going to the top, whether they are individuals as in America, or ethnic groups like those in Hong Kong, Formosa and Singapore, or groups of derivative Chinese culture such as those in Korea and Vietnam.

URBAN: What is there in Chinese culture that makes the Japanese and Chinese adapt Western technology so easily? It could surely not be Confucianism.

KAHN: Confucianism can be a handicap unless it is used cleverly. The Japanese have been able to turn paternalism, communal loyalty, filial piety into a driving force for economic development. Both the Chinese and the Japanese have a great deal of family pride, a family willingness to make great sacrifices for education, a family willingness to save, to invest, to work very long hours, a real talent for finance, an exceptionally good mechanical ability and, in general, a whole set of qualities which make them adept at modern, industrial civilisation. You can see this at work in America where, apart from the Scotch Presbyterians and the Jews, the Chinese and the Japanese are the most successful.

Now the Russian ethos is entirely different. The traditional concern of Russian literature is a mystical kind of preoccupation with man's estate, and the typical Russian character is often thought to be enshrined in Goncharov's character Oblomov—a hero who is as lazy as he is ineffective. It is very possible that the Russian skill does not lie in the field of industrial culture. I'm not saying this in any pejorative sense for the life-style and values of industrial culture leave a great deal to be desired. Be this as it may, industrialisation, modernisation, organisation, efficiency, are not qualities in which the Russian people generally excel, although there are, of course, special fields where, through a heavy concentration of scarce resources, outstanding results are produced. Soviet missile technology is one example.

URBAN: It is all the more intriguing that, in the world Communist movement, the fountainhead of political Messianism is not millennial Russia but China with its down to earth, Confucian tradition.

KAHN: This is a recent development. Under Stalin there was a good deal of Messianism in the Soviet message. Peking's militant evangelism, on the other hand, is entirely bound up with Mao's personality, and Mao's stance isn't really very distant from the Confucian ideals, whatever the language of Chinese propaganda. The cultural revolution is about forging the right kind of person—a human being that is selfless, dedicated, hard working, communal and respectful of the right kind of authority—and all this is in harmony with classical Chinese tradition.

URBAN: You are saying that the Russian and Japanese examples are not fully comparable. Would you say that Japan's experience might be more relevant to the Czech, Hungarian, Polish or Rumanian economies? These countries are making brave efforts to distance themselves from the Soviet model.

KAHN: No, I think they are not comparable either, partly because these are small countries, and partly because their backgrounds are very different from the kind of traditions which Japan had when she began industrialising. But they are comparable with the West because, with the exception of Moravia, Bohemia and parts of East Germany, Eastern Europe belongs to the underdeveloped estate of the Western world. Now, if you ask me: 'who is doing best in the West today?', I would say it's those parts of the West which were left behind in the industrial revolution: Spain, Portugal, Southern Italy, Greece and the European parts of Latin America which are generally growing at the regional rate of over ten per cent per annum. And if you were to tell me that the East European countries would be doing well economically if they were allowed to abandon the Communist model, but at the very least break away from the Soviet economic prototype, I would absolutely agree. Rumania is doing it *under* Communism but away from Moscow's supervision; the rest could do it faster and better without Communism. They could avoid the kind of misinvestments which follow from the Soviet example: building a cement factory where there is no sand, or a steel works where the coal has to be transported from thousands of miles away, or using high-cost wood to make high-cost paper which you then sell cheaply, and, more generally, undertaking a lot of irrational industrial and agricultural operations for which the population has to pay an inordinate price in terms of better living standards foregone and the oppressive aura of an unpopular, command economy.

URBAN: If there were an institute such as yours in the Soviet Union, could it conceivably drive Soviet planning, Soviet investment policies in more rational and more efficient directions?

KAHN: If such an institute lasted I think it would entirely change Russia. But let me point out to you it is most unlikely that such an institute would be permitted to operate in the U.S.S.R. In fact, you can't have my kind of institute anywhere in Europe, not just Russia. The European countries can't even have a RAND Corporation although the benefits of having one are now widely recognised. Why is this? Well, there is in European institutions a strong streak of conservatism. There is a government unwillingness, both financial and political, to support this kind of speculative, independent, free-wheeling and basically critical research which is also, and has to be, of uncertain quality. Then there is government compartmentalisation and government secrecy, both of which militate against a European RAND or a European Hudson enterprise. All this goes with added emphasis for the Soviet Union where conservatism is even much stronger than elsewhere in Europe and the secrecy much heavier. Add to this the ideological objection to any research that would escape official guidance and that would not base itself on Marxist analysis, and you can see why the Soviet Union would provide about *the* most inhospitable setting for a RAND type of research institute. Now the Russians have planning organisations of great skill; in fact, they were the initiators of large-scale planning. But when one looks at the results, one can't escape the feeling that these organisations either cannot or are not allowed to think very hard and with any degree of sophistication.

URBAN: Let me go back to Japan and ask you: why has the Japanese example not had a greater impact on the Afro-Asian countries? Why did they all opt for 'Socialism' of one kind or another rather than 'Japanism'? If, as we are often told, Afro-Asian 'Socialism' is about industrialisation and modernisation, surely Japan rather than the Soviet Union should be the right model.

KAHN: As a matter of fact, from 1905 to about World War I, Japan was a source of inspiration for these underdeveloped nations; they saw that Japan had beaten the Russian empire. But that disappeared when Communism came in—it took the action away from Japan, so to speak. Japan suddenly lacked charisma, mainly perhaps because Japan's advance was not decked out with ideology. The Japanese didn't claim that their industrial achievements had universal application or that it represented a higher stage of development in man's history. Now underdeveloped countries *like* this sort of assurance and the Japanese didn't give it to them. There was also another reason. From the very start of Westernisation there has been a dichotomy in Japan between the government and the intellectuals who tended to downgrade the importance of industrialisation and modernisation. And because these intellectuals were Japan's main channel of communication with the Third World, the underdeveloped countries hadn't enough convincing information to look to Japan for inspiration. Today there is an ideologically inspired, systematic belittling of Japanese achievement by Western intellectuals and Japanese intellectuals alike. They are uneasy about recognising the success of the elasticity of Capitalism, especially in a non-Western milieu. This is a form of wilful myopia which has to be regretted because it is very damaging to the developing countries.

URBAN: I should have thought that hard-pressed nation-builders would be a little more pragmatic than that and take their lessons from wherever they could take them cheaply and efficiently. If an African 'Socialist' government wants to cut corners, Japan has much to offer that no other country has.

KAHN: The Afro-Asians have a lot to learn from Japan, but they cannot learn the entire Japanese lesson. Japanese industrialisation is more than a hundred years old and, as I have already tried to point out, it rests on a particular adaptation of the Japanese character to Western, Capitalist institutions. It is a perfect example of how a non-Western country can use every bit of its resources, but also of how it can carefully modify, submerge or control those aspects of the national character which would get in the way. Now if one thing is characteristic of most of the Afro-Asian governments today it is that they simply haven't that capability. The Chinese, sharing a basic civilisation with Japan, are the only other people who could do as well at the Japanese, but there Mao's 'more red than expert' philosophy has erected a barrier to progress. Of course, the Maoist position is often contradictory. Some official Chinese argue that you can't beat the price system for allocations, but at the same time they feel there is something indecent, un-Communist in using the price system for *incentives*. So the Japanese example has not found effective followers, and I feel that it is in the nature of Japan's rise to great-power status that its example should be very difficult to imitate.

URBAN: You seem to be a great believer in national, perhaps even racial, characteristics which, as you say, predispose people

247

to do certain things rather better, or worse, than others. First, you tied in Japan's industrial progress with certain elements in Japanese tradition, then you said that the Russians as a nation were somehow ill-equipped to run an industrial civilisation with any degree of efficiency, and a few weeks ago in London you said that the British people lacked the kind of ambition which leads to competitive economic achievement, because in England success went socially unrecognised and financially unrewarded. Do you believe, then, that nations have permanent characteristics and that social scientists are justified in building these into their analyses as given factors?

KAHN: From the point of view of cultural characteristics very much so. There is a remarkable degree of accuracy in many of the clichés people use about their own nation and about other nations. The latter are usually unfriendly stereotypes, but if you get behind them you begin to see that there are qualities which give rise to these clichés.

I don't think national characteristics are genetic; they are generally formed before you are ten or twelve, but everything reinforces them from that point on at least as long as you are in the same milieu. You can take an Italian boy of twelve, bring him to America and so transform him that, if he goes back to his native village when he is twenty, he will be thought of as *the* American for the rest of his life. The specificity of a nation is a lasting and stubborn quality, and while it changes, it changes very slowly; and a political scientist would be doing himself a disservice if he left these characteristics out of account. Many otherwise intelligent people do not like to admit that, taking a cross-section of a population, there are differences of taste, temperament and ability among nations. There is a fear, which is perhaps exaggerated, that the implications of recognising such differences may prove politically explosive. But you can't wish these problems away by denying their existence.

URBAN: You are saying that national peculiarities are not inherited but that they are largely formed before the age of ten

248

or twelve. Yet, a minute ago you said that Americans of Scotch Presbyterian, Jewish and Chinese origin are doing better than other Americans. You would appear to recognise, among American-born adults, certain ethnic characteristics which Americanisation does not seem to have overcome and by which you can judge them.

KAHN: The differences exist; however, they are not due to race but to certain similarities in cultural traditions, such as the great stress laid on education, thrift, frugality and solidarity in the family, which these groups share and which make them successful in the context we have been discussing.

URBAN: If one assumes, as I tend to, that there is a connection between industrial accomplishment and making war efficiently, would you say that there are national characteristics to be read into the fact that the Germans and the Japanese made war well and are also the world's leaders in industrial growth since the end of the war?

KAHN: I would not argue that making war and industrialisation were identical qualities, but there is, clearly, an overlap which is important. Modern war requires organisation, devotion, sustained effort and sustained discipline in addition, of course, to an excellent industrial sub-structure. So any nation that has these, and is large enough to matter, is in a position to be extremely dangerous when it makes war and extremely competitive when it puts its shoulder to peacetime pursuits in industry or elsewhere.

URBAN: How would you apply this to England? One could argue the British have done very well in the war, or one could argue that they have not done so well, or would perhaps not have done so well without American help. Today they are certainly doing badly as an industrial nation.

KAHN: Well, I'm an Anglophile but it would be useless to deny that the problem in England is the disappearance of the war-making type of qualities which helped her in 1939–45 but have been absent since: there is simply not enough dedication, devotion, intensity, work-orientation, achievement-orientation or admiration for success. These are not the pleasantest qualities to live with, but they are essential if England is to stay competitive with her commercial rivals. Now the curious thing is that the English live quite well—well according to their past yardsticks—well enough to justify the Conservatives' election slogan in 1960 'You've never had it so good'. England is decaying economically compared to the other large powers: Japan, Germany, France and China, yet British economic conditions continue to improve. The trouble is that the British economy continues to grow at a mere two per cent annually which is as much as it ever achieved over a sustained period in British history, and the result is that, of the five economically comparable powers, Britain has now been overtaken by Germany and Japan and may soon be overtaken by France and China too. In 1945 Britain was economically the strongest of these five countries. If we extrapolate from current trends, in the year 2000 Britain will have fallen from the wealthiest of the five powers to the poorest, even though her GNP will have grown by five per cent.

URBAN: Has Britain changed her national character since 1945?

KAHN: That a nation is successful in winning a war may, but does not have to, mean that she will also make a success of peace and reconstruction. Britain has made no peacetime use of the qualities which made her win the war. One may look upon this as a sign of maturity and wisdom or as a sign of national demoralisation. I would say that, from the British point of view, there is nothing in the world that would jolt the British public into changing its habits. A nation judges its current state by its past experience and not by those of foreign countries, and going by Britain's past experience it is still true to say 'You've never had it so good'. That others have it a lot better and that British exports will have to compete with nations that are more achievement-oriented, is not readily appreciated, not, at least, at grass-root levels where it really matters.

There are, naturally, many excellent firms in England which are as good as any in the world. It is the average performance in England that is low, and England's prospects aren't helped by the fact that the country has not been particularly well governed since 1945. It hasn't been as badly governed as some, but in the economic field big and expensive mistakes have been made, and it is difficult to ask a mature nation to make enormous sacrifices to correct them.

URBAN: You say in your book, *The Year 2000*, that although Fascism and Communism are both discredited today and out of fashion, there is no guarantee that totalitarian solutions will not spring up again in the coming thirty years. What specific forms might totalitarianism take if we discount the obvious possibility of some relapse into straightforward dictatorships of the visionary and moral kind? In other words, how far is society even in the democratic countries likely to be totalitarian in the sense that mass society is bound to impose stringent standards of discipline, uniformity and predictability?

KAHN: Mass society requires no such thing as uniformity. This is an intellectual invention. The idea that the big factory can force you to consume the things it wants to produce is just not true. Big factories are often more flexible than small ones. They can change more readily because many of them have better capitalisation and better management. Generally speaking modern Capitalist industries respond to market pressures most effectively. Of course it is true that the individual—and especially the intellectual—finds himself oppressed by mass society. The television repairman cheats him, his car is badly serviced, he becomes a mere number in too many ways for comfort. All this is true, but it's not necessarily dangerous. Danger usually comes from other forces.

Now this is a very hard thing for me to say—ten years ago I

couldn't have said it, five years ago I began to think it—but the knowledge and technology that are now becoming available are very hard for society to absorb, so we may well need an index of forbidden knowledge. There is a whole list of things that are either causing or may cause serious problems in the next ten or twenty years. Not all should be on the index, obviously, but there are a great many that should. A good deal of genetic engineering looks to me as though one might be better off without it—sex determination you are better off without, cosmetology is not going to make anybody happy. You will be able to design your children in the next twenty to twenty-five years; I doubt that that will increase human happiness, and there are many other examples of dysfunctional knowledge that seems likely to be available.

URBAN: How do you design an index that would guarantee the freedom of research *and* suppress the unwanted initiatives? Who is going to be judge and how will you enforce the judgement?

KAHN: This is a problem we are looking at. At the moment the index is just a phrase, I don't know what we mean by it. One thing I do know, though, is that society should not be satisfied with a scientist's vow similar to the Hippocratic oath. Scientists have been poor judges of the consequences of scientific issues. They do not raise the right questions or raise them intelligently. Their self-discipline might leave us worse off than we are today.

Well, one tentative pattern for an index which we may want to work from is the controls the U.S. Government exercises over nuclear and missile technology. We have certain weapons technologies which our adversaries know but which we do not give to the French or the British or the Germans. So in effect we keep certain types of knowledge secret from our own friends because the arms race is a danger to humanity. That fits roughly what we mean by an index. One should be able to do the same with physics and biology but, of course, this will need a great deal of circumspection and international cooperation of an intricate nature. Whatever the intellectual dangers of an index, they pall in comparison with the danger of not having one. A society that hasn't the moral capacity to absorb new knowledge without putting itself in mortal peril has to have restraints imposed upon it.

URBAN: I can see that the unrestrained growth of technology can be a danger to society but that, in itself, would not speak for a totalitarian society.

KAHN: It most surely would if you don't restrain the spread of knowledge in some way. Genetic engineering has in it the makings of totalitarianism the like of which the world has never seen.

But there is also another source of totalitarianism and that is the New Left with its contempt for bourgeois boredom, with its proneness to intolerance, violence and total solutions. Its attitude to the middle classes is identical with that of the Fascists. They use the same language.

Now much of the effectiveness of the New Left is due to the low morale of the Western democracies. We have forgotten how to stand up for our rights; we have lost the sense for recognising central policy issues. There is this terrible lack of reality-testing of which I have already spoken. In America there is also a permanent crisis of leadership. There is simply not enough wisdom in high places to cope with the issues as they arise. It takes sensible people to run a country; they've got to know what they are doing, and my impression is that very often they don't. It is almost statistically established in the U.S. that from the early sixties to the present day there has been an inverse correlation between education and common-sense in politics. This is a terrible remark. It wasn't true before. I hope it will not be true for too long.

The silliness of American society has become extremely widespread. You can see it in the way the law-and-order issue has been distorted. Law-and-order is supposed to be anti-

Negro, but it was never used in that sense by responsible people. We have in America a great many cities where it is unsafe to go out at night or even during the hours of daylight. The call for law and order was raised because people wanted to make the cities safe; that's all. There was no backlash against the Negro; in fact, if you look at it closely, the slogan expressed the grave dissatisfaction of the white lower-middle class American with the white upper-middle class American, the white, educated class, if you like. Everyone in America had a very clear understanding of this except the intellectual press and the representatives of the foreign press in the U.S. Someone aptly remarked in one of our papers 'Is it true that the U.S. has raised the silliest educated class in history? Not quite, but almost.'

Now it is in this atmosphere of self-deprecation, uncertain values, low morale that the New Left can make excellent headway and totalitarianism again becomes a danger.

URBAN: In other words we are faced with a moral issue rather than anything one could mechanically attribute to the way in which modern society is developing.

KAHN: That is so. The danger comes from the breakdown of moral standards and authority. A mass man *has* been created, but he is not the result of the size of society or any uniformities predicated by the production process, but of the removal of all taboos and charismas.

URBAN: And what is the answer to the moral problem?

KAHN: Morality, obviously, perhaps a new morality, perhaps the rejuvenation of the old. Now there is a lot of talk of change in Western culture. I can't see the need for fundamental change. I can see, though, that Europe as a whole deals with these issues a lot better than the U.S.

URBAN: You say in your book that Americans are to Europeans what Romans were to Greeks.

KAHN: Yes, and I would go further and say that we'd be happier in America if the Greek ethos could assert itself in America. We need to be Athenised. Greece was conquered by Rome and Rome, in turn, intellectually conquered by Greece. Someone in America has called for the Europeanisation of the States; I think that might be the answer to the problem. The new morality looks to me very much like Athens without the slaves—the slaves replaced by the computer.

URBAN: You're not expecting a Christian revival?

KAHN: Well, in the U.S., we have a swing back to traditionalism, back to patriotism, back to the flag, back to religion. This was touched off by the student rebellion which is now condemned by ninety-five per cent of Americans. Part of this reaction is a return to Christian fundamentalism which has always been strong in America and which Europeans have difficulty in understanding. For the coming decades I believe this revival of Christian traditions will be the nation's moral cement, and from there America might gradually evolve a new morality, hopefully on Greek–European lines.

URBAN: Wouldn't the same lessons apply to a good part of Europe too?

KAHN: Not really. If you take out the largely Protestant, Northwestern cultural area (the U.K., Scandinavia, Holland, part of Germany), Europe will do rather well under the modern system. It has shown its ability to cope. Scandinavian Europe has had a love affair with God. Having lost God, it hasn't found a substitute. The Catholic countries of Europe have never had this relationship with the same inwardness and intensity. Not having lost God in the sense the Protestants have, they are in a better position to take the afflictions of our time well in their stride.

CHOOSING
THE FUTURE

FRANÇOIS BOURRICAUD

The Preconceptions of
University Protest in France

François Bourricaud is Professor of Sociology at the University of
Paris and one of the most important French writers on the causes of
student unrest. His publications include *Esquisse de l'autorité*
(Paris, 1961), *Pouvoir et societé dans le Pérou contemporain* (also
in English, 1969) and *Université en crise* (1971).

URBAN: I should like to ask you some questions about the
social and intellectual background of the French student rebellion, but before doing so I wonder whether unrest among the
young is really as new as we're often told it is. Every student
movement worth its salt had grandiose ideas of setting the world
to rights, and, of course, such intentions are not usually compatible with membership of the French Academy or polite
society in Victorian England. The vagrant scholars of the
Middle Ages were the intellectual forebears of the Cohn-
Bendits and Dutschkes of our time and, by all accounts, they
were every bit as offensive to conventional society as their
modern successors. These men were the vendors of unorthodox
news, they were carrying disease, they lived off the kitchens of
other men, they mocked the authority of the Church and were
lechers to boot, though many of them were monastics or even
ordained priests of the Church. In other words, they were the
Hippies of Europe in mediaeval times and for centuries after.

Another thought that occurs to me is that in 18th-Century
France more than one *philosophe* urged the reform of education
in the direction of reason and enlightenment. You had men like
Helvétius and Condorcet saying that the study of dead lan-

guages, of history must discontinue and that the new instruments for the discovery of truth were the natural sciences. But there was soon a violent reaction to this philosophy in the shape of the arrival of the Romantics. These men spoke in the name of the neglected human imagination. They were interested in the remote, in the irrational, in the rejection of systems. A cult of eccentricity followed. These were expressions of the revolt of the passions against the cool classifications practised by scientists and administrators. The *Lumières* (in the phrase of Sir Isaiah Berlin) were accused of spreading darkness.

Well, here again, it is awfully tempting to say that the slogans our young rebels have nailed to their mast are slightly worn by use.

There is, however, a third issue where the analogy with the vagrant scholars and the Romantics does not fit, and that is the role of the university in the life of society. A strong section of our dissenting young would like to fashion the organisation of the university, the nature of the studies conducted at the university, into a microcosm of what should go on outside its walls. The university is supposed to be a model for the rest of society: if you can put through reforms of a radical nature inside the university, somehow, it is assumed, the outside world would follow suit. But would it?

BOURRICAUD: Quite clearly, the student unrest is not new. Equally clearly, it is a strange mixture of often contradictory ambitions and traditions. I propose a clarifying distinction between two types of unrest—the unrest that stems from alienation and the unrest that is action-directed. The Hippy type of rebellion with its tendency to opt out of society and its cynicism belongs to the first type, and it is interesting to ponder that the cynical variety goes back to the Greek Cynics—a school of philosophy which taught that the virtuous life consists of a course of conduct which is independent of all factors external to man. Antisthenes and Diogenes attempted to live the natural life in the midst of a civilised Greek community, renouncing all desires and appetites that were imposed by civilisation. The parallel with the alienated strand in the Hippy movement is clear enough.

The second type is the militant ascetic who wants to change the structure of society with fire and sword. This type is deeply committed to ethical values, he believes in the freedom and equality of men and will fight for them.

Unfortunately this nice analytical distinction falls down in life where the two are found together in a contradictory and unstable pattern, not only between people but very often within the same person. This makes the moral and intellectual texture of the rebellion more colourful: you get the monastic and revolutionary element in the same breast. The monastic self dreams of Arcadia of sorts which can assume Christian, Buddhist or Confucian overtones. The revolutionary ego nurses a social commitment and spoils for a fight.

Now, when you say that the university serves as a microcosm of society, one has to make a distinction again between the prophets and the rebels. For the monastic dissenters the university is a place in some way distinct from the world where your freedom is absolute and you can live out your dream untarnished by any contact with the corruptions of civilisation. It is not a microcosm of the outside world—it is its mirror image. It is a microcosm in the sense that it could be taken as a symbol of how the world could order its affairs but, in fact, does not.

The militant ascetics take the university as a microcosm of society—a microcosm you use against society as a pilot-venture for social experiment.

URBAN: It seems my neat parallel between the vagrant scholars and the Hippy movement has been slightly deflated by a much more convincing type of distinction.

BOURRICAUD: I don't think it has. When I talk about the monastic element, one has to be much more precise and specify what sort of monasticism one is talking about. There is the Franciscan variety—lenient, passive, contemplative—and there is the much more activist Benedictine sort. I think the Hippy movement is cast more in the Franciscan mould. Yet, of the puritanical values of discipline and self-discipline, which are certainly important ingredients of the monastic life, there is not much evidence in California. There is a great deal of sexual licence and social permissiveness, rather of the sort of which your migrant scholars were the early protagonists.

URBAN: May I take you back to my suggestion that the student rebellion may also be analogous with the Romantics' reaction to the French *philosophes*?

BOURRICAUD: Indeed it is, but there the thing reacted against is as much in evidence as the reaction. Youth is both for enlightenment, rationalism, the deflation of authority *and* for spontaneity, the free play of the passions, even mystic experience. Our young rebels want to have it both ways: they hate the aridities of science and technology—the Germans speak with disdain of the *Fachidioten* (idiots of specialisation)—and they are all intent on showing that they are men of profound vision who just failed to make the grade but may yet make it if their revolution creates the right context. Yet, almost in the same breath, they demand a society that would be much more effectively controlled than is the one they reject. A variety of nice phrases—all revolving around some conception of 'autonomy' or 'self-government'—have been put forward to reconcile the contradiction. It is, of course, not difficult to achieve a synthesis on the verbal level. One can attractively talk of creativity, spontaneity, dynamism, and mix it with words such as social responsibility, interdependence, common ownership and the like, but the contradiction cannot be wished away by eloquence.

One of the best known exponents of this synthesis is my good friend and colleague Professor Alain Touraine, who insists that the post-industrial society will be achieved through a sort of student rebellion. To me this is close to nonsense, but the idea is expressive of the impossible dream that motivates student thinking.

261

URBAN: Obviously Touraine's revolution would not be a revolution by the working class, nor would it be a bourgeois uprising. It looks like being a rebellion of frustrated artists.

BOURRICAUD: Exactly: the power behind the student unrest has artistic-aesthetic origins. Some of the most vocal advocates of the students' cause are potential painters, potential musicians, potential conductors who (as the saying goes) have been called but not chosen. Psychologically this is a painful and destructive state to be in, so we have to show them some sympathy. Their hazy notions of an ideal society are transpositions from the realm of art, where they are appropriate, into the realm of politics, where they are not.

But the picture is even more complicated. Touraine shows, and in this respect he is right, that the mood of rebellion is also fed by people who hold down jobs at fairly senior administrative levels but feel frustrated by the small amount of power they wield in decision-making. These men are usually experts of one kind or another in industry or the French civil service. They are highly qualified but, although they enjoy a certain status in the administrative hierarchy, they don't feel that the knowledge they have is being correctly used, or used at all.

All this has a great deal to do with the backwardness of French society, where the man who commands knowledge still has to kow-tow to bureaucrats or the inexpert heads of private firms. So you have a large floating population of excellent men, for whom France's traditional enterprises and the French civil service either have no room or no room for power. The famous dictum of Saint-Simon, that we have a wealth of talent who are unemployed because the structure of society is archaic, has a direct relevance to France's problems in the 1970s. Of course, these talents *will* express their grievances, and they express them in the same confused manner in which the students vent their anger on society. Some of them are rational about the cure they want us to take, others are dreamers. But they are behind the student rebellion and they subscribe to the famous Saint-

Simonian word *l'amour* as their motto for the new society.

URBAN: A forerunner of the ' beautiful people' and the 'love' lore of Venice, California?

BOURRICAUD: Well, today the word would mean a mixture of creativity, originality, devotion and so on, all of which fits in with that nebulous fund of ideas on which the 'beautiful people' erect their fantasies. What I find most preposterous and fascinating in this extraordinary alliance is that it is precisely the people who should be fair game for the lures of the technocracy that fall most easily into the romantic trance and lecture us about creativity and spontaneity. There is the example of M. Rocard (a member of the National Assembly) and some of his friends in the Parti Socialiste Unifié. M. Rocard is a civil servant in the higher regions of financial administration. He has a reputation of being a very austere bureaucrat, but when he walks out of his office he sheds the air of rectitude and becomes a visionary of *auto gestion*.

URBAN: Perhaps Galbraith was right in predicting that the man who has been taught to use his critical faculties in science and technology will not stop there but extend the questioning to the political issues of society. Of course, he was hoping that this is what would happen in the Soviet Union. It has not been happening there to any great extent (most of the protest coming from the liberal arts people), but it would seem to be happening in France. The corollary is that the technical intellectuals in France, those at any rate who are supporting the students, feel that the structure of French society is just as repressive and alien to them as, according to Galbraith, Soviet society is to the Soviet scientists and technical experts. The implications are flattering for the durability of the Soviet system, less so for the French.

BOURRICAUD: I don't know whether the Soviet system will prove more durable than other tyrannies in history. It has cer-

CAN WE SURVIVE OUR FUTURE?

tainly lasted longer than any other one-party state in this century, and it would be a very bold thing to assume that it will be brought down or even basically liberalised by a small number of scientists and technocrats. The French situation is entirely different. French society, inadequate as it is, has some safety valves built into it, which Soviet society has not. In France you can, whether you are right or wrong, whether the state feels jeopardised by your views or not, join in any protest without risking your neck. Now it is quite another matter how far the protest of the French technical intelligentsia is justified or rational. As I have just said, I think it comes from resentment, muddled thinking and millennial hopes. But one has to take these into account and ask oneself: what are the roots of the unrest and what can one do about it?

URBAN: But aren't these experts and administrators also questioning the anarchistic, destructive element in the student rebellion?

BOURRICAUD: They are, but they regard these as excesses, as untypical blemishes on the body of a larger movement of which they approve. This goes to extraordinary lengths. They talk of the rebellion as *The Movement*, and if you tell them that *The Movement* has involved itself in vile acts of extremism or plain foolishness, and ask them 'surely you can't approve of *that*', they will shrug their shoulders and say something to the effect that all this is regrettable but 'you don't expect me to be cut off from *The Movement* for such trivia'. Here you have the devotional element creeping in: if you are 'cut off from *The Movement*' you are excommunicated from the Church or the Party. It comes to the same thing. This is the reason why a great many Frenchmen in important positions of the kind I have described will keep a deafening silence when university halls are smashed by militant Maoists or lecture courses disrupted by anarchists. The dream is that the only vital energy of our society comes from this irrational stream, and to be cut off from it is worse than to condone its aberrations. Behind it all lies the perennial resentment of the men who have been shunted off the main line of development: they know it in their bones that their knowledge would serve society better than the conventional wisdom of tenured bureaucrats, and there is, in this aspect of their resentment, a great deal of truth. Their view of themselves is not perhaps that of potential leaders of a revolutionary vanguard—that they accept will be led by the young—but they do tend to think of themselves as the midwives of history.

URBAN: Going back to the movement as a whole, would you say there is a coherent philosophy behind it? I said in my opening statement that some of these young rebels do not appear to have done their homework and are not aware how old-fashioned they really are in their protests. I was glancing through the *Confessions* of St. Augustine the other day, and there one finds Augustine, writing in the 5th Century, complaining that 'the licence of students in Carthage has reached extraordinary proportions: they break into the lecture rooms disrupting discipline with their frenzied demeanour. In their miraculous blindness they commit numerous felonies which are really punishable by law, but are not so punished because they are condoned by public apathy.'

One should not perhaps expect our Hippies to have read Augustine or the Goliardic verse of the 12th-Century *Carmina Burana*, but I feel somewhat uneasy when I discover that they are barely on nodding terms with Marx and the early Socialists of France, England and Germany. Whatever one may think of the 19th-Century Social Democrats who prepared the October Revolution, there can be no question that they were serious and extremely able men with a genuine revolutionary situation around them which they were determined to, and did, exploit.

BOURRICAUD: Nothing of the sort exists in Western society today. The working class has become a conservative force, its pauperisation has been stopped and reversed. The trade unions are pillars of the establishment. Such revolutionary sentiments as we know of among the workers centre on higher wages—a contemptible form of 'economism' if you ask a thoroughbred Leninist. So we have the students and, in France, some of the disgruntled technical intellectuals. Speaking for myself, I have not the slightest respect for what passes for their philosophy. It is a hopeless hotch-potch—misunderstood Marx mixing uneasily with Mao, Debray, Fanon, Black Power prophets, even Stalin, in a huge melting pot. But the elements won't melt. The 'philosophies' are fragmented as group fights group with bell, book and candle—and I think the metaphor is not wholly inappropriate. I have a certain respect for Marcuse, for he states his aversions with commendable frankness: he hates the kind of society he has to live in. Now there is nothing in a value judgement of this kind you can argue with. Marcuse has every right to dislike our civilisation. Value judgements are free. The nonsense arises when people who think on the same intellectual frequency start telling us that revolution is around the corner. And when they say—and that is the really nauseating part of the rebellion—that *they* have the secret of running the motor of the future society on a mixture of creativity *and* control, spontaneity *and* rational organisation, that is when we have to be quite clear in our minds that we are confronted with Utopia.

URBAN: Mightn't there be also another factor at play in the student rebellion? I think it was Arnold Toynbee who said a few years ago that small wars, an increase in civic disobedience and even localised violence had to be expected because we are now twenty-five years after the last war, a new generation has grown up that doesn't know war from personal experience; what it does know is that it wants to run its horns into something hard and resistant, that it wants to be fully stretched and challenged. The only tough targets young men can find in an affluent and unadventurous society are their fathers' institutions —the established order of society. So these are the ones that attract their ire and hostility.

BOURRICAUD: Well, it is a great pleasure to touch base again with Professor Toynbee's qualified optimism, and I dare say what he says is part of the story. It is certainly true that our aggressive energies lack targets, so targets have to be created. It is a very valid psychological observation that man needs a good hatred as much as he needs good love. Student unrest, even on the scale on which it appeared in Paris in May 1968, is certainly preferable to a nuclear war. So the troubles we have been having at the universities may be a blessing in disguise, though I would hold, in the words of Churchill, that the disguise has been heavy.

I would add yet another factor to our list, and that has to do with the insecurity of our young men and women, in France at any rate, when it comes to preparing themselves for life and a livelihood. The stable career structures have disappeared and we have put nothing in their places. Time was when the career pattern of a young Frenchman was relatively clear. If he was born into a middle-class family, he would go to a *lycée* to get his *baccalauréat*. Then he would go to the university and move into a profession as a doctor, or a lawyer. If he was gifted he would try for one of the *Grandes Ecoles* and make a career at the universities. If he was born into a peasant family he would most likely stay on at the farm, or if he decided to move out, he would still stay in his village as a shopkeeper or artisan. All that has vanished. In the last twenty years many more of our young men have to map out a career for themselves than did their fathers, and this makes for uncertainty. There is a new fluidity in society, which is still relatively stable and static if you compare it with America, but extremely disturbed by French standards.

To put it in a sentence: the young are concerned for their future, their career and their location in society. All this calls for a moratorium to extend the duration of youth. You are still a very young man at twenty-five or twenty-eight. You may be a father but you are still an adolescent, and you fight for all the causes that used to cease to appeal at eighteen but have now a following among men in their late twenties and even thirties. From the educational point of view the late ripening of the young is certainly not objectionable if it means that people stay at the universities or go on studying in some form because they feel that the normal four years cannot do justice to the growing corpus of knowledge. But if it means that you want to stay young because it is easier to be irresponsible and easier to raise absurd demands under the protection of the youth image, then the rather sympathetic figure of the eternal student turns into that of the eternal teenager, and that is less sympathetic.

URBAN: I'm struck by the numerical preponderance of sociologists, psychologists and historians among the student rebels. One knows from the experiences of 1968 that a great many of the social science students had very real grievances. One was that the French universities turned out, if I remember correctly, some 5,000 sociologists each year but there were less than 500 jobs waiting for them to be filled. There were others. But my feeling is that the ideological impact of educating social scientists is more important. People who have been trained in sociology, for instance, tend to take a very critical look at the society in which they live. They tend to compare what was taught them at school and at the university with what they find in real life. They soon discover that the world is not governed by reason, good-will, justice or fair play. This discovery sets the time-bomb ticking and it explodes whenever conditions are most favourable for spectacular action. It can be inside the university or it can be outside it.

BOURRICAUD: It is perfectly true that we are turning out an increasing number of so-called sociologists and psychologists. My impression is that these people are an up-dated version of the traditional arts-student without the latter's dedication. To acquire a good degree in philosophy or classics or one of the literary disciplines takes years of very hard work. Now the young men and women who protest are not primarily concerned with learning. They pick up a few nebulous notions from the odd book that comes their way and create out of these, and what they learn from the Maoists and anarchists, a home-spun ideology of sorts. This gives them a basic vocabulary with which they can berate their enemies. And their vocabulary is basic indeed. It comes down to the consumer society manipulating the individual from the moment he is born to the moment he is buried. This society (they say) perverts you and undermines your identity as a human being. It is therefore a violent society which can only be broken by violence. These are the basic propositions. Later they are decked out with more refined theory, and some young men start talking about social cost, capital investment, etc., but, as I say, the underlying idea is that bourgeois society is intrinsically evil and has to be done away with.

URBAN: It sounds remarkably simple.

BOURRICAUD: It is simple, for the so-called sociologists, psychologists, economists, etc. who go to the barricades are not normally willing to tangle with anything that cannot be reduced to a very small number of ingredients. They deal in a coinage that Raymond Aron has called the 'lingua franca of Marxism' —a concoction of borrowed ideas that I tried to describe earlier in this conversation. I think you are far too charitable when you say that the disaffection stems from the discovery that there is a credibility gap between school and society. I don't think most of our would-be sociologists and psychologists have any idea of how society operates, for they have never taken the trouble to study it. I am most pessimistic on this score. The level of information of our students who take sociology, for instance, is very low, and the examination standards have also been allowed to fall, very largely under student-pressure. What is high is the students' 'ideological equipment', in other words, the body of preconceived ideas with which they enter the university.

URBAN: It is really surprising that at a time when science and our technologies get more and more sophisticated, there should be this deterioration of standards in the social sciences and a tendency for the bad money to drive out the good.

BOURRICAUD: Well, it is not all that surprising. The poverty of thought, the lack of analytical perception starts from the top. Why should the young be more sophisticated and discriminating when they have the example of M. Sartre before them, with his terrible simplifications?

Sartre's monumental *Critique de la raison dialectique* boils down, after a wide and long-winded analysis, to three propositions, each highly questionable. He distinguishes two forms of social structure: the 'series' and the 'group'. You are standing in a bus-queue at Saint-Germain des Prés, but you don't like waiting in a queue. You are a number and a rival of all the other numbers in the queue. There is a shortage of seats in the bus, and everyone in the queue wishes that the others were not there. You all agree to take it in turn to get on the bus, forming an orderly series to avoid a fight. Thus the people in the bus queue form a plurality of solitudes, and Sartre maintains that the whole of the social life of mankind in a Capitalist society is permeated by series of this kind. Clearly 'series' is a bad thing.

Now the opposite kind of social togetherness is the 'group': a collection of people who, unlike those in a series, do have a common purpose. The football team, Sartre says, is an example of the group just as the bus-queue is an example of the series. A group has cohesion, social purpose, loyalty, and its highest embodiment is the revolutionary movement. But, says Sartre, all groups are in danger of dissolving into seriality, hence 'Terror is the statutory guarantee, freely called for, that none shall fall back into seriality.'

This is the kind of analysis you get at the pinnacle of intellectual sophistication. It is all extremely crude and naïve but good enough to seed mythologies.

If you run a red chapel at your university, you are obviously a 'group', and if you enforce your will against those who would not readily agree with you, you are exercising Terror (a good thing) to prevent your group from backsliding into a Capitalist 'series'. On such platitudes were the rebels of May 1968 raised, and such thoughts furnish the background to the dissenting generation today.

URBAN: Has there been anything positive about the French student movement?

BOURRICAUD: Well, it has certainly called attention to the archaic and chaotic structure of our universities. Reforms are being attempted, but it is too early to say with what success. Also it has shown us very convincingly that the critics of society do not come exclusively from the ranks of the young hotheads. In this respect General de Gaulle's call for 'participation' fell on receptive ears. The area of 'participation' is now being widened and that, too, is an interesting departure though it cannot be ascribed to the success of student agitation alone. In a more general sense, it is, I suppose, true that every society needs to be reminded periodically that it is creaking at the joints. The problem is, as always in history: how do we cure the disease without killing the patient.

HELLMUTH BÜTOW

Youth and the Unfulfilled Expectations of German Democracy

Born in 1925, Professor Hellmuth Bütow studied Philosophy, Sociology and History at the universities of Heidelberg and Berlin. In 1958 Professor Bütow joined the East European Institute of the Free University of Berlin of which he is currently the Chairman. He published *Die Entwicklung des dialektischen und historischen Materialismus in der Sowjetzone*, in three parts (1960–63), *Philosophie und Gesellschaft im Denken Ernst Blochs* (1963) and *Radikale Demokratie oder Demokratie der Radikalen* (1969).

URBAN: A great deal has been said and written about the spirit of revolution at our universities. Yet I'm not sure if we have a clear picture of what it is all about, why it has come at the time it has, or even whether one can legitimately talk of a unifying theme behind the unrest. The unifying theme, if there is one, is more in the gesture than in the substance: whether the level of instruction is high or low, whether there are too many lectures or too few, whether students are rich and coddled by both the university and their parents as they are in America, or whether—as in Italy—there is a yawning gap between students and teaching staff, it doesn't seem to make much difference: the students want something that appears in some measure revolutionary, something smacking of 1789, or Maoism, or Che Guevara. The will to revolution is overshadowed by the will to don the mantle of revolutionaries, to embrace their poses rather than their policies.

Yet it would be presumptuous to suppose that intelligent young men and women all over the world would wreck the buildings which are there for their education, disrupt their

272

careers and challenge governments for frivolous reasons alone. When due allowance is made for student frivolity and imitativeness—and these factors can be as powerful as they are silly —one is still left with a feeling that it will not really do to ascribe the restiveness of the young to some technicality in the educational system or some flaw in the way we are governed in a democracy. Aren't we in fact faced here with a deep moral concern over the state of modern society? Or are the students' grievances predominantly educational, inflated perhaps for the benefit of those who might otherwise miss the point?

BÜTOW: It isn't an either/or proposition; a great many factors are at play here. There is distress over the state of a society which is (whether in the East or in the West) now almost exclusively concerned with material values; there is a feeling that work has been dehumanised by the methods of production and by an endless, and apparently aimless, drive to increase the gross national product; there is a crisis of authority which derives from contradictions between the words and deeds of politicians, especially on questions of war and peace, where any links between political speeches and reality tend to be more and more tenuous. To these one has to add the educational factors which merge imperceptibly with the political issues.

If a society imparts independent knowledge in politics and the social sciences—and such knowledge must always contain a certain amount of criticism of existing institutions—it does so at its own risk; for how can it expect students not to exercise their new-found powers of criticism when they leave the university and start on their careers? Can they be expected not to ask themselves how to put what they have learnt into practice and seek a better ordering of society? When society does not show itself resilient enough to accept some of the reforms suggested, then revolution alone seems to present a way out: revolutionary ideas are taken over and revolutionary visions are seen, for it is then clear to the reformers that society is no longer susceptible to reform from within, that it cannot be patched up by tinkering with this or that institution, that change must be

S   273

radical change, from the ground up. Once this point has been reached, the leap from it to a visionary type of Marxism, Maoism, Stalinism, anarchism or whatever else has caught on in this or that particular group, is not a very long one.

What is interesting to observe is that the rebellion of youth is first and foremost a rebellion of bourgeois youth, secondly, a rebellion of students, and only in the third place a rebellion in the schools. The rebel ranks can be shown, by study of their social origins, to belong to quite specific sectors of the population. The working-class youth is, by and large, outside the revolutionary movement.

URBAN: Has the working-class youth then ceased to express its dissatisfaction with bourgeois society—or has it ceased to *be* dissatisfied?

BÜTOW: Neither. There are other ways in which working-class youth has expressed its antagonism. In Germany that protest was peaceable and went on for some years. I'm thinking of those gangs of youths in working-class districts who dressed as Rockers or Hell's Angels and tore about on their motorbikes, scaring the daylight out of the citizens. That was a form of protest, though a non-political one. Political opposition today presupposes university education for the reasons I have just mentioned. The German working class has been, and still is, very thinly represented at the universities.

URBAN: Beguiling theories have been put forward to explain why rebellion burst on the universities at the time it did, but none carries conviction. Up to about 1960 a great deal had been written about the apolitical attitude of youth throughout Europe. I remember a perceptive series of articles by Arthur Koestler in the *Observer* which made just that point. Indeed, the fashionable complaint was to deplore the students' lack of interest in ideas, their lack of concern with any philosophy of life. 'If the students won't put the world to rights, who will?'— was the sort of question one heard among concerned educationists. The young were thought to be far too ready to conform, far too pragmatic and pliable for their age. This was the time when Daniel Bell wrote his *The End of Ideology* and there was some other influential writing in the same vein.

Then, quite unexpectedly, everyone got interested in politics; oil drilling off the coast of California, admission to the girls' dormitories at Nanterre, the Shah of Persia, car exhausts and molecular biology were all politicised. In 1968 the French students came pretty close to overthrowing de Gaulle and his government. What were the causes of the sudden change? Did the rebellion spring from a genuinely revolutionary situation, or was it a revolution of memories—psychodrama, as Raymond Aron put it, writing about the French upheavals? Your point about the social criticism imbibed at the universities and then applied outside its walls, though important, would seem to me insufficient to explain the suddenness and ferocity of the change. There have, after all, always been political theorists in academia who fitted more or less comfortably into society, and those who didn't (Lenin, Hitler or Castro) knew better than to build their movements on the shifting sands of university life.

BÜTOW: The incubation period of revolutions and rebellious upheavals is always a very complicated matter to understand and it is especially difficult if one wants to reduce totally different situations, such as those we had in America and Germany, to a small number of common denominators. That is not to say that the upheavals in Germany, the only ones of which I have personal experience, were unconnected with what went on at Berkeley or New York. The connections were obvious and I shall come to them in a moment. Yet the rebellion in Germany was *sui generis* in its most important aspects.

For at least ten years after the war reconstruction was the only thing Germans were seriously interested in, and clearly this had to be so. But because reconstruction was such an all-absorbing activity, the older generation found it convenient not to find time, or occasion, to remember Germany's recent past, and the young were consequently brought up in the kind of political and moral isolation you describe. Now one has to remember that Germany had just been relaunched as a democracy, and it wasn't long before this apolitical attitude of the young was subjected to serious criticism both in Germany and abroad. It was said that the pursuit of democracy required greater curiosity, a keener consciousness of history and a deeper sense of personal commitment than one could find at the German schools and universities. Steps were taken to remedy the situation; a *political* youth was held to be desirable. Well, we have it.

Next, sociology, a subject which had been long banned from German universities, was imported, one might say from America, and in the process ideas such as those that were later to make their appearance in Berkeley and elsewhere were also imported, and when Berkeley erupted, the German students followed suit using, of course, local incendiary materials. And of these there was no shortage.

The German people had, or ought to have had, genuine grievances to which the students responded, influenced, unquestionably, by the mood at the American universities. What was the dry tinder that could be used for their purposes? There was the gap between the declared aims of German democracy and its actual practice—this was the supreme issue. In 1949 the Federal Republic started off with a thoroughly democratic, almost social-democratic, mandate at least on paper: private property was to be at the service of the common weal, education was to be made universally available, the universities were to be fully integrated in society and so on. None of these brave words were followed up by deeds. The revolt of the students was a revolt against hypocrisy, against a façade of democracy behind which the hand of the manipulator was, as they thought, only too easily discernible.

The pressures had been building up since 1964–65, but I have no precise answer to your question why the dam broke in 1967–68. In America the catalyst was the Vietnam War; in Germany it was the discussion surrounding the visit of the Shah of Persia. It focused attention on the social condition of

Persia, on the curious partiality of Federal politicians towards right-wing conservative regimes, and their bitterly critical attitude to the proletarian dictatorships in East-Central Europe. The erection of the Berlin Wall clinched the matter.

URBAN: Isn't there also another partiality involved here? It is astonishing that young people who profess to be so sensitive to suffering in Guatemala and Vietnam are less moved, if they are moved at all, by the plight of the Danzig workers, or the treatment of minorities by the Soviet authorities? There was no great enthusiasm—in Germany or elsewhere—to take up the cudgels on behalf of Solzhenitsyn, Siniavsky or Daniel, and when Czechoslovakia was occupied by its allies in 1968, even the non-bloc Communist parties were more articulate in their condemnation than the ostensibly left-of-the-Party, militant groups at the universities. Isn't this a case of double standards?

BÜTOW: It is indeed—there is political prejudice, but we have to ask ourselves: what has brought about that prejudice and is it in any way legitimate? Well, for many years now the German press and radio have given the public an even blacker and more exaggerated picture of the East-Central European regimes than they truly deserve. The use of terror, the stupidities of centralisation, the excesses of bureaucracy have all been depicted on an outsize canvas, and if you were a student who could see what was going on around him in Germany but had only a hazy knowledge of East-Central Europe, you would probably have come to the conclusion that the blackening operation was a cover-up for imperfections nearer home. So for me it is an open question whether this unilateral way of looking at things isn't in some measure the pay-off for the diversionary tactics which journalists and intellectuals have exercised for many years. If you go on presenting an outside source as the main danger to your people, and all the while blow your trumpet about your successes, it can easily happen that people grow suspicious and change their minds: the foreign threat seems less and less formidable, and you start questioning conditions in your own society. Then, simply because the elements which hinder reforms are precisely those which are most vociferous in spreading anti-Communism of the crasser kind, there follows a form of blindness—prejudice, double standards, etc.

Of course, the extent to which this has happened varies from group to group. The anarchists are entirely impervious to any argument whether parliamentary democracy of the Westminster kind is better, or worse, than Socialism as it is practised in Czechoslovakia. It is not the form of government, but government they object to. Then there are certain groups which describe themselves in Germany as the proletarian Left; their latter-day avowal of Marxism–Leninism has had the consequence that their attitude to certain events in the Eastern bloc is identical with the official line. Then there is another left-wing group which is still in its infancy and has done very little to catch the public eye. This group condemned the Soviet intervention in Czechoslovakia and it has been very critical of the treatment of Solzhenitsyn, Siniavsky and Daniel. It argues that while under certain conditions it is easy to set up a dictatorship of the proletariat, it can be pretty difficult to get rid of it. But it is as well to remember that this group is no more friendly disposed to the Western democracies than their anarchist or Marxist–Leninist critics.

URBAN: Do these groups represent something larger than themselves? I asked you earlier whether there was, in the Western democracies, a revolutionary situation which these groups of young men and women could exploit. I'm thinking of Marcuse's argument that the working class in the industrially developed countries has ceased to be a revolutionary force and that its place will be taken by revolutionary students and intellectuals.

BÜTOW: I would agree with Marcuse, although there are fringe groupings of unskilled and trainee workers that are still potentially revolutionary; but certainly there is no revolutionary proletariat in Marx's sense. This means that young left-wingers who have opted for revolution find themselves in exactly the same position as Lenin did—there weren't *as yet* enough proletarians in Russia when Lenin needed them, there are *no longer* enough proletarians in the West to fuel a revolution today. In this situation it seems to me almost inevitable that revolutionaries should knock-up for themselves an ideology and use it as a substitute for the real thing.

URBAN: Would this substitute still be governed by Leninist principles?

BÜTOW: Entirely so: once it is clearly understood what the 'objective' situation of the working class is, it *has* to be revolutionary (or so runs the argument). If you look at it from this point of view you will find that, now as before, the working class is excluded from any sort of control of the means of production. On the other hand it is perfectly clear that the proletariat is mentally unprepared to destroy the existing structure of society. So if you are a young revolutionary, you can cogently argue that the revolutionary situation today is neither less nor more genuinely ripe than it was in Lenin's time, and the next step to take is to say that now, as in 1917, revolutionary consciousness has to be inseminated in the working class by an outside donor. And if you are a keen young revolutionary with a degree in sociology to your name, it is not too difficult to say who that donor should be.

URBAN: The attempt to inject this consciousness was very clear, and futile, in France in May 1968.

BÜTOW: It was repelled or ignored in Germany too. Efforts were made to establish contact with the workers, to form cells in the factories and so on, but they came to nothing. The workers were not prepared to jeopardise their prospects of material prosperity by engaging in revolution. As Hochhuth said: 'Revolutions are dangerous,' and these workers seemed to agree with him. But if you have arrogated to yourself the right to be the *avant-garde*, you must adopt the principle of the dic-

279

tatorship of the proletariat, and if your proletariat does not want to exercise such a dictatorship, you can resolve your dilemma by exercising your dictatorship *over* the proletariat in the name of the proletariat, your explanation being that you are anticipating the time when, through re-education, the working class will have become fully conscious of its role as the revolutionary force in history. The story of the Red Cells in Berlin is a perfect illustration of Kautsky's thesis that it is the intelligentsia that is called upon to lead the working class, since the workers are not in a position to know and correctly evaluate their situation —that is to say, they are not able to govern themselves. This is the idea Lenin worked into his book *What is to be done?* and has become the lynchpin of Leninism.

URBAN: Isn't this a most un-Marxist thesis?

BÜTOW: The question seems to turn on Marx's view that, as the class struggle develops in an industrial society, class awareness begins to form at the base, and this awareness has only to find a mode of expression for revolution to break out. Marx's dictum 'The idea becomes a material force as soon as it is taken into the hands of the masses' has two implications: first, the idea must be there, second, the masses must be ready to take this idea into their hands. The question is: was Marx right? For, as industrial development proceeds, the material improvement in the lot of the workers tends to lead them further and further away from the idea of revolution. That is after all the history of Social Democracy. Lenin was certainly logical in arguing as he did that if a Socialist revolution is at all possible, it must be carried out at a time when Capitalism is already operative but industrialisation is not yet advanced. That means, if my interpretation is correct, that Lenin transfers the revolution from the *end* of the Capitalist industrialisation process— where Marx places it—to its *beginning*. And this seems to me to imply that Lenin was in no doubt that the chances of successful revolution would decrease among a proletariat that had a taste of successful industrialisation.

URBAN: This would exonerate Lenin from the grosser kind of heresy, yet it does not speak well of his understanding of Marx's humanism. If industrialisation improves the lot of the workers to the extent that they cease to be a proletariat but, on the contrary, begin to have a large stake in the wealth of society, why have a revolution in the first place? I can't help feeling that our young revolutionaries are aware both of this dilemma and of the fact that their isolation in society is due to it. We have a young generation which is keen to play a historical role, but a situation in which a historical role could be played is simply not there. And because youth can find no realistic outlet for their ambition, they attach themselves to Marxism–Leninism, Maoism, anarchism, even Stalinism—anything in fact that promises to lend their eagerness a sense of reality.

BÜTOW: The radicalisation you mention is a function of the hopelessness of the undertaking. At first it was thought that the intelligentsia itself could produce a new revolutionary class. When that was given up, there was a tendency to feel that the revolutionary intelligentsia might find a base for its operations in the Third World—an idea of Marcuse's. That had to be given up too, at least in Germany. Today the argument runs as follows: the revolutionary class is the proletariat, and the Socialist countries provide the base for revolution. Once a successful revolution has been carried out—still under the leadership of the revolutionary intelligentsia representing the interests of the proletariat—the revolution can count for support on the Socialist countries. The trouble with this programme is that it is a search for ways and means to legitimise whatever action its exponents want to take anyway—it has no basis in society. But when society is confronted with programmes of this kind and takes measures to counteract them— for example, by bringing in the police—then, in the long run, these movements may gain the sort of influence which they could never have gained had they been left alone in the first place.

281

URBAN: Your assumption is that under the surface bourgeois society is violent: by provoking it, this violence can be brought into the open. Isn't this rather like saying: 'I suspect that man over there is violent. I'll punch him on the nose to see whether he hits back. If he does, I was clearly right in my assumption that he was violent'?

BÜTOW: The question is whether a society that lets itself be provoked in this way isn't a society to which the criticism customarily made of it indeed applies. We have to be very careful here and distinguish between the cogency of the criticism levelled at society on the one hand, and the irrational, romanticised aims of those making the criticism on the other. If society uses the irrationalism and immaturity of the aims as a pretext for ignoring the criticism, then one day society may be in for a big surprise.

URBAN: You said a moment ago that revolutionary thinking in Germany assumes that, if a revolution were to break out in the West, the Socialist countries would provide it with a life-line. In what sense exactly is it possible to regard the Socialist states as revolutionary agents in our time?

BÜTOW: I don't think they are revolutionary in any sense; they are highly conservative, Socialist-monopolist countries. But to the young revolutionaries we have been discussing they appear in a very different light. Partly (as I said earlier) these young men and women start off with a heavy bias; partly they have only the most superficial knowledge of the political and social realities in these countries. They get most of their information from books which they are not really able to assess critically, and their reaction to any criticism of the Socialist states exhausts itself in an ignorant intransigence not unlike that of any reactionary bourgeois when he hears democracy or his nation criticised. To put it bluntly: they swallow hook, line and sinker whatever official party propaganda offers them. The leaders of the revolutionary groups usually know a little more about the Socialist states, but they take care not to let on; their purpose is to instil a revolutionary spirit in the rank and file, not to run a debating society—so they keep them in the dark. The psychology of this is simple: once the leaders have made up their minds to take a certain course of action, the observance or non-observance of truth shrinks to the status of a merely tactical consideration.

URBAN: Never let facts interfere with a good theory?

BÜTOW: One could call it that.

URBAN: The critical faculty, then, which these young revolutionaries are busy exercising against the Capitalist societies of the West is not turned eastwards?

BÜTOW: No, and that makes life difficult if you are a teacher at a German university. I can follow students in their criticism in so far as it goes beyond such undifferentiated concepts as Capitalism, Socialism, working class, revolutionary consciousness, etc. The difficulty arises when they come up with some remedy or other which they have quite ingenuously accepted, but which is often highly questionable and could do with thorough scrutiny. But even that is not to be. One could attain a certain balance here if the students were prepared to analyse the state of the Soviet Union too—the way Russia is ruled, its social conditions, its educational system, its handling of the arts and literature—but even that has become virtually impossible. Any critical approach to these questions is taken as proof that you are a hopeless bourgeois. There is just no contact.

URBAN: I take it you are speaking about Berlin. I find it somewhat puzzling that all this should be taking place in a city where daily life is one long reminder of the presence of a very powerful military despotism which has cut the city into two. Is this a case of learning to love your interrogator?

283

BÜTOW: Difficult to say. Berlin is a watershed in Germany: what happened in Berlin in 1967–68 is now becoming virulent at certain West German universities. The feeling of being threatened has led to more extreme forms of conservatism than is to be found in other university towns in Germany. The Berlin *Landesverband* of the SPD is so conservative that it is some-times jokingly called the CSU of the SPD [CSU is slightly to the right of CDU with which it works in electoral alliance]. The Berlin trade unions too are decidedly more conservative than those in the Federal Republic. The man in the street in Berlin is heavily influenced by the Springer press which owns about seventy-five per cent of the daily papers. So there is here a combination of many factors—and of course there is the Wall. There is a feeling in Berlin that we must learn to live with the Wall, that the Wall can only be overcome if we approach what happens on the other side with a little more understanding. Now the young revolutionaries go further than that. They say that the whole purpose of the Wall can be invalidated by approach-ing it from the Eastern point of view. This looks to me like an over-reaction to earlier Western designs to push the frontiers of Communism further back east. The policy has, as it were, turned back upon itself to become an aggressive design against the West.

URBAN: You have satisfied my curiosity as to the place of the upheavals, but I'm still puzzled by the *dramatis personae*. How has it come about that Stalinism has reappeared as a currency in these transactions? Has the great terror been white-washed or forgotten?

BÜTOW: Originally the rebel groups adopted Marxism–Leninism mainly via Maoism (and to a lesser extent via Ho Chi Minh and Che Guevara), and in Maoism Stalin was taken over in fairly undamaged condition. Then, to the great disappoint-ment of these rebels—of whom Rudi Dutschke was one of the leaders—the Cultural Revolution turned out to be a showpiece manipulated from above, and there was a swing to Soviet ideas and to the Soviet Union itself where Stalin had just come in for partial rehabilitation. Now the revolutionary left has gone further than anything done so far in the U.S.S.R. towards rehabilitating Stalin's image: Stalin is presented as a man who, at a given moment in history, was forced to act as he did in order to assure the preservation of Socialism. This is, of course, the line peddled by the Communist press in innumerable articles.

The main point here is that the student groups I am talking about want to give themselves a sense of historical continuity. I would not say that they either propagate or practise Stalinist methods, but there is a conscious attempt to present the development of the Soviet Union as a seamless piece of history, a history without gaps and errors, for that makes it easier to take the dictatorship of the proletariat as a model for the organisation of the future society.

URBAN: Well, this is a highly philosophical kind of explanation. I rather feel that a French or Italian group, if it were to turn to Stalinism, would do so for more practical reasons. Why this urge for a seamless texture? Why this strong ideological component?

BÜTOW: For an easy answer, perhaps it has something to do with the German penchant for perfectionism; but I don't want to make things as easy as that for myself. The return to Marxism–Leninism and even Stalinism seems to me to be a way of shedding a national guilt complex, of over-compensating, if you like, for twelve years of National Socialism. Then, the myth of *das Volk*—always very strong in Germany—is reappearing in some of the revolutionary philosophies. The 'people' are now identified with the working class, and one has an uneasy feeling that in some cases Marxism–Leninism is only a vehicle for giving fresh expression to this missionary Volk-ideology. Also we are in Germany just beginning to learn something that other countries internalised a long time ago—how to live with Communists in our midst. Abroad, no one finds it strange that, at the universities for example, a certain percentage of teachers should be Marxists or Communists; no one disputes on that score their ability to do a good job. In Germany, thanks to National Socialism and a particular kind of National-Socialist anti-Communism, a natural pause ensued after the war in which no one took the trouble to think seriously about Communism. A climate of opinion developed which made it virtually impossible for any Marxist or Communist to hold a post at a German university. Some of this went to ridiculous lengths. To give you an example, when the Red Cells in my Institute wanted a tutorial course in Russian and insisted that a Marxist should be appointed as tutor, the ensuing quarrel was not about whether the man was academically qualified to hold the job, but whether a Marxist should be allowed at all to hold such a post at a German university. Of course, it is taken for granted that a university teacher—like anyone else—has some sort of ideology in his head, but he must not be a Communist.

Another reason for giving the Soviet side every benefit of the doubt, and making the Soviet story a seamless piece of history, is that the German authorities do not seem to have the same sort of allergy to teachers who blotted their copy-books during the Hitler period. A very large percentage of these have been allowed to retain their posts at the universities. I am not saying that, taken together, these factors justify the distortions which mar the revolutionaries' presentation of Soviet history, but they go some way towards explaining the mood in which the Soviet story has come to be decked out to serve as a model.

URBAN: I often wonder whether the proper context for understanding these revolutionary philosophies isn't the confessional, or psychoanalysis—whether we aren't faced here with some repressed yearning for authority and a father figure.

BÜTOW: Let me tackle the father-complex first. Alexander Mitscherlich says in one of his books that our society is turning the young generation loose at a time when the leaders have vanished and the elders of the tribe have lost their authority.

I would add to that that the young generation do all they can to facilitate the process. The strange thing is that they can't get on without fathers and authoritative elders. They ditch their natural fathers to provide themselves with new, one might say 'ersatz' fathers, whom they can pin up on walls or carry in front of them in demonstrations. To these 'ersatz' fathers they submit unconditionally in a way they would never submit to their own, or to whatever authority obtains in their society. This also happens to be very convenient, for to the new fathers it is relatively easy to submit as one does not have to live with them under the same roof.

Coming to psychoanalysis and the confessional, I feel that both the revolutionary Marxist and the anarchist solutions are answers to a deep malaise which derives from the Utopian deficit of democracy. By Utopian deficit I mean that with the passing of time democracy grows more and more complacent and is no longer in a position to discharge the tasks it set itself in the first place. Liberty, equality, fraternity are guaranteed, in one form or another, in all democracies, yet in practice they are no more than ideal goals which have entirely lost their dynamism. In Germany, for instance, at the time of the foundation of the Federal Republic, property (as I have already said) was not a hallowed concept but something to be treated with the public interest in mind. There was, for instance, the CDU politician Ernst Lemmer who wrote an article in 1947 asserting that unless landed property was nationalised Fascism would revive in Germany. When a student reads this today and contemplates the political and economic history of the Federal Republic, he may well come to the conclusion that Lemmer was right. Then we had a professor at the Free University of Berlin, a very important members of the CDU, who said in a paper in 1946 that socialisation was necessary, making it very explicit that socialisation could only be brought about democratically if the workers were given self-government. These were views expressed by *conservative* politicians; so have we any reason to be surprised if our Social Democrats, for example—young and old—feel that the shifts of emphasis in the SPD's programme (and especially the Godesberg instruments which renounced the Party's revolutionary heritage) have removed German democracy from the road it set itself after the war? They feel that democracy tends to rest content with the way things are, that it belittles what is still to be done, thus drugging public awareness and determination to see change brought about.

URBAN: How widespread is this attitude among the younger generation? My impression is that we are dealing here with a small but vocal minority.

BÜTOW: It is not so simple as that. So far as criticism of democracy is concerned, it is a very widespread phenomenon indeed. Disregarding for the moment the fact that most young people—like most of their elders for that matter—are not very interested in politics, the activists alone make up thirty to forty per cent of the German university population. The great majority of these are convinced that democracy is a failure, so relative to the total student population this is in fact a mass phenomenon. It is true that the number of those who advertise their Marxist–Leninist nostrums is small, but this minority is fanatical and very active. They do not hesitate to give up two or three terms of their university careers to give practical currency to their ideas.

URBAN: You have mentioned several morally attractive but irrational and irrelevant alternatives to the bourgeois–democratic model. Are there any that can offer a constructive and practicable solution?

BÜTOW: Recently new groups have appeared who reject both the ideological and governmental monism of the Eastern bloc *and* Western society with its monopolies, its manipulative devices and establishments. They seem to be aiming at a pluralistic Socialist democracy. This implies on the one hand the rejection of every sort of dogmatic ideology, especially of the Marxist–Leninist brand in its ossified forms we know from

East-Central Europe, but it also implies the rejection of the Western political model with its dependence on capital. It has set its sights on creating a society in which several parties are allowed, most property is held in common ownership, but which will at the same time safeguard the citizens' personal freedoms, the freedom of scientific research and artistic expression.

URBAN: Is there any connection here with the Yugoslav example?

BÜTOW: Some of the inspiration came from Yugoslavia, but I would not go so far as to say that Yugoslavia provided the model. These groups, perhaps the most sophisticated of all, have given themselves considerable trouble to check up on their facts; they are, therefore, fully aware that there is a fault in the Yugoslav model—a gap between the one-party state and the workers' self-government (also, they cannot shut their eyes to the Michailov affair). Their readiness to adopt, and reject, elements from both East and West is quite remarkable: for instance they are ready to acknowledge social advance in places where others are not so disposed to see it, as, for example, in the Soviet Union, in Poland and the GDR, but they want that advance without the system of government which accompanies it. They would like to expand the scope of democracy, but they do not agree that you can start enlarging democracy by destroying it. This is a third-road type of movement and is perhaps the most hopeful departure we have seen for some time.

URBAN: We have already briefly touched on the point that the university population is a shifting population. Students generally spend four years at a university, and at the end of their studies they do seem to fit themselves into what one might call civilian life. At twenty-seven they begin running out of revolutionary steam; at thirty-two they start looking around for a bit of real estate for their families, and by the time they reach forty their revolutionary past tends to be looked upon with the kind of disdain officers have for the days they spent in the ranks.

Looking at the revolutionary generation from this point of view, isn't it foolish to suppose that students could be a historical force? There is surely some truth in the saying 'If you are not a Communist at twenty you haven't got a heart—if you are still a Communist at forty you haven't got your head properly screwed on.'

BÜTOW: The power of revolutionary ideas to survive a man's apprenticeship at the university interests me a great deal. It is perfectly true that from the moment a young man leaves the university the pressures of society to make him conform, fit in, moderate his ideas, renounce his fancies are very powerful. This being so, it cannot harm society if a young man's rebellious phase is lived through with great intensity, because this would seem to hold out some hope that a modicum of his critical attitude may be preserved to be of use in later years. Perhaps I need not stress the importance of this for Germany where a traditional respect for *Obrigkeit* (Authority), has repeatedly pushed the country into disaster. And I would venture to say that we are moving towards a new era in which more people will carry a critical mode of thought with them into their maturity, if only in diluted form. And that for me spells hope.

URBAN: You are talking of a critical mode of thought, yet one is often under the impression that there is a form of lunacy abroad in the ranks of the student movement with which even the most open-minded of bourgeoisies could not make its peace.

BÜTOW: This is an exaggeration. I have with me here a pamphlet called *Socialist 1st May, 1968* which caused a great commotion at the time. I have seen it described as an attempt to destroy German democracy; Social Democrats who took part in its distribution were disciplined. Yet when we read the demands made in this pamphlet it is very difficult to see why people got so hot under the collar. For example we read: 'We demand that workers, engineers and scientists should have a say in the use of their labour, in the management of the natural and

technical resources of the economy of our people and in relations between peoples. We demand that workers, engineers and
scientists should have a say in what is produced in their factories, offices and laboratories. We demand self-government at
the place of work through democratisation of the factories and
their management by organs freely chosen by the whole labour
force. We demand schools, technical colleges and universities in
which pupils, apprentices and students can work together, and
in which they can learn things that will be of service in freeing
man from his rulers and be of use to him once he has been freed.
We demand that all living space be treated as communal property and the erection of houses shall be put under control
of those who will live in them' and so forth.

Now one could spend a great deal of time arguing for and
against some of these points. But one thing is clear : at the time
this pamphlet appeared—and it was subsequently endorsed by
the student movement as a whole—the students were not demanding a dictatorship of the proletariat; radical measures like
the expropriation of the means of production were not so much
as mentioned. All the talk in the pamphlet is about joint decisions, joint control, turning man into a responsible citizen, seeing to it that he is no longer a pawn in the hands of the political
parties and so on. These aren't demands that should upset any
democrat; at most he should raise purely practical points : how
is this to be brought about, will such and such a measure promote our progress or hold it back, and so on.

At the time, the students' demands were flatly rejected on
the grounds that they were not in line with the principles of a
free democracy. Well, one wonders who exactly ought to be
blamed for the stink bombs, the stone-throwing, the car-
daubing that followed. No one in a responsible position was
prepared to talk things over with the student opposition while it
was still in a mood of rational argument. Aren't the disturbances
really to be seen as actions of a minority aware of its impotence
and desperately trying to make society take note of its grievances? Suppose a man is trying to put a case he believes to be
right but finds that the other fellow just will not listen—in fact

CAN WE SURVIVE OUR FUTURE?

he won't even allow himself to be approached: hasn't the man with the message *some* right to make himself unpleasant until the other man does pay attention?

And this brings us back to where we started this discussion: the degree of violence and irrationalism which the young use in their protests depends on the nature of the society in which they are growing up. In so far as the student generation have set themselves irrational aims, this is because they despair of the so-called rationality of the society they see around them, and despair of finding a way out. If a society wants to have a rational youth, then it must create the conditions in which a rational desire for social reform can thrive; and it must not fob off young protesters by telling them they are too young to afford the luxury of an informed opinion on such matters. I firmly believe that every society gets the sort of younger generation it deserves.

URBAN: Would you apply this to the youth of Hungary and Czechoslovakia, and to the actions they saw themselves constrained to take in 1956 and 1968?

BÜTOW: I would indeed.

MAURICE DUVERGER

The Scope of Technological Convergence *

Maurice Duverger is one of the most distinguished political scientists in Europe. He is Professor of Political Sociology at the University of Paris and Director of Studies and Research of the Fondation Nationale des Sciences Politiques. His many publications include *Les Parties politiques* (1951), *Méthodes de la science politique* (1959), *Sociologie politique* (1966). He is a frequent contributor to *Le Monde*.

URBAN: The idea that industrial societies are coming to be more and more alike almost irrespective of the political and cultural conditions in which they operate, is principally associated, in the Anglo-Saxon world, with the name of John Kenneth Galbraith. Galbraith suggests that the Western and the Soviet type of industrialised societies converge for three broad reasons: first, the size of industrial organisations—whether nationalised or private—and the nature of the technologies employed, demand planning, and planning has its own imperatives. Second, while in the East European societies the efficiency of planning demands a decentralisation of power from the state to the enterprise, in the West the size and structure of the corporations require managerial techniques which amount in fact to more centralisation and a basic form of planning. If you have a large-scale, complex technology, the similarities in which that technology is organised will leave their imprint on the social organisations surrounding it. Galbraith mentions Novosibirsk in the Soviet Union, and Gary, Indiana, as examples of industrial cities which have more in common

* *Original contribution, unrevised.*

293

than what separates them. The fact that these complexes require planning, a high degree of discipline and certain types of predictable behaviour in the men and women employed is more important, according to Galbraith, than the fact that the workers in Gary, Indiana, work for private shareholders and live in a pluralistic society, while in Novosibirsk the factories are state-owned and the society in which the workers operate is totalitarian. Third, Galbraith believes that as the two societies converge, Communist society will become culturally and politically more free because, he says, the demands of science and advanced technical specialisation cannot be reconciled with political regimentation. How realistic are the reasons for believing that convergence is, in fact, inherent in industrial societies?

DUVERGER: Well, I must claim primogeniture, for ten years ago I used very much the same arguments Galbraith is now using. I put them in a book (*Introduction à la politique*) which came out in 1964 in Paris and had an English version a year later. It is certainly true that, in the West, the evolution of technology means the centralisation and the concentration of the means of production. In Eastern Europe it demands the continuation of planning with different methods, including the method of decentralisation. It is also true that the evolution of Communist societies tends to arouse, in the class of technologists and scientists, expectations of greater intellectual freedom. However, I think this is much more a scientific than a psychologically-motivated need. Any science that cuts itself off grows weaker. There are some striking examples of this in Soviet science: Soviet genetics declined disastrously when Lysenko dominated the scene; Russian economics, which were off to a good start, suffered a grave setback in the last years of Stalin because there was a block to any progress in mathematical economics; all of Freud's theories arrived in the Soviet Union after very great delays and, more recently, we know how very slowly sociology was accepted as a discipline in its own right, and the legitimacy of political science is still disputed in some Soviet quarters. All this has put the clock back in Eastern Europe.

However, it is equally striking that the Soviet Union and the other East European Communist countries are beginning to see all this and have started developing intellectual contacts. The amount of freedom Soviet scientists and intellectuals are allowed is in direct relation to the importance to the science of the intellectuals concerned. If you are an important figure, especially in the natural sciences, like Professor Sakharov, you have, in practice, a great deal of elbow room and your criticisms can go quite far. If you are less important you can criticise less, and this goes for all the sciences at all levels. So I am in broad agreement with Galbraith's views, but I would perhaps formulate some of the factors which make for convergence in a different way and I would also add some others.

In the industrially developed countries—and today a great part of Eastern Europe is so developed—the number of people who have had a higher education grows all the time, and because of this education these people need contacts, foreign books and travel. Here the East European countries are making considerable progress, though the Soviet intellectuals are still kept on a shorter lead than the Czechs, Poles and Hungarians. There is, in the latter, also the growing influence of tourism which, together with the foreign money it injects into the country's economy, also, and quite inevitably, injects the ideas, customs and fashions of the Western countries from which the hard-currency tourists come. Then there is the amazing development of radio and television. The Czechs and Hungarians can pick up German and Austrian television, to say nothing of the East Germans who are really part of the radio and television audiences of the West German stations. In a few years television by satellites will cover the whole world. Of course, efforts will be made to block some of the information broadcast, but I am profoundly convinced that when society has reached a certain technological level it is impossible to curtail people's demand to be informed, or to muffle the freedom of expression. For all these reasons there comes a time when forbidding doesn't work and jamming isn't possible.

Coming to the idea of centralisation and decentralisation, I would stress another imperative of technological progress. I think the characteristic distinction between East and West is expressed not so much in that contrast as in the dichotomy between the Socialist style of production and the Capitalist style of production. Yet within that dichotomy, too, there is a tendency for convergence which Galbraith hints at but does not bring out quite clearly. What I mean is this: in a *laissez-faire* liberal economy, free enterprise and the individual are the driving forces of progress. Invention, research, success are all tied to a small number of men who have personal stakes in what they are doing. But today what drives industry and indeed the whole economy is neither the individual nor the small workshop but fundamental research which requires large material resources and the application of the results of research on a vast scale.

Also, the lead-time makes this kind of research all but impossible not only for the cottage industries but even for the medium-size factories which still dominate the scene in many European countries: between the moment an invention is made and the moment that invention is turned to profitable use there is usually a long delay. Thus even in Western Capitalist countries scientific research is conducted under state auspices by non-Capitalist organisations. From then on the driving force is public intervention, which means state credits and state direction.

URBAN: Can you give an example?

DUVERGER: Well, how was atomic energy discovered and put to use? The nuclear technology was developed because there was a war on and the United States and Britain decided to give priority to the enormous sums required to finance atomic research. No private corporation could have afforded to do so or can do so now. This means that, in the Capitalist

THE SCOPE OF TECHNOLOGICAL CONVERGENCE

countries too, state-socialist organisations are the driving forces
of research.

There is yet another point where I would slightly differ from
Galbraith. I have been saying this since 1964—and today it is
part of conventional wisdom—that in a Capitalist, profit-based
system some needs, private needs, tend to be satisfied very well,
but social services, urban planning, the protection of the environment are given less than adequate attention.

URBAN: I think Galbraith expressed this in the phrase
'private affluence, public squalor', but he was referring exclusively to the United States.

DUVERGER: Yes, what Galbraith was saying about American
conditions which, incidentally, persist to this day, used to apply
in the same sort of measure to the West European Capitalist
countries until shortly after the Second World War. The need
for public intervention was then recognised, and the state began
to look after public health, education, housing and so on. That
means that, in Western Europe at any rate, it is the public, non-
profit-motivated sector which is developing and there is no
doubt that it is serving the general good. This too seems to me
to be an important factor that makes for convergence.

URBAN: Galbraith uses a basically Marxist argument: the
economic base, he says, determines the super-structure. It is
dressed up in modern language, but the idea that a sophisticated
technology and managerial techniques require such-and-such
a type of society and culture is a Marxist idea. Well, I am not
sure how far you subscribe to the deterministic element in Galbraith's position—whether you think that convergence is automatic, as Galbraith implies. I find the notion that somehow
the will of historical development is inexorably written into our
modes of production, and especially into the size of our production units, very difficult to support by evidence. Galbraith
mentions Novosibirsk and Gary, Indiana. This is a hypothetical
comparison. But it is not necessary to deal in hypotheses. Take

the cities of Cologne and Coventry in 1939–45. These were comparable in size, in the nature and distribution of their industries, in the technologies employed in them, in the patterns of occupation, and I suppose one could pursue the parallel down to the number of hospital beds, cinemas, motor-cars, refrigerators and perambulators. On Galbraith's thesis the two ought to have been busy converging in 1939 and years after, for no two cities could have had a more tellingly convergence-prone industrial and technological structure. Yet no two cities in modern history were more clearly set on a collision course; Hitler made it his business to rub out Coventry, and Britain destroyed Cologne with great single-mindedness. It seems to me that Galbraith commits the basic mistake we all commit when we are led by wishful thinking rather than evidence, namely: he examines one section of facts and applies the conclusions he has drawn from them to a much larger area where the conclusions do not apply. But one need not restrict oneself to these two cities or to the Second World War. I am certain one could find comparable communities between France and Germany in 1912 or, if we want to take the same example, one could compare Cologne and Coventry in 1930, before Hitler came to power.

DUVERGER: The problems you have raised are important. Let me first go back to what you say about Galbraith's way of reasoning. Yes, it is close to Marxism; '*marxisant*', I would say, not fully Marxist. But here a footnote is in order. What is interesting to observe in the development of Western society— interesting because it is one of the factors of ideological convergence—is the increasing *de facto* Marxism of a great deal of our thinking, going back to 1950 or thereabouts. Let me explain: the basic proposition of Marx is that civilisations, political organisations, social institutions, the family are all based on, indeed reflect the character of, the technological level of the economy. Before the Second World War this idea was rarely popular except among Marxists. Today we talk of developed and underdeveloped, or developing, countries, and 'development' for us means industrialisation. That is, we differentiate between various countries on Marxist lines, using the state of their productive apparatus as our yardstick because we realise that differences in economic structure entail formidable differences in the political, social and cultural estates. This recognition is clearly reflected in our policies. Imagine a French or British lawyer trying to draw up a constitution for an independent African state in 1930. Well, he would have written an attractive, democratic, pluralist document with ample provisions made for individual liberties, a fine mechanism to balance conflicting sectional interests and so forth. It would not have worked. Today we know that we cannot make the Westminster type of pluralistic, liberal democracy work in underdeveloped countries because they lack the industrial base that would give them the social structure for liberal-democratic institutions. We have given up trying. Now all this amounts to the tacit acceptance of a good deal of Marxism.

URBAN: Isn't there, I wonder, another explanation? African Socialism is 'Socialism' in name only. Does it do more than provide fashionable cover for a very old-fashioned type of authoritarianism? The African and Asian states simply haven't the time, or the will, or the tradition to go through those slow and painful processes which have preceded Western liberal democracy. They believe they can cut corners, that there is a direct line to democracy through 'Socialism'. I dare say a poor country in a hurry may have no choice but to apply such shock tactics in its economy and social organisation, but I think the inference that the absence of a highly developed industrial base makes a country unripe for democracy does not quite follow.

DUVERGER: When I say that in the West the Marxist approach has wider currency than it had twenty or thirty years ago, I am clearly not saying that there has been any direct transposition of Marxist theories. Few people in the West would insist that the world is ineluctibly set for the public ownership of all means of production. But what we do think in the West almost universally is that the machinery of production, economic conditions, technology have a very important, almost fundamental, influence on our culture and all our institutions. And it is surely fair to call this a Marxist influence.

URBAN: But is it a fundamental influence or just one of many?

DUVERGER: For an orthodox Marxist the economic conditions are the all-important, almost unique, factor moulding the super-structure. For us in the West they cannot be the only factor. I'm not going to argue the relative importance of this factor or that, but it is the case that in the last twenty years we have tacitly accepted a vaguely Marxist frame of reference, attaching more and more importance to economic determinants while, on the other side of the divide, there has been a slow movement away from stressing the economic factor to the benefit of more traditional ones such as a nation's cultural background, its history and specific way of doing and thinking things. All these factors are given growing importance in Eastern Europe, and on this score, too, one can cautiously talk of a slow convergence of our unspoken assumptions.

But let me go back to your fascinating comparison between Cologne and Coventry. First, if you were to compare the two cities in 1930, as you later suggested, you would find very considerable differences in the non-economic sphere: language, social behaviour, traditions, town planning, etc. would all underline the dissimilarities rather than the similarities, and, as I have already said, it would be naïve to assume that these do not matter. At the same time you would find both cities based on the private Capitalist enterprise. The ownership of factories would be handed down from father to son, in other cases a bank would act as midwife, but the mechanism would be the same. You would find a work pattern in which the mass of workers earned wages or salaries but had no job security; they would be dependent on the goodwill of the owner with the, perhaps false, impression (I won't argue this point) that the boss's profits were taken out of their pay packets. You would find two cities sharing an identical, Christian civilisation and an identical code of values. You would also find two towns which looked very similar. So a comparative analysis would yield signs of convergence and signs of divergence. What one would like to know is: are the similarities due to similarities in the economic and technological structure or are they independent from it?

URBAN: It is here that one senses a flaw in Galbraith's 'Marxism'. If the theory of convergence à la Galbraith were true, then the imperatives of strictly privately owned exploitative societies should logically lead to convergence with the same force as they allegedly do between state-owned industries in the U.S.S.R. and the privately owned, but faceless, large U.S. corporations. This has never happened and Marx never said it would. Marx foresaw that the 'rapacity' of the private Capitalist would prevent such neat solidarities from arising, and in this he has been borne out by history. But if one took Galbraith in the narrow sense, there should have been convergence between Baltimore and Hiroshima in the 1940s or, to get away from war-time examples, between Lyon and Leipzig in 1928. There was not—there was trade war.

DUVERGER: I think you are stretching the point slightly. I cannot speak for Galbraith, but from the very few things he has said on this subject it would be unfair to conclude that he sees a crude kind of determinism operating between technology and social organisation. I do not think he ever thought, and *I* certainly never thought, that one day Western Europe, the U.S. and the Soviet Union would resemble each other so much in their technological and social structure that you would be able to say they are identical. I think we will not reach that point in the foreseeable future, because even if you had a fully Socialist United States with all firms in public hands, and even if you had a planned and centralised economy there, you would still have to take account of an American culture, of American traditions of behaviour and a whole range of historically-determined factors

301

which make the U.S. into what it is and what the U.S.S.R. cannot be. Conversely, if there were liberalisation, decentralisation, pluralism in the East European states, there would still remain the difference that these countries started from Socialism and the reforms were only grafted on to the main trunk of Socialism rather than the reverse, which would be the case in the U.S. where Capitalism would provide the starting point. So the framework would be different at the start, and consequently the resulting structure, even after many changes, would show important differences.

Now coming back to Cologne and Coventry in the early 1940s: I do not think one can take Germany under Hitler as an example and draw conclusions from it. In my personal view, Nazism in Germany was an historical accident. This kind of totalitarian Fascism had never before arisen in an advanced industrial country and, when all is said and done, it lasted no more than twelve years, from 1933 to 1945—a very short time on the time-scale of history. All the other examples we have of Fascist regimes come from semi-developed countries like Portugal, Spain, Greece and Italy which was also an underdeveloped country in the 1920s.

URBAN: It is interesting to reflect that before the Nazis took office, Germany was one of the educationally and socially most advanced countries in Europe, and in its technology it was probably *the* most highly developed. Germany had excellent social services, exemplary schools and more Ph.Ds per head of population than any other country in Europe. Yet when the crunch came, the German intellectuals, especially those in the technological occupations, did not make a name for themselves by their resistance to Hitler; on the contrary, the great majority of them went along with him. And at the end of the war one could see how easily men like von Braun and the other rocket technologists switched to working for Soviet and American interests, and my reading of this would be that their loyalty was more to the hardware that excited their imagination than to the human or inhuman ends which their gadgets were made to serve. Now I don't know whether this could be intepreted as a specifically German phenomenon or whether one should cast some general doubt on Professor Galbraith's third point—his assumption namely that the requirements of technical sophistication cannot be reconciled with intellectual regimentation.

DUVERGER: I do not think any of the German experience should be ascribed to characteristics peculiar to the German temperament. I do not believe in characteristics peculiar to any race or nation. Of course history cannot be conjured away from the cultural milieu; but then Germany had a very respectable liberal tradition as well as an authoritarian tradition, and the latter was not in any way predestined to get the upper hand. In 1918 Germany went through a Freudian trauma, what with the defeat that overwhelmed it and then seemed to engulf it, driving as it were a wedge into a country which had a formidably dynamic economy and which was thus made politically impotent. Then came the great depression. In one of my books, *Les Parties politiques*, I set out in a graph the curve of National Socialist Party membership and the curve of growth of unemployment in Germany. The two lines run parallel.

If you take a closer look at intellectual protest in Hitler's Germany you will find there evidence of what Galbraith is saying and what I am saying about a highly developed industrial society demanding freedom through its intellectuals. From the moment Hitler took over, the German scientific élite, not just the Jews, began to leave the country. The beneficiaries were the American universities where large numbers of the most brilliant German scientists—Jews, Socialists, Christians—found fresh room for their talents. And this meant that German science gradually lost some of its former excellence. If I had the wit of a Voltaire I would write a philosophical parable explaining how Germany lost the war because the regime despised its intellectuals and, in fact, got rid of some of its very best brains. One could almost boil it down to one man, Albert Einstein: if he had stayed in Germany, Germany would quite likely have got the atom bomb before the U.S. and, with it, it could have won the war. So, broadly speaking, the case of Hitler's Germany does not contradict Galbraith's ideas or mine.

URBAN: I wonder if one can generalise quite as broadly. I think in a dictatorship intellectual dissent is quite likely to occur among high-level scientists, writers and artists, but I am not so sure that the run-of-the-mill technologists aren't more likely to be fairly willing supporters of the regime, or at any rate keep their mouths shut. Your examples in Germany all refer to leading, independent scholars, and the personalities involved in dissent in the Soviet Union—Sakharov, Sinyavsky, Daniel—also come from that group. The man one step down the ladder —that is, the large majority of technically trained people—has not shown himself to be a great fighter for freedom.

DUVERGER: I would say that the managerial class, including the technocracy, would, generally speaking, fight for greater efficiency and freedom only if efficiency is a function (as I am sure it is) of more freedom. Nevertheless I am convinced, as I have said earlier in this conversation, that the demand for more personal liberty becomes universal as society gets more technologically sophisticated and the standard of living reaches a certain level. Freedom becomes one of the creature comforts. We know from personal contact with East Europeans that it is the ordinary man who feels himself deprived if he cannot see American films, or listen to Western music, or visit Western countries. I will admit that the process may have to be a slow one and, with it, convergence is bound to be very slow too, but it is inevitable.

URBAN: I often feel that some of the protest in the Soviet Union is part of an international challenge of the establishment by the younger generation—and it does not seem to matter whether the establishment is the industrial–military complex in the U.S. or the Party apparatus in the U.S.S.R.

DUVERGER: What seems to me important is that there can be such a challenge under a Communist regime. You realise that you have just defended the idea of convergence, because you are saying that when your young Russians or Czechs defy their governments, they are acting in a very similar manner, and for the same kind of reasons, as your American or French students? Well, thirty years ago, under Stalin, such a challenge to the establishment was unimaginable. It was not possible because of the terror and also because people imagined that it was impossible. But today, the challenge is growing all the time and this in my opinion is proof that Galbraith and I were right in saying that the questioning cannot stop at the drawing board. Where I differ from Galbraith is his judgement of the power of an authoritarian state to hold back or slow down the process. Convergence will come up against many obstacles. The apparatus is very strong. It would be a mistake to under-estimate the power of the dictatorship. Convergence will not be a mechanistic affair, it will not be a straight progression. It will, I think, follow a jagged line with moments of convergence alternating with moments of divergence. In the Soviet Union nowadays there is visibly less freedom than there was under Khrushchev and even for some time after Khrushchev. Liberalisation is in retreat, but if you look at the facts closely, even now you have more liberty than you had before Khrushchev and, above all, you have a greater resistance.

URBAN: How far is convergence likely to go in the coming twenty or thirty years? What forms is it likely to assume, which segments of life can it possibly affect? Will it simply mean that the factory worker in Moscow and New York will have the same kind of motor-car and like the same sort of musical, or will it mean something more profound than that?

DUVERGER: It is impossible to make a forecast in terms of future institutions. That would be political science fiction. All one can say is that future institutions will be very different from what they are today in the East and in the West. Possibly we shall have societies which will all look very much alike, but the cultural traditions will not disappear. Basically, in any new-style political and economic institution two features can be expected to predominate: in Eastern Europe society will reach a stage where there will be freedom of discussion and pluralism, not necessarily of the multi-party kind; in the West we'll have a large, centrally planned, Socialist sector.

Of course one has to realise that convergence has been greatly hampered by the virtually permanent economic crisis in which the East European states have found themselves over the last ten–fifteen years. This is a grave structural crisis, and liberal thinkers like Raymond Aron will tell you: this proves that Socialism works badly while Capitalism, as we can see in France and the EEC, works well. That is not necessarily the right conclusion. If we had recorded this interview in 1932, I would have told you that the West's economy was in a catastrophic state and many people would have drawn the conclusion (and many did) that Capitalism was on its death bed. But it wasn't finished. I will not go into explaining why the East European countries have got themselves into their current economic difficulties—the reasons are as well known as the remedies are difficult to find. What matters for the purposes of my argument is that, in a crisis situation, authoritarian countries find it extremely hard to make themselves more liberal. An authoritarian state, where the apparatus is in the hands of a single party or one individual, is always frightened of freedom; and if things are not going well, liberalisation will be halted or postponed. So that is another reason for not expecting convergence to come about overnight.

URBAN: It seems to me that the theory of convergence, especially when it is propounded by American scholars, lacks historical dimension. Galbraith—a horizontalist—talks about the contemporary scene as though nothing had happened in history before 1930 or thereabouts. But one could surely talk of convergence with equal justification in a vertical, historical sense and say, for instance, that the similarities between Stalin and Ivan the Terrible tell us more about the reasons why Soviet society is in the state it is, or about the East–West conflict, than anything that links the worker in Nowa Huta with the worker in Gary, Indiana. This conception of 'convergence' underlines the specific gravity of nations and the way in which national governments tend to repeat the policies of their predecessors, and such factors are surely every bit as important as those technologically determined. One could also speak of the enormous influence of language, the English language for example, which has made for significant similarities between the U.S. and Britain in almost every field of life, and so on.

DUVERGER: If we want to adopt an approach that is scientifically dependable, we must combine the two methods: explaining Stalin in terms of Ivan the Terrible or Peter the Great is one aspect of the problem, a valid aspect of truth, but you must also explain Stalin in terms of the evolution of society, of the conditions after the October Revolution, of the needs of industrialisation within a Communist framework. There is, as you intimate, a tendency in all Western countries, not only in the U.S., to belittle or write off the historical factors in our culture and to concentrate instead on the contemporary scene. It is easier but it is wrong and dangerous. If it is allowed to go on, in not so many years our cultural heritage will be something for antiquarians to know about in underfinanced university departments.

URBAN: Can you foresee a state of affairs arising in the U.S.S.R., say, before the end of the century, where one can go to that country, make any speech one likes and where the Soviet citizen, too, can get up and criticise the government on any issue he likes? I am not even thinking of a pluralistic democracy on the Western pattern, but I wonder whether such freedoms might be attained within the general framework of a Socialist one-party state, but one that might provide certain openings for pluralistic interests.

307

DUVERGER: I have to summarise here the views of a friend of mine from Eastern Europe who visits me periodically. There was a time when we could not meet for he could not get out of his country, then there was a time when we saw each other very freely. Well, about three years ago we were sitting together here in my study discussing more or less the same questions we are discussing now, and this is what he said: 'Some years ago I thought the evolution towards liberalisation would be very rapid. I now think it will be a long and difficult process. There will be reversals, but it will happen all the same.' Now that is pretty well what I think myself: it will be slow and difficult for many reasons, the main one being that a dictatorship has great difficulty ceasing to be a dictatorship. It needs a slow but continuous pressure. But the changes will come, always excepting some drastic deterioration in international relations, threats of war and so on. But so long as things stay roughly as they are, I think it will inevitably happen.

URBAN: Talking in terms of industrially developed societies, Czechoslovakia and East Germany, and to some extent, Hungary and Poland too, would seem to be nearer to the West in their economic structure than the Soviet Union and therefore more convergence-prone if your thesis is correct. Can we expect a faster tempo of liberalisation in these countries than in the U.S.S.R.?

DUVERGER: Well, there are two points to be made here. First, I do not hold with Galbraith that economic structure is all-decisive; there are national and cultural traditions which also play a great role. In some of the East European countries, notably in Hungary and Poland, there is a tradition of armed struggle against oppressive regimes, especially if they are foreign oppressions, and we have seen how that tradition reasserted itself in Hungary in 1956 and in a somewhat un-Polish, bloodless fashion in Poland too. The Czech tradition is of a more peaceable nature but no less important.

Now as against these traditions, we have the almost equally

traditional policy of the Soviet Union (and earlier of Russia under the Czars) to keep the members of its group together, so that if they march in this or that direction, they must march in step. I had a long conversation the other day with a Soviet scholar, and one of the things I told him was what you have just raised with me: Czechoslovakia, with its deep-seated democracy, liberal traditions and sophisticated industrial base was surely cut out to provide a liberal model of socialism from which the whole Soviet camp would benefit. His reply was very striking: 'That is possible,' he said, 'but so long as we are confronted with Capitalist states, we must maintain the close-knit, cooperative unity of the Socialist side. We cannot allow any one country to leave it, or even any one country to advance more rapidly towards a liberal system than the others.' This argument is, of course, debatable from many points of view but it is a valid argument. So I believe it would be misleading to expect that the more industrially or politically advanced of the East European countries will be allowed to get out of step and converge more rapidly than the rest. One need not approve of the reasons that lie behind this policy but one can understand them: news and views have a way of spreading with extra-ordinary speed in Eastern Europe. A spectacular advance in liberalisation in one country would have immediate repercussions in the others, with consequences that may escape Soviet control. For all these reasons one would do well to base one's estimate of the possible speed of convergence on the speed of the Soviet steam engine rather than on the faster motors that propel the other East European countries.

URBAN: There is perhaps a kind of perverted convergence in the way in which Western Europe and Eastern Europe have tried to hammer out their respective unities. It is a striking fact that the philosophy behind the European Economic Community is *'marxisant'*. The Community was established on the assumption that if once the economic interests of the Six were inextricably woven together, their political policies would follow suit, first by simply eliminating national political antagonisms, and later by causing economic integration to spill over into political unification. Eastern Europe, on the other hand, has been proceeding in a decidedly anti-Marxist, and I would say typically conservative, fashion, putting political considerations persistently in command of economic considerations. This goes for Comecon, and until quite recently for most of the Communist economic plans and it certainly explains the disequilibrium of the Soviet economy. So if *we* go on acting as good Marxists, and *they* in Eastern Europe as good conservatives, perhaps there is more in convergence than meets the theory.

DUVERGER: There *is* this paradox you describe and there are more of a similar nature. The development of Western political institutions over the past sixty years shows very clearly that it runs exactly parallel with the development of industrialisation. The West provides a marvellous example of Marxism at work deep in the sinews of our society. Now on the other side of the fence, the *political* will came first and everything else followed from there. Lenin and the Bolsheviks took *political* power in 1917; after the Second World War it was Soviet *military* and *political* power that helped the East European Communist parties into the saddle and, as you say, the East European economies themselves were, and still are, in most cases functions of political policies. In a sentence: the Socialist regimes provide a good example of how a Capitalist economy is installed and run. Whether this is convergence, I do not know, but it is a paradox worth pondering.

THÉO LEFÈVRE

The Fallacy of
Technological Convergence

Théo Lefèvre is Minister in Charge of Politics and Scientific Development in the Belgian Government and Chairman of the EEC Committee for Space Research and Technology. Between 1961 and 1965 M. Lefèvre was the Prime Minister of Belgium. Earlier he was President of the International Union of Christian Democrats and held several other posts in national and international organisations. M. Lefèvre is Flemish by birth and a lawyer by profession. Between 1940 and 1945 he was a member of the Belgian resistance. He has been a member of the Belgian Chamber of Representatives since 1948.

URBAN: It is one of the fashions of our time to believe, if one is an optimist and a liberal intellectual, that the nature of technology and the scale on which technology is applied, have an imperative of their own and that this causes industrial societies to converge. An important element of this convergence is said to be the decentralisation of the economy and of power from the state to the firm in Eastern Europe, and a slow growth of planning in the West European and American societies. From this it is inferred that the similarities in the industrial and technical organisation spin off to the related social organisation so that the two societies become more and more similar in their culture, style of living, silent assumptions about the meaning of the good life and so on.

The reason usually cited for thinking that the spillover will occur is that you cannot have a technologically sophisticated system without sophisticated scientists and technologists to run it. It is assumed, for instance, that in a Soviet-type of dictatorship a man who makes a good mathematician or electrical en-

311

gineer would also want to question the unfreedom in which he lives, that he would demand some say in the social control of the factory in which he works, that he would want to support trade unions that really defend the workers' right even against the state and so forth. In England the late Aneuran Bevan was one of the early protagonists of this theory, and more recently Maurice Duverger and J. K. Galbraith have identified themselves with it in different degrees. Do you believe that a shared technology does in fact lead to such profound similarities as would justify the use of the word 'convergence'?

LEFÈVRE: Let me say at once that I do not believe that a technological civilisation is in itself a good thing. It possesses no innate virtue. When one puts the Communist and Capitalist systems side by side with each other, there are indeed certain similarities between them, but to conclude from that that the two systems converge would be extremely far fetched. Usually those isolated aspects of the two societies which seem similar from a distance reveal themselves, on closer examination, not to be similar after all : they have to do more with the civilisation in which they are historically rooted than with the technological context in which the naked eye perceives them. I am not denying for a moment that science and technical skills influence civilisations, but it is an extremely slow process.

I would say, however, that there is a sense—a rather sad sense—in which the Communist and Capitalist worlds do converge. The Communists are materialists in their ideology, but capable of great devotion and of showing certain spiritual qualities, while in the Capitalist world we are theoretically heirs to a Christian civilisation but in practice we are gross materialists. That is one way we are converging but, from the moral point of view, this is a depressing prospect rather than an elevating one.

When you say that in a totalitarian system a mathematician or an electrical engineer is expected to enforce the habit of enquiry outside his specialism, questioning the political and ideological system in which he lives, then again my response would have to be hedged around with reservations. If this questioning is supposed to coin a common intellectual currency between the two societies, I for one can see no sign of it. I have noticed in the twenty-five years I have spent in public life that a man can be a competent scientist and ask profoundly intelligent questions in his field without being able, and often without being willing, to apply the same degree of intelligence outside his bailiwick. Ortega y Gasset says in one of his books that inside every man there lurks an average man: I belong to the general mass of humanity as soon as I go outside the field I have learnt to understand and deal with; there my judgements have exactly the same validity as those of the man in the street. I do not believe the technical intelligentsia have a hot line to truth or some predestination to pursue justice and liberty. I do not believe that a technologist in Kiev is more likely to question the Soviet system than a disgruntled housewife, or that his judgements would be more pertinent, or deserve greater respect, than hers.

URBAN: What if the technician were allowed to be a culturally more rounded man than he is today? Would you still say that his questioning would have no special value outside his field? We know that in Eastern Europe the fully cultured person is not trusted. Technologists are thought to be politically less dangerous than men steeped in such thought-provoking, and therefore ideologically sensitive, activities as philosophy, psychology and sociology. In Soviet high schools even the study of Greek and Latin is heavily restricted—the fully literate person is suspect. From the historical point of view this fear of literacy is perhaps not very surprising, for it was not more than a century ago that the unauthorised teaching of the alphabet was a seditious activity in Czarist law and carried a heavy prison sentence.

LEFÈVRE: The problem is extemely relevant to the future of our own society. In America and some of the other technologically advanced countries the demand for specialists is receding, and parallel with that recession there is a striking demand for men with broad educational backgrounds. The meaning of this trend is that, given the rapid advance of technology, society has a greater need of men who possess a sound critical sense than of those who have special skills in this or that area. As you say, in the Communist countries it is this type of fully developed person they are afraid of. The underdeveloped person is an easier fit. A conversation I have recently had with two young Czech fugitives brought this point home to me: they had carefully not been taught history. The schools kept them from their past—for them history began with the Communist regime. In the very short run this sort of indoctrination may pay off. In the long run, however, an educational system so lopsided is bound to boomerang on Communist society. Soviet technology can boast of remarkable successes—though I should add that they have all occurred in highly circumscribed fields—yet it is entirely predictable that the unbalanced education which the technically trained Russians are now given is bound to slow down their country's economic and technological development.

URBAN: But isn't the trend in America rather similar? The American technologist is also highly specialised and is less and less familiar with what goes on in the humanities—he even has a slight disdain for them as 'soft' options. Speaking in this series, Professor Philip Rieff of the University of Pennsylvania, said in a striking phrase that the sign of modern barbarism is historic amnesia, a complete lack of historic memory. This would apply to the two Czechs you describe but also to the worship of modernity and change that characterises much of American society. So perhaps one could talk here of a convergence of intellectual approaches, if only a negative one.

LEFÈVRE: A negative one, certainly. However, we must be fair and not see the American situation through too narrow an aperture. In Western Europe, and to a lesser extent in America too, over-specialisation and historic amnesia are trends which are open to correction. We are free to protest and criticise, and we do. But it ill becomes a European to condemn in a fit of self-righteousness the confrontations which take place from time to time in American history. They can be brutal and I do not like this brutality, but I think it is a healthy sign that a great nation like the American holds itself up for self-questioning practically once every two generations. One can only hope that one day there will be convergence with the Soviet Union in this matter of self-examination. So far there is no sign of it.

URBAN: Coming back to the general question of convergence, you are implying, if I understand you correctly, that traditional factors such as history, nationality, language, literature are more important in determining the way in which a civilisation, even a technological civilisation, advances than technological factors.

LEFÈVRE: It is not quite that; in order to understand a civilisation and to be able to judge the direction in which it is going, one cannot stress in isolation one particular aspect of it such as its technology and industry. Those who do so are unconsciously adopting a Marxist point of view—the technological base determining the 'super-structure'. It is precisely the use of this kind of a distorting mirror, the practice of stressing one aspect of the needs of society to the exclusion of all others, that has sparked off the protest at our universities and especially in America. If the American schools tend to turn out the same type of technically skilled but under-educated people as the Russian universities, then the American dissenters certainly know what they are doing—they are protesting against this one-sided and inhuman ethos. But here is the big difference: in the U.S. you can sound the alarm; in the Soviet Union the alarm bells don't ring.

URBAN: Wouldn't you say that young people will rise against the establishment whatever its political complexion? In America it is the military-industrial complex—in Eastern Europe it is the Party and the police state.

LEFÈVRE: In every country the revolt of youth is the revolt of life against the machine. But in the West the protests are listened to, in the Soviet lands they are stifled.

URBAN: But aren't the mechanisation of life, cybernation, automation, part of the price we are paying for modernisation and technological progress? Aren't they a necessary, even an inevitable, price?

LEFÈVRE: I am borrowing from Bergson when I say: life is against the machine. Society becomes an ant-hill as soon as it makes its peace with the proposition that man is there for the progress of science and technology. But once we hold firm to the idea that science and technology exist for the benefit of man, society will, or may, go in an entirely different direction. There is nothing inevitable about the price of technology, but we can see what happens if we get our priorities wrong or allow our senses to be dulled by double talk: the Communist regimes too claim that in their societies technology is there for the good of man, but for fifty years now they have been sacrificing millions of their people to a scientific and technological mirage which has not given their citizens greater freedom or more human dignity. Their means have been terrible, their results nugatory.

But looking around in our part of the world, one has no reason to be pessimistic. Science and technology have given the individual in Western Europe more freedom and they have endowed him with a fuller sense of his dignity than he had before. I have only to look at my own country, Belgium: what a change there has been for the better since the Second World War! And I am certain that the scientific revolution of the 1970s will produce further improvements. Today large sections of our population which, until the 1950s, had no share in the economic, intellectual and spiritual wealth of our country, have a chance of sharing it and do indeed share it; and all this has been achieved without forfeiting any portion of their freedom as citizens or individuals.

URBAN: I am disturbed by one forecast shared by future-oriented researchers on both sides of the Atlantic. Norbert Wiener says that there is no place in modern industry for anybody below an IQ of about 110, and that means below the top quarter of the population. Dennis Gabor shows that in the post-industrial civilisation we are now entering less than half the working population will be fit for any useful employment. 'Soon,' he says, 'the minority which has to work for the rest may be so small that it could be entirely recruited from the most gifted part of the population. The rest will be socially useless by the standards of our present-day civilisation.' When you say: science and technology can be harnessed to serve man—how can they serve man if, precisely because of the high brain-power which the running of an electronic-industrial society requires, every second man and woman will become simply superfluous and, indeed, a burden on society? Therapeutic employment has been suggested as a palliative, and this is already established practice in some factories where over-manning is an accepted arm in the distribution of welfare benefits. But with all that, it is bizarre to speak of the triumph of science if that relegates half the population to socially second-class citizenship. Lafargue's impassioned defence of man's right to be idle has never found much acceptance in the West. People who have been made to feel superfluous usually get themselves, and the society they blame for their redundancy, into deep trouble.

LEFÈVRE: I do not share this pessimism. On the contrary, I believe that the age of the computer opens up exceptional educational opportunities. It would eliminate the spectre of people never stretched to the limit of their innate capacity. Educational methods are making such rapid progress that it is possible to foresee a period of overall advance and a completely new form of interplay between educators and the educated—everyone, in fact, educating everyone else. What is even more important, the computer, far from depersonalising the educational process, will cater for and underline the sovereignty of the individual, as it can be programmed to satisfy the needs of vast numbers

317

of people with great precision in minimum time.

But I am convinced that over and above the methods of education, the motivation for acquiring an education will also change. Until quite recently a young man would study because he would want to have status, climb up the social ladder and earn more money. In the society that is now opening up before our eyes the general level of education will be higher, working hours shorter and the pressure for higher earnings less acute. So people will study not so much for material benefit as to raise the quality of life. Of course there will be pitfalls, but despite the depressingly materialistic atmosphere in which we are now content to live, Western society is open and free enough for the pitfalls to be avoided. In a totalitarian society this is not so, or at any rate much less so, and when I say 'totalitarian' I make no distinction between totalitarian regimes of the Left and Right.

URBAN: How is our freedom to guard against these pitfalls best used? What is the ideal mix in education—technological training overlaid by a coating taken from the humanities, or a humanitarian education which recognises the utility of technological expertise but looks upon it as a means to an end? I can hardly see the two pulling equal weight in a common harness.

LEFÈVRE: The split between the two cultures is one of the great ills afflicting industrial civilisation both of the Capitalist and Communist variety. We must try and create a new humanism in which the two cultures are reunited, but that cannot be done unless we have an educational system which is both pluralistic and provides certain guide-posts for the attainment of new philosophical and spiritual horizons. This in turn presupposes a sound background of historical culture. If men do not feel that they are part of a tradition, if they forget that they must build on the past and not destroy it every time they set out to build a new city or a new enterprise, civilisation will relapse into barbarism. This, too, was put very eloquently by Ortega y Gasset (I suspect a long time before Professor Rieff thought of it). Ortega says that the average man is deficient in historic

318

memory; he believes that everything around him is given and that he is not responsible for the maintenance and development of the material and intellectual goods which have been handed down to him by previous generations. This is a form of adolescence which must be fought.

URBAN: There would seem to be powerful forces in the world of science which are hostile to the new humanism you mention. They would deplore any attempt to keep in touch with historic cultures as a dangerous anachronism. Looking at these problems from the commanding height you occupy both in your country and in EEC, would it be your opinion that certain questions and perhaps whole problem areas should be debarred from scientific enquiry for the simple reason that the results might be too dangerous?

LEFÈVRE: Even if it were possible and desirable to construct an index of such problems it would be illusory to hope that an index could be enforced. Man has an urge to know things and, natural disasters apart, nothing will stop his quest for a deeper scientific understanding. Scientific freedom must remain intact and freedom itself must remain intact enough to make it possible for non-scientists to bring their influence to bear on the uses of science and technology. For we must constantly bear in mind that the exact sciences do not have all the answers, and we must make it quite plain that in a new humanism scientists and traditional humanists alike must learn to be humble and more sceptical about the value of their work and pay much more attention to what the man on the other side of the fence is doing. Today each tends to believe that his own field is just that little more important than any other.

I must refer here to something Bergson said time and again in his books, so much so that it has become a commonplace: at a time when man's knowledge is increasing and his power over other men is increasing, what he needs most is 'soul'. Morally man has not made anything like the same progress as he has made with his scientific faculties. This is the great problem of our age, and I do not think the scientist can disclaim all responsibility in the matter: he cannot say with Kaiser Wilhelm II '*Ich hab' es nicht gewollt*'. Clearly one cannot, and perhaps one should not, hold up the progress of science, but that does not mean to say that every invention should be translated into a practical means simply because the technology for its manufacture is at hand. Outside controls are needed and these inevitably rest on a conception of man, on a conception of what is useful to humanity and what is not. Science cannot be its own judge; man alone can.

URBAN: I wonder if it is wise or adequate to rely on man's ability to judge. You are saying that science is neutral, that technology has no predilections either Left or Right. But the human material is very unreliable. I can't think of anything to put one in a more pessimistic frame of mind than a look at the history of the 20th Century. In this age of ostensible enlightenment we had the largest numbers of crimes perpetrated by men such as Stalin and Hitler, with the passive connivance of many others. The fallibility of the moral judgement of man has shown itself to be extreme. If, as you say, man is the measure, is he a measure all to himself? What should be his lights for telling good from evil, a desirable end from one which is undesirable?

LEFÈVRE: You mention concrete examples and they are a warning. I nevertheless remember one or two which show that there is a certain point at which man can say No. When I was a boy we used to be told that in the next war poison gas would be used. Well, poison gas wasn't used. Gas has never been used because everyone realises that the consequences would be suicidal. I have the impression that in the case of the atom bomb too we have come to the same point: everyone has it, but there is a hesitation to use it.

As far as I am concerned, the guarantee that man's judgements are based on an equitable yardstick is his moral sense based on faith, and this may also be the guarantee of his survival. I am a Roman Catholic but I do not suggest for a moment that one has to be a Catholic, or even a Christian, in order to have such a faith, but one must have *a* faith that provides guidelines. And I believe all positive faiths that I know are summed up in the words of St. Paul (*Romans* 8, 14–15): 'For all who are moved by the Spirit of God are sons of God.' It is, I know, rather bad form to say these things today and it makes one immediately thought of as a hopeless reactionary. Nevertheless, it has to be said clearly that the moment one has given up faith, one has disarmed oneself of all moral restraints and the way is wide open for the ghastliest crimes of war and peace.

URBAN: Would you say that the Soviet version of Marxism, especially as it was practised under Stalin, provides one kind of faith you have in mind? Earlier in this discussion you said that there was a spiritual element in Communist practice.

LEFÈVRE: No, I find Communism is the very opposite of faith.

URBAN: Even the Maoist variety?

LEFÈVRE: Even that. It is a sign of the cultural muddle in which we live that the distinctions between faith, ideology, politics and propaganda should be so hopelessly blurred. I am talking of faith in its proper sense. It is only by an act of doubtful extrapolation that one can call Fascism a faith, or Communism a faith. These two in particular enclose man in an entirely manmade universe.

URBAN: Faith, then, in your definition must have an element of the supernatural, of God, in it?

LEFÈVRE: Yes, that is my deep conviction.

URBAN: Maoism relies rather obviously on Confucian and Christian models. Mao's moral yardstick is not very different from the yardstick of a rather overbearing *pater familias* in

Victorian England. It seems to me that when Mao appeals to the ordinary Chinese to sacrifice himself for the revolution, to lead a frugal life, etc., he is appealing to a genuinely religious type of sentiment.

LEFÈVRE: I would no more call Maoism a religion than I would call idolatry a religion. Christianity has liberated man from the worship of idols, yet we are coming back to precisely that in modern civilisation. Communism is one case in point, Fascism another. And if tomorrow the objects of worship are the wonders of technology, then the whole of our scientific civilisation too will degenerate into a form of idolatry. The first signs of that tendency are already well visible.

URBAN: Is there some practical manner in which we can attack this problem, some institutional way of reversing the reversal?

LEFÈVRE: I can only repeat that our moral and, as part of that, our political consciousness has not kept up with the development of science and technology. We can do more than we can do responsibly. We must, by degrees, heighten our sense of moral vigilance so that it can draw level with whatever we have achieved by our practical faculties alone, but that cannot be done without thinking of our problems in terms of a global order. Yet, a global order will not happen overnight; it will require patient work, predominantly educational. When I said a minute ago that it is by positive faith alone that humanity can escape the new idolatries, I did not imagine for an instant that this could be done by the use of force or pressure. Under the broad umbrella of faith we should foster, at the heart of the educational system, pluralistic conceptions. As these come into being, there should be scope for everyone to work out for himself a code of conduct fully in keeping with his religious or philosophical convictions.

URBAN: Isn't there a danger that the large units which a global order would require might impose on the individual a much greater degree of uniformity than would be compatible with the pluralistic outlook you envisage? We have proof of pluralism thriving in the small European principalities of the 17th and 18th Centuries, but large units such as the U.S. and Soviet Russia would seem to push in the opposite direction.

LEFÈVRE: Unification, such as the one we are witnessing in Western Europe today, does not and must not be allowed to mean uniformity. Unification must be our aim, but unification must, and does, take account of differences, whether they are national, cultural or religious. That is why I am stressing the importance of unification in those fields where non-unification might be suicidal, but I am also stressing the need of pluralism in those where life isn't fully lived unless it is lived in its full variety. If unification is allowed to make us all uniform, then there will be nothing to choose between our kind of society which we still like to think of as free, and the tyranny of the monolithic social model over the individual—Communism. But there is nothing in our experience in Europe to suggest either that we are insufficiently alert to the danger, or that we are insufficiently determined to fight it if it arises.

JAMES FAWCETT

The Anachronisms of Sovereignty in a Technological World

James Fawcett, who has been Director of Studies at the Royal Institute of International Affairs, Chatham House, since 1969, is an international lawyer with special interest in space research. He was a Fellow of All Souls College, Oxford in 1938 and again between 1960 and 1969. Between 1945 and 1950 Mr. Fawcett was Assistant Legal Adviser to the Foreign Office and worked at the United Nations, FAO, UNESCO and the British Embassy in Washington. In 1950–55 he was the Editor of *International Law Quarterly* and between 1955 and 1960 General Counsel to IMF in Washington. Since 1969 Mr. Fawcett has been Vice President of the European Commission of Human Rights of which he has been a member since 1962. He published *British Commonwealth in International Law* (1963), *International Law and the Uses of Outer Space* (1968), *The Law of Nations* (1968) and *The Application of the European Convention on Human Rights* (1969).

GLENNY: A distinguished economist at the London School of Economics, E. J. Mishan, has recently published a book in which he attacks the idea of economic growth as such. There are also some people who would say that Western Capitalism and Soviet-type Communism at present share a common rationale, namely that maximum growth plus a maximal application of technology equals good, and that this is the complete justification of all government economic policies. Mishan, on the other hand, says that growth is something that is not necessarily good *per se*, but that certain criteria must be applied to growth when planning our economy or when planning for the social results of economic growth. Are you in agreement with him or otherwise?

FAWCETT: I am largely in agreement with him. I have read his book and my reaction to it is as follows : I would agree with him that economic growth as the single goal, i.e. the steady increase of production of material goods, is insufficient. There are —or there ought to be—three kinds of objectives for our society. One is economic growth. The second, with which we are now becoming much more concerned than we used to be, is the conservation of the environment and all its resources. And the third objective is the securing of certain elementary rights and freedoms. These objectives have emerged, let us say since the war, as being broadly the kind of objectives that most communities in the world are aiming at, regardless of their political systems. Now these objectives are really in conflict with each other, and herein lies the difficulty. While I do not think economic growth is bad in itself, what is bad about it is its 'open-endedness', and this is where it collides with the proper treatment of the environment and the wise management of our resources. It collides because in a state of nature any group of plants and animals—including man himself as long as he doesn't interfere with nature too much—always attains over time a certain stability, an equilibrium. In any particular eco-system there is a balance between the species, and this balance is achieved at the cost maybe of some species being gradually eliminated, but a balance is achieved and this is, if you like, the objective of an eco-system. Now economic growth seems to me to have no such objective: it simply goes on indefinitely. And it is this inability of economists so far even to try to define at what point economic growth reaches the natural climax that is its most dangerously negative characteristic. And I think it's only by formulating some positive objective for economic growth that we can balance it against extensive damage to our environment.

GLENNY: Mishan recommends that all manufacturing and service industries be subjected to some form of curb through which the real social cost of disamenities and diseconomies produced by a manufacturer's products or services should be reflected in the cost of that product to the manufacturer. Therefore, if a manufacturer makes something which in itself produces harmful consequences to society such as the exhaust gases given out by motor-cars, or if the manufacturing process, for instance, covers the surrounding countryside with smoke and fumes, then the manufacturer must be deterred economically by being obliged to calculate the economic result of this disamenity into the cost of the product or the process. Now it seems to me that Mishan, who describes the mechanics of this proposal in some detail, is shirking the political problem which this will raise, namely that to enforce such a process of control across the entire spectrum of manufacturing and service industries will mean deploying a super-bureaucracy with enormous powers. And yet at the same time Mishan is an advocate of the hundred per cent competitive economy. First, have you any thoughts on how to reconcile such direct interference with the economic process in a free-enterprise economy, and second, on whether such an apparatus (in the Soviet sense of 'apparat') would not very soon become a potentially oppressive form of bureaucracy?

FAWCETT: Mishan's solution, i.e. the imposition of some charge for the disamenity on the manufacturer who creates it, is obviously right in principle. But I don't think it is of nearly wide enough application in practice to be sufficient, and for two reasons. One is that the kind of economic growth we are talking about is nothing so simple and straightforward as the building of, say, a single factory that might make smoke. Of course I recognise that for Mishan this is a model only, but, nevertheless, we are dealing with activities on a very large scale indeed, in which, as in the case of the *Torrey Canyon* disaster, when the entire contents of a giant oil-tanker poured into the sea off the coast of England, the kind of damage that is involved is far beyond what individuals or even very large companies can easily control or correct.

My second reason is that in this problem of economic growth creating disamenity, there may be situations, albeit temporary ones, in which it is in the social interest to tolerate the dis-amenity. And therefore, if I find that Mishan's approach has limitations, it is in the fact that it is too individualistic. For example, somebody pointed out not long ago that if the same attitude had been rigorously adopted in the early 18th Century, the same analysis made of the products of coal, the smoke that it put into the atmosphere and the hazards that this had for health, I think it's arguable that the Industrial Revolution would never have been allowed to take place. We have to recognise that the solution of many of these problems is a matter of balance. Now it may be that people in a particular neighbour-hood dislike the noise of aircraft—and legitimately—but I think the real problem here, which can't be dodged, is this: who is really to be allowed to decide between the demands of expand-ing transport and local interests? The placing of nuclear energy plants may also create the same kind of difficulty. We have been lucky so far and there have been no accidents, or no major ac-cidents, in British atomic energy plants, but presumably there could be; they would certainly have a local effect, but probably much more than local effect. Therefore I see the matter as basi-cally a problem for the whole community and one which can't really be left to the people in the locality, at least not in most cases. The whole use of fossil fuels, for instance, is something that has to be considered in the light of their non-renewability and exhaustion. They will probably be exhausted within another century from now. We just cannot, in my view, allow private enterprise to go on quite freely using these resources *ad in-finitum*.

So I find Mishan right in stating the principle of trying to correct and control disamenities involved in industrial growth and economic growth, but I think his philosophy is too in-dividualistic and his solution really too narrow. And this is where I would come back to the objective I mentioned earlier—the securing of elementary rights and freedoms. These I think are very important, but if we look at the ways in which these rights and freedoms have been formulated, at least inter-nationally, in the last twenty years, we find that almost all the rights and freedoms are subject to some agreed restrictions. And this is what the whole argument is about. The whole argument isn't about some ideal of freedom about which nobody basically disagrees; it is about how far and in what circumstances that freedom can be restricted. And since it involves restrictions, the problem of trying to manage economic growth is essentially a social matter which needs social decisions.

GLENNY: The imposition of one part of society's views on another, which this would involve, means, in fact, political decisions; it means institutions set up in order to perform this. It might be thought that this would be an intolerable encroachment on jealously guarded democratic freedoms at a time when democracy is being questioned all over the world and when it is, many people think, on the defensive.

FAWCETT: What I meant by a social decision was a decision in the general interest of society. Any decision based on social policy is, as you rightly say, a political decision. Now in questions concerning the application of technology, including perhaps the need sometimes to limit its operations, one must be quite clear about which of the problems that arise are soluble in terms of purely technical solutions, and which need political solutions. And at present I think these two concepts are being confused. There is a tendency to treat a good many of the undesirable consequences of technology as being matters simply for some kind of technical solution. I don't think they are. They must be settled politically, and where I believe our political institutions are inadequate is in failing to organise themselves so as to tackle these problems in the best way: that is to say, to make a political decision when it is required. There is in Great Britain, for example, a Parliamentary Committee on Science and Technology of enormous size—it contains about four hundred people—and such a committee, I would have thought, is not one that could give Parliament any really effective advice. What are needed instead are Parliamentary Committees of real expertise. Another difficulty here is—and it is particularly true of international bodies—that there is a belief that if you put a few experts on a committee in a particular field—oil pollution at sea or whatever it may be—they will somehow come up with the right advice, or even be able to solve the problem themselves. I think this is mistaken. You want a clear distinction between the scientific advice, the expertise, the technological knowledge on the one hand and the functions of the social body or political institution that ultimately has to make a decision of policy, i.e. whether the particular process in question is to be limited or is to be allowed to expand, on the other. But the vital factor is that the political body must not have the power to suppress or distort the scientific advice. And this can very often happen where scientific bodies are mere dependencies of the administrative machine. This is where I think a danger to our political freedom lies.

However, if the two functions—the technical and the political—are clearly separated; if the scientific advice is made fully public; and if the political body is given the power to decide, I think one can bring some clarity into this process without seriously reducing political freedom. Some of our freedom may well be reduced; there may be activities that have to be suppressed altogether. Some would say, for instance, that to devote a lot of the land in Scotland to shooting grouse may be very wasteful and could very properly be stopped; if so I don't think the essentials of political freedom need necessarily be destroyed if we go about making and enforcing such decisions in the right way.

GLENNY: It seems to me that the obvious corollary of what you have said is that such control bodies must inevitably extend beyond national boundaries, because, of course, the problems raised by technology are international. There is the well-known case of the complaint by the Swedish Government that industrial gases derived from the Ruhr, from Holland and from Britain, were all, in certain weather conditions, combining to destroy considerable areas of forest in Sweden. So there is an obvious case for the institutions you adumbrate to be international, and therefore to have power which, in varying degrees, would encroach upon the sovereignty of nation-states. Now we know that this is a very sensitive subject. Some nations, or some blocks of nations, react extremely nervously to any suspicion of encroachment on their sovereignty, and indeed the United Nations Security Council itself has constantly encountered this problem when dealing with the most vital problems of peace and war. How much more difficult may it not be, therefore, when it comes to dealing with the much more sophisticated and less obvious problems of the kind that we're discussing. Don't you foresee great international difficulties on these grounds?

FAWCETT: There are great difficulties but they're psychological rather than real, or even more imaginary than real. They too derive, I think, from what I suggested earlier, that our political institutions, indeed our very conception of sovereignty, are already out of date. At the beginning of this century it was no doubt true that most states found it extremely difficult to enter into agreements with each other. It was even harder to delegate authority to some international body. But in 1970 this has now become really very familiar. This has been going on for half a century, and both ministers and civil servants, who after all are the chief instruments of sovereignty, are quite familiar with the situation in which they go to an international consultative body, where there may not be an obligation that binds them to accept decisions. But the general procedure in such an international body is that of a process of organised persuasion, and no reasonable man, civil servant or minister, finds it easy in such a body to resist the organised persuasion of the others if that is based on expert advice and is reasonable. After all, there are certain areas, as you suggested, which are by their nature international, and governments have no choice. It isn't a question of having some mysterious sovereignty that they can protect. If they want to get the benefits of good management they have no choice but to get it this way. And you'll find, if, for example, you look at the international commodity

agreements, which have an important bearing on the proper use
of our natural resources, that the U.S.S.R. has acceded to
recent agreements—on wheat and on sugar. It had not ten
years ago. But it finds now that this is the practical way to
manage certain commodities.

So I think there are great possibilities in international cooperation. Of course there are hundreds of international bodies;
some are effective, some aren't. The effectiveness of an international body depends on two things. One is whether its area of
activity is organic, in the sense that it is a necessary part of the
general international process. That is the prime condition. A
good example of this is the way that the International Monetary
Fund has developed from being rather the Cinderella of
financial institutions to a major organ in world monetary cooperation. Although it is a body to which not all nations belong
—the Soviet Union is still not in it, but some East European
countries are associated with it—it is an example of what I
would call a going concern, because it is serving a real organic
need.

The second point of course is that the body must be reasonably well administered, and that it doesn't try to impose
decisions where the problem it is dealing with does not need or
won't tolerate that kind of pressure. You can do it by organised
persuasion or you can do it by exercising the decision-making
power of the body, but whatever the method, it must be done
with a sense of international tact. A very good international
example here is the North-East Atlantic Fisheries Commission
which has had a good deal of success (not total success, because
there are great difficulties in fishery conservation); it is a body
which makes decisions for governments—that is to say governments are part of it, but it is a combined decision-making body
—and it uses the International Council of the Exploration of
the Sea as its expert adviser. That Council is wholly independent and always publishes its findings. Here is a union of
the two methods which works very well.

GLENNY: I think you'll agree that what you have said on the

question of the international control of technological exploitation applies to an even greater degree to the problem which may be said to be literally universal—namely that of space research and space exploration. I am sure you would agree that there ought to be a supra-national body of some kind, supervising and controlling space research, and yet there is no such body. If one were set up it could only exist at present by mutual consent between the U.S.A. and the U.S.S.R. Do you feel that this is necessary and that it is feasible?

FAWCETT: I don't think that a general international agency to control or manage space activites and space research is necessary. And I stress there the word *general* agency. I think there are a number of uses of outer space which need to be and are in fact already under some kind of international management. But that refers rather to specific uses.

GLENNY: Of course there is the question of whether or not radio-active waste may be disposed of in space, which has a clear application to every country in the world, and not only to the super-powers who are actually doing space research. Then there is the control of meteorological satellites and telecommunication satellites. Clearly there is a functional need to control such matters. However, we get into a much more delicate area of international politics if some attempt is made to legislate, for instance, for the control of the military use of space. Do you not believe that here would be perhaps the most difficult area to achieve any kind of agreement?

FAWCETT: Yes, the military area is always the most difficult to reach agreement about, but I also think it is an area—and this is especially true of the uses of outer space—that is extremely difficult to define. By that I mean that of many of the uses to which outer space has been put since 1956, it is extremely difficult to say whether these are military uses or not. And this is why in the UN General Assembly Resolutions on Outer Space, the worthy statement that space must be used for 'peaceful purposes' has very little real meaning, because 'peaceful' can mean non-aggressive, but including measures of defence or what people call defence. It can also mean 'non-military', though people generally treat it as meaning the first. I think the hard reality of space research is that it has a broad military base and that 24 billion dollars would never have been expended if it had been simply to meet the demands of astronomers saying 'We'd like to see what the moon's made of, will you give us this money to go and do it?' Annual Federal aid for all basic scientific research in the U.S. is little more than the cost of one moon-landing. And there is no question that probably more than half of the entire space effort, both by the Soviet Union and the United States, is military in the sense that it is conducted in great part by the military authorities and has military purposes of various kinds. These are not necessarily the development of immediate strategic positions or the immediate placing of new weapons, but in military terms it is exploratory and experimental. It is possible that the whole *Apollo* operation has had no purpose except to learn how to operate a man-managed satellite, which has basically a military purpose. So to try to isolate the military element in space activities would be virtually impossible. This is a beautiful example of technology reaching the point where war and peace are becoming indistinguishable.

GLENNY: Have you any thoughts as to the entire rationale lying behind space research and exploration? Professor Dennis Gabor in his book *Inventing the Future* is inclined to describe the whole process of space research as not a rational pursuit in itself but as, whether consciously or not, a device for the disposal of surplus resources. In other words, certain sophisticated electronic products and dynamics products are now so complex that we can think of no way of employing these resources in a socially useful fashion. Therefore we feel impelled to employ them in a conspicuously wasteful and indeed, it might be argued, socially useless fashion. Do you subscribe to this view?

333

FAWCETT: No, I don't. The theory of conspicuous waste is attractive in many ways, and there are certain aspects of space research which come very close to confirming it, but I think it overlooks the actual usefulness of some space activities. And it would be as reasonable to say of some space activities that they were simply wasteful means of disposing of surplus resources as to say that the placing of ocean weather ships in the Atlantic was simply a way of getting rid of surplus resources. And here I think there has to be made a fundamental distinction between earth satellites on the one hand, and the *Apollo* programme, the moon programme and any exploration of the planets, such as the *Mariner* Programme for Mars and Venus, on the other. Earth satellites are extremely useful and the services they will provide for mankind are going to increase. The fact that an earth satellite can tell you where the fish are, has already helped the fishing industry, and satellite surveys can also be made of mineral resources. We are going to have here quick current knowledge on a scale which can be most effectively applied and which is quite unparalleled. The use of satellites for meteorology is already enormously important, and may have a great effect, if it is properly handled, on food production round the world. If farmers can know what weather is coming, still more if you can influence the weather, the possibilities are enormous; and the earth satellite for telecommunications, for meteorology, navigation surveys, is a real breakthrough. But I regard the Moon and Planetary exploration on an entirely different basis as being pursued, enormously expensive though it is, primarily for military purposes. I think both the United States and the Soviet Union are mainly interested in the military uses of a manned satellite. They want to be able to reach a position where satellites can be put in orbit round the earth and be flexibly managed by a crew who can, with reliefs, stay there perhaps indefinitely. Now the fact that the Russians have very clearly held back from putting a man on the Moon but concentrated on space docking operations rather indicates that this is their major interest; and the fact that President Johnson put the manned orbiting laboratory programme of the United States back into the Defence Department and away from NASA underlines this. Now in the journal *New Scientist*, when various scientists were asked to comment on the *Apollo 11* landing, some said that its scientific value was at least controversial and others partly denied it. One distinguished astronomer said, 'Give me fifty milligrams of moon dust and I'll tell you the origin of the solar system.' But characteristically of course of all knowledge, the more knowledge we have the greater is our ignorance: now that we've sixty or seventy pounds of moon rock, the controversy about the origin of the solar system is greater than ever. And so I don't think the scientific value is obviously great, certainly as regards manned landings. This aspect of the space programme —the planetary explorations, landings on the moon and so on —comes very close to the conspicuous waste about which Professor Gabor has been talking.

GUNNAR RANDERS

NATO and the Environment

Gunnar Randers is the Assistant Secretary General of NATO for
Scientific Affairs and also Chairman of the NATO Committee on
the Challenges of Modern Society. He is a distinguished astro-
physicist of Norwegian birth with a long record of service with
international scientific organisations, the UN and the International
Atomic Energy Authority. His publications include *Atomic Energy*
(1946), *Atoms and Common Sense* (1950) and *The Reactor and*
the *Bomb* (1968).

URBAN: How has it come about that NATO, which is
generally known as a military organisation, has formed a
Committee on the Challenges of Modern Society of which you
are Chairman?

RANDERS: NATO is not a military organisation, it is a
defence organisation. Its purpose is defence, the common
defence of the Western countries, and defence can and does
take many forms. One main method of NATO's work is political consultation which goes on incessantly, several days a
week, among all the fifteen NATO countries' Ambassadors.
NATO is the only organisation where these nations regularly
meet and consult on a very intimate basis and give each other
the information that's necessary, and do what is necessary, to
avoid war. This of course is not a military but a political function. However, it might be said that all this would not be so
valuable if these countries didn't go a step further and take
military precautions in case their political methods should fail.
    NATO's non-military background goes back to its inception.
One of NATO's aims, as stated in the second Article of the

Treaty, is to promote the welfare and improve the quality of life of the peoples in the alliance. Very soon, in addition to the political consultations, a so-called 'Science Committee' was set up to support pure scientific research and development in the member countries, and I mean scientific work in the broader sense and not simply the development of weapons or new methods of warfare. The idea is, as the Committee's mandate makes clear, to strengthen Western science. Obviously such work is also of value for military defence, but if you look at our programme you will find that we support meetings, conferences and research projects in pure mathematics, astrophysics, in the behavioural sciences, micro-biology—subjects which have nothing to do with defence.

URBAN: Am I right in saying that this development is still fairly new in NATO? I should have thought that, some years ago, when NATO was in Paris, the predominant concern was more or less entirely with military affairs and it is only in the last few years that there has been this extension into the non-military field. These non-military activities, which are now assuming a fairly prominent place in NATO's work, are really a way of establishing a closer political and cultural cohesion between the NATO countries; they are a way of putting over NATO a common roof that covers a great many things beyond the purely military.

RANDERS: There is something in what you say, but you are not right in assuming that the emphasis on the scientific and intellectual side is of such recent origin. As I said earlier, Article 2 of the Treaty was there from the beginning, twenty-one years ago; the 'Science Committee' was created twelve years ago, and it is only the Committee on the Challenges of Modern Society that is new, just over a year old. I think it would be misleading to say that NATO has taken a new direction, or that there is any intention of changing its character. I think it is implementing the original idea, the only difference being that today the feeling among the West European countries is different from what it was twenty years ago. In the early 1950s people were so preoccupied with the spectre of military aggression that preparation for defence against attack was their main concern. Today, rightly or wrongly, people increasingly believe that there is less need for military defence. My own view is that military considerations are less overwhelming than they used to be, and for this reason NATO now places more emphasis on its peaceful activities.

URBAN: For all one knows, such peaceful activities may strike a responsive chord in the Warsaw alliance. Are some of NATO's non-military activities, in fact, envisaged as building bridges between West and East, between NATO and the Warsaw Pact? Is there a tendency to select neutral topics which might promote a subtle convergence between the two blocs?

RANDERS: Yes, there is. To work for a *détente* between East and West is, after all, one of NATO's express purposes, and in establishing the new Committee which deals with environmental problems, the question has been raised at practically every one of our meetings: how should we get our results across to the East and how can we ensure that our own work also benefits Eastern Europe? Could our work be used as a bridge between East and West? The Committee has taken a unanimously positive attitude to this problem and it has been decided that all our results, all our papers, all the information we have on environmental questions and questions of modern society shall be made available to the East. We have even decided that, as the Eastern countries are often in an awkward position in that they feel it is politically difficult for them to accept information from NATO or to cooperate with NATO, all our information may be passed on to them, for example, through the Economic Commission of Europe, of which both the Western and East European countries are members. ECE has its own ecological committee and this will channel our results to Eastern Europe. The East European governments will then get the benefits of our work without any heart-searching about the ethics of cooperation; and the benefits are very real, for some of the problems on our agenda obviously concern the East as much as the West.

URBAN: Could you give an example?

RANDERS: Take pollution. If one asks who is poisoning the waters of the Baltic, the answer is that the Russians, the Swedes and the Danes are polluting it together. Or take the river Danube which crosses the East–West frontier, carrying poisonous effluents from the West to the East. There are other rivers which end up in Western countries or in seas adjoining Western shores. Then there is air pollution. Dust and soot generated by factories in Eastern Germany and Poland rise into the atmosphere and come down in Norway and Sweden. The only way in which this can be corrected is through co-operation. On the other hand, it is true that some of these problems of highly industrialised modern societies, like the pollution question, are so difficult to handle that it would be hopeless to attack them primarily as problems concerning both East and West. It's difficult enough to get NATO's fifteen countries to agree to taking action on any problem; if we started off by trying to persuade Poland, Czechoslovakia and Russia to agree with us on a common course of action, it would probably take ten years to do what we now hope to achieve in one. Our attitude is to do what we think is useful, to do it as fast as possible, and then to offer our methods and results to our opposite numbers in the East. In addition we feel there is much to be said for direct contact on problems which present realistic possibilities for East–West cooperation.

URBAN: But would this be really tantamount to building bridges? There has been a spate of conferences in the last few years on deliberately dehydrated topics, and the hope was that if you could run a good meeting on corneal transplantation in Nairobi or work up a shared dislike of smog-producers, somehow the spirit of good fellowship created at these conferences

339

would spin off into the political field. But it didn't or at any rate not effectively. How would you rate the chances of your Committee going beyond these neutral probings?

RANDERS: All this has been discussed by our Committee. What is more, in the guidelines of the SALT talks these topics are included as problems which could be taken up if there were difficulty in getting ahead with the really touchy political points. One could discuss pollution and so on. I believe such discussions would be useful from the scientific point of view, but I have less hope about their political importance. International meetings have been held for many years on astronomy, physics, chemistry and so on, and the Russians, Czechs, Americans all met together and talked. There has never been any difficulty in arranging such meetings; I have myself been to Russia several times to discuss technical matters with Russian experts. It is a useful exercise but rather limited in its effects, and it doesn't seem to grow at a rate fast enough to make a real difference as far as the immediate purposes of our Committee on the Challenges of Modern Society are concerned. Of course, in East European eyes perhaps we do not fit the neutral formula and also, as I said, we are not really a scientific or technical body but one which sees its purpose as a spur to practical action.

Now if we could get the most influential people supporting our Committee to meet their opposite numbers in Moscow, that could be important because these are people who have direct access to their President's or Party's high-level decision-makers. If one could proceed at a very high level and pursue this kind of cooperation, its significance would be far greater than that of a purely scientific cooperation.

URBAN: You are saying that suitably neutral, scientific, technological matters have never caused walls to go up between the two sides. Where would you say the difficulties start arising?

340

RANDERS: When one comes to social questions, to history, to sociology, the meaning of man's creative work as an individual and a social being, to human values—then the going gets much tougher. These problems cannot be thrashed out freely in public in the Soviet Union. These are the kind of questions that people would normally discuss in their homes but, as you know, it is difficult to do so in Russia. You can't get together with a friend or two and sit in a corner and argue for or against Marxism or Leninism. Most Russians I have met don't feel free to discuss anything like that. Self-censorship makes the subject a non-starter.

URBAN: May I now go into the mechanics of what your Committee is doing? What problem-areas has it identified as worth studying and working on?

RANDERS: The Committee was first suggested by President Nixon in 1969, and you might say it was Nixon's personal enthusiasm and interest that has overcome the original caution in Europe. It is no secret that several member countries were at first rather reluctant to take up environmental problems under NATO. President Nixon's argument for farming out some of these problems to NATO was that NATO is, in many ways, the only organisation that is accustomed to managing big operations like building oil pipelines, communication networks, harbours, airports and so on. Other international organisations are usually geared to making reports and passing resolutions. This time the idea was that the organisation should act; it should not make scientific reports but induce the governments in the NATO Alliance to act. We are an action committee, we do not do scientific research, we do not develop new knowledge but we do forcefully persuade our governments to act upon our recommendations, based as they are on the best knowledge available at the time.

Take traffic safety on the highways, for example. It is a fact that people react strongly to killing in the course of war and demonstrations, and they complain and write about it, but

341

they are somehow resigned to accepting the fact that we in the NATO area kill 140,000 people a year on our highways. This carnage is unnecessary and the only reason we accept it is that we have, in Western society, not yet put enough energy, money and effort into avoiding death on the roads. Our NATO Committee wants to do something about it, so we have a programme, led by the U.S., to develop a 'safety car'. We have projects for car safety inspection led by Germany, for medical assistance led by Italy, for the prevention of drunken driving led by Canada and so on. Also, we have discussed the introduction of a safety air bag for motor-cars. This is a plastic bag mounted on the dashboard of the car. When you are involved in a collision, the plastic bag blows up, fills the whole space between you, your passenger and the windscreen, and so a fraction of a second later, as you're thrown forward, you hit the bag and stay alive. The bag has been developed and it works; but does it work well enough, and would it now be possible to introduce it? Car manufacturers in America feel more work is needed. In addition it would add to the cost of the car which would put the U.S. makers at a disadvantage on the European market; the *European* manufacturers would suffer a loss if such improved cars were introduced in America by law because then *they* would be at a disadvantage on the U.S. market for a while. So we organised a meeting in Detroit, where not only the NATO area's car manufacturers—Opel, Fiat, General Motors and so on—but also Volvo from Sweden and the Japanese makers were present. We demonstrated the usefulness of the air bag, ran cars against each other and showed that at a speed of fifty miles an hour, head on, passengers could walk out of the car unhurt. Now it is possible that the U.S. Department of Transportation will try to introduce such air bags in cars in America as compulsory accessories. But if that is done, the Department will probably first consult our Committee and so have the benefit of the reactions and recommendations of all the West European car manufacturers. The manufacturers, on their part, will then have been warned that these changes may come about in 1973 for example, so they should be able to prepare themselves for production. Technically, this warning could take the form of a recommendation from our Committee to the NATO Council.

URBAN: This is most interesting but can you 'forcefully persuade' governments?

RANDERS: We can't force anyone but we can apply a lot of pressure in NATO.

URBAN: Given the structure and the character of NATO, would your Committee's work not be inclined to restrict itself to recommending, or even thinking about, the kind of measures that lend themselves to this kind of command methodology?

RANDERS: Certainly this is the intention. As I've already said, there are lots of organisations (for instance OECD in Paris) which have worked for many years on environmental problems on a scientific basis. They are concerned with developing knowledge and suggesting new research fields for different countries; what we can do is to pick out areas which are ripe for practical action and to encourage action. For it is in that no-man's land, between study and action, that we usually trip up.

URBAN: What are the priorities of your Committee? Can you list some of the problems in order of importance that are ripe for solution, ought to be solved and can be solved by your methods?

RANDERS: I am afraid your question can't be answered that simply because our method of work is such that it is not left to us to set up priorities. Each project is tied to a pilot-country, and when a country comes forward with a project which we believe can result in action, we launch it. We do not do the detailed work here at NATO Headquarters; we simply organise the exercise. Take again highway safety; the U.S. has offered to provide the pilot project. The work goes on at different universities and governmental institutions in America and, for the time being, it's being led from there. Gradually some European nations are now beginning to participate in special sub-problems. The Committee cannot, therefore, draw up priorities, but it can suggest projects to member countries: and this is what we have done. The Belgians have agreed to become the pilot country for pollution along the coasts of Europe. This of course, is a very important and high-priority subject because the coastal waters along Northern Europe are so badly polluted that it is often considered unsafe to swim in them, and that is where all the continental and British sea resorts are. Portugal, France and Canada are Belgium's co-pilots. They have already started taking measurements along the coast using a variety of research vessels. They are, first, trying to establish the real seriousness of pollution and then the sources of pollution. This pilot project has a very high priority; whether it is higher than highway safety we don't really bother about as these are two different problems. Then take air pollution: here the U.S.A., together with Turkey and Germany, have offered to be pilot countries. They have decided to pick three of the most difficult towns—Ankara, Frankfurt and St. Louis—and try to see if they can solve their problems. We reckon that if we can do something about these three towns we have the answers to the problems of many others.

URBAN: Why did you pick those three cities?

RANDERS: Because Ankara is probably the most difficult city of all the NATO capitals. It has a new industry run on brown coal; it lies in a large bowl with a heavy concentration of inverted air on top so that the soot and smog aren't regularly flushed out by the air currents; they stay on top as they do in Los Angeles. But Ankara's pollution is worse than Los Angeles's and could be critical in the long run. So if we can find some solutions here we hope that a lot of other cities could simply copy its methods. Frankfurt is a different case. There we have an over-whelming concentration of industry, surrounded by another in-

344

dustrial belt, so that there is a vast amount of filth in the air which a million or more people helplessly breathe in every day; yet Frankfurt's great industrial plants have to go on, so we must find answers to the city's problems. This is our second project. The third pollution project is inland water pollution. There, some of the rivers and the Great Lakes in America, Lake Erie for example, come to mind as the worst offenders. Canada has offered to be the pilot country for this project because the Canadians are the ones worst hit by the destruction of Lake Erie. Some hydrologists say that the poisoning of Lake Erie has virtually made it impossible for it to be restored now or perhaps ever. We want to learn from that and see to it that no one else commits the same mistake.

We also have a project called 'Disaster Assistance'. One of its aims is to use NATO's central information network and our organisation for civil defence in cases of floods, earthquakes or other natural disasters. The idea is to put our sophisticated organisation to some constructive, peaceful use.

URBAN: Your Committee's work reminds me a little of the arguments used in Britain after the war to support the idea of a planned economy. In 1943, 1944 and 1945 large squadrons of hundreds of Royal Air Force bombers were sent over Germany to destroy German cities and cow Hitler into submission. They took off from dozens of airfields, rendezvous'd over some point in France or Holland, were led on to their targets by pathfinder aircraft, dropped their bombs in carefully arranged waves—a high degree of precision and coordination was required and, above all, central planning. After the war, when Labour was elected, it was argued by the Labour Party that if the British people wanted welfare services, socialised medicine, subsidised housing and education, an export-worthy economy, all this could only be achieved in the same sort of way in which Nazi Germany was bombed into surrender, and the Labour Government's programme was drawn up on this analogy. It was an impressive argument: if you could win the war by a crash programme, you could win the peace in the same way.

Labour tried it and did not succeed. Britain's economy has been relatively stagnant since the end of the war and shows no signs of improving.

Doesn't the 'Disaster Assistance' project, and don't some of your other philanthropic programmes take their cue from a similar analogy? Aren't you really saying: NATO can organise men, it can coordinate divisions, it can get the aircraft and pipelines and airfields in the right places; if we apply the same methods to solving some of our seemingly intractable human and environmental problems, we can come out on top in that area too?

In other words, you may be selecting problem areas that look like military targets and you may be assuming that they can be bombarded into solution by military–scientific types of techniques. I don't mean to imply that there is anything derogatory in using such techniques, for I'm aware that the roots of the first rational management of society go back to the military history of the late 18th Century, when the needs of mobilising, keeping fed and supplied large numbers of men demanded a high order of managerial skill which was entirely new in those days. Would you agree that there is a subtle transfer of methods in your work from the military to the non-military field?

RANDERS: No, I would not, because there is one aspect of NATO's working method which invalidates what you are saying. In the NATO Council, which is the highest authority in the Organisation, every member has a veto; we can't do anything in it unless each nation, large or small, agrees. So if there is any body which has to struggle with individualists in international relations, it is NATO. The military way of doing things is not NATO's way. We cannot, like the United Nations, take a vote and get a two-thirds majority or a fifty-one per cent majority; it has to be an absolutely unanimous decision, so you can see that your analogy is really far from being correct: we do not use that kind of military planning. This is shown by NATO's own progress, or the lack of it you may say, in its defence programme. We have never managed to standardise our aeroplanes, for example. We have some Swedish aircraft, some British, some American, some French planes. They use different screws, different propellers, different wheels. We have never been able to standardise by higher order. In wartime one can do that by simple fiat. One might say that this is done to a certain extent by Russia in the Warsaw Pact, but NATO consists of fifteen genuinely independent and sovereign countries where no action can be taken without the agreement of the fifteen governments, and without public opinion supporting that action. Of course it is true to say that the Soviet results are impressive in certain fields, but there are other fields where the centralised method doesn't work at all. Think of Soviet agriculture or their distribution of consumer goods. It is hard to imagine a more consistently disastrous variety of central planning.

Another project our new Committee deals with will show you how far we are from following any military pattern in our work. The British have undertaken to run a pilot project for us on what might be described as 'taking care of human happiness in a technological society': how does the individual survive among the computers, automated shops and machinery, in our de-personalised cities, in families where TV has suppressed the will and ability to talk and discuss? People can be terribly miserable in advanced technological societies. The British, as our pilot country here, are trying to find out what has gone wrong with our progress, and it would be absurd to suggest that they are doing this by military analogy.

URBAN: Let me use another tack and ask you with all respect: wouldn't a military organisation, after twenty years of existence, feel a psychological need to superimpose on its military tasks, which are inevitably pessimistic and unpleasant in their implications, something that sounds good, that smells of optimism, that is humanitarian and philanthropic?

RANDERS: Practically all international (and national) organisations today have taken up the question of environment. Why?

Is it because it smells of optimism? This may motivate some of these organisations, but the problems are real enough and would need ten times the number of organisations that are active on them and ten times the amount of resources.

One must remember that our concern with the environment is not an exercise in propaganda. We are looking for concrete recommendations: what can we do to protect people from the evils of growing technology? This has to be done; you can regard it with suspicion or pleasure or surprise; nevertheless, it's one of the things it would be awfully wrong not to worry about.

URBAN: I'm intrigued by the ambivalence of the work you are doing. On the one hand you are preparing for the unpleasant task of having to fight a nuclear war, and I think this preparation is highly necessary; on the other hand you are worrying about how to make people happy in peacetime and how to make their lives more humane and comfortable. There is a curious dualism—a concern with destruction and construction—in these two activities. I find it admirable that you can pursue both under one roof. Now let me take this a step further. Is there a parallel service offered by the Warsaw Pact countries? Do they provide anything by way of humanitarian work from which NATO could benefit, where you could say: well, the Warsaw Pact people are trying to rid the Socialist states of their shortcomings, they have a scientific committee to analyse what's wrong with workers' alienation in their factories, another, perhaps, to see how central-planning undermines the initiative to innovate at the grass-roots of industry, a third to study how forced industrialisation is upsetting the ecological balance of their countries and so on? Are we getting the benefit of their experience in these fields? Can we talk of an exchange of scientific information in these peaceful areas?

RANDERS: Not that we know of, not in the Warsaw Pact. They are concentrating, as far as we know, purely on military defence. There is, generally, very little to compare between the

Warsaw Pact and NATO. At this moment the Warsaw Pact forces are being built up all over the world. Their fleets have come out into the oceans; we don't quite know why, but they are increasing their potential all the time. NATO's naval forces have, if anything, shrunk until quite recently, not to speak of our land forces. There is obviously a completely different rationale behind the two organisations. The kind of thing you seem to suspect NATO of, a command-methodology in the civilian sphere, is what the Warsaw Pact countries are using. The Warsaw Pact governments are increasing their military strength, but their peoples have no voice in the matter. NATO on the other hand has been reducing, not because it wants to, but because, rightly or wrongly, our peoples are not willing to sacrifice more for defence.

Now you say we are planning for nuclear war. Of course we are planning for nuclear war; what choice have we? But the purpose of NATO is to avoid war, and that is why political consultations have the highest priority in our counsels. At the same time we know that our peaceful work will not be taken seriously and will not be effective unless we have ready what is necessary to guarantee our security, and that means the ability to meet a nuclear attack. So there is really no duality in NATO. Unfortunately we live in a world where there are people who might, under certain conditions, resort to attack with nuclear weapons, and so our first requirement is to have nuclear weapons. When you have them and you are seen to be having them, you may be on the best way to deterring war.

URBAN: Is there any agency in NATO that is trying to think of ways of alleviating the ideological antagonisms between Eastern Europe and the NATO countries, of finding some common ground between the Marxist type of interpretation of man's place in history and the much more diffuse and pluralistic Western interpretations?

RANDERS: Not in NATO. I think it would be very difficult to get any such thing going in NATO because each government would be highly sensitive about it. They all have their own feelings of how history should be represented. After all, some of this work is going on at UNESCO where they're trying to write an unbiased kind of world history. We may get to the point where NATO may take on a project of this kind, but the time is not yet ripe.

URBAN: Is there any actual contact between your Committee and any organisation in the Warsaw Pact that may have a similar interest?

RANDERS: Every year our Science Committee supports some sixty different meetings to which, from time to time, Russians and other East European scientists and experts are invited. Well, as might be expected, the Russians never come. However, every now and then we see Czechs, Poles and Rumanians at these meetings; this is the only kind of contact we have with their side. Sometimes these non-Russian scientists are slightly surprised that they are invited to a NATO-sponsored meeting at all, but their governments are more permissive in these matters than is the Soviet Government and they allow their men to participate.

BERNARD CAZES

Opportunities and Pitfalls
of Future-oriented Research

Bernard Cazes is a senior French civil servant with special responsibilities for future-oriented studies in the Commissariat Général du
Plan, and Rapporteur Général of the Groupe d'Etudes Prospectives
du VI Plan. He has published *La Planification en France et le IV
plan* (1962), *La Vie économique* (1965), and edited, with his wife,
Baron d'Holbach's Selected Writings: *D'Holbach portatif* (1967).
He is also the author of several articles on economic planning and
the methodology of planning, published in France, the United States
and the United Kingdom.

URBAN: A number of attempts have been made since the
beginning of the century, most of them by historians and
literary men, to tell us something about the future. But most of
these were impressionistic, literary types of forecasts. There
was a famous series of books in this genre, published in the
1920s, with people like H. G. Wells and Bertrand Russell par-
ticipating. These books usually appeared under some title drawn
from Greek mythology to personify or typify the subject, and
dealt with the future of medicine, the future of architecture
and so on: Haldane wrote *Daedalus, or Science and the Future*,
Russell contributed *Icarus, or the Future of Science* and there
were others. These were very idiosyncratic and one-shot affairs,
not, I think, what would today pass for precise research. Then,
in the 1930s, we had Huxley's *Brave New World*, Orwell's
1984 and the books of H. G. Wells, who inspired most of these
efforts, still straddling the stage with such timeless favourites
as *The Time Machine, Anticipations, The Wonderful Visit*,
etc. All these depicted for us Utopias, usually frightening

Utopias, and we were advised to guard against them.

The last ten years have seen a great resurgence of interest in the future. Men have always tried to read the entrails of animals in order to know something about their fate, and, in a sense, the works I have just mentioned still come into that category: they were meant to be read as opinion and had no broader claim. What we have today—future-oriented research —appears to be a completely different enterprise. Modern planners talk about a systematic, analytical study of the future which, they say, has a claim to be ranked as science—a far cry from the divine madness which, in the words of Plato, is the spring of 'that most glorious art whereby the future is discerned'.

How would you describe the salient features of these modern future-studies?

CAZES: You are quite right in stressing the novelty of future-studies. It was not so many years ago that Raymond Aron said: 'We are too much obsessed by the 20th Century to spend time speculating about the 21st. Long-range historical predictions have gone out of fashion.' And here we are today—members of what is rapidly becoming a futurological industry—turning out forecasts on every conceivable subject whether short-range or long-range.

The books you mentioned suffer from one basic fault: their authors were *prophets* of the future; they had no notion of how society hangs together, which elements are more susceptible to change than others, how society as a system really works.

Modern future research is trying to correct this deficiency. Two distinctive features of this new orientation may be put forward. First, there is a very strong connection between future-oriented research and the apparatus and methodology of the social sciences—not only of economics but also of sociology and perhaps, very modestly, political science too. In other words, modern future-oriented research explores the boundaries of social systems, the interplay of values, motivation and resources, and the interactions of social systems as they come into contact with each other. My second point, which is perhaps still more important, is that there is a very close relationship between this kind of future-oriented analysis and policy-making. Governments have discovered that by using some of the information provided by forecasters—long-term forecasters—they can avoid certain mistakes in their planning and improve the quality of their decisions.

URBAN: How do the social sciences and future-oriented research share a methodology?

CAZES: This sharing of a methodology seems to occur on two levels. First, future-oriented research as a set of probabilistic statements on the future has to rely on the scientific approach of the 'if ... then' type. Second, if one considers future-oriented research as a way of shaping a future we desire, that is, if one relates prediction to planning, the most profitable method to use is the one provided by so called policy-analysis which tries to relate statements about the future to alternative kinds of action. But I should add that, quite naturally, the scientifically reliable content of policy-analysis and of other sorts of cost-benefit studies is weaker than that of any causal type of *ex post facto* work. Prediction is, by the nature of it, a much more risky enterprise than explanation because, where human affairs are concerned, the 'other-things-being-equal' clause is something we can simply not rely upon.

URBAN: Systems analysis and cybernetics would appear to be ideal tools for such work, for they interrelate more efficiently than do other methods various developments in a nation's economy, demography and so forth.

CAZES: Well, to put it in very simple terms: since the social sciences are able to explain a situation, it is a natural temptation for them to say: 'We can also try to *predict* a situation.' After all, a prediction is an extrapolation from the present, so a scientific analysis has both retrospective and predictive applications. It can explain how things happened in the past, and from there it can try to predict a variety of alternative situations which might occur in the future.

URBAN: Systems analysis then assumes that men and societies act by rational considerations and make rational choices. Your analogy would appear to be drawn from the management of a factory. But is human society constructed in that way? Do you think that the rationalism which we think governs economic decisions—and even there it is disputed whether rationalism is the decisive factor—can be legitimately attributed to what people do in their private lives, as consumers, producers, trade unionists, etc.?

CAZES: No, such an attribution would be invalid, and I think it was not by accident that the first efforts in future-oriented research began with the more reliable, 'hard' disciplines. These studies were concerned with technological forecasting, the study of economic growth, population trends and so forth. Even here errors were made, but, within the set of possible candidates for futurology, those with a record for reliability and manageability had to be selected.

But after that, by a kind of natural urge to move further ahead, some scientists began to ask: would it be possible to say something about the future of 'soft' variables? Could one predict leisure patterns, religious attitudes, changes in the perception of human values with any certainty? But here, of course, the questions become more awkward—and considerably more fascinating.

URBAN: You are saying that in the technological field it is easier to make realistic forecasts because technology is quantifiable and therefore lends itself to prediction. I should have thought forecasting from simple intellectual models is not as new as people imagine. Every time we make a hypothesis of how an institution works, or how a policeman reacts to a driving offence, one has a primitive model in mind. So forecasting is perhaps no more than an informed and intelligent type of guesswork by people steeped in economics, sociology and other disciplines. What is new today—or so it would seem to a layman—is that we tend to quantify many factors to which it used not to be fashionable (and possible) to assign a number.

CAZES: I agree. It is perfectly true that great political philosophers and historians, such as Machiavelli or de Tocqueville, used an implicit model of human and social behaviour. For instance, in de Tocqueville you find the crucial idea that there is in modern societies a trend towards increasing equality, and if you start from that point in your analysis you can come up with a certain number of illuminating statements about various aspects of social life and human relationships. Quantification is, of course, a dangerous procedure, for now that we have computers at our beck and call we tend to quantify variables that are not clearly quantifiable, and yet the temptation to quantify is too persuasive to be resisted. Therefore, one can go very badly wrong by quantifying without due caution. The Romans were quite right when they expressed their distrust of counting heads in the phrase 'to number is to err'.

URBAN: Reading Herman Kahn's book, *The Year 2000*, I was struck by the fact that he and his co-author, Wiener, do not really talk of any particular future but of alternative futures. They talk of choices, and the purpose of their exercise seems to be to outline for the policy-makers, or for society in general, a number of choices. What they are saying is: *if* you decide to live in your own homes in a rural area rather than in blocks of flats in the city, then you have to build certain roads that lead to your houses, certain schools for your children, certain amenity centres, swimming pools, shopping areas and so on; also such and such strains might develop in your neighbourhood. But then they stress that *if* you decide to do something else, other things will follow. But it is striking that they do not say that (A) or (B) will *necessarily* be the future. So governments and societies, individual cities, local governments have it in their power to choose or not to choose between certain alternatives. Would you say that this way of looking at the future is the accepted method of futurology: you do not forecast any particular development but provide options from which governments and their advisers can choose?

CAZES: You have described rather precisely what good futurology should be and what it isn't always. It should really present alternative images of the future to enlarge the options and the wisdom of the policy-makers. *The Year 2000* offers an extremely rich choice of alternatives, and my only real criticism of the book would be this, that the wealth of possibilities is perhaps too large to be fully credible. I wonder if the kaleidoscopic options offered us aren't too much for our brains and our stomachs to take in. We are almost drowned in an ocean of alternative worlds, canonic variations and so forth. I would compare the book with the situation of a shopper who walks into a deparment store to find himself surrounded by so many goods that he is unable to decide what he really wants.

URBAN: I am also struck by a certain lack of originality in the choices offered. If one were to ask an intelligent layman with some grounding in politics and history to say what sorts of developments he would expect in the next thirty or forty years in economics, urbanisation, Sino-Soviet affairs and so forth, I think his forecasts would not be very different from those which Kahn and Wiener give us in their book with an apparatus of great sophistication. A broad spectrum of possibilities is always easily depicted. If you depict contingency A, and then its very opposite, B, and also a number of compromises between the two, one of these predictions is bound to come tolerably close to reality. Can futurology get away from these generalities and pick the winner?

CAZES: The kind of futurology you question—which we French would call *'propos de Normand'* ('perhaps yes and perhaps no')—is the occupational disease of every scenario-writer. This is especially so in the geopolitical and military fields where the policy-maker is supposed to be prepared for every contingency. These scenarios are the raw material of what one might call 'political science-fiction': U.S. President goes mad, Mao murdered by angry young colonels, etc. My own position may be summed up in two points:

First, scenario-writing is a poor substitute for a sound theoretical framework that gives some focus to one's analysis of the future. Take again de Tocqueville's view that the world is moving towards greater equality: in forecasting the future of industrial societies, he did not have to give us a catalogue of every conceivable alternative, because he knew perfectly well what were the possible and what were the impossible developments within the limits of his conceptual apparatus.

Second, scenarios are relevant only if one is able to identify the roots and/or causal factors of the projected alternatives, and reason in terms of the 'if . . . then' paradigm, that is, if one's various predictions of the future are not purely gratuitous. They may then serve to highlight the uncertainties which face the policy-maker.

URBAN: But coming back to techniques of forecasting, how would you describe the way in which a surprise-free technological forecast is made? Take housing, or population, or public transport—these are fields which are more easily quantifiable —how are predictions made and how are they used by governments?

CAZES: Basically, two broad methods are used. The first, which is typically quantitative, is the projection from past trends into the future. You can, for instance, extrapolate the growth of electricity-generating capacity from past trends. You can talk about the likely speed of the diffusion of certain patterns of consumption, because all these things can be based on past evidence, and you can reasonably make forecasts for twenty years or even longer. The second method is more qualitative or, if you like, more impressionistic. It is a very modest method, for it simply consists of asking people engaged in research and development activities for their advice as to what are, or are likely to be, technological innovations in their particular fields : what machinery is likely to be invented, what discoveries are being worked on and so forth. They will then tell you about the kind of computers we can expect to have in ten or fifteen or thirty years' time, of new chemicals, of the uses of atomic energy and so forth. The role of the technological forecaster is to assemble these items of information about new technologies and to ask himself how, in their togetherness, these new technologies will affect his particular field or a much larger field surrounding that particular field, between, say, 1975 and 1985 : what will be their implications in terms of manpower employed, in terms of the skills which will be necessary, in terms of regional development, in terms of the structure of industry and the like. Then he has to ask himself—and this is particularly important for small countries—whether within a wide array of possible new technologies, technology A or B or C should be selected, or whether, in fact, the whole bag of new technologies should be put to use; should the country specialise, selecting one or two of these new technologies, leaving the rest for other countries to adopt for such-and-such economic or social reasons? Having done all that, he has a file on the choices open to governments and parliaments, and he can present these choices to the decision makers.

URBAN: But the decision is ultimately a political matter.

CAZES: Not always. I would rather say that every important decision has political connotations even if it concerns an ostensibly non-political issue. Take, for instance, the decision by Ford to put up a car-manufacturing plant near Bordeaux. It was certainly taken on sound financial grounds, but willy-nilly it was also an element in the political competition between the French Prime Minister and M. Servan-Schreiber. Or take the textile industry: an investment in labour-saving devices may have a big impact on regional employment, on the exports of developing countries and so forth.

URBAN: How are these bits of information put together? The layman's picture of a systems analysis approach to social problems is that the systems analyst is a man who looks upon society as a kind of organism. Is this in fact so? Is this the formula systems analysts use when they integrate their disjointed pieces of information? Or is there some other method that one ought to know about?

CAZES: In systems analysis every aspect of a problem to be solved is related to every other aspect. But the efficiency of your analysis depends very largely on whether or not you are dealing with 'hard' variables. In a systems analysis of an engineering or economic issue one can generally identify the probable impact on the 'output' (e.g. the volume of employment) of any change in the 'inputs', such as birth-rate, man-hour production and so on. In the 'softer' areas one faces much greater difficulties. In trying to pinpoint the social or cultural implications of primary school reform or law reform, for instance, it is much more awkward to make a reasonable prediction. Or take the problem of women in the United States: if during the 1970s there is pressure on the American woman both to reduce her participation in the labour force and to reduce the size of the American family—will there be a conflict of roles in American women, and if so, how will they react?

I should add, however, that if there is great uncertainty in trying to estimate the long-range implications of doing something, it is easier to identify the consequences of inaction—of letting things drift on. For instance, in our current report on the year 1985, prepared for the Groupe d'Etudes Prospectives du VI Plan, we have tried to show that maintaining the French educational system in its present form is probably the surest way of not rising to the social, cultural and economic challenges of the coming, post-industrial society.

URBAN: I wonder whether it wouldn't be a mistake to confine one's forecasting to the simple, linear type. One astonishing forecast in the Kahn/Wiener book concerns the volume of research and development in the United States in the next thirty years. There is an extrapolation of the future cost of research and development from present trends. The cost forecast for the year 2000 has a surprising ring about it, for the Kahn/Wiener curve shows that the United States would be spending more on its research and development than its entire gross national product. Now this is surely absurd.

CAZES: Predictions are arrived at either inductively (i.e. you infer the future from certain regularities observed in the past) or deductively (e.g. the part cannot be larger than the whole). Extrapolation-to-absurdity is clearly a case of deductive thinking. As I see it, Kahn and Wiener didn't predict that in the year 2000 the United States would devote the whole volume of its GNP to research and development; rather they warned against the assumption that a share of the total resources—namely that taken up by research and development—may grow indefinitely. And they were right, because since 1969 the curve has been declining. Obviously extrapolation cannot be the only approach to getting our perspectives right about the future.

URBAN: What criteria do you use when you make a forecast?

CAZES: This is an important and difficult question. I am deeply involved in future-oriented research, and I have reason to believe that we don't pay enough attention to this problem. On what basis do we select our facts? What are our images of the future? I must confess that our criteria are predominantly commercial criteria, and criteria of feasibility and practicability. It is only very seldom that one selects wider criteria that do not concern themselves solely with financial, economic and technological problems. It is sad but true that in a large number of cases we are driven by the machine: whatever can be made will be made; whatever can be invented will be invented. If a machine *can* be produced we can be quite certain that it *will* be produced. From this flows a more general and equally depressing fact: we generate a type of forecasting that leaves broad human, environmental and social considerations completely out of the picture. To the expert forecaster, reared as he is in a technological frame of reference, the more humanitarian considerations appear too vague to be quantifiable.

URBAN: I expected you to say something totally different. There is a school of thinking in historiography and the philosophy of history—and Collingwood comes to mind as one distinguished representative—which holds that history reflects the historian's idiosyncrasies more than the events as they 'actually' happened. I thought you were going to suggest that in futurology, too, the scholar's pet preferences are rationalised into outwardly objective types of predictions. What in fact you are saying is that the machine is in charge rather than the driver.

CAZES: I don't agree with you entirely. What I have just said I said in my capacity as a civil servant, and I was thinking mainly in terms of policy-oriented futurology where in fact it is true that the machine is more important than the man who runs it. But there is also another kind of forecasting which is totally different from the one I have just mentioned and where people, when describing the future, are really describing their pet Utopias. It would be unfair to mention names, but although I consider some of these endeavours with personal sympathy, and although I am very often in complete agreement with the kind of desirable futures some of these Utopian writers depict, I cannot, in all conscience, see that their forecasts differ from the literary type of 19th- and 20th-Century Utopias which you mentioned in your opening statement. The 'wishful thinking' type of prediction lives side by side with the 'sovereignty-of-the-machine' type of forecasting.

URBAN: Going back to the question of criteria: how do they rank in order? What are the priorities, how do you arrive at your decisions?

CAZES: Let me take transportation as a concrete example. First, you have the considered judgement of experts on the technological feasibility of an invention or a suggested new technological process. Then you consider correlations between levels of income, which is an independent variable, and dependent variables such as the use of the various modes of transportation: rail, road, air travel and so on. Then you come to the purely commercial criteria such as: is technology A to be preferred to technology B because it promises to be more competitive on the market? Then there are criteria which are not always taken into consideration at a low level but come into government considerations, such as non-market effectiveness. One of these would be national prestige, or such macroeconomic considerations as the balance of payments. Both are non-commercial criteria because no private firm is interested in the balance of payments, or how its product will affect national prestige. It is the Minister of Finance and the Minister of Technology and the Prime Minister who are interested in such questions.

These are, by and large, rather pedestrian considerations; but in certain studies, which are not always future-oriented but simply policy planning analyses, one sees the beginnings of a widening of the criteria. For instance, French ecologists are now studying the impact of road building on urban dislocation, and the effects of large engineering works on landscape, the purity of the air and water.

URBAN: It is interesting that such ecological considerations should still be so rare. Now surely it must be extremely difficult to embody such considerations in quantitative terms.

CAZES: It is difficult enough to identify these considerations in physical terms, and it would be even much more difficult to put a monetary value on them. In the majority of cases this cannot be done with our present techniques. So all you can say to your policy-maker is that you have a list of non-quantifiable benefits which ought to be taken into consideration, or you can say that you have a list of non-quantifiable diseconomies and these ought also to be looked at before a certain project is approved or rejected.

URBAN: I should have thought that despite these manifest difficulties, systems analysis would offer some language for transposing qualitative factors into statements that make sense to the men and machines that deal in quantities. If the domain of qualitative differentiation remains a closed book to the systems analyst, we have not really advanced much beyond counting heads, except that we do it faster, in which case systems analysis is a big name for a small innovation. Of course, the name sounds attractive, and one knows that in the social sciences that can be important.

CAZES: One can try to translate quality into quantity, and this has been done by the Roskill Commission for instance. One can try to find equivalents—some translation of intangibles into market terms. One can try to compute fresh air, sun, lack of noise and the like by examining their market value. You can say to yourself that in neighbourhoods which have fresh air and where the sun is not blotted out by soot and exhaust fumes, and where the traffic does not generate an awful lot of noise, houses have a higher value than comparable houses in neighbourhoods which suffer from air pollution, noise, etc. If you do this you get a very awkward and a very rough yardstick. It is incomplete and very imperfect.

URBAN: Now if these intangibles are not easily incorporated in hard and fast formulae because they can't be accurately measured, does this not imply that future-oriented studies tend to be self-fulfilling simply because only a certain type of future can be envisaged, and therefore *that* is the type of future that planners, technologists and governments are likely to work for?

CAZES: That is true. Let me give you one example. Demographic projections for the coming decades say that seventy per cent of the population in the Western industrial countries will live in megalopolises, that is, in huge urban concentrations. Well, this tends to be a self-fulfilling prophecy, because when business people read this kind of forecast and when the planners read it, they say to themselves: well, this is what the future will be so we'd better concentrate our businesses, our economic activities in the areas where this kind of dynamism is likely to take place; therefore we'll invest in the large cities and not in the country, and we'll put our businesses and our banks into these huge concentrations.

URBAN: So in fact this is a good example of how commercial investment and thinking follow these forecasts and bring about developments that are often not desirable in themselves, but simply happen because they have been predicted.

CAZES: Yes, and I suspect that public investment very often follows the same path.

URBAN: There is clearly a case here for ethical considerations. Would you say that certain types of forecasts, those that are socially undesirable, should perhaps not be published? I realise the enormous difficulty in defining what is and is not socially desirable. It is enough to remember the recent controversy whether Gallup polls should be published before a general election. Also this takes one directly into the even more controversial question of whether scientific enquiry itself should have limits imposed on it on moral grounds. One has only to think of recent biological findings which show a correlation between race and intelligence, to realise the size of the problem. In the United States, where these IQ tests have been most widely conducted, the nexus between race and IQ rating is politically explosive and susceptible of being exploited. Should such findings be made public knowledge?

CAZES: This is a formidable and intricate question. In my own field, one is, first, very often up against an unbalanced situation. You have too many studies dealing with one type of

364

future, and therefore the question we should ask ourselves is whether we should prohibit the publication of these one-sided studies, or diversify our research and publish only after the net has been thrown wider. Of course, the second situation is the one to be preferred, and if you have your research really diversified there should be no restriction on publication.

There is also another difficulty which is common to all futurological studies, and that is that our emphasis on hard facts does not allow sufficient elbow-room for imaginative types of prediction. It is very difficult, not only for the layman but also for the technologist, to design a really meaningful picture of the future because you express your forecast in material and therefore largely mundane terms, such as private and public consumption, number of francs earned, tax paid and so forth, and from these it is almost impossible to imagine what the future will be like. It is very difficult from such factors to enact for yourself the day to day life of people in the year 2000.

URBAN: You are in fact saying that the life of society is more than the sum of its parts : when you have computed consumption, earning power, technological progress, the energy resources used and so forth, you still know very little about the feel of living thirty years hence. So we come to the methodological problem : how can the study of the future take some account of factors that are elusive and often irrational? How can futurology allow for the emergence of the imponderables : of Messianic faiths, dictatorships, currency crises, anarchistic movements? After all, we have witnessed all these things in the last fifty years in a supposedly enlightened and scientific world, and they —more than consumption or urbanisation—have been decisive for our history. I, for one, can see no reason why we should not expect similar imponderables to rule us in the coming thirty or fifty years. Do your analyses take some account of these factors, or are they impossible to write into your calculations?

CAZES: Well, it is almost impossible. One can initiate a scientific study of social paranoia or social disturbances such as

Jean Baechler has done beautifully in his *Phénomènes révolutionaires*. But I am unable to say whether the day will ever come when we can identify the key variables which account for the eruptions of irrational forces in society. Secondly, and this is more disturbing still, even if we knew the recipe, I wonder whether we could prevent these forces from having a national or international impact. I don't know the answer because I am not sure whether pathological phenomena in society are really phenomena that ought to be cured, or whether they are simply the reverse side of a period of fertility and creativity. Are these not unavoidable by-products of basically creative waves of activities which we suppress at our peril? Or, at the very least, are they not the accidents of history?

To be a good futurologist one has to have a lively sense of philosophy and history. If one could, in this particular example, believe with Spengler or Toynbee that there is periodicity in the lives of civilisations, if one had reason to believe, for instance, that fifty years of classicism is bound to be followed by thirty years of romanticism and so forth, not just in the arts but in the broader field of political thinking and cultural conventions as well, one could then depict alternative futures based on at least plausible hypotheses. In such envelope forecasts one could vaguely make room for social unrest, hero-worship, the surfacing of irrational desires, etc. But here we are right outside the narrow field of futurology which, as far as I'm concerned, is the one we are pursuing for the benefit of policy-makers.

In any case, even if some superior futurologist could tell his government 'look out, for you are entering an era of chauvinism', what should a government do? Some historians have identified slow-moving trends in the attitudes of societies. From the beginning of the 18th Century we can talk of a scientific civilisation which is, of course, still very much with us. But suppose that a perceptive historian identified a new trend within that larger trend: I can't see that the implications of such an identification could be translated into terms of policy-making decisions. All one could say, as a practical student of the future, is that you cannot modify capital formation, or your budget for health, or education, or transportation to tackle some long-term change detected by this perceptive historian. Historical trends move very slowly and imperceptively, and in my view governments are simply not in a position to change them with problem-solving methods. There is a very apt sentence in *Dr. Zhivago* where Pasternak says: 'History is not made by anyone. You cannot make history; nor can you see history, any more than you can watch the grass growing.'

Perhaps the only people who have some influence on these long-term, subterranean trends are the cultural pace-makers, the ideologists, the religious leaders, the social prophets. But even the influence of these is open to question—what determined the Anglo-Saxon countries' new attitude to death which Geoffrey Gorer describes in *Death, Grief and Mourning*, or what are the springs of our new conception of family life so penetratingly discussed by Philippe Ariès in *Centuries of Childhood*?

OSSIP K. FLECHTHEIM

Marxism and
the Third Road

Ossip K. Flechtheim is one of the best known European academic futurologists and a leading spokesman of the 'bridge-building' school of future-oriented research. He is Professor of Political Science at the Free University of Berlin and editor of the journal *Futurum*. His numerous publications include: *Eine Welt oder keine* (1964), *Weltkommunismus im Wandel* (1965), *History and Futurology* (1966) and *Futurologie* (1970).

URBAN: Future-oriented research—futurology to use a word you have coined—has found little favour in Eastern Europe. The Communist attitude to futurology is that there is simply no need for a special scholarship to concentrate on a scientific prediction of the future, for all that can be known about the future is spelt out, directly or by implication, in Marx's analysis.

How does Marxism as predictive analysis stand up to the scrutiny of a modern futurologist?

FLECHTHEIM: You are quite right, the official assumption was that Marxism, or Marxism–Leninism, is the combined science of politics, sociology, economics and philosophy, and for that reason no other form of social science was possible and permissible. That is why there was so much hesitation before the title sociology was accepted in Eastern Europe. This attitude has gradually changed as contacts were made with the West and certain empirical investigations were carried out. So now there is in almost every Communist country—China is an exception —an official sociology. Also one can see the beginnings—and that is an even more difficult case—of a rudimentary kind of political science, still very closely connected with official doctrine and constitutional law. More recently, some Communist countries can boast of a kind of futurology or social prognostics. All this is new. For a very long time it was assumed that one could study the future within the scope of Marxism–Leninism, with the traditional tools of historical and dialectical materialism and a combination of official disciplines. With the coming of predictive studies in America and Western Europe, social scientists in the Communist world had to make a decision whether to go along with the West or do something else. Needless to say, they decided that Marxism–Leninism has itself a claim to be regarded as futurology, and they said that a more precise explanation of the writings of Marx and Lenin would yield better prognoses than could be obtained in other ways.

URBAN: You said 'within the scope of Marxism–Leninism'. Is there no contradiction here? If one speaks of the prognostics of Marxism, can one at the same time speak of the prognostics of Leninism? Leninism in the strict sense is surely incompatible with the Marxist prognosis. Lenin's idea that a small group of professional revolutionaries can inject a sense of class-consciousness and revolutionary rectitude into a proletariat that might otherwise not realise its mission and miss out on history, is a most un-Marxist notion. So if one wants to take Marx at his word—at any rate, at his word in the Communist Manifesto—Lenin's success in 1917 should be enough to cast doubt on much in Marx that is predictive.

FLECHTHEIM: You are quite right. Nevertheless, it is a fact that in the Communist countries such distinctions are forcefully discouraged. There, Lenin's version of the teaching of Marx continues to be *the* science of the future in much the same way (if I may use a flattering parallel) as the geocentric view of the universe, though 1,200 years old in the 16th Century, continued to be the official dogma of Christendom even after Copernicus, Kepler and Galileo had shown it to be scientifically untenable.

In the West, however, the future is becoming the object of new and more thorough studies, and we have suddenly discovered that we have been engaged in this kind of work all along. It is a little like Molière's Monsieur Jourdain, who suddenly realises that he has been speaking in prose all his life. In a sense all great plans and projects beginning with, say, the first five-year plan in 1929 in the Soviet Union, contain the two basic elements of futurology: the actual planning and the long-range prognostics.

But let me add a footnote here, before we go any further, on the adventures of the term 'futurology' in Eastern Europe. The Communist countries were in a bit of a dilemma when the term first became common currency. There was some hesitation. Then the Czechoslovaks began using it in 1968. They even founded a futurological society and they are still using the term in their official documents. It is sporadically also used in Poland. In the Soviet Union there was first a hesitant attempt to talk of 'futurology'. Recently I happened to come across an article in a technical journal: 'Futurology, the Science of the 20th Century.' Now Soviet social scientists tend to say that the notion of futurology is linked with non-Communist ideas, that it reflects a 'third-road' ideology and is a bourgeois product. They emphasise planning as their answer to future-studies and have settled for the term 'social prognostication', which is now the principal term used, both there and in East Germany.

URBAN: How would you describe the differences between the methods employed in 'social prognostics' and those we use in future-oriented research in the Western countries?

FLECHTHEIM: We must differentiate between three aspects of futurology. First, there are the actual forecasts—projections, plans, etc.—which are based on the extrapolation of specific developments in a restricted field, for instance the increase of motor traffic in a specific town. These are very technical matters where statistics, cybernetics, computers, etc. are used. In this field there is, generally speaking, no difference between the kind of futurology we pursue in the West and the one they have in the East. Let me give you an example.

I received an invitation the other day to a manufacturers' and managers' conference in Düsseldorf. One could tell from the fee they were charging participants—1350 DM—that it was meant for top-notch men in the field. The subject was technological forecasting, especially market investigations. One of the leading speakers was to be a professor from Rumania who was going to lecture West German industrialists on marketing problems! So you can see that on this first score the questions asked and the methods used are the same—East and West. This is a topic where the field for cooperation should be wide open.

The second aspect of futurology where we have to make a comparison is the nature of planning—what is meant by a planned economy. Here the Soviet Union took the lead with its monumental five-year plans which were later accepted by (or foisted upon) the other Communist states.

But the Western countries too have integrated some features of the Soviet type of planning in their economies. Of course the differences are more significant than the similarities. There is hardly a non-Communist country that has anything like the centralised, command type of planning that the Soviet Union and East Germany have. We have in the West adopted various degrees of planning—indicative planning in France, and even the Federal Republic and Holland inject increasing doses of planning into their economies: there is planning in medium-term financial allocations, in traffic management, in regional development, etc. Here I speak with less certainty, but I should imagine that in this area too a certain rapprochement is to be found and an exchange of experiences might be profitable.

Now the third aspect is a difficult one to name. It has to do with the general philosophy of future-oriented research. Sometimes I simply call it the general premises on which the futurologist tacitly relies when he sets out to formulate his questions, and it is here that the great conceptions and visions come in, for it is ultimately these, often hazy, assumptions that determine the direction and tenor of all social, political programming.

And this brings me back to your first question—is Marxism and Leninism a futurology in the Western sense? It was fairly generally believed by Communists in the early years of the century that Marx's ideas could be made to harmonise with revolution in a backward country. Lenin believed it was possible and he acted upon it, but he insisted that the revolution's success depended on how far it would be helped by similar unheavals in the industrially developed world. Then, when those revolutions did not materialise, Stalin responded with 'socialism in one country', and world revolution was postponed. It acquired a quality of the millennium which it was pious to extol but unwise to expect. So Communists are faced with the question: does Marxism–Leninism have any validity as a scientific base for future-oriented research? Is 'futurology' more than a collection of straightforward technological extrapolations of the kind we also use in the West, pepped up by optimistic expectations of the future which are *de rigeur* in Communist states?

You will find a great many people in the U.S.S.R. who believe that with more planning, more social engineering, with twenty-year perspective plans, etc. the Soviet Union will make very great steps forward as an industrialised and rich country: everyone will enjoy a much higher living standard, everyone will live according to his needs, and a classless society will be ushered in. However, the withering away of the Party and state is not mentioned; on the contrary it is emphasised that the maintenance and further improvement of the achievements in the economic sphere demand the continuance of the Party and the state in their present roles. So here we have one significant deviation from Marx's prediction which the Czechoslovak reform Communists tried to put right in 1968 with the results we all know. In the West we have nothing like this closed conception of futurological expectations. We have a variety of conceptions as we move from Right to Left on the political spectrum.

URBAN: Where would you place Herman Kahn's school in this spectrum?

FLECHTHEIM: To the right. Herman Kahn's futurological philosophy is definitely conservative because he assumes that all development in the technical, commercial, social spheres will take place within the existing Western social and economic order. Not only that, but he expects the future to be like nothing so much as an American future. Worse, his model of the future is based not on what America is like in 1970, but what America was like in 1950, coupled with a tremendous technological leap forward. It is a bizarre idea, for one has to ask oneself: how can one operate a space-economy with a steam-engine type of free-enterprise mentality?

I tend to see in futurology a means of seeking out what one might call a 'third road', that is to say a prospect of the future which is different from both what we have in the East and what the majority of the students of this problem expect in the West. I believe that a new social and economic system will finally emerge incorporating specific features from both the Eastern and Western systems of 'Socialism' and 'Capitalism'.

URBAN: What would this compromise be like? Is there anything in Marx and Engels you can build on?

FLECHTHEIM: Yes there is, but of course Marx and Engels had no monopoly of forecasting much that has actually taken place in our time. A long time before social prognoses became fashionable, we had thinkers like Thomas More in the 16th Century and a whole school of Utopian Socialists like Saint-Simon, Fourier, Proudhon and many others. Most Utopian thinking was a child of its time, reflecting some crisis of society, new forces coming up with fresh ideas for moulding the future. Even later Utopian writers such as Wells, who were politically far less committed than the 19th-Century Socialists, didn't see the future as some simple extension or a piecemeal improvement of the present. In many ways they were after something fundamentally different—a better and juster society, a society

CAN WE SURVIVE OUR FUTURE?

in which the old ideals of liberty, equality and fraternity would be realised in a much more authentic way than they had been hitherto.

Marx and Engels belong to the same tradition. Engels published a booklet called *The Development of Socialism from Utopia to Science*, and there are concrete, almost technical, studies by Marx and Engels which show astonishing foresight. One such analytical study is Marx's essay on the political development of France after the *coup d'état* of Napoleon III in 1851. Then we have Marx's remarkably accurate forecasts about the United States. He foresaw the shift of emphasis from the Atlantic to the Pacific, the growing importance of China. I think it was in 1850 that Marx wrote 'One day we will find this inscription on the great wall of China: "République Chinoise, Liberté, Egalité Fraternité ...".' Marx predicted automation and foresaw the possibility that the worker might be rendered more or less superfluous by the machine. (This, of course, brings up the question: what becomes of the class-conscious proletariat when its numbers are so badly reduced?)

There are, therefore, in Marx and Engels quite a few interesting premises for scientific work that go beyond Utopia. But at the same time the Utopian element breaks through very strongly, especially in the dialectic. After all, Marx and Engels remained basically loyal to Hegel's dialectic—and in this respect I can't see much difference between the early and the late Marx—and this has involved their predictions in great difficulties.

URBAN: What exactly were these difficulties?

FLECHTHEIM: The idea that thesis and antithesis result in a revolutionary kind of synthesis—a leap, as it were, in nature —is entirely imaginary. It has not been confirmed by science and lends the Marxist dialectic an air of unreality. We have seen, especially in the industrially developed societies—and that is the proper testing ground of Marxism—that the proletariat has not become a class-conscious vehicle of history and that it has not transformed society from Capitalism into Socialism. On the contrary, there has been an increasing *embourgeoisement* of the proletariat and a dwindling of its numbers.

That is why I would see in futurology, as I understand it, a suspension of Marxism. I mean this in the double—Hegelian—sense, viz. that one would have to reject a great deal in Marx, but one should also preserve what is positive and scientifically valid in him. The synthesis I have in mind would bridge the gap between the Utopian consciousness which is, as I have said, still very much part of Marx and Engels, and the modern, strictly scientific investigation of the future : social prognostics, planning, etc. If my estimate is correct, the result would produce a nice balance between Utopia and science. It would be much more realistic than the impressionistic forecasts of the 1920s and 1930s but would retain some of the imaginative qualities of Utopian thinking. It would spare us both the aridities of empirical science and the flights of the Utopian imagination.

This futurology would draw on the social evolution that has taken place in the Eastern and Western countries, representing, however, neither the first nor the second but an independent, though clearly derivative, third road. It would integrate the growing permissiveness, liberalism and individualism of Western society with an improved, or if you like enlightened, interpretation of Socialism as it is practised in East Europe. One cannot make a precise prediction here but a synthesis that would unite liberalism and Socialism, or democracy in the West European sense and democratisation as it is understood in the East, is entirely within the realm of possibilities. It would mean a new alternative which would go beyond our received notions of democracy. A democracy of this type was being born, to everyone's surprise, in Czechoslovakia in 1968, and it is perhaps not without significance that the Czech reform movement was very much influenced—intellectually, theoretically and spiritually—by the Czech futurologists who had been engaged in this kind of work for several years under the auspices of the Academy of Sciences.

URBAN: The futurology you describe predicates a convergence between the Eastern and Western types of society. The question, as I see it, is: is this convergence written into the nature of the two systems (i.e. is it socially and technologically determined as Sakharov thinks, for instance), or does it require an act of will on the part of the two sides who do not always appear to have the courage of their convergence?

FLECHTHEIM: Your scepticism is amply justified. I can see no automatic development towards convergence in the sense in which we have just discussed it, that is to say, in the positive sense. I would go so far as to say that if the present trend between the two parties is allowed to run its course and follows the kind of curve that is, alas, the normal curve in history—mankind taking no conscious part in the determination of its future—a *negative* type of convergence is the one we'll have to reckon with.

URBAN: How is one to understand a negative type of convergence?

FLECHTHEIM: I would say the most clearly negative kind of convergence is the collective death of mankind. This possibility has to be taken seriously. We have the means, the foolishness and historical precedent for mass destruction. If power-politics and the arms race continue, if we go on showing ourselves incapable of resolving international conflicts, if atomic or biological blows are exchanged over the Middle East or any other part of the world, then we may be facing the possibility that life will be extinguished on our planet or, at the very least, mankind will relapse into barbarism. This relapse would involve not merely the destruction of the occident, as Spengler said after the First World War, but the destruction of all modern culture and civilisation. Now this is our first model.

The second alternative would arise if the negative tendencies, which we have seen gathering more and more momentum, especially in the two super-powers, were further reinforced. I

376

think at the beginning, at least, we would avoid a major catastrophe. But this would only be a reprieve similar to the one we
have had for the last twenty-five years. We would not be solving
the crucial problems of the 1970s and '80s which are all coming up now and many of them have already arrived—problems
like the control of population growth, disarmament, the sanita-
tion of the environment, the democratisation and humanisation
of society, of the state, of education and so on. All this would
remain unsolved. We would muddle along, pushing the problems along with us as we have done in the past. Eventually all
this would produce a state of affairs which one might best describe as a kind of neo-Caesarism. This in my view would not
amount to a repetition of what some of the young people, especially on the far Left, fear most—a revival of Fascism. It
would not be so dramatic, but it would be a slow decline, a
slow petrification and ossification, the sort of thing that happened in late classical antiquity, in the late Roman Empire : the
ruling structures are preserved but without the spirit that used
to move them, and there is an overlordship of administrators,
bureaucrats and technocrats without any vision where we are
all going. More and more armaments would be manufactured.
There would be more and more space travel for military purposes, more and more mass consumption for the minority of
mankind in the rich countries. Therefore the polarisation between rich and poor countries would increase.

URBAN: These tendencies are in effect already visible today
on both sides of the divide.

FLECHTHEIM: Yes, and one has to see quite clearly where
they might be leading. The neo-Caesarism I am talking about
would mean, in the Soviet Union and the dependent countries,
the perpetuation of a more or less authoritarian and bureaucratic society which would, however, enable the people to enjoy a greater prosperity and would give them wider educational
opportunities, especially in the technical fields. But it would
not lead to any real liberalisation. The self-determination of

the masses, in the sense of Marx and Engels, would not be realised.

In the West, neo-Caesarism would bring about the disintegration of the liberal and democratic forces of society; this would mean more regimentation, centralisation and planning from the top, cushioned, however, by a certain prosperity. At the same time the cultural and environmental problems I have already mentioned would be neglected. There is a saying by the Polish writer Lec *'panem et circenses*—the bread gets whiter and the games bloodier'. There is something in that. The bread gets whiter as certain comforts, the value of which is very much open to question, are being achieved : one possesses not one car but probably two. The people at the top of the pyramid now travel to Venus and Mars. The middle class will be spending its holidays on a more accessible place such as the moon, and simpler folks will no longer go to Italy but perhaps to Africa or Australia, hoping that their children will make it to the moon too.

At the same time the cities are turning into slums, not enough is being done for education, health care and science, the crime rate is rising and the non-participation of man in the activities of the state and society, of which he is supposedly a member, create fresh tensions and frustrations. In other words, one notices a disintegration of the humane, liberal, really democratic forces in Western society and a parallel growth of authoritarianism. In the East the worst features of the rule of terror are curtailed but the regimentation of society is maintained. Thus the two systems move closer to each other even though certain differences remain.

The continuing importance of the Party establishment in the East would be matched by the growing strength of the managerial class in the West. On the whole, the two forms of society would meet and perhaps meet for a conscious purpose too : to counter the pressure of the poor and rebellious masses in the Third World. This, of course, would mean a regrettable regression because the kind of society it would make necessary would be militarised, highly regimented, replete with Orwellian and Huxleyan features. Then, one can foresee that some of the industrialised countries would try to steal a march on their rivals by allying themselves with groups in the Third World, creating dangerous tensions and conflicts on fresh lines. So this would be my second alternative: a neo-Caesarism. Unlike Spengler, I do not expect that mankind would, if this alternative came about, technologically relapse into an earlier, primitive existence. I would expect the paradoxical coexistence of cultural barbarism with a high level of technological sophistication.

URBAN: 'Ghengis Khan with a telegraph,' to use Herzen's warning.

FLECHTHEIM: It could be that or it could be the telegraph operator with a technologically-determined whip in hand. It is difficult to say which would be more objectionable.

My third alternative inspires more hope. It would unite the positive features of democracy and Socialism, shedding the negative ones I have just mentioned. In this alternative future, individuals and groups in the West would not lose their identity or autonomy; they would be integrated in larger units by way of a rational and voluntary process and they would look beyond their direct interests. There would be more democratic planning, new kinds of family and group-living would be explored, the liberties and responsibilities of the individual would be extended in the personal, intellectual and social fields. The Eastern countries on the other hand would have to allow for wider liberalisation, create institutional guarantees to respect the rights of the individual and learn to do without the prevailing autocracy which, although not fully totalitarian any more, still contains the makings of a possible return to totalitarianism.

URBAN: This is indeed a hopeful alternative but is it realistic?

FLECHTHEIM: I think it is a possible alternative for a number of good reasons. Today we have a whole range of technological means at our disposal which earlier generations did not possess. These should make it possible for most of us to enjoy a high standard of living. What is more, our technology is still getting both larger and more refined, so that new problems as they arise can be taken care of without diverting funds or expertise away from older ones. New groups of people can become involved in these problems without taking anything away from others. So one could hope to achieve more in the future by way of a new distribution of functions and a new kind of social participation. This is my first reason for being hopeful.

The second reason is a bit more elusive and contains a slightly missionary element. It has to do with our consciousness of what constitute worthy ends of human existence. If you look at the great declarations, the great political programmes of our time—the Charter of the United Nations, the Universal Declaration of Human Rights, the European Convention of Human Rights, UNESCO, even the Soviet Constitution (of which, incidentally, Bukharin was the author), more honoured in the breach than in the enforcement, you will find that, in spite of the differences, they all come down clearly for certain fundamental human rights and democratic principles, and they all have goals for the future which are not entirely dissimilar. So we should, like the Russian dissident writers, take our rulers at their words and demand that they practise what they preach on Sundays at the United Nations. This will not be easy, for hypocrisy is a time-honoured prop in politics, but it would clear the air and bring out the common strands that might accelerate the gradual fusion of a liberalised East with a socially responsible West.

My third point hangs together with the second. It may not strike you as too realistic and its prospects at the moment are certainly dim. I am thinking of non-violent mass action and that strong movement in the study of society and politics which expresses itself in peace-research, future-oriented research, ecology and a paramount concern with the environment. All these may, in their togetherness, help us to realise some of the ideas I have just mentioned, and they may show us new ways of ending the civil war which is dividing mankind. We can no longer afford one.

Of course with Vietnam, Czechoslovakia, the suppression of civil rights in the Soviet Union among our most recent experiences, we cannot be too hopeful. On the other hand there is evidence that a new force, the small countries, may be pioneering a way for us. Great progress along the lines I have briefly indicated has been made in the Scandinavian countries and Holland on our side, while in Eastern Europe, Yugoslavia, Hungary, even Rumania and perhaps, later again Czechoslovakia, are, or will be, moving on a convergent path. The third-road, which to my mind is the only sane road for the future, presupposes a coming together of the non-conformists on our side with the revisionists in the East. This they could not do in isolation. They would have to be supported, as they are being already supported, by the new generation, the technological and managerial classes and the libertarian intellectuals, sharing a vision of the future which neither the East nor the West could claim as its own.

BRIAN ALDISS

Learning to Live
with a Doom-laden Future

Brian Aldiss is one of the most prolific and imaginative science-fiction writers in Britain today. He is a former President of the British Science Fiction Association and the editor of *Science Fiction Horizons*. His many publications include *Canopy of Time* (1959), *The Male Response* (1961), *Best Fantasy Stories* (1962), *Introducing SF* (1964), *Earthworks* (1965), *An Age* (1967), *Intangibles Inc. and other Stories* (1969).

GLENNY: As someone who has spent most of his life imagining what is going to happen in the future, can you tell me whether the future, when it has become materialised in the present, has horrified you, pleased you or surprised you more?

ALDISS: It has surprised me, certainly. I suppose it surprises us all although I suspect that those surprises are mainly disappointments. Nothing has proved quite as beautiful as we expected. Those chaps tramping about on the moon—they didn't perform in quite the spontaneous way they used to in the fiction of my childhood. They didn't take a comic cook along with them, for instance. In the event, some of the glory and sense of adventure have evaporated. Perhaps our imaginations just weren't strong enough. The future—before realisation, I mean—is always a blank; it has no existence. We write on it what we will, and so influence what is going to materialise; I think in a profound sense that is true—we are not entirely helpless, and the terrible things happening in the world must be regarded as our responsibility—must in an obscure way have been willed.

382

GLENNY: When you say that the future is our responsibility, it implies a degree of volition on the part of mankind and it also implies a considerable element of control over the nature of the environment: otherwise you wouldn't talk about it being our responsibility. Now, do you believe that we have reached the stage where we can in fact impose our will on what is to happen in the future? If so, is this not a potential source of as much danger and disaster as it is of well-being?

ALDISS: Yes, I think it is. However, you imply a distinction between volition and control and I think one cannot keep these two quite separate. Supposing you liken civilisation to a speeding plane, then at the beginning of the century we had a bi-plane that was on the whole fairly easy to fly; there weren't many controls, if you had an accident with any luck you could hop out of the cockpit because you weren't going too fast, you could climb out on the wing if a strut broke and repair it with a bit of adhesive tape and a length of wire. Well, our bi-plane has developed into a great big jumbo jet and I feel that we haven't built in enough controls. Building the jet, though, was an act of volition, and now the steering must be improved.

If my analogy is to the point, then it follows that controls must be increased—controls on technology, for instance. Certainly controls bring their own dangers but I don't think we can go on flying blind for much longer, which is what we seem to be trying to do. Paradoxically, I believe that in a profound sense most of us are enjoying the dangers of the flight. It's hair-raising, but all's well so far, it's better than travelling by donkey-cart; this unacknowledged delight in risk-taking is typical of the '60s and '70s. People on the whole like the sense of doom. The fashionable topic at the moment is pollution. Yet no one really cares about it. We sit here smoking our cigarettes and cigars, grumbling about pollution, yet all the time we are polluting our lungs and the atmosphere. In a sense this is something we wish for; more than the risk we fear controls, but more controls must come. After all we're living in a world with many more controls than our grandfathers would have tolerated, and we still don't know how many more controls we should tolerate. If we have failed, it is in not facing up to this question.

GLENNY: From talking to other people on this subject, controls are, of course, the crux of the problems of the future. We seem to have reached the point where some people who take a very radical view say that progress, or if you like, history, must stop. They maintain that we've reached a point where matters just cannot go on as they are, and there must be some cosmic figure who will raise a hand and say 'halt'. Others take a more gradualist attitude and say we must take piecemeal measures to stop this, that or the other harmful phenomena before things get any worse. Where do you stand among the advocates of control? Are you, as it were, a cosmic policeman who'd like to bring the rushing traffic of technology to a halt, or are you more an engineer who'd like to divert it into other channels or perhaps decelerate it slightly?

ALDISS: Well, the very idea of a cosmic policeman scares me a lot more than the mundane perils of the traffic. I would prefer to dodge among the busy roads, although it does seem at times that the traffic will eventually choke to a halt on its own. But controls, yes, they are certainly vital. I believe that if only we learn how to make proper use of it, over the next thirty years we will have available a superb method of control. You see the moon flights wouldn't have been possible without the computers making their instantaneous calculations and handling such a tremendous amount of data; we now have this fine instrument which can handle, not decisions, but the data that lead to the making of decisions. The most crucial of our present-day problems seems to me that no one knows quite what decisions to make. One sees this on national levels, where governments really do not know whether to pursue course A, B, C or so on down to Z. In future they should at least have the data available. Presumably we are at the beginning of a tremendous 'data explosion': at the end of twenty years we could all have a direct telephone line to a world knowledge-store, where we can check on any known fact. The only trouble is that there will be other people with other telephone lines who can check on *us*. This is, of course, where I begin to feel a sense of terror, and one can see straight away that with an unscrupulous government, and governments tend to be unscrupulous, things could become very unpleasant. Everything about us could be recorded in memory-banks. Regrettably, governments seem to want to control individuals more than they want to control the technosphere, whereas ideally, one would like to see a government dedicated to controlling the technosphere.

GLENNY: Do you then see the controls of the future being exerted more over people than over things?

ALDISS: I suppose people would agree that behind this discussion lies the admitted necessity to have better people living better lives. That's a necessity—but is it a possibility? This is what we grope blindly for, and this I think is where the 20th Century differs from any other century except the 19th, because now we can see the instruments and possibilities of solving many human dilemmas, if only they can be seized. This is why, in a sense, our age is essentially so tragic because for the first time we have our hands stretched out and can almost grasp our salvation.

How to do it? Frankly I don't know. Computers could aid us enormously here. I certainly don't see the computer, as many science-fiction writers do, as a menace itself; this is absolute bunk. It's a superb instrument that we've developed to work for us—and unfortunately to work for our governments too. This is where danger comes in. The trick about governments, perhaps, is not to think of them as divorced from us; we must accept responsibility for them. If one had an educated majority in the country, or rather an enlightened majority, then they could make the government work as they wanted it to. At the moment the likelihood of any government really representing the will of the people is about as great as the chance of drawing a winning ticket in a lottery—particularly while 'the will of the people' is a bit of a myth. Now the creation of that enlightened majority is perhaps something which could result from intensive educational use of computers. In *The Shape of Further Things*, I describe the way in which computer-terminals in every home —as we now have television sets—could free scholars from the present-day drudgery of chasing after facts buried in elusive sources. Computer-terminals would give direct access to the information stores in the great learned institutions of the world : or in your nearest branch library. The discipline of learning would still be necessary—the wasteful hours of fact-grubbing would be saved. We'd have a data explosion on an unprecedented scale. In the time saved, children could learn how to live instead of how to earn a living. We would then have a real education for life, the gift of self-knowledge would come earlier instead of later, with a resultant lessening of strain on the individual and on society. If this ever came about—and the chances are pretty remote—it would be a genuine step towards Utopia : towards having better people leading better lives.

GLENNY : You said a moment ago that the transformation of the future is, or should be, the result of the will of the people. Ideally, I don't think anybody would disagree with you. In practice, however, is it ever 'the people' who impose their will on the way that technology or industry develop and change their lives? I suspect that it is more often a combination of technologists, politicians and, above all, bureaucrats who know how to manipulate the machinery for such changes, and that very often 'the people' are mere passive subjects who have to take the consequences of decisions made on their behalf and without their consent. In the future, since decisions of this nature may be infinitely more far-reaching and possibly more dangerous, more unpleasant in their consequences than before, do you not believe that our institutions, whether in the East or the West, are at the moment dangerously lacking in the ability of ordinary people to assert control over the new élite of technocrats?

ALDISS : The drawback in all political institutions anywhere in the world is that the people in power are people with a will to power, whereas what is needed ideally are people in power who don't want power, who aren't obsessed by power. If one could only be ruled by people who weren't so eager simply to retain office, governments might show more collective wisdom and less tendency to form what you call new élites—which is an impossibility, I suppose! Governments notoriously don't vote themselves out of power! With the present state of affairs it can't be imagined, but perhaps with the coming data explosion I have outlined there could be some real diffusion of power in place of the concentration and centralisation so typical of the present day. Certainly the data explosion will affect the structure of our societies. What may happen is that technicians, politicians and bureaucrats will come from a much wider spectrum of society, and see and feel far beyond their own speciality. One hopes this might be so, just as the people who are now at, say, managerial level in the mass media have gained from the paperback revolution of the 1950s, when a lot more knowledge was available suddenly and cheaply to a lot of people. Something of the sort could only be positively good.

GLENNY: This sounds to me rather like pious optimism and little more.

ALDISS: Yes, I admit it. Hope does not spring eternal to the human breast. I prefer to avoid the role of prophet of doom; traditionally no one ever listens to Cassandra's wailing voice.

GLENNY: But surely we must pay heed to some of Cassandra's warnings?

ALDISS: Agreed. One of the snares of an increasing technology is that with every advance it creates terrible side-effects which themselves have to be doctored with another quick technological palliative. The classic instance, of course, is the progress in medicine in the 19th Century which dramatically lowered the infant mortality rate and now leaves us with the population problem. One couldn't say that Pasteur's and Lister's researches should have been squashed at birth, but we are left to face the terrible back-lash of problems arising from their solution.

One question closely connected with medical progress is the fate of people in big cities. Take the 19th-Century model, shall we say London, as a typical example, where a good percentage of its inhabitants was ill-housed, had no amenities, few rights, bad drains, tainted drinking water, polluted air and all the rest of the burdens with which the writings of Mayhew and Dr. Simon have made us familiar; and yet, nevertheless, those people lived in close and dependent units, so that there was a great sense of human empathy, of relationship, in the court or the street or neighbourhood. Nowadays people are infinitely better housed, they take for granted adequate sanitary facilities, they have central heating; if they are lucky they have air-conditioning; they've got television, telephone, radio, lifts up to their flats and so on, but they are often also overwhelmed by feelings of isolation.

GLENNY: What are the effects of this isolation?

ALDISS: Isolation drains all the colours out of life. It diminishes one's sense of one's own worth and compartmentalises one's thinking; this is a dangerous thing because it can make us neglect possible solutions to our problems when they may arise. For instance, it's too easy to talk of technology as something separate from us and I must stress that technology is no accident; it is the outcome of human volition. We long for our machines, they have become component parts of us since the Renaissance, they're now essentially a part of the human psyche. You should not talk of technology in the abstract: technology is people and what people do. Since we have a measure of self-control, we can control our technologies; but the isolation and fear of modern life can render us powerless to take control.

That is what technology means, and that is why it is such a

prominent feature of our lives. We observe the close inter-relationship between us and technology by popping the old basic question: what sort of creature is mankind? My view is that essentially we are still Iron Age people. The human brain is a unit developed rather quickly over the last couple of million years, not exactly shoddy, but perhaps with a few connections missing here and there. It has after all been built up round an earlier model—the animal brain, and the animal brain is still in there somewhere, functioning dimly like an old television set enveloped in cotton wool. We may suppose that it interferes in some ways with the working of our higher brain-centres. If we were all intellect, we would just go ahead with our technology; we wouldn't mind the gasoline fumes, the polluted rivers, the shattered chains of life. But in fact we are divided and the animal still seeks the ways of nature; we have, if you like, a heart as well as a head, and the modern battle is to see that the head doesn't run too far ahead of the heart, that technology supports instead of killing nature. You can point back in history to times when the heart outran the head—religious wars are one of the symptoms—and that wasn't fun either. If we could only get the head and the heart to function in harmony: this I think is the problem: not to banish but balance technological forces.

GLENNY: Let us revert for a moment to the universalist approach to the problem, namely to those who say that the progress of history must stop. In some areas such as the international agreement on nuclear explosions within the atmosphere known as the test-ban treaty, and the conventions which forbid the use of chemical warfare, some tentative attempts have been made to halt the advance of technology. Do you feel that there is further scope for development of the thesis that history must stop?

ALDISS: Well, there is a sense in which history has now stopped of its own accord in the Western World. The sands may have run out without our knowing it. Two instances—one from the natural world and one from the world of ideas. Take the natural world first. A sense of impending doom in the West is no new thing; but there is now very good reason for believing that pollution of our oceans, through dumping and distribution of poisons and chemicals and sewage, may already have reached irreversible proportions. The Great Lakes, the Baltic, the Mediterranean, are rapidly dying, becoming unable to support their traditional life-forms, and there is no reason to suppose that this is anything but the beginning of a terminal process. With dead oceans, the rest of the world will die. It is possible that the most rigorous legal and political controls, applied tomorrow, would already be too late. From the world of ideas, we receive the same dusty answer. We live at the fag-end of the Renaissance. In the golden dawn of the Renaissance, men looked about and believed they could do anything; at sunset, we see clearly that the day has brought us such power that whatever we do has unconsidered side-effects with the balance of nature. The vitalising effect of a new age is hardly likely to come about while we struggle in the mess of our own making. Perhaps the one hope lies in the data explosion I mentioned. This is what I mean by saying history has stopped. We can see only night ahead. Our brave 20th Century is in most of its essentials merely a re-run of the 19th. We are more deeply enslaved to our machines, and the shadow of Malthus lies even longer in the land.

Now that I'm really stuck in this Cassandra role, I'd better add the obvious—that pollution doesn't pollute the globe; human beings do. We can't escape the population explosion and, despite the spiritual impoverishment we've mentioned, the Western nations are still getting richer at the expense of the poorer ones. We tremble on the brink of a catastrophe of unprecedented magnitude, and in getting richer we seem to get poorer all the time. There is only so much cake to slice. Whatever ultimately happened to the dinosaurs, we don't know, but it's fairly obvious that if mankind becomes extinct it will be because it went too far too fast.

GLENNY: Is this connected with the 'population explosion' that you mentioned just now?

ALDISS: Yes it is. There are now many more people as well as goods and services, while paradoxically enough we become more isolated. The more highly populated the world, the more we are forced back on ourselves. For the first time ever, the ordinary man can fly to a holiday by a warm and sunny sea— only to be driven off the beach by thousands of others like him! I'd hate to poach here on Professor Toynbee's ground; he'll say it better than I could, but one of our difficulties is that in man's long history the individual was only accustomed to facing and dealing with his own group, his own family group or his own tribe; and if another tribe came along, you would probably throw stones at it until it moved over the hill again. Now you can't do this nowadays, and in daily life we have to cope with a number of strangers, people whose faces we haven't seen before and perhaps never want to see again. This is probably damaging us in some way, since it is not easy to maintain our identities in the face of indifference or hostility. In the tribal group or the family group, however stupid you are, however maimed or unfortunate you are, you have your identity; even the traditional village idiot had his identity and his accepted role, though I hope this is not taking too sentimental a view of the past. In the over-populated world, identity is at a premium.

I believe that many of the big crises today, crises not only of technology but of the disintegration of the major religions, stem from and feed this same instability of the individual. At the moment people on the whole are insecure about their roles in society, and this may well be part of the reason why we compartmentalise our thinking and talk about technology and the government and the biosphere as though they were in some way entirely separate from us and as though man were separate from nature, for in so doing we seem to lessen our responsibilities. And all the while we need to take up more responsibility, to control both ourselves and the forces of nature we have unleashed. We *are* nature; if one fights nature one is fighting oneself.

GLENNY: This problem of the weakening of identities is a matter that affects the individual. What of the social effects?

ALDISS: One effect is that human beings tend to draw in on themselves more than they did—we spoke earlier about the way communities have vanished with better housing, and in a sense an increase in material goods has driven the family unit back on itself. Families are much more isolated than they were, and even within the family group individuals can become isolated, because better transport means that you may live in London but Granny lives out in the country; you can only see her twice a year and then it's a formal visit before she goes into the old people's home. This trend will presumably increase as there are more and more people and so the anaemia of society will increase. I think it's here that I am at my most pessimistic. If the world population really does double in the next thirty years, the year 2000 will bring severe psychological changes even within the family group; motherhood, for instance, may get a bad name, children in their vulnerable early teens may be turned away from home. It may be accursed to bring forth life, just as it is to slay it, so that motherhood could eventually rank as a major crime along with murder. It's already very evident in this country that there are too many people and the pressures of over-population are going to accelerate, perhaps irreversibly.

GLENNY: In all this discussion we have been circling round the central question: are we on the point of making a technology-based life that is intolerable in the terms that we have known it? Therefore don't you think we are at a revolutionary turning point, rather than merely revolving on the endless wheel, so to speak, of the Industrial Revolution.

ALDISS: Well, the wheel metaphor might come in aptly here; think of the world as a watch with large and small wheels going round at different speeds. Without by any means seeing European civilisation as ideal, one suspects it has greater inbuilt stability than the more rapidly revolving big wheels of the two super-powers. To deal with Europe for a moment, we in Europe have always been cushioned by a number of factors: for one thing our development has been slow and organic from Neolithic man to the present day; perhaps one might say that this process of gradualism is the head and the heart keeping pace! Progress hasn't been too forced. With the Renaissance came the voyages of discovery when the white races discovered parts of the world that the inhabitants didn't even know were lost, and then with the Industrial Revolution the Europeans were able to export their goods, their cheap cottons and their machinery to those parts of the world that they had colonised, so that Europe has undoubtedly been historically extremely fortunate, both as a market garden and in finding markets. This fortune is something that neither the U.S.S.R. nor the U.S.A. ever had. In order to eat, both countries had to conquer nature rather than coming gradually to terms with the environment. Unfortunately matters are such that these two great powers are now setting the pace for the rest; the truth is that most of the rest of us are bent on copying them, and the European virtues of modesty and gradualism are about to vanish. We are opting for gigantism and exploitation all the time; we're building bigger engines, bigger aeroplanes, larger and larger corporations, we're amalgamating into supra-national blocs. I was in Indonesia in the years of its formation and the Javanese then were to be seen parading round the streets with five wristwatches on each arm. This was their ambition, and one laughs at it, but we have our equivalents with people who can't bear to have a black-and-white television set as soon as a colour television set is available at twice the price. This is the spirit of envy, which indeed must have got mankind out of the caves (one always wants a bigger and better cave than the neighbours), but as long as envy and the other basic human emotions and desires—greed, fear, rapacity, the lust for power—hold sway, then in this sense history has stopped because we can never rise above Iron Age Man. This is the wheel going round with a vengeance.

Perhaps there will be a real breakthrough into a new level of civilisation with the coming advances in biology. One just dare not think of these things, but with progress in surgery at the genetic level we can see that it might be possible one day to cut out some of these basic drives of mankind and perhaps in another thirty years, at the turn of the century, we will see people walking around who have been freed from all our hopes and fears by surgery. You and I can only view this with distaste; it sounds too like a symbolic castration; but after all one generation's meat is another generation's poison and vice versa, and many of the things that we find perfectly acceptable would have been utterly odious to our grandparents—so that if we look at the future and shudder, there's no doubt that the future will look back and shudder just as complacently at us. Let's just hope there will be someone ahead there capable of looking back.

INDEX

Affluence of West, dangers of, 16, 24, 108–9, 166–7, 178–9, 388, 392–3; effects on society, 125–6, 190–5, 210, 233, 234–5, 237
Russian, 233
Africa, culture, 217; ecology in East, 214; future development of, 125, 144, 152, 198–9, 212–13; nationalism, 238; socialism, 247, 299
Agrarian societies, defects of, 164–5, 170, 193–4, 212; ecology of, 209–15 *passim*; industrialisation of, 33–4, 38; unemployment in, 164, 225–6
Agriculture, 28, 59, 123, 164, 211, 334
Aristotle, 9, 145, 173, 217
Aron, Raymond, 2, 69, 275, 306, 352
Asia, culture, 110–12; future development of, 125, 144, 157; nationalism, 238; socialism, 299
Atomic physics, 62, 73–88 *passim*; *and see* Nuclear technology
Authority, need for, 173; in Germany, 286–7, 290; rejection of, 170–1
Automation, 144–5, 182, 199, 225, 374
Aviation, 21, 29–30, 74–5, 99, 150, 202

Bacon, Sir Francis, 22, 84, 140–1, 144, 152, 168
Belgium, 316, 344
Bergson, Henri, 10, 316, 319
Berlin, 277, 280, 283–4, 286
Biology, ethics of, 17, 78, 135–7, 159–60; future of, 394; need to control, 252–3; value of, 134–5, 186
Biosphere, 26–9, 36–7, 38, 196, 203, 222
Birth control, 60; failure of, 219; *and see* Population
Bouthoul, Gaston, 225
Britain, agriculture, 211; coal-mining, 179–80; control of science and technology, 328; economic growth, 183, 250–1, 345–6; education, 146, 147, 177, 195; government, 151–2, 177; immigrants, 184; Industrial Revolution, 28, 33, 34, 169, 189, 190; industry, 29, 151–2, 175, 182, 185–6; mental health, 237; as nuclear power, 210–11, 296–7; in Second World War, 171–2, 250, 345; social welfare, 234, 345, 347; stability, 183–4, 218; uncompetitive character, 248–51

Broadcasting, 10, 11, 52, 91, 110, 120, 128–9, 150, 295–6
Buddhism, 31, 167, 260
Bureaucracy, limitations of, 13, 22, 262, 265; power of, 158, 159; Soviet and American, 50–1

Canada, and U.S. aid, 239; pollution in, 344, 345
Capitalism, benefits of, 162, 205, 242–3, 247, 251; and Christianity, 112; compared with Communism, 311–23 *passim*; and Leninism, 280; *and see* Western world
Capitalist countries, *see* Western world, U.S.A., etc.
Centralisation, growing tendency towards, 175–7, 296, 306, 378; in E. Europe, 125, 347
Chemical warfare, 60, 188, 389
China, Imperial, 35–9, 232
China, modern, Cultural Revolution, 135, 244, 284; ideology, 23, 244, *and see* Maoism; as nuclear power, 240; technological backwardness, 37–8
Chinese culture, 243, 244
Chomsky, Professor Noam, 112
Christianity, in Eastern Europe, 232–3; and ecology, 111–12; and the individual, 86, 147, 167, 320–2; and science, 31, 369–70; and society, 17, 97–8, 101–2; in U.S.A., 163, 255; and youth, 231–2, 260
Cities, similarities between industrial, 293–4, 298, 300–1; *and see* Urbanisation
Collectivism, 9–10, 194–5, 270
Communications, modern, 15, 21, 130, 175; *and see* Broadcasting, Mass media
Communism, compared with Capitalism, 311–23 *passim*; discredited, 251; in Germany, 286; ideology, 141–2, 244–5, 311–23 *passim, and see* Leninism, Marxism, Stalinism; in Italy, 149; and science, 18, 141; *and see* Eastern Europe, Soviet Union
Communist countries, *see* Eastern Europe, Soviet Union
Computers, age of, 20, 355; dangers of, 154, 159, 176; uses of, 198, 317–18, 370–1, 384, 385–6
Comte, Auguste, 47
Conformism in modern society, 92, 94, 97, 100–2, 130–1, 143, 148, 251, 290, 322–3

Confucianism, 36, 38, 86, 243, 244, 260, 321–2
Consciousness, search for a new, 12–13, 14, 45, 47, 50, 51, 79, 120, 121, 167–8
Crime, 237, 254
Cybernetics, 113, 316, 353, 370–1
Czechoslovakia, culture, 295, 308–9, 314; economy, 244, 308; and futurology, 370, 375; occupation of, 91, 125, 277, 278, 292, 305, 372, 375, 381

Democracy, dying, 13, 23, 75, 176, 197–8, 217–18, 276–7, 287–8, 290–1, 328, 375, 378; in developing countries, 299
Denmark, 221, 339
Descartes, René, 10, 64, 81
Developing countries, aid to, 110, 239; democracy in, 299; development of, 125, 156, 198, 246–7, 298; future of, 42, 108–10, 125, 144, 152, 198–9, 378–9; industrialisation, dangers of, 125, 143–5, 152, 198, 209–13; materialism of, 108, 393; nationalism in, 238; socialism in, 246–7, 299; Soviet influence on, 49
Dictatorships, 14, 16, 19, 54–5, 153–4, 162, 217–18, 219, 241–2, 251, 303–8 passim
Drugs, 15, 188, 229, 232
Duverger, Maurice, 16, 89, 293–310, 312; Introduction à la politique, 294; Parties politiques, 303

Eastern Europe, conflicts in, 238–9; and ecology, 108, 209, 338–9; economic development, 30, 125, 177, 205, 244–5, 294–5, 304–7; education in, 295, 313–14; and futurology, 108, 368–81 passim; military defence, 348–9; regimes, 277–89 passim; relations with West, 338–49; religion in, 232–3; society in, 120, 295, 302–9 passim, 311–13, 368–81; sociology in, 368–9; and see Economic planning, Soviet Union
Ecology, and Christianity, 111–12; definition of, 207–8; and futurology, 351–67 passim; global, 106–9, 113, 118, 123, 132, 207–24 passim, 329–30; modern concern with, 19, 68, 105, 106, 123, 132, 325; and NATO, 339–40; and planning, 17, 68, 107, 198, 207–24 passim, 324–35 passim
Economic development, as end in itself, 64–6, 106, 177, 199, 324–5; and national characteristics, 246–51; need to control, 19, 41–2, 65, 106–20 passim, 174–86 passim, 191–5, 196–206 passim, 209, 220, 325–8, 384; and see Technology
of Britain, 183, 250–1, 345–6; of developing countries, 125, 156, 198, 246–7, 298; of Eastern Europe, 30, 108, 125, 177, 205, 244–5, 294–5, 304–7; of France, 250; of Germany, 249, 250; of Japan, 30–3, 108, 240–50 passim; of Soviet Union, 107, 125, 200–1, 209, 241–8, 294, 308–9; of Western world, 24, 66–8, 184–5, 311
Economic planning, and environment, 20,

68–9, 107, 198, 207–24 passim, 324–35 passim; and futurology, 351–67 passim, 368–81 passim, 384–9 passim; need for, 67, 103, 122–4; and society, 142–3, 180–6 passim, 293–310 passim; in East and West, 103–26 passim, 174–86 passim, 196–206 passim, 244–6, 293–310 passim, 311–12, 324, 368–81 passim; in West, 65–8
Education, advances in, 317–18, 386; defects of, 12, 134, 142, 175, 176, 194–5, 229, 230, 272–3; of élite, 71, 76, 385; importance of, 68, 159, 171, 182, 201; need for a broad, 147, 148, 269–70, 318, 322, 386; of public, 71–2, 123, 128–9, 131–2, 161–2, 182, 208–9
in Eastern Europe, 295, 313–14; in West, 146, 147, 165–6, 177, 194–5, 229, 230, 359; and see Universities
Elite, dangers of, 13–14, 386–7; education of, 23, 71, 146–7; in future, 144–5, 146–7; and political role, 146, 147, 157, 381, 386–7; and society, 74–7; in Soviet Union, 163; in West, 146–7
Employment, in agrarian societies, 212, 226; and automation, 144–5, 146, 182, 199, 255–6, 274; in cities, 165–6; and I.Q., 225, 317; problems of, 21, 66, 67, 179–80; and see Migrant labour
Engels, Friedrich, 169, 373–5, 377–8
Environment, man's relationship with, 26–9, 39–40, 52, 58, 64, 78–9, 81–3, 101–2, 105, 113–14, 116–17, 123, 131, 132–7, 207–24 passim, 233–4, 325; need to plan for, 325–31, 336–48, 362; and see Ecology, Pollution
Ethics, see Moral values
European Economic Community, 309–10, 319

Family life, changes in, 78, 149, 169, 189–90, 191, 359, 379, 391, 392
Fascism, 251, 253, 287, 302, 321–2, 377
Fisheries, 221, 331, 334
Foulness (London's Third Airport), 20, 68, 193–4, 363
France, ecology, 132, 344, 362; economic development of, 250; education, 146, 147, 359; intelligentsia, 262, 263–4, 266; society, 262–5, 267–8; student unrest, 14–15, 122, 258–71, 275, 279
Freedom, discussed, 97–8, 101–2, 198; planning for, 325, 327–9; restriction of, 113–15, 142, 170, 197–8, 216, 328, 329, 385, 394
in Eastern Europe, 294, 304, 311–12, 316, 318, 341, 350; in West, 152, 316, 318
Freud, Sigmund, 11, 48, 294
Futurology, 13, 19, 20, 41–3; and ethics, 22–3, 79–80, 364–5; and man, 20, 117; methodology of, 351–67; need for, 67–9, 85, 103–26 passim; and science, 81–3; Western and Soviet compared, 104–5, 107–8, 368–81 passim

Gabor, Professor Dennis, 17, 34, 53, 56, 145–6, 196–206, 235–6, 317; Inventing the Future, 196, 203, 225, 333, 335

Galbraith, J. K., 263, 293–310 *passim*, 312
Genetic engineering, 16–17, 20, 99, 252, 253, 294, 394
Germany, East, economic development of, 244, 308; pollution in, 339
Germany, West, Communism in, 286; democracy in, 276–7, 287–8, 291; economic growth of, 249, 250; effects of war, 275–7, 285–7; and futurology, 371; migrant labour in, 184–5, 189, 190; national character of, 16, 249, 285–6, 290, 302–4; pollution in, 20, 344; social unrest, 273–84 *passim*; student rebellion in, 14–15, 122, 261, 274–91 *passim*; in First World War, 303; in Second World War, 226, 239, 302, 345; *and see* Hitler, Nazism
Greece, development of, 244–5; Fascism in, 302

Hegel, G. W. F., 374–5
Heisenberg, Werner, 12–13, 17, 73–88; *Das Naturbild der heutigen Physik*, 81, 82; *Der Teil und das Ganze*, 87
Hellenistic culture, 11, 21, 36, 39, 115, 217, 255, 259–60
Herzen, Alexander, 140, 153
Hippy culture, 231–2, 258, 259–61, 265
History, biased, 361; and futurology, 366–7; lessons of, 11, 12, 13, 14, 23, 27–43 *passim*, 46, 61, 70–1, 98, 167–9, 200, 227, 229, 230, 306–7, 333–4, 366–7, 390; need for unbiased, 230, 350; rejection of, 11–12, 47, 48, 142–3, 229, 230, 232, 306–7, 314, 318–19
'History must stop' (Gabor), 34–6, 53, 56, 196, 384, 389–90
Hitler, Adolph, 54, 153–4, 226, 238, 275 298, 302–4, 316, 345
Hobbes, Thomas, 147, 166–7
Housing, 21, 177
Hudson Institute, 225, 227, 245, 273
Hungary, 125, 244, 292, 308, 381
Huxley, Aldous, 52, 351

India, 156, 164, 198–9, 219–20
Individual, the, alienation of, 14, 52, 120–1, 148, 259, 260, 388, 391–2; cult of, 167–8; in modern society, 9, 108, 110, 120–1, 125, 143, 147–8, 259, 261 ff., 341, 388, 391–2; *and see* Man, nature of
Industrial Revolution, 28, 33, 34, 169, 189, 190, 327, 392–3
Industrialisation and employment, 148–9, 169–70, 184, 189–90, 280–1; *and see* Automation, Developing countries
Industry, and ecology, 59, 68, 123, 133, 193, 326–7, 329, 339, 344–5, 362; gigantism of, 175–7, 202, 251, 293–4, 296; need to control, 220, 325–8
Intelligence Quotients, and employment, 146, 225, 317; and race, 364
Intelligentsia, role of, 162, 280, 281, 313, 381; in Eastern Europe, 295; in France, 262, 263–4, 266; in Germany, 302–4; in Soviet Union, 295, 304
International co-operation, need for, 105–8, 329–33, 339, 341–4, 381

Italy, Fascist, 65, 153, 302; industrialisation and employment, 149, 169, 185, 189–90; Southern Italy, development of, 244–5

Japan, culture, 31, 243, 248–9; economic development, 30–3, 35, 108, 240–50 *passim*; and fisheries, 221; population control, 221

Kahn, Herman, 15, 17, 22, 225–55, 373; *The Year 2000*, 67, 251, 254, 355–6, 359–60
Keynes, J. M., 234–5, 237
Koestler, Arthur, 274
Krushchev, N., 118, 240, 305

Lafargue, Paul, 236, 317
Leisure, problems of, 145, 234–5, 236–7, 317
Lenin, V. I., 32, 33, 34, 275, 279, 280, 310, 369, 372
Leninism, 79, 168, 266; *and see* Marxism–Leninism
Liberalism, in E. Europe, 309; in Germany, 16; Lockean, 147; future of, 375, 378
Locke, John, 147

MacLuhan, M., 90
Malthus, T. R., 17, 20, 390
Man, nature of, discussed, 23, 27, 43, 48, 56, 64, 96–8, 100–3, 116–21, 145, 166–9, 236–8
    aggression of, 16, 17, 105, 226, 229, 237, 266; development of, 19, 26–43 *passim*, 117, 188; and environment, 49, 105, 113–14, 116–17, 123; and futurology, 20, 117, 354–5; immaturity of, 128–9, 137, 230–1, 318–20, 389, 393–4; irrationality of, 16, 17–19, 80–1, 97, 117–21 *passim*; limitations of, 18, 20–1, 167–9, 230; responsibility for future, 105, 106, 115, 122, 382–90 *passim*; as social being, 18–19, 37, 38, 84, 130–1, 132, 143, 168–9, 172–3, 197
    mass-man, 23, 52, 89–90, 97, 130–1, 142–4, 147–8, 150–2, 251, 254; *and see* Individual, Religion, Technology
Maoism, 79, 109, 135, 244, 247, 264, 268, 272, 273, 284, 321–2
Marcuse, Herbert, 94, 151, 169, 266, 278, 281
Marx, Karl, 47, 100, 197, 233, 280, 372, 373–5, 377–8
Marxism, 33, 49–51, 79, 100, 104, 142, 168, 266, 269, 274, 278; Marxism–Leninism, 278–89 *passim*; and futurology, 368–72, 374–5
Mass media, 11, 91, 120, 277, 387; *and see* Broadcasting
Materialism, dangers of, 128, 149, 221; of Communism, 49, 312; of modern society, 108, 163, 195, 208, 273, 393–4
Medical science, 22, 60, 74–5, 175, 207, 212–13, 387–8
Mental illness, 237, 365–6; *and see* Social unease
Metaphysics, 59, 63–4, 80, 83–4, 97–8, 98–9, 134, 156, 168, 231–2; *and see* Religion
Middle East, 41, 201, 217–18, 376

Migrant labour, 149, 169–70, 184–5, 189–90
Military defence, 201, 336–8, 346–7, 348–9; and space research, 332–5, 377
Mishan, E. J., 177–8; *The Cost of Economic Growth*, 191–3, 324–7
Moonshots, 21, 99, 121, 202–3
Moral values, contemporary underdevelopment of, 20, 22, 28, 37, 46, 56, 64, 71, 233–4, 253–5, 312, 318, 319–20, 388–9, 390; and economic development, 64–5, 105–6, 192; and futurology, 22–3, 79–80, 364–5; need for new, 12, 16, 17, 56, 61, 69, 73, 78, 85–6, 106, 110–20 *passim*, 129–37 *passim*, 157, 160–1, 163, 254–5, 318–23; and power, 27–43 *passim*, 54–5, 64–5; and science, 18–19, 136, 156–7, 173, 364–5; sexual, 56, 60, 187–8, 261; and technology, 12, 27, 60–72 *passim*, 76–88 *passim*, 96, 127–8, 133–7, 173; in Soviet Union, 162–3; in West, 162–3, 253–5, 312, 318
Motor-car industry, and congestion, 29, 30, 54, 128, 178–9, 199; need to control, 178–9, 180, 200, 341–4; and politics, 358; and pollution, 20, 123, 128, 178–9; 'safety car' project, 341–2, 343–4, 358

National characteristics, and economic development, 246–51, 300–8; and politics, 285–6, 290
NATO, purposes of, 336–50
Natural resources, location of, 169–70
  scarcity of, 16, 27, 58, 59, 69, 105, 109–24 *passim*, 131, 132, 211–22 *passim*, 327; may lead to war, 16, 109–10
Nature, conservation of, 68, 132–3, 134–5, 325; control of, 27–8, 41, 59–61, 85, 151; as enemy, 28, 41, 60, 61, 85, 112–13, 393; laws of, 77–8; loss of contact with, 99, 117–18, 131, 133, 142, 149, 389; man's use of, 27–8, 81–3, 85; symbiosis with, 106, 113, 132–5, 137, 142, 144; *and see* Ecology
  of man, *see* Man, nature of
Nazism, 46, 55, 65, 302–4
Norway, 221, 339
Nuclear technology, control of, 389; U.S. controls, 252–3; dangers of, 85, 188, 210, 227–8, 327, *and see* War, nuclear; development of in U.S.A. and Britain, 296–7; *and see* Atomic physics

Ortega y Gasset, 313, 318–19
Orwell, George, *1984*, 52, 152, 351

Plato, 11, 20, 21, 22, 54, 75, 352
Pluralism, in E. Europe, 306; value of, 162–3, 322–3
Poland, 244, 289, 295, 308, 339, 370
Political philosophy, 17th Century, 140–1, 147, 160, 166–7; 18th Century, 45–6, 61–3, 141–2, 258–9, 261; 19th Century, 46–8, 85, 137, 140, 153, 161, 163, 166, 373
Politics (and politicians), and economic planning, 66–8, 124, 293–310 *passim*, 345–6, 358–9; and environment, 68, 107, 208, 326–30, 336–48; and futuro-

logy, 353, 355, 384–9 *passim*; limitations of, 20, 43, 75, 151, 158–9, 171, 208, 273, 330, 384–7; and technology, 14, 20, 70, 90, 141–2, 157–8, 161–2, 172–3, 176–7, 195
Pollution, dangers of, 41–2, 59, 118, 198, 223–4, 326–7, 344–5; need to control, 19–20, 27, 30, 68, 108, 123, 193, 204, 210, 221–2, 339, 383–4, 389–90; research into, 344–5
  chemical, 59, 123, 211, 212, 221–3; industrial, 59, 68, 108, 123, 193, 202, 326–7, 329, 339, 344–5; radio-active, 210, 332; thermal, 210–11
  of air, 20, 27, 30, 118, 128, 199, 204, 221–2, 329, 339, 344; of inland water, 20, 27, 30, 118, 204, 223, 345; of sea, 210, 223, 326, 329, 344
Population explosion, dangers of, 20, 22, 24, 68–9, 105, 109, 123–4, 131, 173, 175, 220, 387–8, 390–2; future, 363–4; need to control, 19–20, 124, 214, 216, 219, 392
Portugal, 244–5, 302, 344
Primitive societies and ecology, 209, 211–15 *passim*
Proletariat, future unemployment of, 144–5, 146, 182, 225–6, 317, 374; non-revolutionary, 14–15, 265–6, 274, 278–81, 369, 374–5
Protestantism, 255; and ecology, 111–12; and the individual, 147, 232
Psychology, 48; and revolution, 286–7; students of, 268–9; of the individual, *see* Man, nature of

Quality of life, and economic growth, 180–1, 192–5; measurement of, 392; threatened, 125–6, 142, 150–1, 392

RAND Corporation, 245–6
Rationalism, and faith, 83–4; 18th Century, 45–6, 62–3, 258–9; limitations of, 14, 15, 17–19, 63, 80–1, 83–4, 86, 292, 354; need for, 123; power of, 131
Religion, and biology, 17, 134–7 *passim*; discredited, 23, 43, 84, 92, 96, 134, 163, 232–3; in E. Europe, 232–3; man's need for, 37, 79–80, 97–100, 129, 131, 132, 231–4, 255, 321–2, 367; new forms of, 80, 86–7, 98–100, 232; and science, 77–8, 84, 86–7, 134, 135, 369–70; and technology, 31, 98–100, 101–2; *and see* Christianity, Roman Catholicism, etc.
Roman Catholicism, 47, 232, 255, 320–1; and ecology, 111
Romantic Movement, 62–3, 167, 259, 261
Rousseau, Jean-Jacques, 141–2, 143
Rumania, 244, 381
Russell, Lord Bertrand, 236–7, 351
Russia, Imperial, 30–4, 49, 242, 307
Russia, Soviet, *see* Soviet Union
Russian Revolution, 241–2, 265, 279, 289, 307, 310

Sakharov, Professor, 294, 304, 376
Sargent, A., 134, 135–6, 137
Sartre, J.-P., 270

Science, benefits of, 155–6, 163, 198, 316, 334; dangers of, 154, 197–8, 208; East–West interchange, 340; and liberty, 142; and moral values, 18–19, 136, 156–7, 173, 364–5; and NATO, 337; need to control, 22–3, 116, 197, 216, 220, 252–3, 319–20, 328–9; neutrality of, 115–16, 320; prestige of, 156–7, 230, 294–5; and religion, 77–8, 84, 86–7, 134, 135, 369–70; and society, 13, 17, 18, 48, 73–88 *passim*, 128, 140–1

Scientists, education of, 160–1; power of, 22, 154–61, 160–1, 171, 172–3, 204, 218, 252

Sexual revolution, 56, 60, 187–8

Social sciences, 18, 273; role in futurology, 352–67 *passim*, 368–70; *and see* Sociology

Social structure, changes in, 13, 28, 93–5, 159, 171–3, 175–86 *passim*, 187–91, 216–20

Social unease, 13–15, 62–3, 92–3, 120–1, 169–70, 184, 190, 228–9, 234, 237–8, 251, 347–5, 365–6, 388, 391; in France, 262, 267–8; in Germany, 273–84 *passim*

Social welfare, in Britain, 234, 345, 347; in West, 297

Socialism, in developing countries, 246–7, 299; future of, 375; in E. Europe, 296–310 *passim*; in Germany, 285–90 *passim*; New Left, 168, 253; in Soviet Union, 33, 34, 285, 372, 375

Socialists, Utopian, 351–2, 361, 373–4

Societies, industrial, convergence of, 293–310, 311–23, 376

Society, and economic development, 66–9, 174–86 *passim*, 192–5, 293–310, 325–8; evolution of, 368–81 *passim*, 387; future of, 351–67 *passim*, 376–70, 387; and the individual, 18–19, 36, 130–1, 132, 216–17, 261 ff., 273, 388, 391–2; need for controls, 21, 217–24 *passim*; and technology, 26–43 *passim*, 45–8, 51–6, 57–72 *passim*, 73–88 *passim*, 89–90, 92–6, 101, 128, 130, 132–3, 140–52 *passim*, 159, 164, 165–6, 169, 174–86 *passim*, 190–1, 203–4, 209, 224, 251–2, 311–23 *passim*, 164, 165–6, 169, 174–86 *passim*, 190–1, 325–9, 347–8, 360–1, 380, 386–8

Sociology, defects of, 116; in E. Europe, 368–9; students of, 268–9, 276, 279

South America, 217–18, 220, 244–5

Soviet Union, culture of, 50–1, 162–3, 243–4, 248, 295, 304, 313–15; and ecology, 209, 339; economic development of, 107, 125, 200–1, 209, 241–8, 294–5, 308–9; foreign policy of, 118, 239–40, 331; and futurology, 104–5, 107–8, 368–81 *passim*; industrialisation in, 49–50, 241–2, 307, 393; as nuclear power, 41, 227; planning, 103–4, 245–6, 308, 370, 371, 380, 381; regime of, 51, 239, 242, 263–4, 305, 310, 315, 341, 350, 380, 381; science in, 9, 218, 294–5, 303; socialism in, 33, 34, 285, 372, 375; society in, 219, 304, 306–7; sociology in, 294, 368–9; space research in, 202, 332–4

Space research, age of, 20, 21; effects on man, 99, 121; military uses of, 332–5, 377; need to control, 332–3; value of, 70, 101, 202–3, 382

Spain, 244–5, 302

Spengler, O., 366, 376, 379

Stalin, Joseph, 54, 153–4, 241, 273, 281, 284, 285, 294, 305, 306, 320, 321, 372; Stalinism, 49, 266, 241–2, 244, 285

Student unrest, 258 ff., *and see* Youth

Sweden, 92, 177, 329, 339

Switzerland, 184–5, 190

Technologists, failure of, 45–8, 51, 53, 151; power of, 70, 90, 154–5, 156–61, 171, 172–3, 204

Technology, acceleration of, 27–8, 53, 119, 163–4, 174–5, 187, 201–2, 390; benefits of, 59, 94–5, 151, 155, 163, 202–3, 221, 316; dangers of, 22–3, 29, 45–56 *passim*, 58–62, 82–5, 132–3, 135, 186, 187, 325–7, 388–9, 392; environmental, *see* Pollution; political, 52, 54–5, 140–1, 144–5, 152, 153–4, 156, 159, 174–5, 197–8, 218–19, 384–5, 386–7; dissent against, 14, 63, 127, 172; and futurology, 354, 357–8, 360–1; and man, 17, 18–19, 22–3, 27, 29–30, 33–4, 48, 52–3, 56, 62–4, 73–4, 76, 89–93, 97–100, 130, 184, 185, 315, 347–8, 388–9, 392; and moral values, 12, 27, 60–72 *passim*, 76–88 *passim*, 96, 127–8, 133–7, 173; need to control, 29, 36–7, 38, 40–2, 53–6, 59, 63, 69–70, 85, 127–8, 133, 141, 151–2, 153–72 *passim*, 197, 216, 220, 252–3, 319–20, 325–31, 348, 383–5, 389, 392; and religion, 79–80, 99, 101–2; *and see* Automation, society

Technosphere, 26–9, 36–7, 38, 39, 43, 196–7, 203

Third World, *see* Developing countries

Totalitarianism, danger of, 17, 54, 55, 90, 100, 102, 152, 175–6, 197–8, 216, 251–4, 318, 377–9

Touraine, Professor Alain, 261–2

Toynbee, Arnold J., 13, 14, 22, 26–43, 129, 228, 266–7, 366, 391

Transport, problems of, 21, 29–30, 54, 120, 128, 200, 362

Turkey, 34, 344

Unemployment, *see* Employment

UNESCO, 230, 350, 380

United Nations, 108, 131; Charter, 380; Development Decade, 110; Resolutions on Outer Space, 332–3; Security Council, 332–3

United States of America, affluence of, 109, 125–6, 233–4; culture of, 15–16, 47, 94, 125–6, 162–3, 249, 301–2, 312–15; economic planning, 67, 103–4, 181–3, 199, 200–1, 204; education, 146, 147, 171, 229, 230, 253–5; foreign policy, 118, 239–40; immaturity of, 118, 239–40, 253–5; industrialisation of, 34, 40,

INDEX

94, 189–90, 233, 393; moral values of, 162–3, 253–5; and motor-car safety, 342, 343–4; Negroes in, 181–2, 189, 254, 364; nuclear controls, 252–3; as nuclear power, 41, 227, 296–7; politics in, 171, 182, 323; and pollution, 54, 123, 132, 344; population control in, 219; research and development, 359–60; science in, 18, 157; social problems in, 164, 181–2, 253–4, 297; space research in, 202, 332–4; universities in, 12, 15, 45–6, 171, 229, 276, 315; youth in, 228–32, 272–91, 315–16

Universities, contemporary, 12, 162, 272–5, 286; in Britain, 195; in France, 258 ff., 275; in Germany, 230, 274 ff.; in U.S.A., 12, 15, 45–6, 171, 229, 275, 276, 315

Urbanisation, advantages of, 29–40, 164–6, 193–4; defects of, 20, 39–40, 164–5, 212, 214, 218, 344–5, 388, 392; development of, 39–40, 364; in Italy, 149, 189; in U.S.A., 40, 175

Vietnam, culture, 112, 243; War, 238, 276, 277, 381

War, causes of, 16, 42, 225, 226–7, 266–7, 238–9, 249; results of, 240–1, 296
nuclear, possibility of, 41, 42, 62, 118, 188, 348–9, 376; unlikely, 227–8, 238, 240

War, First World, 227, 242, 303

War, Second World, 28, 154, 171–2, 226, 238, 250, 297–8, 302, 345

Warsaw Pact, 338, 347, 348–50

Weizsäcker, Carl Friedrich von, 83, 87

Wells, H. G., 52, 351, 373

Western world, centralisation in, 293, 296, 306; culture of, 15–16, 44–55 *passim*, 293–310 *passim*, 311–23 *passim*, 393–4; economic growth of, 24, 30, 34, 65–7, 177, 209; and futurology, 305–6, 368–81 *passim*; military defence in, 346–7; moral underdevelopment of, 128, 233–5, 312, 318, 393–4; and pollution, 123, 209, 337–45 *passim*; science in, 296–7, 337; social welfare in, 297; *and see* Affluence, Economic planning, *and see* Britain, U.S.A., etc.

Wiener, Norbert, 317, 355–6, 359–60

Youth, anarchism of, 114, 261, 264, 273, 278, 287; and drugs, 15, 229, 232; ideology of, 114, 229–32, 261–6, 269–70, 272–91; importance of, 208–9, 261; rebellion of, 11–13, 14–15, 63, 87–8, 93, 121–2, 199, 228–32, 258 ff., 272–91, 315–16; sexual morality of, 187–8, 261

Yugoslavia, 289, 381